EMPLOYEE RELATIONS IN CONTEXT

David Farnham is Professor of Employment Relations at the University of Portsmouth. His other publications include: *Personnel in Context*; *The Corporate Environment*; *Managing in a Business Context*; *Understanding Industrial Relations* (with J. Pimlott); and *Managing Academic Staff in Changing University Systems*. He has also co-edited or co-authored with Sylvia Horton: *Managing People in the Public Services*; *Public Management in Britain*; *Human Resources Flexibilities in the Public Services*; and *New Public Managers in Europe*. Marjorie Corbridge is Programme Area Director for Postgraduate Courses in Portsmouth Business School, Sylvia Horton is Principal Lecturer in Public Sector Studies at the University of Portsmouth and Stephen Pilbeam is Principal Lecturer in Human Resources Management.

The Chartered Institute of Personnel and Development is the leading publisher of books and reports for personnel and training professionals, students, and all those concerned with the effective management and development of people at work. For details of all our titles, please contact the Publishing Department:

tel. 020 8263 3387
fax 020 8263 3850
e-mail publish@cipd.co.uk

The catalogue of all CIPD titles can be viewed on the CIPD website:
www.cipd.co.uk/bookstore

EMPLOYEE RELATIONS IN CONTEXT

David Farnham

CHARTERED INSTITUTE OF PERSONNEL
AND DEVELOPMENT

First edition published in 1997
Reprinted 1999
Second edition published in 2000
Reprinted 2002

An earlier version of this text, *Employee Relations*, was published in 1993 by the
Institute of Personnel Management

Phototypeset by The Comp-Room, Aylesbury
and printed in Great Britain
by the Short Run Press, Exeter

British Library Cataloguing in Publication Data

A catalogue record for this book is available from the British Library

ISBN 0-85292-876-9

Chartered Institute of Personnel and Development, CIPD House,
Camp Road, London SW19 4UX
Tel: 020 8971 9000   Fax: 020 8263 3333
E-mail: cipd@cipd.co.uk
Website: www.cipd.co.uk
Incorporated by Royal Charter. Registered charity no. 1079797

Contents

v

Contents

Contents

Contents

Contents

Contents

List of figures

List of tables

List of exhibits

List of abbreviations

AC	*Akademikernes Centralorganisation*
ACAS	Advisory, Conciliation and Arbitration Service
ADST	approved deferred share trust
AEU	Amalgamated Engineering Union
AEEU	Amalgamated Engineering and Electrical Union
AF	*Akademikernes Felleorganisasjon*
AFL-CIO	American Federation of Labor-Congress of Industrial Organization
AMMA	Assistant Masters and Mistresses Association
APEX	Association of Professional Executive Clerical and Computer Staff
ASB	Amalgamated Society of Boilermakers
ASOD	action short of dismissal
ATL	Association of Teachers and Lecturers
BIFU	Banking Insurance and Finance Union
BMA	British Medical Association
BSAS	British Social Attitudes Survey
BV	best value
C and P	custom and practice
CAC	Central Arbitration Committee
CBI	Confederation of British Industry
CCT	compulsory competitive tendering
CFDT	*Confédération Français Démocratique du Travail*
CFTC	*Confédération Français du Travail Chrétien*
CGT	*Confédération Général du Travail*
CGT-FO	*Confédération Général du Travail-Force Ouvrière*
CIPD	Chartered Institute of Personnel and Development
CIR	Commission on Industrial Relations
CMK OS	Czech Moravian Chamber of Trade Unions
CNV	*Christelijk National Vakverbond*
CO	Certification Officer
COHSE	Confederation of Health Service Employees
CPAUIA	Commissioner for Protection Against Unlawful Industrial Action
CPSA	Civil and Public Services Association
CRE	Commission for Racial Equality
CRTUM	Commissioner for the Rights of Trade Union Members
CSOP	company share option plan
CWS	Co-operative Wholesale Society

CWU   Communication Workers Union

DDA 1995   Disability Discrimination Act 1995
DfEE   Department for Education and Employment
DGB   *Deutscher Gewerkschaftsbund*

EA 1980   Employment Act 1980
EA 1982   Employment Act 1982
EA 1988   Employment Act 1988
EA 1990   Employment Act 1990
EAT   Employment Appeal Tribunal
EEC   European Economic Community
EETPU   Electrical Electronic Telecommunications and Plumbing
               Union
ELM   external labour market
EMU   European monetary union
EPA 1975   Employment Protection Act 1975
ERA 1996   Employment Rights Act 1996
ERA 1999   Employment Relations Act 1999
ERL   employee relations
ESO   employee share ownership
ET   employment tribunal
ETUC   European Trade Union Confederation
EWC   European works council

FBP   fall-back position
FWRs   Fair Wages Resolutions

GDP   gross domestic product
GMB   General Municipal and Boilermakers
GNP   gross national product
GPMU   Graphical Paper and Media Union

HRM   human resources management

ICFTU   International Confederation of Free Trade Unions
ICTU   Irish Congress of Trade Unions
ILM   internal labour market
ILO   International Labour Organisation
IMF   International Monetary Fund
IPD   Institute of Personnel and Development
IPM   Institute of Personnel Management
IRA 1971   Industrial Relations Act 1971
ISP   ideal settlement point
ISTC   Iron and Steel Trades Confederation
IT   information technology

JCC	joint consultative committee
KOZ SR	Confederation of Trade Unions of the Slovak Republic
LIFO	last-in first-out
LLM	local labour market
LO	*Landesorganisationen i Sverige*
LO-D	*Landesorganisationen i Danmark*
LO-N	*Landsorganisasjonen i Norge*
MSFU	Manufacturing Science and Finance Union
NALGO	National and Local Government Officers Union
NAS/UWT	National Association of Schoolmasters/Union of Women Teachers
NCU	National Communications Union
NFC	National Freight Corporation
NGA	National Graphical Association
NHS	National Health Service
NSAs	new-style agreements
NUCPS	National Union of Civil and Public Servants
NUM	National Union of Mineworkers
NUPE	National Union of Public Employees
NURMTW	National Union of Railway Marine and Transport Workers
NUT	National Union of Teachers
OECD	Organisation for Economic Co-operation and Development
PF	Police Federation
PRB	pay review body
PRP	performance-related pay
PSBR	public sector borrowing requirement
PSTCU	Public Services Tax and Commerce Union
QMV	qualified majority voting
QWA	quality work assured
RCN	Royal College of Nursing of the United Kingdom
RSP	realistic settlement point
SAYE	save as you earn
SCPC	Standing Commission on Pay Comparability
SCPR	Social and Community Planning Research
SOGAT	Society of Graphical and Allied Trades
SOSR	some other substantial reason
TGWU	Transport and General Workers Union

TQC	total quality control
TQM	total quality management
TUC	Trades Union Congress
TULRCA 1992	Trade Union and Labour Relations (Consolidation) Act 1992

UCATT	Union of Construction Allied Trades and Technicians
UMA	union membership agreement
UN	United Nations
UNICE	Union of Industrial and Employers' Confederations of Europe
USDAW	Union of Shop Distributive and Allied Workers

WERS 1998	Workplace Employee Relations Survey 1998
WIRS 1990	Workplace Industrial Relations Survey 1990
WTO	World Trade Organisation

Preface

Since the last edition of this book, the Blair administration was elected to office with a landslide majority in May 1997, there have been important changes in the European context – such as the Working Time Directive – and the Workplace Employee Relations Survey 1998 (WERS 1998) (Cully *et al* 1999) has been published. This edition takes account of the changes associated with these developments and of recent research findings, including those of WERS 4. In this introductory book – written from a managerial perspective – students and teachers are provided with a study guide to employee relations, rather than a conventional textbook, which focuses on the diffuse roots, complexities and varieties of British employee relations practices. Like earlier editions, this one puts employee relations into its wider socio-economic contexts and seeks to provide a framework within which students of personnel and development can identify and understand the role of management in managing the employment relationship, contextually, operationally and strategically.

Employee relations is defined as that part of managing people that enables competent managers to balance, within acceptable limits, the interests of employers as buyers of labour services and those of employees as suppliers of labour services in the labour market and workplace. Within this framework, the main task of those responsible for managing the employment relationship is to develop appropriate institutions, policies and rules to promote 'good' working relations with those whom they employ. This means preventing unnecessary conflict between management and employees over those matters in which both parties have mutual, though sometimes diverging, interests. A second related task for management is to try and obtain the commitment of employees to the goals of the organisations employing them, in ways benefiting both employer and employees. The 'balance of interests' strategy and 'commitment' strategy are sometimes used in parallel in organisations. In other cases, the emphasis is on one or other of these approaches, with the balance of interest strategy being based on the collective employment relationship and the commitment one on individual, non-union aspects of the relationship.

This does not mean that this book is written from a narrow, prescriptive viewpoint. The text seeks to be analytical, academic and rigorous in its approach and emphasises the contingent nature of employee relations management. Contingency means that that there are not only choices and alternative approaches for management in taking decisions in employee relations, but also constraints and limitations on areas of managerial discretion in managing employees.

In line with its managerial thrust, and compared with other texts on the subject, this one also provides opportunities for developing the competency of students, by enabling them to apply their knowledge and skills of employee relations to practical situations. This practical approach to employee relations management is underlined by the conceptual, theoretical and empirical content of the chapters and by the assignments at the end of them. These assignments require students to do wider reading, undertake activities and problem-solve real-life issues. Assignments may be done individually or in groups and they may be presented orally, in writing or by a combination of these methods. Where an assignment refers to 'your organisation', and the student is not currently employed, this may be interpreted by the reader as meaning 'any organisation with which you are familiar'.

This book focuses largely on British practice in employee relations but also incorporates some international comparisons, where this helps illustrate how other countries deal with similar issues. This is to enable students to understand some of the external trends and alternative approaches to employee relations in countries and national cultures other than their own.

The book consists of two Parts and 11 chapters. Part 1 examines the 'Institutions and Background' to employee relations. This section of the book outlines the parties, processes and contexts of employee relations. Chapter 1 provides an overview of employee relations by examining the interests of the buyers and sellers of labour services, the agreements and rules they make, the conflict-resolving processes they use and major influences on the behaviour of the actors in employee relations. In Chapter 2, the major players in employee relations – management, management organisations, employee organisations and state agencies – are identified and their roles discussed. Chapter 3 analyses the main processes and outcomes of employee relations including management-led approaches, joint approaches, third-party intervention, industrial sanctions and Western European patterns of worker co-determination.

Chapter 4 examines the impact of economic and legal policy on employee relations. The topics discussed range from Keynesianism and supply-side economics to statutory employment protection rights and the law on trade disputes. In Chapter 5, the changing economic, technological, social and political contexts within which employee relations management takes place are analysed and discussed and the implications for managing employee relations are considered.

Part 2 concentrates on 'Employee Relations in Practice'. In Chapter 6, the growing phenomenon of the non-union firm is examined. This chapter then goes on to discuss aspects of workplace communications, including employee involvement, employee commitment, employee communications and worker participation in management decision-making. Chapter 7 focuses on collective bargaining and joint consultation by looking at some of the theoretical issues relating to collective bargaining, emerging patterns of bargaining and the major theories underpinning effective negotiating practice. It also considers the nature and scope of joint consultation in its various institutional forms. Chapter 8 links with Chapter 7 by concentrating on management and its relations with trade unions. This includes developments in union policy, structure and practice, union responses to the changing employee relations environment, the law and union membership, and union recognition – including the new statutory recognition procedures incorporated within the Employment Relations Act 1999.

Chapter 9 moves on to examine the role of public policy in employee relations and explores the 'social dimension' of the single European market. It discusses the traditional role of the state, the 'Employee Relations Consensus' between 1945 and 1979, the subsequent breakdown of that consensus and the Labour Government's approach to employee relations since 1997. It also examines the impact of the EU's social dimension on British employers and workers.

In Chapter 10, attention is concentrated on collective industrial action, including its functions, patterns of activity, what influences it and how it can be managed. Finally, in Chapter 11, we turn to the basic employee relations skills required of managers in managing the employment relationship, including negotiation, grievance handling, dealing with discipline in the workplace and managing redundancies.

In getting this new edition to press, I would particularly like to acknowledge the support and co-operation of Richard Goff and Chris Jackson at CIPD House. I would also like to thank my colleagues – Sylvia Horton, and Stephen Pilbeam and Marjorie Corbridge – for updating Chapters 6 and 11 respectively. Other colleagues – Derek Adam-Smith, Dr Peter Scott and Dr Steve Williams – kindly commented and corrected me on parts of the manuscript. I thank them for this, but would remind readers that I alone remain responsible for any remaining errors of fact or observation. Thanks are also due to Rosemary Wright of the CIPD for producing the author and subject indexes. The result is, I hope, a new, up-to-date text which is well informed and one that will be of practical benefit to both students and teachers of contemporary employee relations.

David Farnham
April 2000

REFERENCE

CULLY M., WOODLAND S., O'REILLY A. and DIX G. (1999) *Britain at Work: As depicted by the 1998 Workplace Employee Relations Survey*. London, Routledge.

Part 1

INSTITUTIONS AND BACKGROUND

1 An overview of employee relations

Employee relations in market economies take place wherever work is exchanged for payment between an employer and an employee. The essence of employee relations, therefore, is paid employment or the pay–work bargain between employers and employees. An employee is someone who works under a contract of employment, sometimes called 'a contract of service', for an employer. A contract of employment contrasts with 'a contract for services'. A contract for services is made between independent contractors and those buying their specialist labour services, such as fee-paid, self-employed management consultants (for example trainers) selling their consultancy skills to companies, or building subcontractors (for example carpenters or electricians) selling their labour services to a construction company. In contrast, section 230 of the Employment Rights Act (ERA) 1996 defines a contract of employment as 'a contract of service or apprenticeship, whether express or implied, and (if it is express) whether oral or in writing' between an employer and an employee. To determine whether or not a worker has the legal status of an employee or that of an independent contractor, the courts apply a number of tests. These include the type of work, the nature of the orders given to the worker, the method and frequency of payment, the power to dismiss and the understanding between the parties. But the crucial test is that of 'control'. In other words, who has the ultimate right to tell the worker what to do? If one person can tell another what job to do, how it is to be done and when, where and with whom, then that party is the employer in law and the other is an employee.

The pay–work bargain between employer and employee is influenced by a series of factors, including:

- the institutional arrangements by which employment decisions are made
- the structure and ownership of the industry, sector, organisation and workplace where employment takes place
- external factors such as the political, economic, social and legal contexts of the exchange relationship
- the ideas and values underpinning employment activity.

Organisations, whatever their ownership, size or outputs, employ people to work for them, hiring them for the knowledge, skills and capabilities that individual workers possess, and the employer rewards them accordingly. People, in turn, seek paid employment to earn incomes so that they can spend the money they earn, as consumers in the market place. There are

3

also other, more complex reasons why people work, but the economic imperative is the fundamental one.

Employee relations, therefore, are concerned with the interactions among the parties to the employment relationship. These consist of three groups: the primary parties, secondary parties and tertiary parties. The primary parties pay for work and provide work in the labour market (employers and employees). The secondary parties act on behalf of the primary parties (management or management organisations and trade unions) in the negotiation and regulation of employment contracts. The third-party role is provided by state agencies and European Union (EU) institutions, which attempt to mediate between employers and employees, and employers and unions, in the interests of stable employee relations or to provide a 'floor' of employment standards below which no individual worker should fall. It is the interaction between the primary and secondary parties that result in employee relations practices. In organisations, employee relations practices are a product of a number of factors. The principal ones are:

- the *interests* of the buyers and sellers of labour services (or human resources skills)
- the *agreements and rules* made by them and their agents
- the *conflict-resolving processes* that are used
- the *external influences* affecting the parties making employment decisions.

INTERESTS IN EMPLOYEE RELATIONS

The economic imperatives

Today employers are normally organisations. As employers, organisations vary widely in their patterns of ownership, size of employment units, numbers of employment units and types of workers employed (Cully *et al* 1999). Business organisations in the private sector are characterised by being driven by the profit motive and market factors and are found in the primary economic sector (such as agriculture, mining and fishing), secondary sector (such as manufacturing and construction) and tertiary sector (such as services). Larger enterprises operate on several sites, employing a wide variety of human resources skills, including managerial, professional, technical, administrative and what are traditionally called 'manual' groups of workers. Some private enterprises are heavily unionised, whilst others are non-unionised. Larger firms tend to have well-organised, professional personnel or human resources departments; smaller ones do not.

Public-sector organisations, other than a few commercial public corporations such as the Post Office, are generally driven by welfare or political goals, having been set up by the state to provide a series of services to the general public (Horton and Farnham 1999). These enterprises are normally financed by general taxation on individuals or corporations but their services are 'free' at the point of use by those consuming them. The public sector is usually classified as consisting of public corporations, central government, including the National Health Service, and local authorities (Fleming 1989, Central Statistical Office 1991, Office for National Statistics 1997). Public-sector organisations tend to be large, complex enterprises, employing a wide variety of occupational groups and skills, with relatively high levels of union membership and bureaucratically driven personnel policies and departments.

Business organisations are driven by the profit motive and market values, so one of the main aims of those directing them and those responsible for their economic effectiveness is to obtain a financial surplus of revenues over costs at the end of each accounting cycle. Unless they achieve this financial target, businesses cannot, in the medium term at least, survive as viable economic units. At the extremes, firms may be either labour intensive, as in parts of the service sector, or capital intensive, as in high-tech production industries. In both cases, the cost-effective utilisation and managing of human resources is essential to organisational success. Private employers can stay profitable only where:

- total pay and employment costs are kept within planned human resources budgets, and/or
- worker productivity per head is increased, and/or
- human resources budgets are exceeded, pay is cut or the numbers employed in the enterprise at current pay levels are reduced.

Public-sector organisations are not driven solely by market factors, in that they are 'not for profit' enterprises (Starks 1991). But they have to operate as efficiently as possible and provide 'value for money' to their political stewards, in Parliament or local government, and to those who pay for them as taxpayers. Like their private-sector counterparts, they also have to utilise and manage their human resources cost-effectively, especially since they tend to be labour-intensive organisations where some 70 per cent of their costs are labour or human resources costs. If labour costs increase in public-sector organisations, a number of governmental and employer responses are possible. These include:

- raising taxes
- increasing public borrowing
- introducing 'charges' for services
- increasing labour productivity
- cutting back public services
- reducing staffing establishments.

Individuals in employment, or those seeking work, have their own economic interests when working. They typically want:

- the best pay available to them
- good promotion prospects
- the best fringe benefits, such as pensions, medical insurance and job training

5

- the best working conditions, such as short hours of work, holidays with pay, and sick pay
- a safe and healthy working environment
- security of employment.

All of these elements of the employment package involve economic costs to employers, which include employment costs such as wages and salaries, National Insurance and pensions.

Labour market and managerial relations

With employers buying labour skills and work effort and workers selling these in the labour market, there are potential conflicts of interest in the determination of the pay–work bargain or in the market relations between them. Put crudely, the economic interests of employers are such that they want the lowest possible employment costs commensurate with obtaining and retaining the best-qualified staff with the skills that the organisation needs. Employers also want the commitment of their workforces to the organisations employing them. The economic interests of the workforce, in contrast, are that they want the best possible terms and conditions of employment commensurate with their job security and employment prospects. The more that is paid out in pay or non-pay benefits to employees, however, the less is available to corporate shareholders or for investment purposes by the organisation and vice versa. Even in the public sector, the higher the employment costs for hiring and retaining staff, the higher the taxes that are needed or the higher the level of public borrowing required to pay and employ staff. These, then, are the underlying conflicts between employers and employees in the labour market under the market economy.

There are other potential conflicts of interest between employers and employees once labour has been hired in the workplace. These derive from the managerial relations between the parties arising out of the pay–work bargain (Flanders 1968). Employers generally want employees who are compliant with or committed to employer rules and policies and to management decisions. If organisations are to achieve their economic targets of profitability, efficiency, productivity and growth – or, at a minimum, economic survival – managers, who are responsible for organisational success and effectiveness, want employees who respond willingly and flexibly to managerial decisions and initiatives. Managers want to be free to take and implement decisions in the interests of enterprise efficiency and workplace order, without being constrained by individual or collective employee resistance to them.

Employees, on the other hand, normally want a say in how their work is organised, how the decisions affecting their working lives are taken and how any complaints and grievances relating to their rewards, working arrangements and job content may be resolved. It is potential conflicts over job control that are at the root of the managerial relations between managers and employees in the workplace.

6

Where conflict between employers and employees remains unresolved, in either their market or managerial relations, industrial or workplace conflict can result. Employers may take sanctions against their employees, or employees and their unions may take sanctions against their employers. The situation then becomes a power struggle, with the stronger side trying to force the weaker side to concede to its demands. The outcome of such conflicts depends on the balance of power between the two sides and on other factors, such as the availability of third-party intervention, the law and public opinion. Even where trade unions are not recognised by an employer (as is increasingly the case), covert or 'unorganised' conflict may arise between the employer and its employees. This may take the forms of absenteeism, low morale amongst employees, high labour turnover or withholding effort from the employer. In some respects, unorganised conflict in the workplace is more difficult for employers to manage than is formal, 'organised' conflict between employers and trade unions.

Common interests and 'good' employee relations

Since there are heavy economic costs to all parties to the employment relationship if they fail to reach agreements, accommodations and understandings amongst themselves, employers and employees – and trade unions where these are recognised – normally emphasise their common interests in the pay–work bargain, rather than their differences. Amongst other things, employers seek predictable labour costs, a stable workforce, co-operative employees, some flexibility amongst their employees between the tasks and functions they do, employee commitment to the organisation and its management, and willingness by employees to work as members of teams. Employees, and recognised unions, in turn, seek amongst other things reasonable terms and conditions of employment, continuous and secure employment, fair management decisions, equality of opportunity, opportunities for training and development, job satisfaction, family-friendly policies and ability to influence the organisational decisions affecting their daily working lives.

It is to the benefit of both employers and employees, therefore, to focus on their common interests and the mutuality of the employment relationship through the pay–work bargain and other institutional arrangements between them. This can be done by resolving any potential conflicts between the parties, either constitutionally through relevant procedural arrangements or by interpersonal negotiation or by managerial discretion, to avoid any damaging and expensive conflict between them. Both employers/managers and employees (and the unions representing them) do not want any intra-organisational or workplace conflicts between them to threaten the stability, operational success and ultimate viability of the enterprise in which they work. The common interests of employers and employees thus demand that for most of the time they prefer to build on the mutual interests between them, rather than their diverging ones.

For employers, any organised or informal conflict with their employees in the workplace results in lost output, lost revenues and loss of reputation for fair dealings with those whom they employ. For employees, in turn, industrial conflict creates bad will between them and their employers and means lost pay and possible job losses if the employer's business prospects are damaged. 'Good' employee relations, from both the employers' and employees' points of view, means establishing sensible institutional arrangements between the parties to engender mutual trust between them. It requires the provision of rules and procedures aimed at reconciling any potential conflicts between them, when they arise. In this way, employers and employees and management and unions can build on their common interests together and avoid any costly employee relations' confrontations between them.

The state also has an interest in 'good' employee relations. This is expressed through government policies, the law, the state's employee relations agencies and its role as an employer in its own right. One concern of government, as the ultimate source of power in society, is to ensure that any unresolved conflicts between employers and employees, especially where there are trade unions involved, over either their market or managerial relations, do not degenerate into what it considers to be unacceptable or unlawful behaviour. Government's main concern is that such conflict might either damage the economy or threaten social disorder. This is a difficult role to fulfil, since if government is seen to intervene in a way which is perceived as being too much in favour of one of the parties, at the expense of the other, then the legitimacy of its actions may be disputed. Second, government seeks to provide a framework of law, including state enforcement agencies, within which the parties to employee relations are expected to conduct themselves. Employment law provides the parties with rights and responsibilities and the means for adjudicating them (Wedderburn 1986). Third, as an employer, government seeks to provide its own 'good' employment practices, so as to facilitate the effective recruitment and retention of appropriately qualified public servants (Farnham and Horton 1996b; see also Chapter 9).

AGREEMENTS AND RULES

Formal, written agreements and rules in employee relations are the principal means for containing any potential conflicts arising from the pay–work bargain between employers and employees. But there are also unwritten 'understandings' (custom and practice) that provide guidelines to behaviour between the buyers and sellers of labour services in the labour market and the workplace (Brown 1972, Terry 1977).

Employment rules may be made unilaterally, bilaterally or trilaterally. Unilateral rules are made by:

- employers and managers (company or management rules)
- management organisations (policy statements)
- workers (customs and practices)

- trade unions (union rules)
- the state (statute and common law)
- European Union (EU) (directives and regulations).

Agreements are made bilaterally between:

- employers and employees (contracts of employment, workforce agreements)
- employers or employers' associations and trade unions (collective agreements).

Substantive agreements or substantive rules cover the pay and conditions of employment associated with particular jobs. They include rates of pay, additional payments, overtime pay, hours of work, holiday arrangements, holiday pay, sick pay, maternity pay and so on. By specifying the economic rights and obligations attached to particular jobs, substantive agreements or substantive rules regulate the market relations between the buyers and sellers of labour services. Procedural agreements or procedural rules, such as grievance, disciplinary and redundancy procedures, adjust any differences between the parties to the pay–work bargain, whether in interpreting existing agreements or rules (conflicts of right) or in making new agreements or rules (conflicts of interest).

Substantive and procedural agreements and rules may be regulated internally or externally. Company and management rules, for example, are internally regulated, as are customs and practices, since changing them does not require the consent of external authorities, such as trade unions, management organisations or the state. All other types of substantive and procedural arrangements – whether policy statements by management organisations, union rules, statute and common law, EU directives and regulations, contracts of employment, collective agreements – are externally regulated. In practice, although each of these methods of determining employment rules shades into the others, differentiating them conceptually is useful for analytical purposes.

The employee relations agreements and rules, outlined above, are made at different decision-making levels. Customs and practices are made at workgroup and departmental levels, with company rules, contracts of employment, company collective agreements and workplace collective agreements being determined at employer or site levels. Industry-wide (or sectoral) collective agreements and the policy statements of management organisations are determined at multi-employer level. Statute and common law stem from the United Kingdom (UK) Parliament and the courts respectively, while European directives and regulations, such as the Transfer of Undertakings (Protection of Employment) Regulations 1981 and the Working Time Regulations 1998 derive from decisions made in EU institutions.

CONFLICT–RESOLVING PROCESSES

Unilateral employer regulation – company rules or 'the right to manage' – is only one of several types of employment rules. Given the potential conflicts of interest in the employment relationship between employers and employees, there are a number of institutional arrangements by which those between the primary parties to the pay–work bargain (employers and employees) and the secondary parties (management or management organisations and trade unions) may be resolved. Some are individual processes; others are collective ones. Individual processes are those where there are direct, face-to-face contacts between employers or managers and their subordinates. Collective processes are those where employees are represented indirectly in employment decision-making with employers and managers, by either trade unions or non-union staff associations or non-union staff.

Both individual and collective processes, in turn, can be subdivided into voluntary or legal methods of conducting employee relations. Voluntary methods are those determined independently and autonomously by the parties to employee relations, such as 'free' or 'voluntary' bargaining between employers and trade unions. Legal methods are those supported by the law, whether derived from common law, statutory or European sources. They provide the parties with legal rights and obligations and are ultimately enforceable by the courts, such as in employment protection, health and safety matters or the regulation of industrial conflict.

Combining individual and collective processes with voluntary and legal methods, as shown in Figure 1, we observe that there are four major approaches to resolving employee relations conflict. These are:

- employer regulation
- joint regulation
- state regulation
- regulated collectivism.

Figure 1 Conflict resolution and employee relations

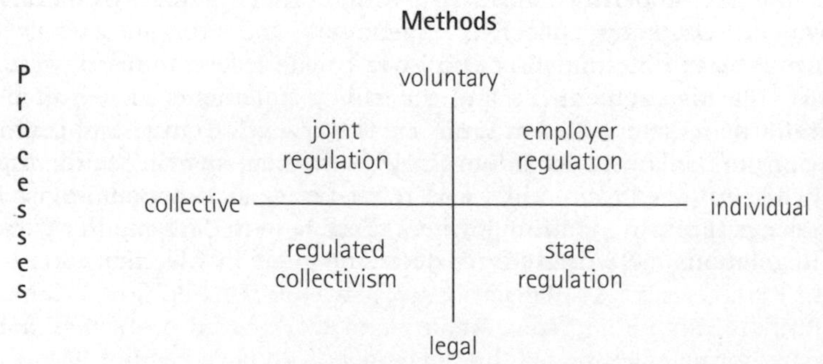

At any one time, the ways in which the pay–work bargain is determined, interpreted and implemented – within any organisational or national setting – involve, to varying degrees, a combination of these approaches to resolving potential conflict in the employment relationship. But any one of them may be the dominant approach, within a country, an industry, an organisation or a workplace.

Employer regulation

This involves a combination of individual processes and voluntary methods, which are employer and management driven. Unilateral employer regulation has traditionally been the preferred way by which employers and managers have managed employees. Its variants include:

*   the right to manage
*   employee involvement
*   profit-sharing
*   pay review bodies.

The right to manage is basically the claim by managers that it is their exclusive 'prerogative' to unilaterally take decisions, over all employment and managerial issues in the organisations that they manage, which they alone have the exclusive right to determine. Managerial prerogative was originally rooted in the nineteenth-century claim that it was the owners of industrial capital, or their appointed agents, who had the legal right to do as they wished with what they owned or for which they were responsible. A more recent justification for the right to manage is the 'economic efficiency' argument, which asserts that it is professional managers alone who have the technical expertise and managerial knowledge to take the 'right' decisions in the organisations in which they work (Farnham and Pimlott 1995). Where trade unions are absent, the employer's freedom to make decisions unilaterally is restricted only by what the law prescribes. Where unions are recognised by the employer, however, management's right to determine and apply employment rules is further restricted by union influence and power. But there are always areas of organisational decision-making, normally incorporated into company or 'works' rules, which remain exclusive to management alone (Storey 1980, 1983).

There are a number of types of employee involvement. One is team briefing. This is a system of direct communication between line managers and their work teams, based on the principle of cascading information downwards, on a regular and formal basis, from management to employees. It aims to inform employees and work groups of what is happening in their organisation, and why. It also reinforces the role of line managers as leaders of their work teams. Another type of employee involvement is quality circles. These comprise small groups of employees meeting regularly and voluntarily to discuss and solve quality and work-based problems. Quality circles are normally led by first line managers who have been provided with training to improve the effectiveness of quality circles. Quality circles are sometimes monitored by steering committees higher up the organisation. Other types of workgroup employee involvement practices include Total Quality Management arrangements, team working and information and communication committees (see Chapter 6).

Profit-sharing is also an employer-driven employee involvement process, principally in the private sector. It is primarily aimed at emphasising the common, rather than the divergent, interests of employers and employees within their organisations and at reinforcing this financially. Profit-sharing is where cash bonuses are paid voluntarily by employers to employees out of corporate profits. In practice, these cash bonuses are provided in one of the following ways:

- on a discretionary basis
- as a fixed proportion of profits
- as a proportion above a stated profit threshold
- in relation to dividends paid on share capital.

Profit-sharing does not provide employees with a share in the ownership of an enterprise but simply with an additional monetary claim, over and above their pay and non-pay rewards, based on corporate success (see Chapter 6).

Pay review bodies (PRBs) are appointed by the prime minister for certain groups of public servants. It is a politically-driven approach to employee relations. The role of PRBs is to make recommendations to the prime minister about the pay for particular public servants, although the government is not automatically bound by the decisions made. PRBs are established where it is felt that collective forms of pay determination for particular groups – such as top civil servants, doctors and dentists, and the armed services – are inappropriate. In most cases, however, union evidence is given to the review body, such as for schoolteachers, nurses, midwives and the professions allied to medicine, and this is taken into account in the PRB's recommendations.

Joint regulation

This involves a combination of collective processes and voluntary methods and includes:

- collective bargaining
- joint consultation.

Collective bargaining takes place between the employer and union representatives. It is based on the assumption that both the market and managerial relations between the primary parties to employee relations are power based, and that without collective bargaining the balance of power is weighted in favour of employers and individual managers rather than with individual employees. This is because any individual employee has a far greater need for a particular job, and the pay–work bargain attached to it, than the employer has for any particular worker (Webb and Webb 1913: 172). Without collective bargaining, individual workers are disadvantaged in the labour market since, where labour supply is plentiful, each worker is competing with others for jobs, enabling pay and conditions to be cut to the lowest possible standards by market-driven employers. Equally, in their managerial relations, without collective bargaining, workers are subject to internal, unilateral employment decisions about their work, over which they have no influence or control. Thus in the absence of collective bargaining, individual workers have to accept, in selling their labour skills, what the employer determines is 'the market rate' through what is strictly an individual bargain. According to the Webbs, however:

> if a group of workmen [sic] concert together, and send representatives to conduct the bargaining on behalf of the whole body, the position is at once changed. Instead of the employer making a series of deals with isolated individuals, he meets with a collective will, and settles, in a single agreement, the principles upon which, for the time being, all workmen [sic] of a particular group, or class, or grade, will be engaged.

With collective bargaining, then, there is assumed to be a fairer balance of bargaining power in the market between the buyers and sellers of labour, with employers and unions being jointly responsible for implementing the substantive and procedural collective agreements determined between them. These terms, conditions and procedures then become incorporated into the individual contracts of employment of the employees covered by the bargaining arrangements. In this way, collective bargaining is a process for identifying, institutionalising and resolving any conflicts of interest or of rights between the parties in employee relations (see Chapter 7).

Joint consultation is the process whereby employer and employee representatives, who may or may not be union representatives, come together, normally at workplace and/or employer levels, to discuss matters of common interest. There are a number of different approaches to joint consultation (Marchington 1989) but the basic distinction between joint consultation and collective bargaining is that it is a collaborative rather than an adversarial process. Joint consultation tends to exclude matters that are subject to negotiation and to focus on matters of a non-controversial nature. It also discusses issues prior to management taking a decision, or prior to negotiation, but it does not itself generally involve the taking of decisions. In this sense, the joint consultative process retains the power of management as a group to take and implement decisions, after consultations with union or worker representatives have been completed (see Chapter 7).

State regulation

This combines individual processes with legal methods and includes:

- contracts of employment
- employment protection rights for individual workers
- individual conciliation by the Advisory, Conciliation and Arbitration Service (ACAS)
- union membership rights
- laws regulating employee share ownership.

Contracts of employment are, in many respects, the focal point of relations between the primary parties to employment – employers and employees, or individual managers and their staff. In essence, a contract of employment is a legal agreement between an employer and an individual employee about terms and conditions. It is a legal arrangement, under common law, whereby the employee undertakes to obey the lawful and reasonable orders of the employer, or its managerial agents, and to take reasonable care in carrying out his or her employment duties, in exchange for remuneration. There is also a duty of fidelity to the employer. The employer, in turn, is bound in duty to pay wages, take reasonable care for the employee's safety and exercise due consideration in dealing with the employee. In practice, many features of the contract of employment are undefined, since the courts settle them through the legal device of 'implied terms'. The other main legal sources of the contract of employment include (Lewis and Sargent 2000):

- statutory statements
- collective agreements
- works rules
- customs and practices.

Employment protection rights for workers are incorporated in legislation providing a floor of minimum statutory employment rights for individuals, below which no one may fall. These rights include (see also Chapters 3 and 4):

- the right to a statutory minimum wage
- the right not to be 'unfairly' dismissed
- the right to minimum periods of notice
- the right to itemised pay statements
- the right not to be discriminated against on the grounds of sex, nationality or ethnic origin
- the right not to be made redundant without a minimum compensatory payment
- the right to maternity pay and leave
- the right to a series of family-friendly policies.

ACAS is empowered by the Trade Union and Labour Relations (Consolidation) Act (TULRCA) 1992 to provide individual conciliation where employees think that their employment protection rights, such as not to be

14

'unfairly' dismissed or to statutory maternity pay and leave, have been infringed by an employer. Cases unresolved by ACAS may go to employment tribunals.

There are a number of union membership rights for individual trade unionists. These include the right:

- not to be unreasonably excluded or expelled from a trade union
- to elect union office holders by secret ballot
- to endorse official trade union industrial action by secret ballot
- to determine union political funds by secret ballot
- not to be unjustifiably disciplined by the individual's union (see Chapters 4 and 8).

Employee share ownership (ESO), introduced by the Finance Acts 1978 and 1980, provides employees with not only a stake in the ownership of the firm in which they work but also a right to participate in the distribution of its profits. Technically ESO is a legal regulation of an optional, voluntary employee relations practice. It is government and employer driven and is aimed at increasing the identification of employees with their employers, making them more conscious of the market pressures on their firms and ensuring they gain financially from corporate profitability. There are certain types of ESO that attract tax advantages, such as Approved All Employee Profit Sharing Schemes and Save As You Earn Schemes. Under approved schemes, employees are not liable for income tax on gains in exercising share options.

Regulated collectivism

This involves collective processes underpinned by the law and includes:

- wages boards
- conciliation, arbitration and mediation
- trade union rights
- pension fund trustees
- industrial sanctions
- in the European context, co-determination.

Third-party intervention and trade union rights

Wages boards for agricultural workers in England and Wales and in Scotland were established in law in the 1920s to settle minimum hourly rates of pay, where there was no collective bargaining machinery. They consist of employer, union and independent representation, including an independent chair, and now regulate minimum hourly rates, overtime pay and related conditions of employment. Wages boards issue wages 'orders' setting out their decisions, which are legally enforceable on all employers covered by them.

Voluntary conciliation, arbitration and mediation in Britain is provided by ACAS, through the TULRCA 1992, where either a trade dispute is threatened, or negotiations between an employer and a union have broken down.

Collective conciliation is the process whereby, with negotiations having broken down, and normally when the agreed procedures to avoid disputes are exhausted, ACAS officers provide assistance to both sides to get them talking again. Their intervention often provides a basis for resolving such conflicts. Arbitration is the process whereby a third party, normally a single arbitrator or a panel of arbitrators, hears the cases of each side, deliberates on their evidence and determines a settlement. Each side agrees in advance to be bound by the decision of the arbitrator and to accept the award. Mediation is the process whereby a third party, normally an individual nominated by ACAS, with the approval of both sides, makes recommendations to the parties that may provide a basis for settling their differences.

Certain legal rights are provided for 'independent' unions having a certificate of independence from the Certification Officer (CO), where they are recognised by employers for collective bargaining purposes. These legal rights include (see also Chapters 3 and 9):

- the appointment of safety representatives and the establishment of safety committees
- consultation on collective redundancies
- information and consultation on business transfers
- secret ballots on employers' premises.

Independent unions, which are not recognised by an employer for collective bargaining purposes, have a right to make a claim for statutory union recognition where an employer refuses to recognise the union voluntarily (see Chapter 8).

Pension fund trustees, whether employee or union representatives, have the right to be consulted by employers, under the Social Security Pensions Act 1975, on matters relating to contracting out of the state scheme through an occupational pension scheme.

Industrial sanctions

Industrial sanctions are normally taken, within a framework established by the law, where there are no alternative conflict-resolving processes left between employers and unions or between managers and employees. Sanctions may be used unilaterally either by employers, management organisations and managers against employees and their unions, or by employees and their unions against employers. They are a method of last resort in employee relations and are used by one party to force the other to concede a demand, often of principle, which cannot be resolved by persuasion, negotiation, compromise or third-party intervention. Industrial sanctions involve the blunt use of employer, union or worker power against the other party. To remain 'constitutional', in other words within the accepted rules of employee relations, they should be taken only after any agreed procedures for avoiding conflict have been used and a 'failure to agree' has been recorded. Where sanctions are outside the framework of established rules between the parties, they are 'unconstitutional'. Where they are outside the framework of established legal rules, they are 'unlawful'.

Employers use a range of industrial sanctions. These include, in increasing order of severity:

- tight supervision
- harsh discipline
- demotion
- withdrawing overtime
- changing working practices unilaterally
- lockouts
- closing sites or workplaces
- reinvesting in plant and machinery elsewhere.

Formal sanctions by employees and unions against employers and management, in turn, include (see also Chapter 10):

- lax time-keeping
- working inefficiently
- working to rule or 'to contract'
- banning overtime
- stoppages of work.

Co-determination

Co-determination, which does not exist in Britain, is the process embodied in law whereby employees are enabled to participate in certain areas of managerial decision-making within the business organisations employing them. In Germany, for example, the law provides for the establishment of works councils at plant or site level (Berghahn and Karsten 1987). The workforce in all plants or sites, for example, elects works councils where five or more employees are employed. Works councils exist to protect the interests of workers in the plant and to ensure that effect is given to legislation, safety regulations and collective agreements affecting employees. They also have the right to participate in certain management decisions relating to the operation of the plant, the conduct of employees and the distribution of working hours. Employers also have to seek the consent of works councils on certain other issues.

Federal law in Germany also provides for other forms of co-determination by employee representatives in management. These operate at company level. In the mining, iron and steel industries, for example, there is numerical parity of 'capital' and 'labour' representatives on the (upper-tier) supervisory boards of these enterprises. These appoint and dismiss members of the (lower-tier) management board and supervise them. Additionally, the labour director, who is a member of the management board, cannot be appointed against the wishes of the majority of employee representatives. In limited companies employing more than 2,000 persons, 50 per cent of the supervisory board are shareholder representatives, with the employees' side divided between those employed by the company and external trade union representatives (see Chapters 3 and 6).

EXTERNAL INFLUENCES

Employee relations in the labour market and workplace do not take place in a vacuum. The resolution of potential employment differences and conflicts between the buyers and sellers of labour services are affected by a variety of economic and political factors.

The microeconomic level

A major determinant of pay rates and numbers of workers employed by an organisation is the demand for labour relative to its supply. Other things being equal, where labour demand exceeds labour supply, pay rates rise. Where labour supply exceeds labour demand, pay rates fall. There is also the union 'mark-up' differential between union and non-union labour. This is the extent by which unions are able to raise pay rates for their members over and above the market rates for equivalent non-union labour. The union mark-up varies widely across occupations and over time. Stewart (1983), for example, indicated a union mark-up of about 8 per cent in British manu-facturing as a whole, with shipbuilding and paper and printing, at that time, having mark-ups of around 18 per cent and 11 per cent respectively. Clearly, the union mark-up varies amongst occupations and industries and over time, but these figures give some idea of the 'gap' between union and non-union pay.

The determinants of an employer's demand for labour are complex. It depends partly on the structure of the external labour market, its internal labour market and its local labour market, but more particularly on the buoyancy, or not, of its product markets (Brown 1973) or, in the public ser-vices, on the ceiling placed on public spending by government (Beaumont 1992, Farnham and Horton 1996b, Corby and White 1999). The total supply of labour available to the economy is determined by the size of the population of working age, with the amount supplied being a function of the labour force participation rate, the number of hours that people are willing to work and the amount of effort provided by people at work. From an employer's point of view, the quality, relative mobility and potential pro-ductivity of labour affect its available supply.

A firm's external labour market (ELM) is the number of workers that are either available for work or potentially available for new jobs. Within the ELM, pricing and allocating decisions are controlled largely by economic variables, but employer decisions are crucial (Rubery 1989). In practice, because of differences in the quality of labour, in terms of aptitudes, skills and training, the ELM is highly segmented by occupation, industry, geog-raphy, gender, race and age (Dex 1989, Jenkins 1989 and Ashton 1989). One theory, the dual labour market hypothesis, is that the ELM is dichotomised into primary and secondary sectors. The primary sector is characterised by 'good' jobs and the secondary sector by 'bad' ones. Good jobs have high pay, high status, excellent promotion prospects, attractive fringe benefits and security of employment. Bad jobs, with the opposite characteristics, are allocated to those excluded from the primary sector, because they lack investment in 'human capital' or are discriminated against. In the secondary sector, where unions are weak or unrecognised, pay rates are established largely by competition and market supply and demand. This is because with full employment there are sufficient jobs available for all those seeking work at current pay rates, or, in conditions of unemployment, labour supply exceeds labour demand and pay rates fall. Work in the secondary sector is generally low paid, unattractive and unstable.

An internal labour market (ILM) is an arrangement by which labour is supplied and demanded within a firm without direct access to the ELM. Employment policies are directed towards those employed in the firm, with most jobs being filled by the promotion or transfer of workers who are already working in the company (Robinson 1970). ILMs, therefore, consist of sets of employment relationships, embodying formal and informal rules, which govern each job and the relationships amongst them. The reasons for ILMs include:

- union pressure for internal promotion, based on seniority
- on-the-job training, which makes the jobs unique
- low-cost recruitment
- good employment practice
- more reliable selection
- scarcity of skills in the ELM.

Local labour markets (LLMs) are largely the consequence of the financial and psychological costs and disadvantages, to workers, of extensive time spent travelling to work. These costs further segment a labour force already stratified by the characteristics outlined above. Such costs tend to restrict a firm's labour market to that which is accessible from a limited geographical area, for less-skilled occupational groups at least. This definition of LLMs assumes that their key characteristic is that the bulk of an area's working population continually seeks employment there and that local employers recruit most of the labour from the area.

The macroeconomy

Government economic policy also affects the buyers and sellers of labour. One approach is Keynesian demand management, which dominated British macroeconomic policy during the 1940s, 1950s and 1960s (Worswick and Ady 1952, Dow 1964, Worswick and Trevithick 1984). Its focus is on the level of aggregate demand in the economy. This is the total sum spent on goods and services, consisting of consumption, investment, government expenditure and expenditure on exports less imports. With the economy expanding and aggregate demand rising, demand for goods, services and labour increases, unemployment falls and union bargaining power is strengthened. When the economy slows down, because of falls in consumption or investment, demand for goods, services and labour decreases, unemployment rises and union bargaining power is weakened.

Governments using Keynesian demand management techniques seek to influence the level of aggregate demand by counter-cyclical fiscal and monetary policies. These are aimed at trying to slow down the economy when it is booming, because 'full employment' contributes to pay and price inflation, and at trying to boost the economy during recession, because unemployment is rising. Governments cut their spending and raise taxes when the economy is overheating and increase their spending, by public borrowing, and cut taxes when the economy is in recession (see Chapter 4).

The ways in which employers and unions in the private and public sectors react to these policy instruments is crucial in determining whether or not governmental policy succeeds. If pay bargainers fail to respond to the labour market signals given by government, and pay increases rise faster than national productivity, then the 'pay–price' and 'pay–tax/public borrowing' spirals are fuelled, resulting in inflation, low growth and balance of payments problems. If, on the other hand, employers resist 'felt-fair' union pay claims, then increases in trade disputes are likely. For these reasons, Keynesian demand management policies are normally linked with 'prices and incomes' policies, necessitating employer and union co-operation with government, aimed at restraining price and pay rises in line with rises in productivity and efficiency in the corporate sector (Jones 1987; see also Chapter 9 below).

Another approach is where governments focus on 'supply-side' measures, as they have done in Britain and the United States since the mid-1970s. Supply-side economics emphasises that the principal determinant of the rate of growth of an economy, in both the short and long run, is the allocation and efficient use of labour and capital. It is a restatement of neo-classical macroeconomic principles. These are based on the notion of 'rational expectations' and a 'natural rate of unemployment' that emerges as a result of efficient market clearing. By this view, raising aggregate demand cannot reduce the natural rate of unemployment and attempts to disturb this equilibrium are self-defeating, because they will be anticipated and neutralised by economic agents in the market place (Brittan 1988, Green 1989, Levacic 1988).

Supply-side economic policies focus on removing impediments to the supply of and efficient use of the factors of production. Such policies are concerned with the determinants of the natural rate of unemployment, rather than with the level of effective demand in the short run as in Keynesian macroeconomics. Among these impediments are claimed to be disincentives to work and invest, because of tax structures and tax levels, and institutional barriers, such as trade unions, to the efficient allocation of resources. The policy prescriptions flowing from this analysis are (see also Chapters 4 and 9):

- deregulating labour and product markets, thus making them more competitive and efficient
- privatisation
- cutting public borrowing
- cutting taxes.

The employee relations implications of these supply-side policies are the strengthening of employer bargaining power in the labour market and managerial rights in the workplace. In the private sector, in order to remain competitive in tight product markets, companies seek increased workforce productivity and efficiency, which are only made possible by reducing unit labour costs and increasing labour flexibility. This results in rising unemployment – unless pay rates fall, new product markets are found or growth rates are high. This weakens union wage bargaining power. In the public sector, there are similar employer pressures to raise efficiency, keep public spending under control and resist union pay claims that are 'not affordable' or not responsive to 'market forces'. The right to manage, in turn, is reinforced at the workplace, because of fear of unemployment and job losses, and union resistance to changes in working practices, new technology and managerial assertiveness is weakened.

Politics, the state and the law

Politics, the state and the law are never neutral in employee relations. The roles of the state – as legislator, manager of the economy, employer or third-party conciliator – its governmental agents, and the courts are crucial in determining the contexts within which employee relations decisions are taken (see Chapter 9).

During the nineteenth century, in the age of classical *laissez-faire*, or the doctrine that economic decisions are best guided by the autonomous decisions of free individuals in the market place, the state's role in employee relations was a minimalist and restrictive one. This reflected the dominant power structures in a society based on landed wealth, a growing entrepreneurial class of manufacturers and merchants and an elitist Parliament and undemocratic political system (Fox 1985). Wide differentials in wealth, class, status and power separated 'master' from 'servant', capitalist from worker, entrepreneur from wage earner and even craftsman from labourer. And common law regulation of the master and servant relationship, described by Kahn-Freund (1983: 18) as 'a command under the guise of an agreement', dominated the employment contract between the primary parties to the pay–work bargain.

By the early twentieth century, with the slow emergence of trade unionism amongst working people and the gradual democratisation of the parliamentary system, there were three main political and legal legacies of classical *laissez-faire* for employee relations. One was the emergence of a unified 'labour movement', linking the now legally emancipated unions with the newly created Labour Party (see Chapter 9). This political alliance was in

21

reaction to the dominance in Parliament of the business and commercial classes and meant that employee relations were now inevitably politicised and dichotomised between those representing the interests of the capitalist and labouring classes respectively (Farnham 1976, 1996). Second, there was a mistrust of the law by working people, especially of the courts, in the ways it affected trade unions, collective bargaining and the regulation of industrial conflict. Their preference was for autonomy in collective bargaining with employers and for non-intervention by the courts and the judges in employee relations. The third legacy was the central importance of the common law in regulating the individual contract of employment.

With the steady growth in the size, power and scope of the state in the twentieth century (White and Chapman 1987), and the continued democratisation of society (Middlemas 1979), it was inevitable that the roles of government and the law would increase in employee relations. Crouch (1979) provides four models of state or public policy on employee relations under advanced market capitalism. These are summarised in Figure 2. He describes them as:

- voluntary collective bargaining
- neo-*laissez-faire*
- corporatism
- bargained corporatism.

The model that predominates depends on whether the state is organised on 'corporatist' or 'liberal' principles and whether the position of trade unions within it is 'weak' or 'strong'. A corporatist state is where the economy is largely privately owned but the interests of capital, workers and government are integrated and mediated, through centralised institutional mechanisms, to ensure political and economic stability. A liberal state, in contrast, is one based on private enterprise but where, as far as possible, the political and economic spheres are disassociated. Economic decisions are decentralised, with businesses, individuals and workers exercising freedom of choice in the market place. A crucial development in economic liberalism is the acceptance of trade unionism, or collectivism. Combination of workers takes place to offset the inequalities between workers as sellers of labour services and capitalists as buyers in the market place, resulting in 'collective' liberalism or collective *laissez-faire*.

Governments, with their economic and legal policy preferences, determine whether employee relations operate in corporatist or liberal contexts and whether trade unions are weak or strong. The centralised, corporate state, with weak trade unions – as in post-war Japan – provides an example of corporatism as the employee relations model, comprising a combination of supply-side economic policies, union pay constraint and legal limitations on trade unions. Where unions are strong in a corporate state, the model is described as one of bargained corporatism. This is a situation as in Britain during World War II and in the late 1970s. It was also the dominant model in parts of central Europe, such as the Federal Republic of Germany, for

22

much of the post-war period, where only recently has the consensus on the integrity of the 'social market' become weakened (Jacobi *et al* 1998). Employee relations in Ireland have also been characterised by a revived form of bargaining corporatism in recent years, centred around an agreement between the 'social partners' negotiated in 1996, known as 'Partnership 2000' (von Prondzynski 1998). Here union leaders accepted politically imposed restraints on 'free collective bargaining' in return for other gains for their members, such as concessions on social policy, laws favourable to union organisation and a share in economic and political decision-making (Crouch 1994).

In the liberal, market-centred state, voluntary collective bargaining provides the model for employee relations where unions are strong. This was the dominant model for much of the post-war period in Britain, especially in the 30 years after 1945, apart from 1970–71. It was characterised largely by bi-partisan Conservative or Labour governments, with demand management economic policies and legal abstention in employee relations. Where unions are weak in the liberal state, the model is described as neo-*laissez-faire*. This was the case in the inter-war period and since the early 1980s. During this period, Conservative governments supported supply-side economic policy and legal intervention in employee relations. These proscribed union activities and industrial action (Moran 1977, Gamble 1988, Farnham 1990; see also Chapter 9).

With the return to the Labour Party to power under the leadership of Tony Blair, and the economic policies supported by the Chancellor of the Exchequer Gordon Brown post-1997, the 'New Labour' Government continued to pursue supply-side economic policies (Horton and Farnham 1999). Although it did not change the laws proscribing union activities and industrial action, it did enact, in the spirit of the 'Third Way', the Employment Relations Act (ERA) 1999. This provides *inter alia* a statutory right to trade union recognition, the promotion of family-friendly policies and other related employment protection rights for individual workers and trade unionists.

Figure 2 **State policies on employee relations**

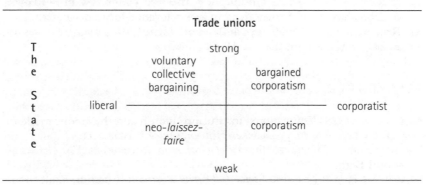

Source: Crouch (1979)

ASSIGNMENTS

(a) Why do people work? What do they get from working? And what are the main implications of employee needs at work for employers and their employee relations policies? Give examples from your own organisation.

(b) Provide examples of employment costs to your organisation for employing various categories of staff, breaking them down into costing classifications. What factors have to be taken into account by the employer in costing the likely effects of a stoppage of work by a key group of employees in the organisation?

(c) Read Brown (1972) and Terry (1977) and analyse what is meant by the term 'custom and practice'. Why do workers use it and why do employers accept it? Looking at your own organisation, identify some current 'customs and practices', indicating management's reaction to them and why they are tolerated. Provide other examples of 'C and P' that management have recently claimed back, how this was done and why.

(d) Interview some managers, including someone in personnel, at least one trade union representative and some employees, and ask them to define what they consider to be 'good employee relations'. Comment on and compare their answers and approaches. Rank in order of relative importance the conflict-resolving processes in your organisation used to maintain 'good employee relations', commenting on them as appropriate.

(e) Identify and evaluate the types of labour market from which your employer recruits its employees. How are these labour markets segmented and what are the implications for employee relations?

(f) Read Lewis and Sargent (2000) and identify the main common law duties of employers and employees under the contract of employment.

(g) Summarise Flanders' analysis of the trade unions' role in politics (1970: 24–37). Examine the relevance of his arguments today. Alternatively, discuss his analysis of job regulation and its part in rule-making in employee relations (*ibid*: 86–94).

(h) Evaluate Kahn-Freund's 'reflections on law and power' in employee relations (1977: 1–17). Outline how the role of the law in employee relations has evolved since then and its relevance for management.

(i) Read Cully *et al* 1999, pp14–22, and identify the main features of British workplaces in the late 1990s.

REFERENCES

ASHTON D. (1989) 'Educational institutions, youth and the labour market', in D. Gallie (ed.), *Employment in Britain*, Oxford, Blackwell.

BERGHAHN V. and KARSTEN D. (1987) *Industrial Relations in West Germany*. Oxford, Berg.

BEAUMONT P. (1992) *Public Sector Industrial Relations*. London, Routledge.

BRITTAN S. (1988) *A Restatement of Economic Liberalism*. London, Macmillan.

BROWN W. (1972) 'A consideration of custom and practice'. *British Journal of Industrial Relations*. X(1), March.

BROWN W. (1973) *Piecework Bargaining*. London, Heinemann.

CENTRAL STATISTICAL OFFICE (1991) 'Employment in the public and private sectors'. *Economic Trends*. 458, December.

CORBY S. *and* WHITE G. (EDS) (1999) *Employee Relations in the Public Services*. London, Routledge.

CROUCH C. (1979) *The Politics of Industrial Relations*. Glasgow, Fontana.

CROUCH C. (1994) *Industrial Relations and European State Traditions*. Oxford, Clarendon Press.

CULLY M., WOODLAND S., O'REILLY A. *and* DIX G. (1999) *Britain at Work*. London, Routledge.

DEX S. (1989) 'Gender and the labour market', in D. Gallie (ed.), *Employment in Britain*, Oxford, Blackwell.

DOW J. (1964) *The Management of the British Economy 1945 to 1960*. Cambridge, Cambridge University Press.

FARNHAM D. (1976) 'The Labour Alliance: reality or myth?' *Parliamentary Affairs*. XXIX(1), Winter.

FARNHAM D. (1993) 'Human resources management and employee relations', in D. Farnham and S. Horton (EDS), *Managing the New Public Services*, Basingstoke, Macmillan.

FARNHAM D. (1990) 'Trade union policy 1979–89: restriction or reform?', in S. Savage and L. Robins (eds), *Public Policy under Thatcher*, Basingstoke, Macmillan.

FARNHAM D. (1996) 'New Labour, new unions and the new labour market'. *Parliamentary Affairs*. 49(44), October.

FARNHAM D. *and* GILES L. (1996) 'Human resources management and employment relations', in D. Farnham and S. Horton (eds), *Managing the New Public Services*, Basingstoke, Macmillan.

FARNHAM D. *and* HORTON S. (EDS) (1996a) *Managing the New Public Services*. Basingstoke, Macmillan.

FARNHAM D. *and* HORTON S. (1996b) *Managing People in the Public Services*. Basingstoke, Macmillan.

FARNHAM D. *and* PIMLOTT J. (1995) *Understanding Industrial Relations*. London, Cassell.

FLANDERS A. (1968) 'Collective bargaining: a theoretical analysis', in A. Flanders, 1970, *Management and Unions*, London, Faber & Faber.

FLEMING A. (1989) 'Employment in the public and private sectors'. *Economic Trends*. 434, December.

FOX A. (1985) *History and Heritage*. London, Allen & Unwin.

GAMBLE A. (1988) *The Free Economy and the Strong State*. London, Macmillan.

GREEN F. (1989) *The Restructuring of the British Economy*. London, Harvester.

HORTON S. *and* FARNHAM D. (EDS) (1999) *Public Management in Britain*. London, Macmillan.

JACOBI O., KELLER B. *and* MUELLER-JENTSCH W. (1998) 'Germany: Facing new challenges', in A. Ferner and R. Hyman (eds), *Changing Industrial Relations in Europe*, Oxford, Blackwell.

JENKINS R. (1989) 'Discrimination and equal opportunity in employment: ethnicity and race in the United Kingdom', in D. Gallie (ed.), *Employment in Britain*, Oxford, Blackwell.

JONES R. (1987) *Wages and Employment Policy 1936–85*. London, Allen & Unwin.

KAHN-FREUND O. (1977) *Labour and the Law*. London, Stevens.

KAHN-FREUND O. (1983) *Labour and the Law*. 3rd edition. London, Stevens.

LEVACIC R. (1988) *Supply Side Economics*. Oxford, Heinemann.

LEWIS D. *and* SARGENT M. (2000) *Essentials of Employment Law*. London, Institute of Personnel and Development.

MARCHINGTON M. (1989) 'Joint consultation in practice', in K. Sisson (ed.), *Personnel Management in Britain*, Oxford, Blackwell.

MIDDLEMAS K. (1979) *Politics in Industrial Society*. London, Deutsch.

MORAN M. (1977) *The Politics of Industrial Relations*. London, Macmillan.

OFFICE FOR NATIONAL STATISTICS (1997) 'Employment in the public and private sectors'. *Economic Trends*. 520, March.

RUBERY J. (1989) 'Employers and the labour market', in D. Gallie (ed.), *Employment in Britain*, Oxford, Blackwell.

ROBINSON D. (ed.) (1970) *Local Labour Markets and Wage Structure*. Farnborough, Gower.

STARKS M. (1991) *Not for Profit Not for Sale*. Bristol, Policy Journals.

STEWART M. (1983) 'Relative earnings and individual union membership in the UK'. *Economica*.

STOREY J. (1980) *The Challenge to Management Control*. London, Kogan Page.

STOREY J. (1983) *Managerial Prerogative and the Question of Control*. London, Routledge & Kegan Paul.

TERRY M. (1977) 'The inevitable growth of informality'. *British Journal of Industrial Relations*. 15(1).

VON PRONDZYNSKI F. (1998) 'Ireland: corporatism revived', in A. Ferner and R. Hyman (eds), *Changing Industrial Relations in Europe*, Oxford, Blackwell.

WEBB S. *and* WEBB B. (1913) *Industrial Democracy*. New York, Longmans.

WEDDERBURN, Lord (1986) *The Worker and the Law*. Harmondsworth, Penguin.

WHITE G. *and* CHAPMAN H. (1987) 'Long-term trends in public expenditure'. *Economic Trends*. 408, October.

WORSWICK D. *and* ADY P. (1952) *The British Economy 1945–50*. Oxford, Oxford University Press.

WORSWICK D. *and* TREVITHICK J. (1984) *Keynes and the Modern World*. Cambridge, Cambridge University Press.

2 The parties in employee relations

In advanced market economies, employee relations are largely institution-alised. This means that the primary parties to the employment relationship (employers and employees) are bound together by a network of formally agreed rules, agreements and procedures, such as contracts of employment, employment handbooks, grievance, disciplinary and promotion procedures, and by informal customs and practices. These networks of formal and informal employment rules provide both parties with a series of interdependent, individual rights and obligations, emphasising the mutuality of their relationship, which are aimed at reconciling any potential conflicts between them with authority and consistency. These rights and obligations between employers and employees are economic, legal and constitutional in character, but they are underpinned by a set of normative and moral values associated with fairness, equity and trust in the employment relationship (Hyman and Brough 1975, Fox 1974, Fox 1985).

Another institutional feature of employee relations is the secondary nature of many employment relationships. The secondary parties (management or management organisations and unions) are also bound together by a network of formally agreed collective rules, agreements and procedures, where trade unions are recognised by employers. These include union rules, collective agreements and negotiating and consultative procedures (see Chapters 1, 7 and 8). These link the parties together in a web of mutually independent, collective rights and obligations, again aimed at reconciling any potential conflicts between them legitimately and peacefully. These too are economic and constitutional in character, with their own procedural and substantive, normative order (Flanders and Fox 1969).

The last institutional feature of employee relations is the existence of third parties, normally agents of the state. These bodies are created to influence the decisions of the primary and secondary parties in the employment relationship and to ensure either 'fair play' or changes in the balance of power amongst them. The values associated with third-party institutions have varied between those of even-handedness, balance and legitimacy, on the one side, and of bias, controversy and coercion on the other (see Chapter 9).

MANAGEMENT

The term 'management' is used in two main senses. First, management is the set of activities carried out by those individuals with decision-taking and executive responsibilities in organisations. It focuses on the jobs, tasks and

27

activities that managers do. This definition of management incorporates three aspects of managing: what managers do; how they do it; and how they are grouped as 'systems of authority' in organisations, vertically and horizontally. It recognises that managers are themselves employees who are employed for the knowledge, skills and expertise that they bring into organisations as part of the internal and occupational divisions of labour. Management in this sense focuses on four areas of managing. These are: the nature of managerial work (Mintzberg 1975, Stewart 1982); managerial processes (Fayol 1949, Likert 1961, Peters and Waterman 1982); management levels (Chandler and Daems 1980); and the functional areas of management, such as operations, finance, marketing and personnel or human resources (Farnham 1990).

The second way in which the term 'management' is used is to describe the group of people in organisations who are collectively responsible for the efficient and effective running of the enterprises they manage. By this view, management is the authority system or the power group that has the responsibility for ensuring the financial viability, organisational success and ultimate accountability of an enterprise to its primary beneficiaries, whether these are shareholders, government ministers, local politicians or governing bodies. Management in this sense focuses on the agency roles of managers in terms of their responsibilities for enterprise effectiveness, corporate efficiency and employee relations. It is this meaning of the term 'management' that is primarily used in this book.

One objective of management collectively is to ensure the profitability and/or efficiency of the organisations in which they work. They have to ensure the most efficient use of enterprise resources and the achievement of enterprise goals. In practice, however, management also has to take account of the broader social and economic consequences of their decisions, not just the short-term economic ones. In this respect, Brown (1960) amongst others has argued that management has to reconcile a number of conflicting aims and objectives. These include making their enterprises economically viable, whilst at the same time ensuring that organisations are responsive to shareholder, customer, supplier and employee interests. Management, in short, is concerned not only with profits and efficiency in the market sector, or with 'value for money' in the public sector, but also with being socially responsible to the wider communities with which it interacts. It also wants good working relations with its employees. This view of management is one most recently revived in the concept of the enterprise as one consisting of a number of interrelated and interdependent 'stakeholders' (Hutton 1996).

This means that employees are only one of the many stakeholders in organisations and are only one of the executive concerns of management (Farnham 1999). Customers, banks, suppliers and government inspectorates all make demands on the management systems of organisations. Employee relations are an important part of the management function but they are only one of management's many organisational roles and corporate responsibilities. This makes the managing of employee relations problematic in any organisation. At one extreme, management can develop sophisticated employee relations strategies, policies and procedures, which take account of and 'fit with' other, often conflicting, demands made on managers as a group, such as the search for profitability, shareholder value, productivity, performance and effective marketing in private businesses. In the public sector, the emphasis may be on efficiency, accountability, value for money for taxpayers, economy and satisfied clients or service users.

In both cases, the 'good' employer's aim is to promote all these objectives, as well as the best employment practices associated with being 'model' employing organisations. At the other extreme, management may act in ways meeting only the minimum employment standards required by the law and local labour market pressures and it may place much greater emphasis on financial matters, operations management and technical issues, as is the case in small businesses in the private sector. As the Workplace Employee Relations Survey 1998 (WERS) has concluded, whilst it would be over-simplistic to argue that the small business approach to organising work was totally unstructured, small businesses have 'a *less* formal approach than small multiples to the regulation of the employment relationship' (Cully *et al* 1999: 273).

The management of employee relations

For these and related reasons, most large and some medium-size organisations in the private sector and those in the public sector use employee relations specialists. They are variously described as personnel managers, industrial relations managers, employee relations managers or, most recently, as human resources managers. It is these members of management who represent the human resources function within the management structure and in its dealings with line managers, employee or union representatives, and employees. They are the professional managers of the employment contract.

The traditional management role in employee relations was identified as a disinterested, reactive and fire-fighting one. Top management literally did not want to know about employee relations (Winkler 1974). According to Miller (1987), this pattern of reactive, 'non-strategic' employee relations management implies an employee relations function that is characterised by being:

- separate from an organisation's corporate strategy
- short term
- not of interest to the board of directors
- identified with a definition of employee relations focusing principally on unionised groups of manual workers.

During the 1990s, however, the employee relations function took on a more structured and important role in the managing of people, in both the private and public sectors. According to the WERS 1998, the broad picture in the late 1990s was one of relatively well-developed structures for the management of employees in organisations, with control being largely retained by centralised personnel departments, especially in larger organisations. Employee relations was generally seen to be an important part of management, with three-quarters of workplaces covered by the survey having a personnel specialist at workplace or higher organisational level, though some of them were general managers. The proportion of workplaces employing personnel specialists at workplace or higher level varied by workplace size, organisation size, sector, ownership and industry. Larger workplaces, larger organisations, the public sector and foreign-owned organisations were more likely to have personnel specialists than smaller workplaces, smaller organisations, the private sector and wholly UK-owned firms. The industries having relatively high proportions of personnel specialists at workplace or higher level included the public utilities, the wholesale and retail trades, financial services, public administration, education and health. Those workplaces with relatively low proportions of personnel specialists included manufacturing and construction, with hotels and restaurants, transport and communications, and other business services falling in the middle ranges.

The nine most common tasks of managers having employee relations responsibilities were identified in the WERS 1998 as:

- handling grievances (in 95 per cent of workplaces)
- recruiting or selecting employees (94 per cent)
- equal opportunities (93 per cent)
- staffing or manpower planning (91 per cent)
- training employees (88 per cent)
- health and safety (87 per cent)
- performance appraisals (86 per cent)
- pay and conditions of employment (78 per cent)
- systems of payment (57 per cent).

The number and type of duties for which managers were responsible varied by job, however. Over one-third of personnel specialists and general managers said that they were responsible for all nine tasks, compared with almost three-fifths of owners or proprietors of medium or smaller businesses (Cully *et al* 1999).

Traditional and emerging patterns of employee relations management

Figure 3 sums up the main traditional and emerging economic, organisational, social and political contexts within which employers and management, and their workers, have operated and are operating in, especially but not exclusively in Britain. The elements within each of these contexts are derived from the more detailed contextual analyses provided in Chapters 4 and 5. These are obviously 'pure' typologies and, in the 'real world' of personnel and development, the traditional and emerging contexts of

Figure 3 The contexts of British employee relations

Traditional contexts	Emerging contexts
The Economy	
protected economy	open economy
strong national markets	globalised markets
industrialisation	de-industrialisation
strong manufacturing base	dominant service base
national ownership	multinational ownership
large public sector	smaller public sector
mass consumption	customised consumption
steady growth	variable growth
regulated labour market	deregulated labour market
Work Organisation	
Fordist	post-Fordist
bureaucratic/hierarchic	organic/flat
mechanical technology	information technology
mass production	batch production
full-time employment	flexible employment
male employment	growing female employment
single skills and unskilled work	multiskills and deskilled work
task-based work	team-based work
The Social Structure	
young population	ageing population
nuclear family structure	multiple family structure
large working class	small working class
small middle class	large middle class
strong class identities	interest-based identities
class subcultures	diverse subcultures
growing equality	growing inequality
stable society	dynamic society
Politics	
two-party system	multiparty system
partisan voting	issue-based voting
consensus politics	conviction politics
corporatist policy-making	governmental policy-making
national sovereignty	Europeanisation
strong collectivist/welfare state culture	strong individualist/enterprise culture
Keynesian policies	monetarist/supply-side policies
state support for collective bargaining	state support for individual contracts

employee relations management are rarely as clear-cut as Figure 3 implies. These typologies are identified and used as tools of analysis and for the purposes of description rather than of prescription. What is clear, however, is that the traditional contexts, which were established largely in the immediate post-war period, no longer apply. Above all, the 1980s and 1990s were periods of immense change, uncertainty and transition, economically, socially, politically and organisationally. It is a legacy continuing into the twenty-first century. Whilst, in practice, elements of the traditional contexts remain, they are being continually challenged and counterbalanced by the forces of change, as indicated in the emerging contexts outlined in Figure 4.

These external contexts, in turn, are impinging on the patterns of employee relations management currently being practised in Britain, as shown in Figure 4. Traditional patterns of employee relations management, based on collectivism, managing relatively high levels of organised industrial conflict and 'personnel management' strategies, now co-exist with, or in some cases are being replaced by, emerging patterns of employee relations management in both private and public organisations. The 'new employee relations' and emerging patterns of employee relations management, in contrast, are more likely to be based on individualism, low levels of organised industrial conflict and 'human resources management' strategies. There are clearly hybrid forms of employee relations management, which draw on elements of both the traditional and emerging models outlined in Figure 4. But the important factor to recognise is that the predominant patterns, whether nationally or organisationally, evolve largely from the contexts outlined above. When these contexts change, as they inevitably do, so do the dominant patterns of employee relations management. No single pattern of

Figure 4 Patterns of British employee relations (ERL) management

Traditional patterns (Personnel management strategies)	Emerging patterns (Human resources management strategies)
strong unions	weak unions
collective bargaining	employee involvement
jointly driven ERL	management-driven ERL
policy focused on groups	policy focused on individuals
collective agreements	personal contracts
standardised payments	payment by performance
narrow wage differentials	wider wage differentials
common employee benefits	cafeteria employee benefits
employment security	employment insecurity
high levels of organised industrial conflict	low levels of organised industrial conflict
personnel management strategies	human resources management strategies

employee relations management, nationally or organisationally, is either self-evident or axiomatic at any one time, or over time. It is a function of management choice, taking account of the contemporary economic, organisational, social and political contexts in which employers and workers operate.

Managing collective bargaining

The steady growth of trade unions throughout the first part of the twentieth century, together with employer recognition of trade unions and public policy support for collective bargaining, meant that the joint determination of terms and conditions of employment had become the centrepiece of British employee relations by the 1960s (Ministry of Labour 1965). Indeed, the conclusion of the Donovan Commission (1968: 50) was that properly conducted, 'collective bargaining is the best method of conducting industrial relations'. It added, however, that multi-employer, industry-wide bargaining was no longer capable of imposing its decisions on the participants. The Commission therefore recommended that management should take the initiative and responsibility for reforming collective bargaining at company and plant levels. The means was to be the development of proactive personnel policies, management-led authoritative, collective bargaining machinery, comprehensive procedural agreements and joint arrangements for discussing health and safety at work, within companies or plants. Multi-employer, industry-wide bargaining would deal with those issues, such as overtime premiums, length of working week or holiday periods, which it could most effectively regulate (see Chapter 9).

From the late 1960s until the mid-1980s, Donovan's recommendations were gradually extended and acted upon in much of the corporate sector, with parallel developments in the public sector. The changes must not be exaggerated, however, as research by Storey (1992: 259) showed that whilst old-style industrial relations 'fire-fighting' was increasingly disavowed by management, there was hardly 'an instance where anything approaching a "strategic" stance towards unions and industrial relations could readily be discerned as having taken its place'. Nevertheless, the outcome was a steady expansion in numbers of personnel and employee relations specialists to help deal with the workplace issues arising from decentralised collective bargaining, the increasing scope of employment legislation and trade union organisation locally (Millward and Stevens 1986, Millward et al 1992).

In this role, employee relations specialists are a resource from which senior line management can draw advice, expertise and technical know-how in the managing of collective employee relations. The sorts of tasks in which they are involved include:

- participating in negotiating and joint consultation
- assisting in the drafting of collective agreements
- advising on employment legislation
- advising in grievance and disciplinary cases

33

- handling redundancies
- providing inputs to personnel policy-making and decision-taking.

It is a role with both advisory and executive functions that typifies this collective approach to employee relations management.

Human resources management (HRM) and the new industrial relations

Another development, largely since the 1980s, has been the emergence of what are claimed to be more strategic and integrated approaches to managing employee relations, based on employee commitment and common interests in the workplace, rather than managerial control and potential conflicts between employer and employee. Its origins can be traced back to the 1950s in the United States where three 'models' of HRM can be identified. Fombrun, Tichy and Devanna (1984), for example, introduced the 'matching model' of HRM, which emphasised the 'tight fit' between human resources strategy and business strategy, with the assumption that personnel specialists could play an important role in the formulation of corporate strategy. The 'Harvard' model of Beer and his colleagues (1984) identified the different stakeholders in organisations, including shareholders, employees and the community, arguing that HRM strategies needed to recognise these interests and integrate them into human resources strategy and business strategy. Another American, Walton (1985), emphasised the shift from 'control to commitment' in organisations and the importance of HRM approaches in achieving corporate success and employee commitment.

The HRM initiatives that have taken place in the UK have been mainly in some larger organisations, especially in the corporate sector, in response to increased product market competition, changes in market structures and technological change. Some of these developments are identified in the debate about HRM in the UK (Storey 1989, Storey 1992, Sissons 1998). One element in the debate distinguishes between 'hard' HRM, focusing on human resource strategy and employee utilisation, and 'soft' HRM, with its greater emphasis on the 'human' aspects of management and concern with people in organisations. Other UK commentators, such as Guest (1987), have examined the capacity of HRM to satisfy some key propositions, such as 'strategic integration', 'high commitment', 'high quality' and 'flexibility' within organisations. Hendry and Pettigrew (1990), in contrast, have built on the Harvard model linking HRM content to business strategy and taking account of the socio-economic, technical and political-legal contexts impacting on strategic decisions. Critics such as Legge (1995: 339) have argued, however, that 'the widespread implementation of the "soft" normative model of HRM appears as a mirage, retreating into a receding horizon', while for Kennoy (1990) HRM is a very ambiguous concept that means all things to all people. The conclusion of a leading set of industrial relations commentators (Edwards *et al* 1998: 22) was that much of the evidence on HRM in the UK came from relatively large firms, where particular HRM

34

practices have been adopted, 'albeit sporadically'.

Whatever the exact nature of HRM, survey evidence reveals a fairly positive picture of strategic HRM by the early 1990s. At that time, 63 per cent of UK organisations surveyed claimed to have personnel or human resource directors, 83 per cent claimed a corporate strategy and 73 per cent claimed a personnel or HRM strategy (Price Waterhouse Cranfield 1990). Recent evidence from the WERS 1998 indicated that (Cully *et al* 1999):

- 64 per cent of private-sector workplaces had a representative on the board of directors, with specific responsibility for employee relations
- 57 per cent of private-sector workplaces had a strategic plan encompassing employee development, drawn up with the help of the employee relations manager
- 40 per cent of private-sector workplaces had an integrated strategic plan and representative on the board of directors
- 39 per cent of private-sector workplaces had Investors in People accreditation.

Other developments have given rise to a related debate focused on the relationship between the claimed rise of HRM and the apparent decline of trade union power. Bassett (1986) and Wickens (1987), on the basis of limited case study material, proclaimed the arrival of a 'new industrial relations' based on single-union, 'no-strike' deals or even no unions at all. Dunn (1990) noted that the rhetoric of industrial relations has changed. From being based on the metaphor of 'trench warfare', it is now based on that of the 'new frontier', which is more consistent with HRM and the notion of a new industrial relations than it is with traditional personnel management. Again the evidence is inconclusive. Indeed the WERS 1998 (Cully *et al* 1999) concluded that while trade union representation was disappearing at an accelerating rate in the period 1980–98, not all indicators of union presence and activity indicated increasing weakness. 'More plausible is the notion that a number of alternative approaches to employee relations are being adopted in different types of workplace and in different parts of the economy.'

Models of employee relations management and managerial approaches to employee relations

From the outline analysis above, it is clear that the roles and status of employee relations specialists in organisations are now secure but are quite different from what they were when Donovan reported. Employee relations managers clearly operate in a variety of modes and at different organisational levels. Some are operating in roles akin to what Tyson (1987) has described as the 'contracts manager' model of the personnel function. This is where employee relations specialists are particularly valued for their capacity to make quick decisions and informal agreements with trade union representatives, and their other activities are largely advisory. Others are operating as what Tyson has described as HRM 'architects'. This is a creative view of personnel and employee relations that aims at contributing to corporate success through explicit human resources policies and integrated systems of labour control between personnel and line managers. The architect model is particularly associated with the management of change, proactive personnel planning and systems of employee involvement (see Chapter 6).

In its role as agent of the employer, management has a variety of employment activities to carry out. These include: attracting, recruiting, rewarding, motivating, retaining, directing, disciplining, exiting, negotiating and consulting with employees at work. In undertaking these activities, management can choose, explicitly or implicitly, from a multiplicity of approaches to employee relations. A critical influence is management style. Management style, according to Purcell (1987: 535), implies:

> a distinctive set of guiding principles, written or otherwise, which set parameters to and signposts for management action in the way employees are treated and particular events handled. Management style is therefore akin to business policy and its strategic derivatives.

It is management style, in short, that circumscribes the boundaries and direction of acceptable management action in its dealing with employees.

Frames of reference

Some writers suggest that it is management's 'frame of reference' that determines its predominant style of employee relations management. Fox (1966) identified two major frames of reference, the unitary and the pluralist. The main elements of the unitary view are:

- there is one source of authority in organisations, with no oppositionary groups or leaders
- the role of organisational leaders is to act in ways inspiring the loyalty and commitment of employees
- organisations consist of teams of people, working together for common aims, where there are no conflicts of interest between managers and subordinates
- strong leadership is required from management to achieve common organisational purpose
- trade unions are illegitimate intrusions into the right to manage
- conflict in organisations is dysfunctional, disloyal and out of keeping with organisational well-being.

Pluralism, in contrast, emphasises that:

- there are rival sources of leadership and attachment within organisations
- conflict can be functional if recognised and contained within appropriate institutional mechanisms

- organisations are coalitions of competing interests and management's role is to mediate among different interest groups
- trade unions are legitimate representatives of employee interests at work
- stability in employee relations results from concessions and compromises between managers and unions in the collective bargaining process.

Fox (1974) developed his analysis further in identifying four 'ideal' typologies of employee relations management. He described management as being:

- *traditionalists*, with unitary, anti-union policies
- *sophisticated paternalists*, with unitary, enlightened, employee-centred human resource policies
- *sophisticated moderns*, with pluralist, joint management–union decision-making in defined areas
- *standard moderns*, where unions are recognised but employee relations fire-fighting predominates.

Purcell and Sisson (1983) divided the standard modern management style into 'constitutionalists' and 'consultors'. Constitutionalists codify the limits of collective bargaining, whilst consultors place greater emphasis on joint consultation and joint problem-solving.

Another frame of reference is the 'neo-unitary' one, which builds on unitarism but provides a more sophisticated approach to managing people than the unitary framework (Farnham and Pimlott 1995). Managers holding this position:

- aim to integrate employees into their organisations through encouraging commitment and involvement by employees in the business and its business plans
- believe strongly in market-centred, managerialist and individualist values
- seek employee commitment to quality, customer needs and job flexibility
- stress the importance of corporate culture in managing change
- invest heavily in training and development.

Individualism and collectivism

Purcell (1987: 535–6) has claimed that the unitary and pluralist frames of reference are limited in defining management styles. He identified two main dimensions of management style: individualism and collectivism. Individualism focuses on 'the feelings and sentiments of each employee' and encourages the capacities of individual employees and their roles at work. He distinguishes between 'high' and 'low' degrees of individualism. High individualism emphasises the resource status of employees, with employers wanting to develop and nurture their employees' talents and abilities. Related employment policies include careful selection, internal labour markets, staff appraisal, merit pay and extensive communication systems, all of which are associated with a 'neo-unitary' approach to employee relations (Farnham and Pimlott 1995). Low individualism emphasises the commodity status of employees, with employers concentrating on the control of both labour costs and the labour process. Profits are the priority and employment policies include recruiting in secondary labour markets, tight workplace discipline and little security of employment. Intermediate between high and low individualism is 'paternalism'. This synthesises caring, welfare employment policies with the subordinate position of lower-level employees in the organisational hierarchy.

Collectivism is the 'extent to which the organisation recognises the right of employees to have a say in those aspects of management decision-making which concern them' (Purcell 1987: 538). Collectivism is operated through trade union organisation or other forms of employee representative system, thus giving employees a collective voice in organisational decision-making. There are two aspects of collectivism: the levels of employee participation – whether these are 'high' or 'low' – and the degree of legitimacy given to collective organisation by management. High-level employee participation, such as co-determination, pension fund trustees and employer-wide collective bargaining, takes place at the corporate level. Low-level employee participation, in contrast, takes place at workgroup, departmental or workplace levels. Management tolerance of collectivism ranges from willing co-operation, at one extreme, to grudging acceptance at the other.

The important point made by Purcell (1987: 541) was that links between individualism and collectivism in employee relations are complex. While some employers have more individualist management styles, such as American-owned companies, and some have more collectivist ones, such as larger UK companies, elements of both individualism and collectivism are not incompatible with each other, as in some Japanese-owned and British companies. 'Management styles operate along the two dimensions and . . . action in one area, toward individualism, for example, is not necessarily associated with changes in the collectivism scale.'

In practice, individualist styles of employee relations management tend towards non-unionism, while collectivist ones lead to union recognition. Thus whether an employer recognises trade unions for representational, consultative, negotiating or co-determination purposes is a critical and visible expression of management style and its approach to employee relations. This does not mean, however, that internal training, promotion ladders and welfare provisions for individual employees are precluded. On the other hand, where trade unions are recognised and employees are given a collective voice in employee relations, and the unions are subsequently derecognised, this is clearly an expression of a shift towards a more individualist style of employee relations management (Claydon 1989).

Employee relations policies

It is difficult to define the concept of an 'employee relations policy' with precision. In essence, it represents an employer's intentions and objectives about employment-related and human resources matters and the ways in which these are communicated to managers, employees, the wider community and, where they are recognised, to trade unions and their representatives. In practice, employee relations policies are an amalgam of explicit written statements and implicit unwritten assumptions about how employees are to be treated and managed as individuals and as members of trade unions. They are organisationally specific and contingent on the external and internal environments within which organisations operate, but can change over time. Management style is an important determinant of an organisation's employee relations policies, but the internal and external contingencies are crucial.

The contingencies acting on management in determining an organisation's employee relations policies include:

- legislation
- other employers' policies
- organisational size, ownership and location
- union power
- prevailing 'good practice'
- most importantly, the links between the organisation's business strategy and its employment and human resources strategy
- public policy.

Policy choices

One way of analysing management's policy choices in employee relations is outlined in Figure 5. This identifies four possible policy choices for management. First, management can pursue a policy of worker subordination. This is based on low degrees of individualism and collectivism, with high levels of management discretion. Policy is operated through firm management control and management prerogative or 'the right to manage'. Second, the policy of union incorporation is where there is a relatively high degree of collectivism, a low degree of individualism, and policy is operated, in key employment areas, through joint management–union regulation. The third policy choice is employee commitment that incorporates a high degree of individualism and a low degree of collectivism, with policy being operated through management-driven programmes of HRM and employee involvement. Fourth, the policy of worker participation involves high degrees of both individualism and collectivism, with policy being operated through management–employee co-determination linked, possibly, with employee involvement measures. Indeed worker participation policies are not incompatible with union incorporation and/or employee commitment policies. In practice, of course, management can adopt different employee relations policies for different groups of workers or different policies for the same group of workers at different times.

Where an organisation espouses its employee relations policies, they are normally written down and communicated by top management to line

Figure 5 Management policies on employee relations

		Individualism	
		low	*high*
	low	worker subordination	employee commitment
Collectivism			
	high	union incorporation	worker participation

managers and their subordinate staff. Such policies can be broad or narrow in scope and potentially can cover a wide range of possible policy areas. Employee relations policies, which are in effect guidelines to effective managerial action, are put into practice through relevant procedures, handbooks and manuals. These policies enable management to take consistent decisions in employee relations, thereby minimising potential conflicts between employers and trade unions and managers and their staff. The sorts of area where employee relations policy guidelines are developed by management include:

- union recognition (or non-recognition)
- collective bargaining units, levels and scope
- information for the purposes of conducting collective bargaining
- time-off arrangements for in-house union officials involved in employee relations
- pay and conditions
- equal opportunities
- appraisal
- training and development
- recruitment and selection
- promotion
- grievances, discipline and dismissal
- redundancy
- employee involvement
- human resources planning
- health and safety.

The list above is neither exclusive nor exhaustive, but is indicative of the policy choices available to management.

Business strategy and managing personnel

Thomason (1991) has provided a more sophisticated analysis. He examined the links between business strategy and management approaches to acquiring and utilising human resources and identifies three historical shifts in

40

business strategy. They are not watertight compartments but are indicative of the main emphases of business strategy in different historical periods, different enterprises over time and some enterprises at any one time. The three approaches are:

- a *product differentiation strategy*, associated with the early industrial revolution
- a *low-cost leadership strategy*, associated with industrial rationalisation, which began about 100 years ago
- a *customer/client satisfaction strategy*, associated with 'new wave' rationalisations, in response to global competition and technical change, since the 1960s.

The differentiation strategy depends upon a core skilled workforce, supplemented by peripheral workers recruited for less-skilled work, organised in factories and workshops. The low-cost strategy depends upon the external labour market, where jobs are broken down into small tasks and repetitive activities, in line with the principles of scientific management. In contrast, in organisations seeking special relationships with their customers or clients, emphasis is placed on quality, reliability and product or service delivery and intra-organisational teamwork. This business strategy depends on, first, the development of internal labour markets and job training for existing employees. Second, job tasks and activities are reorganised, with the focus being on flexibility, versatility, multiskilling and commitment. Third, management tries to create and transmit new corporate cultures to its employees (Anthony 1990), emphasising the primacy of client relationships, quality and teamwork.

Thomason's analysis leads to four possible labour control processes for management. The first stresses the need for quality output and, where recruitment takes place in the external labour market, uses an *employee selection strategy*. The second, which emphasises low-cost production and recruitment in the external labour market, uses an *employee supervision strategy*. This provides a framework of agreed or imposed employment rules and procedures. The third, based on price competition and demand for high-quality products, relies on a *human resources development strategy*, aimed at staff flexibility. The fourth, stressing customer satisfaction and recruitment from the internal labour market, focuses on a *human resources partnership strategy*. This aims at integrating employees into the organisation and at employee commitment.

MANAGEMENT ORGANISATIONS

There are a range of organisations acting on behalf of management interests in employee relations. Some, such as the CIPD, Institute of Management and Institute of Directors, are based on individual or personal membership. This section focuses on management organisations based on collective or

41

corporate membership that have specific roles in employee relations and related areas.

Employers' associations

An employers' association is defined in law as any organisation of employers, individual proprietors or constituent organisations of employers whose principal purpose includes the regulation of relations between employers and workers or between employers and trade unions. Employers' associations recruit member firms vertically, on an industry-wide basis. It is estimated that membership of employers' associations in industry and commerce, which was 22 per cent in the 1980s and had fallen to 13 per cent in 1990, had risen slightly to 18 per cent of workplaces in 1998 (Cully *et al* 1999).

Objectives, functions and ideology

The idea of employers within an industry combining together for employee relations purposes is not a new one. The first such bodies were formed in the nineteenth century in response to trade union organisation. Their central objective was to protect employer interests collectively in dealings with the unions (Clegg 1979). However, unlike in the United States where, despite anti-trust laws, there have been powerful producer cartels, there has always been a much stronger ideological reluctance by British companies to combine amongst themselves for business purposes. Companies have generally jealously guarded their 'trade secrets' and corporate independence in commercial matters, with the result that membership of employers' associations has often been resisted by some British companies. In recent years, the national collective bargaining function and protective role of employers' associations have diminished, as decentralised bargaining has grown and union power weakened.

One of the main traditional roles of employers' associations was to bargain collectively for their members, with the trade unions, on a multi-employer or industry-wide basis. The theory underlying this was that multi-employer collective agreements on pay and conditions took labour costs out of competition for all employers in the industry, thus allowing companies to compete in product markets other than by undercutting their competitors' employment costs. A corollary to this was that combination amongst employers also protected individual employers against being 'picked off', one by one, by the union(s) during a trade dispute. With the changing ownership and organisation of business enterprises, the decentralisation of corporate decision-making and competitive market pressures, companies are now less likely to engage in multi-employer, national collective bargaining, which has generally been replaced by company or workplace bargaining or, in some cases, union derecognition.

At the end of 1997, the Certification Officer (CO), who is required by law to maintain a list of employers' associations under section 2 of the Trade Union and Labour Relations (Consolidation) Act 1992 (TULRCA 1992), listed 113 such organisations, with another 97 bodies that were unlisted. This compares with 131 listed and 146 unlisted associations in 1992, 148 listed and 187 unlisted associations in 1986, and 196 listed and 280 unlisted associations in 1977 (Certification Office 1999, 1992, 1987, 1978). Table 1 summarises the largest employers' associations in Britain at the end of 1997, which covered a wide range of manufacturing and service-sector employers. Some of them, such as the Engineering Employers Associations, are independent local associations affiliated to national, federal bodies. Others, such as the National Farmers Union, are strong national bodies with local, subordinate associations.

Current activities

In these and similar cases, employers' associations continue to provide a number of services to member firms. These include:

- employer representation in collective bargaining
- intelligence, information and data collection for employers
- assistance in operating procedures to avoid disputes

Table 1 Major listed and unlisted employers' associations in Britain, 1997

Associations with over £2,000,000 income	Number of members
Engineering Employers Federation (EEF) West Midlands	1,201
Engineering Employers Federation	17
Engineering Employers Federation South	580
Engineering Employers East Midlands Association	380
10 other Engineering Employers Associations	2,887
England and Wales Cricket Board Ltd	39
National Farmers Union	127,024
Freight Transport Association Ltd*	11,767
Retail Motor Industry Federation Ltd	11,424
Electrical Contractors Association	1,970
Heating and Ventilating Contractors Association	1,159
British Printing Industries Federation	2,971
Construction Federation	8
Road Haulage Association Ltd*	9,687
Chemical Industries Association Ltd*	175
National Federation of Retail Newsagents	24,886
Newspaper Society	216
British Jewellery and Giftware Federation*	1,996
Federation of Master Builders	14,830
National Pharmaceutical Association Ltd	5,771
Paper Federation of Great Britain Ltd	57
Society of London Theatre*	94

* unlisted association

Source: Certification Office (1999)

- policy guidelines and advice on employee relations
- consultancy and training for managers
- representing employers at employment tribunals
- protection for employers taking part in trade disputes against the trade unions in their industry.

In acting as specialist providers of employee relations knowledge and expertise, employers' associations, like trade unions, are serviced by a cadre of full-time officers who work closely with elected representatives from member companies in determining policy, representing employer interests and fire-fighting on behalf of employers when necessary (Watson 1988).

As indicated above, a main reason why there has been a decline in the absolute numbers and the relative importance of employers' associations in the last decade is the declining importance of multi-employer pay bargaining arrangements in the private sector (Brown and Walsh 1991). Further, the traditional reluctance to combine by private employers has been reinforced by recent changes in business structure, especially decentralised cost centres (Marginson *et al* 1988), increased product market competition and devolved employee relations policies. In these circumstances, companies, and sometimes plants within multi-site companies, are less inclined to join employers' associations for employee relations purposes. They prefer the autonomy of determining their own employment policies, reward structures and decentralised bargaining arrangements for dealing with trade unions. Indeed, some writers argue that decentralised bargaining provides distinct advantages to management by keeping local union officials and full-time officers away from strategic decision-making (Kinnie 1987). In some cases, employers have opted for union derecognition and no bargaining at all (Gregg and Yates 1991).

Another reason for the relative decline in importance of employers' associations is political. Since the late 1970s, governments have adopted market-centred economic policies rather than corporatist ones (see Chapters 1, 4 and 9). Apart from special cases, such as that of the National Farmers Union, this shift in public policy has generally diminished the role of employers' associations as pressure groups representing the interests of employers nationally in discussions in Whitehall and government departments. Moreover, with shifts towards greater EU integration and a single European market for capital, goods, services and certain types of labour (such as footballers), the role of industry-wide employers' associations is further weakened. The political role of employers' associations is now more effectively carried out by central organisations, such as the Confederation of British Industry (CBI), which recruits horizontally across industries and vertically within them, than by industry-based ones. There are also supranational employer organisations, such as the Union of Industrial and Employers' Confederations of Europe (UNICE) (see below).

The Confederation of British Industry (CBI)

Unlike some of its other European counterparts, such as in Germany, Ireland and the Netherlands, the CBI – ever since its formation in 1965 – has been ambivalent about taking on a corporatist role in employee relations in collaboration with unions and government at central level. In recent years, its activities have mainly focused on 'speaking up' for British business. The CBI has a complex structure of committees. These include an Employment Policy Committee – comprising an Employee Relations Panel, Employment Relocation Panel and Equal Opportunities Panel – and an Education and Training Affairs Committee. As a campaigning and management organisation, however, the CBI is only indirectly involved in employee relations and then only insofar as these affect corporate efficiency, productivity and competitiveness.

The CBI's mission is to 'help create and sustain the conditions in which businesses in the UK can compete and prosper' (Confederation of British Industry 1995: 9) and its objectives are:

- to provide the means for British industry to influence economic and related policy
- to develop the contribution of British industry to the national economy
- to encourage economic efficiency
- to provide advice and services to its members.

CBI policy prescriptions on employee relations are limited but direct. First, since the 1980s, the CBI has continually expressed its opposition to a tightly regulated labour market and has been strongly opposed to harmonised EU employment legislation and minimum standards of employment protection. Its arguments are that this would adversely affect business competitiveness and restrict the necessary flexibility of the labour market and it supported the UK opt-out from the Social Chapter, instituted under the Major administrations 1990–97. Second, CBI actions on employment affairs have concentrated on helping its members protect labour cost competitiveness and labour flexibility. The CBI has continually argued the case for linking employee pay to corporate performance and productivity growth. It has also taken part in the public debate about the merits of decentralised pay bargaining (Confederation of British Industry 1991).

The CBI has identified its most important economic, European, education and training, employment policy and international activities and those policy changes by government where it considers its influence has been most felt. These include (Confederation of British Industry 1996a):

- working on the private finance initiative with government
- encouraging the Labour Party in a more pro-business direction
- keeping European business issues on the political agenda
- contributing to a more dispassionate debate about European monetary union

- lobbying Brussels for action on competitiveness and related business issues
- publishing regional business agendas
- focusing on competitiveness
- shifting the Labour Party away from statutory training levies towards individual learning accounts
- raising business concerns on how the quality of the UK skills base might be addressed
- developing a strong small and medium enterprise agenda, oriented towards growth companies
- supporting full implementation of the Uruguay Round Agreements in World Trade Organisation discussions.

The CBI also published an agenda aimed at the incoming Labour Government, elected in May 1997, setting out policies needed 'for sustained wealth creation' in the UK (Confederation of British Industry 1996b: 3). It set out the features of the global context and the resultant challenges that business and government would have to address jointly. These included:

- meeting the challenges and opportunities of a changing world
- maintaining economic stability
- building a Europe that works
- investing to grow
- focusing on making markets work
- working together effectively
- developing skilled and flexible people.

In the latter context, the CBI wanted an education and training system supporting lifelong learning, employment practices focusing on investment in people as individuals and labour market legislation supporting flexibility and responsiveness that 'doesn't stand in the way of job creation' (*ibid*: 10). The CBI therefore supported:

- further improvements in Britain's education and training system
- the attainment of agreed national education and training targets
- a unified and respected qualifications structure for 16–19-year-olds
- tax-incentivised learning accounts for individuals
- Investors in People being made available to small and medium-sized enterprises
- pay linked to performance.

On the other hand, the CBI opposed:

- legislative imposition of specific forms of employee relations
- a statutory enforced minimum wage
- a UK opt-in to the Social Protocol at Maastricht.

In the light of the Labour Government's subsequent enactment of the Employment Relations Act (ERA) 1999, National Minimum Wage Act 1998 and its opt-in to the Social Chapter after coming to office in May 1997, the CBI was singularly unsuccessful in achieving its policy objectives in these three areas.

The CBI claims to represent the interests of more than 250,000 member organisations, embracing all sectors of industry and commerce, and more than 200 trade associations. Many of its members are multinational businesses or parent companies with subsidiaries, but over 90 per cent of its members are firms with under 200 employees. This means that the CBI recruits both horizontally across industries and vertically within them. To fulfil its tasks, it has a President's Committee, a council, a National Manufacturing Council and a number of standing committees. Seven directorates and a chief economic adviser service these bodies. These comprise: membership and commercial; small and medium-sized enterprises; finance; business environment; European affairs; human resources; and manufacturing and international markets. The CBI is also active in Europe through UNICE (see below).

The Union of Industrial and Employers' Confederations of Europe (UNICE)

UNICE is the official voice of European business and industry in contact with European institutions and was established in 1958. It is composed of 33 central industry and employers' federations from 25 European countries, with a permanent secretariat based in Brussels. Its purposes include (Union of Industrial and Employers' Confederations of Europe 1997):

- to keep abreast of issues that interest its members by maintaining permanent contacts with all the European institutions
- to provide a framework that enables industry and employers to examine European policies and proposed legislation and prepare joint position papers
- to promote its policies and positions at European and national level and persuade European legislators to take them into account
- to represent its members in the dialogue between social partners provided for in European treaties.

UNICE's main priorities are:

- improving European competitiveness leading to growth and the creation of lasting jobs
- completing all aspects of the Single Market
- progressing towards economic and monetary union, with a European system of central banks and a single currency
- pursuing economic and social cohesion in the EU
- developing social policies compatible with competitiveness and economic growth

- supporting the restructuring and economic development of central and eastern Europe
- liberalising world trade on the principles of the Uruguay Round Agreement
- promoting European technology, research and development
- protecting the environment based on sustainable development.

UNICE's principal contacts are with the Commission of the European Communities, European Parliament, Council of Ministers and Economic and Social Committee. It also works with other European-level governmental organisations and international non-governmental organisations, such as the European Trade Union Confederation (ETUC). It operates through its Council of Presidents, an Executive Committee, a permanent Secretariat in Brussels and a series of policy committees that assist in policy formulation, suggest actions to be taken and implement UNICE decisions (Union of Industrial and Employers' Confederations of Europe 1997).

EMPLOYEE ORGANISATIONS

There are a variety of organisations representing employees and workers at workplace, organisational, national, European and international level. These include trade unions, staff associations, professional associations, union confederations, national trade union centres and international organisations of trade unions and trade unionists.

Trade unions

A trade union is any organisation of workers, or constituent or affiliated organisations, whose principal purposes include the regulation of relations between its members and their employers, management or employers' associations. The CO listed 224 unions in Britain in December 1998, with a total of 7.8 million members, although some 80 per cent of this membership was concentrated in the 16 largest unions with 100,000 members or more. This compares with 287 listed unions in 1992, with a total of 9.8 million members, 375 listed unions with 10.8 million members in 1986 and 485 listed unions with 12.1 million members in 1977 (Certification Office 1999, 1992, 1987, 1978). It was estimated that in 1980, at the time of the first Workplace Industrial Relations Survey, union density in Britain (or the proportion of all employees organised in trade unions) was 65 per cent in organisations employing 25 or more employees. This had fallen to 58 per cent in 1984, 47 per cent by 1990 and 36 per cent in 1998 (Cully *et al* 1999).

Objectives, functions and ideology

Trade unions organise by occupation or industry or, as in Japan, by enterprise where each union consists solely of members from a single company or firm. Where they are occupationally based, unions recruit horizontally

48

across industries. Where they are industrially based, they recruit vertically within an industry. Because of their deep historical roots, the complex structures of British industry and the variegated patterns of union mergers and amalgamations, British trade unions are rarely based purely on occupational or industrial lines alone. They are job-based organisations and tend to recruit both across and within industries, resulting in membership competition between unions and multi-union representation structures with employers (see Chapter 7 below; Coates and Topham 1988). In the USA, Canada and Australasia, trade unions are also organised on job and occupational lines. In Germany, in contrast, trade unions are organised on industrial lines in 17 *Industriegewerkschaften* or industrial unions. In France, the pattern of union membership is different again, with unions being organised on ideological and religious lines. The main union groupings in France are the socialist *Confédération Français Démocratique du Travail* (CFDT), the communist *Confédération Général du Travail* (CGT), the more conservative *Confédération Général du Travail-Force Ouvrière* (CGT-FO) and the Christian *Confédération Français du Travail Chrétien* (CFTC).

Like employers' associations, trade unions exist to protect the interests of their members. The essential rationale of trade unions, therefore, is to defend and extend their members' individual employment interests, in both their market relations and managerial relations with employers, through collective organisation and strength. Trade union organisation, in other words, is based on an ideology of collectivism, or worker solidarity, summed up in the slogan 'Unity is Strength'. The industrial objectives of trade unions include participating in:

- the determination of pay and conditions
- the maintenance and improvement of health and safety standards within the workplace
- how work and job tasks are organised
- agreed employee relations procedures for resolving grievances, disciplinary and related issues
- 'fair' dealings with management
- improving security of employment in the workplace.

Many unions also have political objectives since, as organisations, they want to influence political decision-making when it affects the interests of their members as employees and citizens, and the interests of unions as employee interest groups. To these ends, the unions seek to influence, first, government economic policies, such as those covering the labour market, the training of human resources, union bargaining power, taxation and public spending. Second, unions are also interested in government legal policy and the ways that it affects individual employment rights and union collective rights to organise, be recognised by employers and take industrial action against employers. Third, they want to influence government social policies in terms of pensions, state benefits and public services so as to raise the 'social wage' to which all citizens are entitled. Fourth, unions also play an international role by seeking links with unions in other countries. They want to influence international labour policy and protest and conduct campaigns when brother and sister unionists overseas are persecuted or discriminated against by employers or the political authorities (see Chapter 8).

Current activities

Unions use a variety of methods to further their industrial objectives as the collective agents of employee participation in employee relations. These include unilateral regulation, collective bargaining, joint consultation and industrial action. In parts of Europe, such as in Sweden, Germany and Denmark, unions also participate with management in co-determination systems, which provide legal rights for employee representatives in enterprise decision-making (Incomes Data Services 1991, Ferner and Hyman 1998).

In furthering their political objectives, unions in Britain use a number of methods. These include lobbying governments, seeking consultations with ministers and maintaining close links with the Labour Party (McIlroy 1988). The political role of the unions is made possible through the device of 'political funds' and the 'political levy'. Under the TULRCA 1992, unions can include the furtherance of political objects among their aims and adopt political fund rules. These provide for union expenditure on political objects, but any payments made in furthering them must come out of a separate political fund. Union members not wishing to pay the political levy may 'contract out' of paying it. The main uses of union political funds include:

- to affiliate union members to the Labour Party, thereby enabling unions to influence Labour Party policy
- to support Labour Members in Parliament
- to conduct political campaigns on behalf of their members.

In 1998, 40 unions had political funds, with some 4.7 million members contributing to them. This compares with 54 unions having political funds in 1990, with 6.1 million members contributing to them (Certification Office 1999, 1992).

Trade unions are voluntary, democratic bodies, with all the strengths and weaknesses associated with these characteristics. With the closed shop unlawful, individuals generally join the trade union of their choice, according to their occupation, where they work and what unions are recognised. Once recruited, members are allocated to a union branch, which is the basic unit of trade union organisation. Branches are linked to regions or divisions which, in turn, are linked to national union headquarters (Farnham and Pimlott 1995).

Unions are democratic bodies in the sense that decisions at workplace, divisional (or regional) and national levels are taken only after membership debate and by majority voting. Every member is entitled to stand for union office, in accordance with the union rule book and the law, and to participate on an equal basis in union decision-making procedures. In workplaces, shop stewards, workplace representatives and health and safety representatives are elected to speak on behalf of their members with management. Workplaces, branches and divisions, in turn, are serviced and supported by full-time, professional union officers.

Staff associations and professional bodies

The term 'staff associations' is difficult to define with precision, but in essence they have three main characteristics:

- their membership is confined to employees of a single employer, where the employees are almost always in non-manual, white-collar work
- they do not normally regard themselves as 'trade unions' in the accepted meaning of the term
- they are generally found in the private sector rather than in public-sector employment, especially in the financial services, such as banks, insurance and building societies.

Staff associations are sometimes encouraged by employers and management in order to keep unions out of their businesses. Such organisations, confined to a single employer, are rarely effective negotiating bodies. They lack adequate financial resources, find it difficult to bargain on equal terms with the employer and, though operating at low cost, are poorly protected against unexpected hostility from a paternalist or benevolent employer (Certification Office 1981). On the other hand, it is sometimes the employees themselves who, in seeking collective representation with the employer, are reluctant to join a union for ideological, political or social reasons. With their relatively low membership subscriptions and lack of militancy, staff associations sometimes provide an acceptable alternative to trade unions for certain types of white-collar employee (Farnham and Giles 1995).

Professional bodies are not primarily employee relations agencies, but they normally seek to:

- control the education and training of new members to the 'profession', acting as 'qualifying associations'
- maintain professional standards amongst members
- advance the standing and status of the profession in the wider community (see Millerson 1964).

Where professional bodies take on a dual function, in seeking to protect and improve their members' employment interests, such as in pay determination or collective bargaining, this is more likely to happen in the public sector rather than the private sector. In the education and the health services, for example, there are groups of professional employees who use their professional bodies in this dual capacity, such as amongst nurses, midwives and teachers.

The Trades Union Congress (TUC)

The TUC is 'the unions' union'. It is a long-established body, formed in 1868, and is the sole central co-ordinating body of the British trade union movement. In comparison with most other European countries, this is fairly unusual since in Europe there are often rival central trade union centres, representing different political, confessional and occupational interests. The TUC is an autonomous body composed of individually affiliated union organisations paying an annual affiliation fee, based on their membership size. In 1997, the TUC had 75 affiliated unions, representing 6.8 million members, which accounted for 85 per cent of total union membership in the UK at that time. This compared with 74 affiliated unions, with 8.2 million members, in 1991; 89 affiliated unions, with 9.6 million members, in 1986; and 108 affiliated unions, with 11.6 million members, in 1981 (Trades Union Congress 1998; 1991; 1986; 1981). The TUC's written mission statement is (Trades Union Congress 1999: 1):

> to be a high profile organisation which campaigns successfully for trade union aims and values, assists trade unions to increase membership and effectiveness, cuts out wasteful rivalry and promotes trade union solidarity.

Within this generic purpose, the specific aims of the TUC are:

- to promote the interests of all or any of its affiliated organisations
- to improve the economic and social conditions of workers in all parts of the world
- to affiliate to or assist any organisation having similar objectives to the TUC
- to assist in the complete organisation of all workers eligible for union membership
- to assist in settling disputes between members of affiliated organisations and their employers, between affiliated organisations and their members, and between affiliated organisations themselves.

The TUC also has a series of targeted, workplace objectives, which are set out in its Employment Charter for a World Class Britain (Trades Union Congress 1997). It is these objectives that affiliated unions seek to deliver on behalf of their members, underpinned by the belief that all working people should be entitled to them:

- a safe and healthy working environment
- equal treatment at work regardless of sex, race, disability, sexuality or age
- a clear written statement from their employer of the key rights provided by their contract of employment
- lifelong access to education and training

52

- equivalent treatment, whether full-time, part-time, temporary, self-employed or working at home
- provision to help parents and carers combine work and domestic responsibilities
- fair pay, working hours, holidays, pensions and sick pay arrangements
- information and consultation on all matters affecting their security of employment
- fair treatment when disciplinary action is taken against them
- fair treatment in cases of redundancy, including levels of compensation that fully reflect their earnings
- proper protection in cases of business transfers, takeovers, mergers and insolvency
- provision to join and be represented by an independent trade union with proper facilities and fair treatment for union representatives.

The TUC's priorities in the late 1990s were to continue championing the cause of working people and their rights at work, through promoting a 'decent platform' of rights 'as a prerequisite for economic growth and a fair society' (*ibid*: 2). These included:

- continuing to work on the national minimum wage and the wider challenge of building a successful economy
- mounting a campaign for fair employment rights
- pursuing a 'new unionism' project concentrating on organisation and recruitment
- advancing the TUC agenda in Europe
- raising the profile of the TUC and its affiliates around training issues.

The TUC gives effect to these aims, objectives and priorities in a number of ways. These include:

- developing policies on industrial, economic and social matters and campaigning actively for them
- assisting unions in dispute
- regulating relations between affiliated unions and promoting inter-union co-operation
- providing services to affiliated unions
- nominating representatives on statutory and consultative bodies
- participating in international trade union organisations.

The TUC's policy-making congress meets annually in the first week of September and is attended by more than 800 delegates. The General Council, which governs the TUC between congresses, is elected by congress and has an executive committee, four task groups and six joint committees, covering a wide range of sub-areas, such as economic affairs, employment law, equality issues, health and safety, and public services. The main committees are:

- representation at work
- full employment
- monitoring group on European social dialogue
- organising and recruitment
- pensioners
- race relations
- TUC regions
- trades councils
- women's issues
- youth forum.

Seven permanent TUC departments service these committees and their activities:

- secretary's
- economic and social affairs
- equal rights
- international
- management services and administration
- campaigns and communications
- organisation and services.

The European Trade Union Confederation (ETUC)

The ETUC was founded in 1973 and, in 1998, had in its affiliation 68 national trade union centres in 29 countries (39 in the 15 countries within the EU) and 15 European industry federations totalling more than 50 million members. Five organisations from the Baltic states and Croatia have observer status. With its headquarters located in Brussels, the ETUC is the voice of organised labour throughout Europe, being by far the most representative all-industry trade union federation within the EU. It is the only general trade union organisation recognised as a 'social partner' by the European Commission. Amongst its membership it has the following organisations:

- unitary trade unions confederations, such as the TUC in the UK, Irish Congress of Trade Unions (ICTU), Czech Moravian Chamber of Trade Unions (CMK OS), Confederation of Trade Unions of the Slovak Republic (KOZ SR) and *Deutscher Gewerkschaftsbund* (DGB) in Germany
- those which are predominantly blue-collar or white-collar union groups, such as the *Landesorganisationen i Sverige* (LO) and the *Tjänstemannens Centralorganisation* (TCO) in Sweden, *Landsorganisasjonen i Norge* (LO-N) and *Akademikernes Felleorganisasjon* (AF) in Norway and *Landesorganisationen i Danmark* (LO-D) and *Akademikernes Central-organisation* (AC) in Denmark
- union federations with particular ideological or political tendencies, such as the socialist *Fédération Générale du Travail de Belgique* (FGTB), the

Christian Confédération des Syndicats Chrétiens (CSC) in Belgium and *Christelijk National Vakverbond* (CNV) in the Netherlands
* 15 European industry federations, drawn from affiliated unions in particular sectors, such as metal, telecommunications, agriculture, public services, textiles and journalists.

The ETUC has a wide remit and works throughout Europe to promote a variety of economic, political and social objectives on behalf of working people and their families (European Trade Union Confederation 1997). These include:

* the extension and consolidation of political liberties and democracy
* respect for human and trade union rights
* elimination of all forms of discrimination based on sex, age, colour, race, sexual orientation, nationality, religious or political beliefs and political opinions
* equal opportunities and equal treatment for men and women
* geographically balanced and environmentally sound economic and social development
* freely chosen and productive employment for all
* the development, improvement and enhancement of education and training for all
* democratisation of the economy
* a steady improvement in living and working conditions
* a society free of exclusion, based on the principles of freedom, justice and solidarity.

The ETUC has the task of carrying out, with the highest degree of cohesion, trade union initiatives at European level so as to attain its goals as part of the process of European integration. To this purpose, the ETUC directs its activities towards (ETUC 1997: 1):

* the EU, with calls for the deepening of its social, political and democratic aspects, in step with that of its economic and monetary dimensions, for its enlargement to other European countries, and for its active commitment to promoting peace, development and social justice in the world
* the Council of Europe, European Free Trade Area and other European institutions that promote co-operation on matters affecting working people's interests
* European employers' organisations, with a view to establishing solid labour relations at European level via the Social Dialogue and negotiations.

The International Confederation of Free Trade Unions (ICFTU)

The ICFTU was formed in 1949. It now has 141 affiliated organisations in some 97 countries on five continents, with a membership of about 86 million. It is a confederation of national trade union centres, with a secretariat in

Brussels and permanent offices in Geneva and New York. Its motto is 'Bread, Peace and Freedom' (International Confederation of Free Trade Unions 1988). The objectives of the ICFTU include:

- promoting the interests of working people throughout the world
- working for rising living standards, full employment and social security
- reducing the gap between the rich and poor
- working for international understanding, disarmament and world peace
- helping workers to organise themselves and secure the recognition of their organisations as free bargaining agents
- fighting against oppression, dictatorship and discrimination of any kind
- defending fundamental human and trade union rights.

The ICFTU helps to defend workers' rights, fight poverty, reduce international tensions and promote peace. It also has very close relations with the International Labour Organisation (ILO), which is the only international body made up of government, employer and worker representatives. Because of ICFTU representation, the ILO has established many international standards to protect workers' rights and denounce violations of trade union rights by governments. The ICFTU insists that all countries should respect basic trade union rights, such as freedom of association, free collective bargaining and the right to strike. The ICFTU represents the trade union movement at international conferences, in the United Nations (UN) and in various specialised UN agencies. Finally, the ICFTU maintains close relations with the International Trade Secretariats associated with it, such as the International Metal Workers' Federation and the International Transport Workers' Federation.

STATE AGENCIES

Employment tribunals (ETs) and the Employment Appeal Tribunal (EAT)

ETs are independent judicial bodies set up to hear matters of dispute in employee relations, quickly, informally and cheaply. ETs have a legally qualified chair, with two other members, each of whom are drawn from panels appointed by the Secretary of State for Education and Employment. One lay member is drawn from a panel of employer members, the other from a panel of employee members. Anyone can present cases at ETs, which deal with a variety of appeals, applications and complaints. ETs also determine questions of compensation delegated to them. About 50 ETs sit daily in England and Wales, with the number of registered applications now approaching over 90,000 per year and the number of hearings approaching 25,000.

The jurisdiction of ETs derives from a series of employment laws and EU regulations, enacted on a piecemeal basis since the mid-1970s. The legal rights stemming from them are largely directed at individual workers and individual trade unionists. The principal legislative provisions include:

- Equal Pay Act 1970 and Equal Pay Amendment Regulations 1983
- Health and Safety at Work Act 1974 and Safety Committees Regulations 1977
- Employment Protection Act 1975
- Sex Discrimination Acts 1975 and 1985
- Race Relations Act 1976
- Transfer of Undertakings (Protection of Employment) Regulations 1981
- Wages Act 1986
- Trade Union and Labour Relations (Consolidation) Act 1992
- Trade Union Reform and Employment Rights Act 1993
- Disability Discrimination Act 1995
- Employment Protection (Part-Time) Regulations 1995
- Transfer of Undertakings (Protection of Employment) Regulations 1995
- Employment Rights Act 1996
- National Minimum Wage Act 1998
- Working Time Regulations 1998
- Employment Relations Act 1999.

Although the matters that may be considered by ETs are wide-ranging (Department of Employment 1991; Dickens and Cockburn 1986), about 60 per cent relate to claims of unfair dismissal. The other main applications relate to the Wages Act 1986, redundancy payments, race discrimination, sex discrimination and equal pay. Exhibit 1 shows the main types of complaint that can be made by employees and trade unionists to ETs.

Exhibit 1 **Complaints heard by employment tribunals**

- unfair dismissal
- disputes regarding redundancy pay
- failure to consult employee representatives about proposed redundancies
- equal pay claims
- sex discrimination
- racial discrimination
- disability discrimination
- breach of contract
- unlawful deduction of wages by employers
- appeals against health and safety improvement and prohibition notices
- not informing and consulting employee representatives about transfers of undertakings
- exclusion or expulsion from a trade union
- unjustifiable discipline by a trade union
- complaints regarding working time and the national minimum wage

---

The EAT was established by sections 86 and 87 of the Employment Protection Act (EPA) 1975. It sits regularly in London and Edinburgh and consists of appointed judges and lay members, with special knowledge or experience of employee relations as employer or worker representatives. It hears appeals from the decisions of ETs on questions of law only. It is not the function of the EAT to re-hear the facts of the case as they were put to an ET. Nor does the EAT have power to interfere with the judgement reached by ETs on those facts. Any appeal to the EAT must show that in reaching its decision the tribunal made an error in its interpretation or application of the law. As in tribunals, any person may appear before the EAT, including employer and union representatives. The EAT hears several hundred cases each year.

The Advisory, Conciliation and Arbitration Service (ACAS)

ACAS was created by the Employment Protection Act (EPA) 1975. Its prime statutory duty, now incorporated in the Trade Union and Labour Relations (Consolidation) Act 1992 (TULRCA 1992), is to promote 'the improvement of industrial relations' (section 209). Until 1993, this duty had included the particular role 'of encouraging the extension of collective bargaining and the development and, where necessary, reform of collective bargaining machinery'. This is now no longer the case. ACAS is independent of government, employers and trade unions, but its governing council is drawn from employers, employee organisations and independent experts in employee relations. In carrying out its statutory duties, ACAS undertakes four main activities:

- preventing and resolving disputes
- providing conciliation services in actual and potential complaints to ETs
- giving advice, assistance and information on industrial relations and employment issues
- promoting good employment practices.

In 1998, ACAS received 1,301 requests for collective conciliation, with 1,214 cases being completed, of which 1,110 cases resulted in a settlement or progress towards a settlement. It dealt with 51 cases that were referred to arbitration and dispute mediation. It also received over 100,000 cases for conciliating in actual and potential claims to ETs, which was the highest ever total. Of these cases, about 93 per cent were completed. These consisted of about 44,000 settlements and 33,000 withdrawn cases, with 29,000 going to ETs. ACAS's network of Public Enquiry Points was also kept busy, with over 500,000 enquiries (Advisory Conciliation and Arbitration Service 1999).

ACAS's role in resolving disputes is through collective conciliation, arbitration and mediation (see Chapter 3). Collective conciliation is the process whereby employers and trade unions are helped to reach mutually acceptable settlements of disputes through neutral, third-party intervention by an ACAS conciliation officer. It is voluntary, and agreements reached in conciliation are determined by the parties themselves, normally only after agreed procedures are exhausted or when both sides agree that there are overriding considerations requiring it. In 1998, ACAS's largest category of completed conciliations was on pay and conditions of employment (48 per cent). This was followed by: dismissal and discipline (13 per cent), redundancy (12 per cent), union recognition (11 per cent), other trade union matters (6 per cent), changes in working practices (6 per cent) and other issues (4 per cent). In 1991 by comparison, ACAS's completed conciliations consisted of pay and conditions of employment (41 per cent), followed by redundancy (19 per cent), union recognition (14 per cent), dismissal and discipline (12 per cent), other union matters (7 per cent) and changes in working practices (4 per cent).

Voluntary arbitration is provided where the parties in dispute invite one or more impartial persons to make a decision that both parties agree in advance to accept. It is normally regarded as a means of last resort for determining a peaceful settlement, where disputes cannot be resolved by other methods. In accordance with the TULRCA 1992, ACAS has to ensure that:

- the consent of both parties is obtained
- conciliation is considered
- any agreed procedures have been used and a failure to agree recorded.

Arbitration may proceed, however, where ACAS believes there to be special circumstances for using it. In 1998, the issues referred to arbitration and mediation were: general pay and conditions (43 per cent), discipline and dismissal (25 per cent), annual pay (22 per cent), grading (2 per cent) and other issues (8 per cent). In 1991, by contrast, the issues referred to ACAS arbitrators (and mediators) were discipline and dismissal (35 per cent), other pay and conditions of employment (22 per cent), grading (22 per cent) and annual pay (17 per cent).

Mediation is where a third party, appointed by ACAS, assists the parties to reach their own negotiated settlement, by making appropriate suggestions to both sides. These recommendations are similar to those of an arbitrator's award, but the parties do not agree in advance to accept them. Mediation tends to constrain the parties more than conciliation does, but is more flexible and decisive.

ACAS also has a statutory duty to promote settlements of complaints, by individuals, which have been or could be made to an ET. The largest part of ACAS's workload in this area concerns unfair dismissal, followed by claims under the Wages Act 1986, breach of contract, sex discrimination, equal pay and racial discrimination.

The advisory and information services provided by ACAS complement its conciliation services. The key areas where ACAS focuses its advisory services are:

- orderly, dispute-free collective bargaining
- the orderly and voluntary resolution of individual employment issues
- effective and felt-fair payment and reward systems

- improved communication, consultation and employee involvement practices
- the effective use of human resources at work, including participative approaches to change.

It is also ACAS's belief, in the ongoing search for competitiveness, that organisations 'must' (Advisory Conciliation and Arbitration Service 1996: 27):

> develop a positive approach not only to change in the workplace but also to the conduct of industrial relations. In particular we emphasise the need to:
>
> - involve all interested parties in a partnership approach and turn away from an adversarial style of industrial relations
> - seek change though co-operation rather than conflict by recognising the importance for employees and their representatives of being informed, consulted and fully involved in all aspects of change
> - understand the importance of people and the benefits of developing them to their full potential.

The Central Arbitration Committee (CAC)

The CAC is a standing, independent arbitration body, working nationally in employee relations. It was set up as 'the Industrial Court' in 1919 and its current status and constitution are embodied in the TULRCA 1992. The CAC has three panels, one consisting of the independent chair and deputy chairs and two of members with experience as employers and employees. A committee of three, with one member from each panel, normally hears cases. The CAC deals with issues relating to national disputes, a single employer or a particular employee group. It provides voluntary arbitration in trade disputes at the request of one party, but with the agreement of the other. It also determines claims by trade unions for disclosure of information for collective bargaining purposes. The ERA 1999 gives the CAC further powers to determine applications for statutory trade union recognition. Where a panel cannot reach a unanimous or majority decision, the chair is able to decide the matter.

The Certification Officer (CO)

The CO, originally established under section 3 of the EPA 1975, had six main functions, stemming from the TULRCA 1992 (Certification Office 1999):

- maintaining a list of trade unions and determining their independence
- dealing with complaints by members that a union has failed to maintain an accurate register of members; seeing that unions keep proper accounting records; investigating the financial affairs of unions; and ensuring that the statutory requirements regarding members' superannuation schemes are observed

- dealing with complaints by members that a union has failed to comply with the legal provisions regarding secret postal ballots in union elections for executive committees, presidents and general secretaries
- ensuring observance of the statutory procedures governing the setting up, operation and review of political funds for trade unions and dealing with complaints about the conduct of political fund ballots
- seeing that the statutory procedures for amalgamations and transfer of engagements between unions are complied with and dealing with complaints by members about the conduct of merger ballots
- maintaining a list of employers' associations and ensuring their compliance with the statutory requirements relating to accounting records, annual returns, auditors, financial affairs, political funds and statutory procedures for amalgamations and transfers of engagements in respect of employers' associations.

The ERA 1999 confers new powers on the CO, which widen the scope for trade union members to make complaints to the CO of alleged breaches of trade union law or trade union rules and give the CO a greater role as an alternative to the courts. The CO has powers to issue orders in the same way as an order of court in relation to, for example, membership registers, inspection of accounts, election of officers, and use of funds for political objects. The CO is no longer able to hear complaints regarding the dismissal or disciplining of union members, but members can still take claims to ETs alleging unfair dismissal or infringement of individual rights.

Schedule 29 of the Act gives the CO new powers to hear complaints about breaches of union rules. These cover the appointment of, or election to, union office, removal of a person from an office of a union, ballots of union members (other than industrial action) and the constitution and proceedings of union conferences and executive committees.

The ERA 1999 also abolishes the Commissioner for the Rights of Trade Union Members (CRTUM). This office was created under the Employment Act 1988 to assist union members contemplating or taking legal action against a union or an official arising out of an alleged or threatened breach of a member's statutory union membership rights. Some of its functions have been transferred to the CO (see above). The Commissioner for Protection Against Unlawful Industrial Action (CPAUIA) is also abolished. Its role was to give assistance to any persons party to High Court or Court of Sessions proceedings, where they were likely to be deprived of goods and services because of industrial action unlawfully organised by a trade union. In practice, both the CRTUM and CPAUIA heard few cases from union members or individuals claiming that their rights had been infringed.

ASSIGNMENTS

(a) Read Hyman and Brough (1975: 229–53) and comment on their analysis of the role of social values in employee relations, particularly the concept of 'fairness'. Alternatively, read Flanders and Fox (1969: 241–76). What did they identify as the sources of 'normative disorder' in British industrial relations at that time and how did these manifest themselves? What relevance does their analysis have for employee relations today?

(b) Interview an employee relations manager and find out the sort of job tasks and activities which he or she does. To whom is this person accountable and what sort of performance targets are set by senior management for this individual?

(c) To what extent is the management style of your employer based on individualism and/or collectivism? Provide illustrations of its employment policies and practices to substantiate your diagnosis.

(d) Read Farnham and Pimlott (1995: 44–9) and compare and contrast the unitary (including 'neo-unitary') and pluralist concepts of employee relations.

(e) What are the pros and cons of an employer joining an employers' association: (i) in a labour-intensive industry, where the firm is medium-sized, is one of many operating in a competitive product market, and where there are strong trade unions in the workplace and industry? (ii) in a capital-intensive industry, where the firm is a large one operating in a heterogeneous product market, and where the unions are weak in the workplace and industry? (iii) in a capital-intensive industry, where the firm is medium-sized and is operating in a homogeneous product market and the unions are strong in the workplace and industry?

(f) Read the Workplace Employee Relations Survey 1998 and report on trends in trade union membership and recognition (Cully et al 1999: 234–42).

(g) Interview some trade union members and find out: why they are union members, including the benefits of this; what they see as the purposes of trade unions; and what the main problems facing their union are.

(h) Read Chapter 1 of ACAS's current Annual Report. What were the major trends in employee relations for that year? How may these trends be explained?

(i) Read Clegg (1976: 309–16). What is his defence of pluralism in employee relations?

REFERENCES

ADVISORY, CONCILIATION AND ARBITRATION SERVICE (1996) *Annual Report 1995*. London, ACAS.

ADVISORY, CONCILIATION AND ARBITRATION SERVICE (1999) *Annual Report 1998*. London, ACAS.

ANTHONY P. (1990) 'The paradox of the management of culture or "he who leads is lost"'. *Personnel Review*. 19(4).

BASSETT P. (1986) *Strike Free: New industrial relations in Britain*. London, Macmillan.

BEER M., SPECTOR B., LAWRENCE P., QUINN MILLS D. and WALTON R. (1984) *Managing Human Assets*. New York, Free Press.

BROWN W. (1960) *Exploration in Management*. London, Heinemann.

BROWN W. and WALSH J. (1991) 'Pay determination in Britain in the 1990s: the anatomy of decentralisation'. *Oxford Review of Economic Policy*. 7(1).

CERTIFICATION OFFICE (1978) *Annual Report of the Certification Officer 1977*. London, CO.

CERTIFICATION OFFICE (1981) *Annual Report of the Certification Officer 1980*. London, CO.

CERTIFICATION OFFICE (1987) *Annual Report of the Certification Officer 1986*. London, CO.

CERTIFICATION OFFICE (1992) *Annual Report of the Certification Officer 1991*. London, CO.

CERTIFICATION OFFICE (1999) *Annual Report of the Certification Officer 1998*. London, CO.

CHANDLER A. and DAEMS H. (EDS) (1980) *Managerial Hierarchies*. London, Harvard University Press.

CLAYDON T. (1989) 'Union derecognition in Britain in the 1980s'. *British Journal of Industrial Relations*. 28(2).

CLEGG H. (1976) 'Pluralism in industrial relations'. *British Journal of Industrial Relations*. XII(2).

CLEGG H. (1979) *The Changing System of Industrial Relations in Britain*. Oxford, Blackwell.

COATES T. and TOPHAM T. (1988) *Trade Unions in Britain*. London, Fontana.

CONFEDERATION OF BRITISH INDUSTRY (1991) *Annual Review and Report for 1990*. London, CBI.

CONFEDERATION OF BRITISH INDUSTRY (1995) *Annual Report for 1995*. London, CBI.

CONFEDERATION OF BRITISH INDUSTRY (1996a) *Annual Review for 1996*. London, CBI.

CONFEDERATION OF BRITISH INDUSTRY (1996b) *Prospering in the Global Economy*. London, CBI.

CULLY M., WOODLAND S., O'REILLY A. and DIX G. (1999) *Britain at Work*. London, Routledge.

DEPARTMENT OF EMPLOYMENT (1991) *Trade Union Immunities*. London, HMSO.

DICKENS L. and COCKBURN D. (1986) 'Dispute settlement institutions and the courts', in R. Lewis (ed.), *Labour Law in Britain*, Oxford, Blackwell.

DONOVAN, Lord (1968) *Royal Commission on Trade Unions and Employers' Associations 1965–1968: Report*. London, HMSO.

DUNN S. (1990) 'Root metaphor in the old and new industrial relations'. *British Journal of Industrial Relations*. 28(1).

EDWARDS P., HALL M., HYMAN R., MARGINSON P., SISSON K., WADDINGTON J. and WINCHESTER D. (1998) 'Great Britain: from partial collectivism to neo-liberalism to where?' in A. Ferner and R. Hyman (eds), *Changing Industrial Relations in Europe*, Oxford, Blackwell.

EUROPEAN TRADE UNION CONFEDERATION (1997) *ETUC Info: About the ETUC*. Brussels, ETUC.

FARNHAM D. (1990) *Personnel in Context*. 3rd edition. London, Institute of Personnel Management.

FARNHAM D. (1999) *Managing in a Business Context*. London, Institute of Personnel and Development.

FARNHAM D. and GILES L. (1995) 'Trade unions in the UK: trends and counter-trends since 1979'. *Employee Relations*. 17(2).

FARNHAM D. and PIMLOTT J. (1995) *Understanding Industrial Relations*. London, Cassell.

FAYOL H. *Industrial and General Administration*. Tr. G. Storrs (1949) London, Pitman.

FERNER A. and HYMAN R. (EDS) (1998) *Changing Industrial Relations in Europe*. Oxford, Blackwell.

FLANDERS A. and FOX A. (1969) 'Collective bargaining: from Donovan to Durkheim', in A. Flanders, 1970, *Management and Unions*, London, Faber & Faber.

FOMBRUN C., TICHY N. and DEVANNA M. (1984) *Strategic Human Resource Management*. New York, Wiley.

FOX A. (1966) *Industrial Relations and Industrial Sociology: Royal Commission on trade unions and employers' associations Research Paper 3*. London, HMSO.

FOX A. (1974) *Beyond Contract: Work, power and trust relations*. London, Faber and Faber.

FOX A. (1985) *History and Heritage*. London, Allen & Unwin.

GREGG P. and YATES A. (1991) 'Changes in wage-setting arrangements and trade union presence in the 1980s'. *British Journal of Industrial Relations*. 29(3).

GUEST D. (1987) 'Human resource management and industrial relations.' *Journal of Management Studies*. 27(4).

HENDRY C. and PETTIGREW A. (1990) 'Human resource management: an agenda for the 1990s'. *International Journal of Human Resource Management*. 1(1).

HUTTON W. (1996) *The State We're In*. London, Cape.

HYMAN R. and BROUGH I. (1975) *Social Values and Industrial Relations*. Oxford, Blackwell.

INCOMES DATA SERVICES (1991) *Industrial Relations*. London, Institute of Personnel Management.

INTERNATIONAL CONFEDERATION OF FREE TRADE UNIONS (1988) *Bread, Peace and Freedom*. Brussels, ICFTU.

KENNOY T. (1990) 'Human resource management: rhetoric, reality and contradiction'. *International Journal of Human Resource Management*. 1(3).

KINNIE N. (1987) 'Bargaining within the enterprise: centralised or decentralised?' *Journal of Management Studies*. 24(5), September.

LEGGE K. (1995) *HRM: Rhetorics and Realities*. Basingstoke, Macmillan.

LIKERT R. (1961) *New Patterns of Management*. New York, McGraw-Hill.

McIlroy J. (1988) *Trade Unions in Britain Today*. Manchester, Manchester University Press.

Marginson P., Edwards P., Martin R., Sisson N K. *and* Purcell J. (1988) *Beyond the Workplace: Managing industrial relations in multi-establishments*. Oxford, Blackwell.

Miller P. (1987) 'Strategic industrial relations and human resource management – distinction, definition and recognition'. *Journal of Management Studies*. 24(2), July.

Millerson G. (1964) *The Qualifying Associations*. London, Routledge.

Millward N. *and* Stevens M. (1986) *British Workplace Industrial Relations 1980–1984*. Aldershot, Gower.

Millward N., Stevens M., Smart D. *and* Hawes W. (1992) *Workplace Industrial Relations in Transition*. Aldershot, Dartmouth.

Ministry of Labour (1965) *Royal Commission on Trade Unions and Employers' Associations: Written evidence of the Ministry of Labour*. London, HMSO.

Mintzberg H. (1975) *The Nature of Managerial Work*. New York, Prentice Hall.

Peters T. *and* Waterman R. (1982) *In Search of Excellence*. New York, Harper & Row.

Price Waterhouse Cranfield (1990) *Price Waterhouse Cranfield Survey 1990*. Cranfield.

Purcell J. (1987) 'Mapping management styles in employee relations'. *Journal of Management Studies*. 24(5), September.

Purcell J. *and* Sisson K. (1983) 'Strategies and practice in the management of industrial relations', in G. Bain (ed.), *Industrial Relations in Britain*, Oxford, Blackwell.

Sissons K. (ed.) (1998) *Personnel Management in Britain*. Oxford, Blackwell.

Stewart R. (1982) *Choices for the Manager*. London, McGraw-Hill.

Storey J. (ed.) (1989) *New Perspectives on Human Resource Management*. London, Routledge.

Storey J. (ed.) (1992) *The Development of the Management of Human Resources*. Oxford, Blackwell.

Thomason G. (1991) 'The management of personnel'. *Personnel Review*. 20(2).

Trades Union Congress (1981) *Annual Report*. London, TUC.

Trades Union Congress (1986) *Annual Report*. London, TUC.

Trades Union Congress (1991) *Annual Report*. London, TUC.

Trades Union Congress (1997) *Annual Report*. London, TUC.

Trades Union Congress (1998) *Directory*. London, TUC.

Trades Union Congress (1999) *Annual Report*. London, TUC.

Tyson S. (1987) 'The management of the personnel function'. *Journal of Management Studies*. 24(5).

Union of Industrial and Employers' Confederations of Europe (1997) *The Voice of European Business and Industry*. Brussels, UNICE.

Walton R. (1985) 'From control to commitment in the workplace'. *Harvard Business Review*. 63(2), April.

WATSON D. (1988) *Managers of Discontent*. London, Routledge.
WICKENS P. (1987) *The Road to Nissan*. Basingstoke, Macmillan.
WINKLER J. (1974) 'The ghost at the bargaining table: directors and industrial relations'. *British Journal of Industrial Relations*. July.

3 Processes of employee relations

There are a number of processes for conducting and managing the employment relationship, as outlined in Chapter 1. Some are voluntary, others are legally enforceable; some are individually based, others are collectively based. Marsden (1999: 3) argues that the employment relationship, in its myriad forms, has revolutionised the organisation of labour services by providing firms and workers with a very flexible method of co-ordination and a platform for investing in skills. Its key feature is that it enables management to 'decide detailed work assignments after workers have been hired'. In his view, the emergence and institutionalisation of the employment relationship owes much to the development of job rules 'that square the apparent circle of providing employers with flexible allocations and employees with limited liability to follow their employer's instructions'. This chapter explores and outlines the main employee relations processes and provides examples of the employee relations rules they determine.

PERSONAL CONTRACTS

With the growth of individualised employee relations policies and practices since the 1980s (see Chapters 6 and 9), the use of personal contracts of employment between employers and individual employees has been extended within some organisations, especially to managerial and professional staff. A personal contract normally incorporates an individual salary for the post-holder and other specific terms and conditions of employment, pertinent to that individual and his or her job. According to the 1998 Workplace Employee Relations Survey (WERS 1998), 59 per cent of the employed workforce in Britain covered by the survey had employment contracts that were not collectively determined.

A personal contract is erroneously perceived as being the outcome of a process of individual bargaining between an employer and an employee. Yet in practice, it more commonly represents a situation where an employer recruits and selects (or promotes) an employee and is prepared to offer terms and conditions that the employer believes to be acceptable and 'reasonable' in the circumstances. These circumstances take into account the employer's labour market needs, its knowledge of the labour market and what the employer can afford to pay. In such cases, it is the employer who normally has a better knowledge of supply and demand in the particular external or internal labour market than does the individual employee. And while the employer may be prepared to make some concessions at the margin of the contract between the parties, the employee's main disadvantage is that he or she has imperfect knowledge of the market and what competition there is for the new job or the promotion being offered. The only occasions where the individual worker has market advantage (such as certain sports 'stars' and entertainers) is where there is a shortfall in the supply of certain labour market skills, usually at the top, skilled end of the market. But, in general, the Webbs neatly expressed the problem faced by individual workers in the labour market (Webb and Webb 1913: 173 – this writer's italics):

> In unorganised trades the individual workman [sic], applying for a job, accepts or refuses *the terms offered by the employer*, without communication with his fellow-workmen [sic], and without any other consideration than the exigencies of his [sic] own position. For the sale of his labor [sic] he makes, with the employer, a strictly individual bargain.

Personal contracts have always been more common among management staff than among non-management employees in large organisations, and for all employees in non-union small firms. However, the practice has spread in both the private and public sectors in recent years and has become increasingly the norm among some groups of employees, such as technical and professional workers, that have traditionally had their terms and conditions of employment determined collectively rather than individually. Personal contracts are typically linked to staff appraisal, performance review, staff development and performance-related pay.

According to section 230 of the Employment Rights Act 1996 (ERA 1996), a contract of employment is 'a contract of service or apprenticeship, whether express or implied, and (if it is express) whether oral or in writing'. For a contract to exist, three conditions must be satisfied:

- a clear offer must have been made and accepted
- the contract must be agreed with the intention of it being legally binding
- there must be 'consideration', ie there must be benefit to each party to the contract.

The identity of the employer in law is normally evident, but there are four main tests for determining whether or not a worker is a 'an employee'. These are:

- the degree of control that the employer has over the individual employee
- the degree to which an individual is integrated into the business
- the degree to which an individual is independent of the business
- the 'multiple text', which takes account of different factors in assessing the individual worker's status.

All employees are entitled to receive written particulars from their employer setting out the main terms of their employment. The information must be provided within two months of commencing employment. Exhibit 2 illustrates the information typically included in such written statements.

Exhibit 2 Written particulars of the main terms and conditions of employment

These include:

- the names of the employer and employee
- the date of the commencement of employment
- the date on which the employee's period of continuous employment began
- the scale or rate of pay or method of calculating pay
- the intervals at which pay is given
- terms and conditions relating to hours of work
- holiday entitlements
- the title of the job
- the place of work
- terms relating to sickness and injury
- terms relating to pensions and pension schemes
- a statement confirming whether a pension contracting-out certificate is in force
- a statement confirming whether the employment is permanent or for a fixed term
- collective agreements affecting the contract
- any terms relating to working abroad
- how grievances and disciplinary matters are to be resolved.

Some terms, the implied terms, are not expressly provided for in the contract but are deemed to be an essential part of the contract because they reflect the true intentions of the parties regarding its terms. Thus employees are obliged to:

- obey lawful and reasonable orders given by the employer
- serve the employer faithfully and not act in ways contrary to the interests of the employer
- perform their duties with reasonable care.

Employers, in turn, are obliged to:

- pay agreed wages and provide work to the employee
- take reasonable care to ensure the safety of the employee by providing a safe working environment
- provide a suitable working environment suitable for the performance of the employee's contractual duties
- treat the employee in such a way as to maintain the relationship of mutual trust and confidence between the parties.

Some terms of employment that are incorporated into the contract of employment are set out in other documents, such as staff handbooks or collective agreements. Thus while terms relating to sick pay, pension entitlement and disciplinary and grievance procedures may be included in the written statement, they can be referred to in other documents. Any document referred to must be readily accessible to the employee. Where any particulars change, the employer is obliged to provide the employee with a written statement setting out the details of the changes. The clearest method of doing this is by express incorporation. Incorporation can also occur where it is established that the conduct of the parties indicates incorporation or where custom and practice establish it.

Where an employer wishes the contract to contain certain explicit terms, then these can be expressly provided for in the contract. Such express terms may cover:

- restrictive covenants to protect the legitimate interests of the employer at the end of employment
- the protection of confidential information
- the protection of intellectual property rights.

A senior management contract known to the author includes most of the items in Exhibit 2. But within it, there is a statement, regarding hours of work (Portsmouth and South East Hampshire Health Authority 1991), that: 'managers are required to work such hours as are necessary for the full performance of their duties.' It goes on to add that continuation of the appointment is 'subject to satisfactory performance', with the duties of the post being reviewed in 'accordance with the Individual Performance Review arrangements for senior managers'.

> The primary objective of this will be to help . . . achieve the best possible level of performance, but unsatisfactory performance, as assessed under the Individual Performance Review arrangements, may be regarded as grounds for action under the Authority's disciplinary and dismissal procedures.

In this case, this could result from failure to meet agreed objectives after two successive reviews where unsatisfactory performance is identified. Clearly, compared with collectively determined terms and conditions, personal contracts give senior managers much tighter control over the job activities, work performance and pay rewards of the employees covered by such contracts. Personal contracts of this sort effectively enhance management control of the work process.

Employers may want to change an employee's contract for a variety of reasons, but unless the employer proceeds within the bounds of 'reasonableness', and the terms of the contract, then the change amounts to a fundamental breach of contract. One way of doing this is by incorporating an express term, giving the employer the right to make relatively minor changes to the contract in specific situations. Where there is no express right to vary the contract, the employer must consider varying it by consent. Change by express consent can be achieved either by varying the existing contract or by terminating it and offering the employee a new one. Implied consent is achieved where an employee continues to work without raising objections. Even where an employee has consented to a variation, 'consideration' should also be made for the contract to be valid. If changes have been agreed through collective bargaining, the individual's contract may be varied where the union is acting as agent of the employee and where there is an express term in the employee's contract incorporating any terms collectively agreed.

There are two ways in which an employer can change terms and conditions unilaterally. The first is by terminating the contract of the employee and offering re-engagement under a new contract including the varied terms. The second is by imposing the changes and presenting the employee with a *fait accompli*. Where an employer unilaterally varies an employee's contract, the employee can:

- continue working under the contract without objection, in which case the employee may be deemed to have agreed the variation by implication
- continue working under protest and bring about a claim for breach of contract or for damages suffered as a result of the variation
- refuse to work under the varied contract
- resign and claim constructive or wrongful dismissal.

Absence of consultation in relation to a variation of a contract of employment does not automatically render any resulting dismissal unfair, but it is a factor taken into account in any hearing before an employment tribunal.

COLLECTIVE BARGAINING

Collective bargaining (or joint negotiation) is a voluntary process involving autonomous employers and independent trade unions and remains a common pattern of employee relations in Britain and many other Western countries (see Chapters 7 and 8). Its purpose is to determine:

- the terms and conditions of employment, for particular groups of employees
- the ways in which employment issues such as individual grievances, collective disputes and disciplinary matters are to be resolved at workplace and corporate levels.

Autonomous employers are normally self-governing organisations, operating in the market or public sectors. Independent trade unions are organisations of workers which are not under the domination or control of an employer and whose activities are not liable to interference from an employer. Unions meeting the criteria for 'independence' set out in section 5 of the Trade Unions and Labour Relations (Consolidation) Act 1992 (TULRCA 1992) may apply for a certificate of independence from the Certification Officer (CO).

Collective bargaining is a power relationship, based on a management policy of union incorporation in the enterprise. It is one of power-sharing or joint regulation with management. Its outcomes, resulting from negotiations between management and union representatives, are collective agreements. In Britain, collective agreements are voluntary and not legally enforceable.

71

In other countries, collective agreements are normally legally binding contracts between employers and unions, with any breaches of such agreements resulting in legal action being taken by the aggrieved party against the other. The relative advantage in collective bargaining is determined by the balance of bargaining power between the two parties in the negotiating process. Where the power balance favours the employer side, this is to the relative disadvantage of the union and its members. Where the power balance favours the union side, this is to the relative disadvantage of the employer and management. The essence of an effective collective bargaining relationship between employers and trade unions is the willingness of both parties to seek negotiated and agreed settlements, by concessions, exchanges and compromises between them, so that each side feels mutually bound, responsible and committed to their joint bargaining outcomes (Clegg 1976).

Any set of collective bargaining arrangements comprises a framework or structure within which the employer and union sides participate. Parker and his colleagues (1971) use the term 'bargaining structure' to describe the permanent features distinguishing the collective bargaining process in any particular industry or organisation. They identify four interrelated features within any collective bargaining structure. These are bargaining levels, bargaining units, bargaining scope and bargaining forms.

Bargaining levels

The bargaining level is where collective bargaining between employer and union representatives takes place. This may be at:

- multi-employer level (otherwise described as industry-wide or national level)
- single-employer or company level
- workplace or plant level.

The WERS 1998 estimated that collective bargaining at multi-employer level determined pay for non-managerial employees in 5 per cent of private-sector workplaces, single-employer level in 14 per cent of workplaces and establishment level in 9 per cent of workplaces. Management, individual negotiation or 'some other method' covered the remaining 71 per cent of private-sector workplaces. In the public sector, the respective proportions were 35 per cent, 15 per cent and 7 per cent, with management, individual negotiation or some other method covering the remaining 43 per cent of public-sector workplaces (Cully et al 1999).

Multi-employer bargaining was common among private-sector employers in Britain in the 1930s, 1940s and 1950s. For multi-employer bargaining to operate, it is necessary for employers to organise themselves into employers' associations or federations (see Chapter 2), thus providing a collective voice for employer interests in the bargaining process. Unions, in turn, often collaborate at national level through multi-union confederations, consisting of a number of independent trade unions working together. Multi-employer bargaining has also been a common practice in the public services such as local government, the civil service and the National Health Service (NHS). This is changing, however, as indicated above, with the public services being broken up into a series of executive agencies, NHS trusts and directly managed units in schools, colleges and universities, where there are different, more-diverse patterns of employee relations (Farnham and Horton 1996a, 1996b).

Multi-employer bargaining is also common in parts of Europe. In Denmark, for example, industry-wide collective agreements in the private sector are concluded every other year between individual unions and industrial employers' associations. Union members must ratify all such agreements, which are legally enforceable, in a ballot before they can be signed and implemented by the negotiating parties. In Italy, industry-wide bargaining has traditionally been important because it is the level at which minimum wage rates are set for each industry. These cover the private sector, publicly owned companies and the small business or craft sector. There are around 25 major industries in Italy and about 100 national industry agreements, which are binding on all employers, irrespective of whether they are members of signatory organisations (Incomes Data Services 1991, Ferner and Hyman 1998).

Single-employer or company bargaining takes place between one employer and the union (or unions) it recognises at corporate level. These arrangements are common either in medium to large multi-site companies where the employer wants standardised terms, conditions and employment policies across the company, or in single-site companies which are not involved in multi-employer bargaining arrangements. Company bargaining is becoming more common in Britain as companies move away from multi-employer bargaining so as to provide themselves with more flexibility, better cost-effectiveness and greater control in the bargaining process. Most collective bargaining in the Republic of Ireland is carried out at company level (Gunnigle and Flood 1990). In the Netherlands, where there used to be a highly centralised collective bargaining system, and where multi-employer bargaining still predominates, company bargaining has increased in importance in recent years, especially in the large corporate sector.

Workplace or plant bargaining in large multi-site companies takes place between local managers and local union officials. This has been a growing trend in Britain since the 1980s. Patterns vary but, in the private sector, some of the driving forces have been changes in business strategy, decentralised cost and profit centres and management wishes to keep union officials away from strategic decision-making levels. Marginson and his colleagues (1988) showed, even where there was plant bargaining, that management freedom to bargain locally may be limited and that guidelines and controls were set at corporate centre. There have also been pressures from government to encourage more decentralised bargaining and pay flexibility in the public services, though not to the extent that has happened in the private sector.

In the USA and Japan, plant bargaining is the norm. In the USA, this is because of its business structures, industrial and commercial regionalisation, immense geographical size and preferred management strategies in employee relations (Kochan *et al* 1986). In Japan, most collective bargaining takes place at enterprise level. Employers favour it because of their paternalist personnel and employment policies. The unions support it because of their co-operative working arrangements with the employers and their origins as factory and company-based wartime production committees (Shirai 1983).

Bargaining units

A bargaining unit, which is closely related to the bargaining level in an industry or organisation, is the group of employees covered by a particular set of substantive or procedural collective agreements. Separate bargaining units, for example, may cover manual workers, clerical and administrative workers and supervisory workers respectively. A bargaining unit may be narrow or wide in terms of the group of workers it covers. A narrow bargaining unit, by definition, covers a limited group, such as the skilled craft workers in a manufacturing organisation. A wide bargaining unit covers a much more comprehensive group, such as all the manual workers within an industry, organisation or plant.

There has been a tendency in recent years for bargaining units, especially at company and workplace levels, to become wider. Bargaining units are more likely than in the past to be of a 'single table' type. A single bargaining table covers all the recognised groups of workers at employer or enterprise level including:

- non-manual and manual groups
- workers represented by TUC and non-TUC unions
- skilled, semi-skilled and less-skilled workers.

It is an approach to employee relations that rationalises and simplifies the bargaining process for employers, harmonises conditions of employment within the employment unit and integrates and focuses collective bargaining for management and the unions.

Bargaining units are interconnected with bargaining levels. The bargaining unit is particularly concerned with the representative function of the trade unions recognised by the employer, while the bargaining level concentrates on the management side of the negotiating table. Within a bargaining unit, it is a joint panel of unions, or a single trade union, that acts as the bargaining agent on behalf of the employees, with the unions normally determining the representative arrangements on behalf of their members. Bargaining levels, in contrast, are predominantly employer-determined and are influenced by a combination of product market, business structure and technological factors (Advisory, Conciliation and Arbitration Service 1983, Palmer 1990).

74

Bargaining scope

Bargaining scope begins where the right to manage ends. It defines the range of subjects and matters covered within procedural and substantive agreements and may be extensive or limited in content. Again, the tendency in Britain in recent years has been for bargaining scope to narrow, and increasingly is limited to pay negotiation, as employers and managers become more assertive and confident in the collective bargaining process. Relatively high levels of unemployment, falling union membership and well-trained management negotiators have helped this. Unless changes favourable to unions and their members are made to the balance of power in the labour market, the legal framework of employee relations and personnel policy, bargaining scope is unlikely to be extended in the future.

Bargaining forms

Bargaining forms are the ways in which collective agreements are recorded. They may be formal and written, on the one hand, or unwritten and informal on the other. The tendency in recent years has been towards greater formality in recording collective agreements. This is to avoid arguments about the content and application of collective agreements and to provide stability in collective bargaining arrangements when those who have negotiated procedural or substantive agreements change jobs or roles.

COLLECTIVE AGREEMENTS

Collective agreements are the outcome of collective bargaining and are jointly determined employment rules and they may be procedural or substantive in nature. Procedural collective agreements set out:

- the responsibilities and duties of management and unions in employee relations
- the steps or stages through which the parties determine employee relations decisions jointly
- what happens when the parties to employee relations fail to agree.

Substantive collective agreements, in contrast, cover the terms and conditions of employment relating to specific categories of jobs and employment groups.

In Britain, unlike in other western European and North American countries, collective agreements between employers and unions are not legally enforceable. They are binding in honour only and, in consequence, their wording is often imprecise. Being non-legal agreements means that neither party can sue the other in the courts when agreements are broken, for example when either management or unions fail to act in accordance with agreed procedures. Collective agreements become incorporated, however, into the individual contracts of employment of all the employees covered by

75

the bargaining unit, whether they are trade union members or not.

Procedural agreements

There is no such thing as a 'model' procedural agreement. Each employer and the union(s) that it recognises determine their own set of procedural agreements according to a number of contingent factors. These include:

- the size and organisational structure of the company, public service or industry
- the level(s) at which collective bargaining takes place
- the history, location(s) and ownership of the organisation
- the dominant style and philosophy of management
- the union(s) with which the management deal
- the union power and organisation.

For the purposes of this analysis, the main types of procedural clauses found in 'traditional' collective agreements between management and unions in the private sector, at employer or enterprise level, are outlined in Exhibits 3–7 below. These clauses typically cover:

- general principles
- union recognition, union representation and facilities
- the rights and duties of the parties
- grievances and the avoidance of disputes
- discipline.

Such procedural agreements, which often include multi-union representation, contrast with a less common form of collective agreement, based on single-union representation, called 'new style' or 'single-union' deals. Their procedural clauses incorporate a different approach from the ones outlined below (see Chapter 7).

General principles clauses

These clauses set out the intentions of the various parties to the collective bargaining relationship and the general spirit with which it is to be conducted. The subject matter of these clauses is illustrated in Exhibit 3.

Exhibit 3 General principles clauses in procedural agreements

---

These may comprise:

- a general statement of the basis on which discussions and negotiations between the company and the unions take place
- a general statement emphasising the need for good working relations between the company and the unions

- a company statement recognising the right of the unions to represent and negotiate on behalf of their members
- a company statement recognising the right of employees to join and belong to a union
- a union statement recognising the company's responsibility to plan, organise and manage the company efficiently and cost-effectively
- a joint statement reinforcing the common, shared objectives of the company and unions in contributing to its prosperity, increased productivity and operating efficiency
- a joint statement committing the company and the unions to refrain from any form of industrial action until agreed procedures have been exhausted.

Union recognition, workplace representation and facilities procedure

These clauses set out the unions having recognition rights and how union representatives are to be elected and treated within the procedural arrangements. The subject matter of these procedures is illustrated in Exhibit 4.

Exhibit 4 Union recognition and facilities procedure

This covers:

- company recognition of workplace representatives, elected in accordance with union rules
- the appointment of workplace representatives, their numbers, constituencies and co-ordination into a joint panel of unions or joint union committee
- the conditions permitting workplace representatives to undertake union duties and activities and the facilities for these, including time off, pay, administrative support and union training.

The rights and duties of management and unions

These clauses define the roles and responsibilities of the parties in the collective bargaining relationship. The subject matter of these clauses is illustrated in Exhibit 5.

Exhibit 5 Rights and responsibilities of the parties within procedure

These cover:

- the importance of the effective use of procedures to all the parties and of mutual confidence and trust among them in the conduct of good employee relations
- the right of workplace representatives to take up grievances, disciplinary and other matters on behalf of individuals and workgroups
- the responsibility of workplace representatives to act on behalf of their members where this is justified

- the responsibility of workplace representatives to act fairly, honestly and in a manner befitting their functions
- the responsibilities of management to ensure that procedures are used, that workplace representatives are treated fairly, honestly and with the respect due to their positions and that the cases presented to them are given a fair hearing
- the rights of management to object to any breach of procedure through union channels and to expect unions to keep to the principles, spirit and stages of agreed procedures
- the rights of unions to nominate elected workplace representatives to designated areas and to the joint panel of unions or joint union committee
- the responsibility of the unions to see that their workplace representatives adhere to the principles, spirit and stages of agreed procedures.

Procedures for settling grievances and avoiding collective disputes

These clauses provide means for settling and resolving grievances and disputes between the parties. They normally follow a series of stages, with both the employer and the unions undertaking to refrain from taking coercive industrial action against the other, including lockouts or stoppages of work (ie to retain existing arrangements – the status quo), while the procedures are being used. Grievance procedures normally cover individual issues (see Chapter 11) and collective 'disputes' procedures normally cover matters of concern to groups of employees. The subject matter of these clauses is illustrated in Exhibits 6 and 7.

Exhibit 6 Procedure for individual grievances

These clauses provide for meetings involving:

- Stage 1: the union member and immediate supervisor
  (if the issue is not resolved, it is referred to . . .)
- Stage 2: the union member, workplace representative and supervisor
  (if the issue is not resolved, it is referred to . . .)
- Stage 3: the union member, workplace representative and next level of management
  (if the issue is not resolved, it is referred to . . .)
- Stage 4: the joint panel of unions or joint union committee and appropriate managers, including the personnel manager
  (if the issue is not resolved, and at the request of either management or the union, it is referred to . . .)
- Stage 5: the personnel manager, union full-time official and other invited parties
  (if the issue is not resolved, it is referred to . . .)
- Stage 6: the human resources director, union full-time official and other invited parties
  (if the issue is not resolved, it may be referred to . . .)
- Stage 7: an external party agreed to by management and the union.

Exhibit 7 Procedure to avoid collective disputes

- For a group managed by the same supervisor, these clauses provide for meetings involving:
  – Stages 2–7 above
- For a group involving members of one union in more than one department, these clauses provide for meetings involving:
  – the joint panel of unions or the joint union committee and the personnel manager (if it is not resolved, it is referred to . . .)
  – Stages 5–7 above
- For a group with members of more than one union in more than one department, these clauses provide for meetings involving:
  – the joint panel of unions or joint union committee and appropriate management representatives, including the personnel manager (if it is not resolved, it is referred to . . .)
  – senior management representatives and appropriate full-time union officials.

Disciplinary procedure

The objective of this procedure is to help individuals whose conduct (or performance) gives cause for dissatisfaction, to improve their behaviour (see Chapter 11). Individuals being disciplined have the right to be accompanied by their union representative. The subject matter of these clauses is illustrated in Exhibit 8.

Exhibit 8 Disciplinary procedure

The stages typically incorporate interviews involving:

- Stage 1: the individual and the supervisor, which can result in a verbal warning
- Stage 2: unless an improvement in employee conduct (or performance) results, the supervisor reviews the situation with the individual, which, following investigation, can result in a first written warning
- Stage 3: where there is still no improvement in employee conduct (or performance), the supervisor consults his or her manager, which, following investigation, can result in a second written warning
- Stage 4: where there continues to be no improvement in employee conduct (or performance), the manager consults with his or her manager who, if still dissatisfied with the conduct, following investigation, can dismiss the individual.

Where appropriate, Stages 2 or 3 above may be the first steps used in implementing the procedure. Cases of defined and established gross misconduct, for example, may result in instant dismissal, with an individual being suspended on full pay pending a hearing. Appeals systems are normally built into disciplinary procedures, thus allowing individuals to appeal against disciplinary sanctions determined by management.

Other procedures

These clauses include procedures covering:

- recruitment
- induction
- promotion
- redeployment
- training
- redundancy
- retirement.

New-style agreements

New-style collective agreements – sometimes mistakenly described as 'single-union deals' – are typically found in 'high-tech', foreign-owned, 'greenfield site' companies (Rico 1987). Some new-style procedural clauses are of the same types as those found in traditional procedures, although they incorporate different provisions and emphases, but others are quite distinctive and different from those in normal procedural arrangements between employers and unions. Like traditional procedures, new-style procedures include clauses covering:

- general principles
- union recognition and facilities
- grievances and the avoidance of disputes
- discipline.

They also commonly focus on (see also Chapters 1 and 9):

- single-union recognition, not multi-union recognition
- the role of employee representatives in procedure, not union representatives
- single machinery for dealing with negotiation, consultation and information, not multiple machinery
- the need for two procedures for avoiding disputes, not a single procedure – with one for dealing with conflicts of rights (for interpreting existing agreements) and the other for dealing with conflicts of interest (in making new agreements).

Additional procedural clauses typically found in new-style agreements include:

- 'no-strike' arrangements
- 'pendulum' arbitration for disputes of interest, where the arbitrator rules for the final position of one side or the other
- 'labour flexibility' clauses.

The subject matter of typical procedural clauses incorporated in new-style agreements is illustrated in Exhibit 9 (see also Chapter 8).

Exhibit 9 **Procedural clauses in new-style collective agreements**

These cover:

- single-union recognition
- employee representation within the company
- single-employment status for all employees
- employee flexibility and multiskilling, with security of employment and opportunities for training and retraining for employees
- a company council, or forum, incorporating advisory, information, consultative and negotiating functions
- no-strike or peace clauses
- binding pendulum arbitration.

Substantive agreements

These cover how much the various groups of employees are paid for the jobs they do, in terms of either immediate or postponed payments (such as pensions), and the conditions of employment associated with these jobs. Substantive agreements define the market relations between the primary parties to the employment contract and they therefore involve financial costs to the employer and economic rewards for the employees. The main categories are summarised in Figure 6, but the lists are neither exclusive nor exhaustive.

Figure 6 **Main categories of substantive agreement**

Pay	Conditions
Hourly wage rates	Working hours
Annual salaries	Length of working week
Shift work payments	Shift working hours
Unsocial hours payments	Shift working systems
Pay structures	Clocking-in arrangements
Payments for performance	Working time arrangements
Pay bonuses	Refreshments facilities
Overtime payments	Overtime arrangements
Holiday pay	Holiday arrangements
Sick pay	Sick pay schemes
Maternity pay	Maternity leave
Redundancy payments	Pensions schemes
'Call-in payments'	Sabbatical leave

JOINT CONSULTATION

In Britain, voluntary collective bargaining and voluntary joint consultation have traditionally been seen as separate and complementary processes, with collective bargaining focusing on the divergent interests of employers and employees and consultation focusing on their common interests. In practice, where bargaining and consultation co-exist, the distinction between them is commonly institutionalised by having separate negotiating and consultative machinery and separate agendas for their activities. This has meant in many cases that collective bargaining has been concerned with pay determination and conditions of employment and joint consultation with welfare, health and safety, training and efficiency, even where the same representatives are involved in the separate processes in the same organisation.

Although Flanders (1964) argued that this distinction between bargaining and consultation is artificial, McCarthy (1966) accepted the distinction but claimed that there was an inverse relationship between trade union power and joint consultation. When union power is strong, joint consultation is neutralised, and when it is weak, joint consultation is reinvigorated. The McCarthy thesis is fairly persuasive, up to a point, since as Millward and Stevens (1986) have shown, there was a significant growth of joint consultative committees (JCCs) in Britain during the early 1980s, which was a period of generally high unemployment, declining union membership and assertive styles of management. By the time of the third Workplace Industrial Relations Survey (WIRS) in 1990, however, the overall proportion of workplaces with JCCs had fallen 'between 1984 and 1990, from 34 per cent to 29 per cent' (Millward *et al* 1992: 153). This could be accounted for by the fact that by 1990, there were fewer larger workplaces with recognised unions, where JCCs had previously been common. However, in the WERS 1998, it was reported that the number of workplaces with local and/or higher-level JCCs had risen to 53 per cent of all workplaces. This contrasted with the 1960s and 1970s, a period of strong trade union power, when successful joint consultation was not widely practised in either private or public industry. Union representatives preferred negotiation because it influenced employment decisions and consultation did not.

One of the problems of analysing joint consultation as an employee relations process is that it has a variety of objectives, subject matter, representative structures and managerial approaches to it. Marchington (1989) identifies four models of joint consultation, in terms of the links between collective bargaining and employee representation. The aims of each of the four models are, respectively:

- to prevent the establishment of independent trade unionism
- to make JCCs a marginal activity within the enterprise
- to upgrade joint consultation, as a substitute for collective bargaining
- to make JCCs a valuable adjunct to collective bargaining.

Clearly, from Marchington's research, management's motives for setting up and participating in joint consultation, and its attitudes towards it, are crucial determinants of its effectiveness, efficacy and impact on employee relations behaviour. Management establishes the *non-union model* to prevent unions organising in the workplace. It is based on information-giving by management either of a 'hard' business nature or on 'soft' welfare and social matters. Non-union consultative committees are normally chaired by a senior line or personnel manager, and the employee representatives, chosen from amongst the workforce, are encouraged to identify with management and not to challenge management prerogatives or management's decision-making authority. JCCs of this sort are usually at establishment level and are not linked to committees on other sites in multi-plant firms.

The *marginal model* of joint consultation is one in which the JCC has a symbolic role and the JCC's employee representatives are kept busy on non-controversial issues. Fairly trivial information is provided to employee representatives. These JCCs tend to be chaired by the personnel manager and both union and non-union members represent employees. Like the non-union model, the marginal model of joint consultation is organised at plant or establishment level, with no links to other parts of the organisation.

The *competitive model* aims to reduce union influence by upgrading joint consultation so as to render collective bargaining less meaningful. Management provides hard, high-level information to shop stewards and other employee representatives. Senior line managers chair meetings at establishment level, although in larger organisations there may be departmental JCCs, allowing ideas and information to be passed up and down the organisation to reinforce the line management chain of command. According to Marchington (1988), this sort of consultation may be linked with other types of employee involvement, such as quality circles, team briefings and similar direct forms of management-employee communications (see Chapter 6).

The purpose of the *adjunct model* of joint consultation is to provide a problem-solving forum, for management and union representatives, at plant and company levels, in parallel with the collective bargaining machinery. With this approach, collective bargaining tends to deal with matters of conflict between management and unions, such as pay and conditions of employment, while joint consultation fills in the gaps left by negotiation. This type of joint consultation deals therefore with issues of common and shared interests between the parties, but may also be seen as a process preceding the negotiation of matters of conflict. The adjunct consultative process tends to be based on high trust and mutual collaboration between management and union representatives, with hard, high-level information, covering trading prospects, business plans and customer relations, being provided by management. Adjunct JCCs are likely to be chaired by the most senior line manager in the plant or company and there are normally links between JCCs at workplace and corporate levels in multisite companies. Management is also likely to encourage workplace representatives to have their own discussions prior to JCC meetings, to reinforce good working relations among management, unions and staff.

CONCILIATION, ARBITRATION AND MEDIATION

Where the secondary parties to employee relations (management/management organisations and unions) are unable to resolve their employee relations differences by agreed negotiating or consultative procedures, or where no procedures exist, then the only means by which they can avoid damaging industrial conflict is by voluntary conciliation, arbitration or mediation. Normally, these are provided through the Advisory, Conciliation and Arbitration Service (ACAS) (see Chapters 1 and 2).

Conciliation

Where the parties in dispute request or agree to collective conciliation, it is ACAS that provides a conciliator. The task of the conciliator is to help employer and unions settle their differences by agreement. Conciliators work through confidential, informal meetings between the parties, sometimes separately, sometimes jointly. They also work with certain broad assumptions. These include:

- that the parties wish to reach agreement
- that they wish to avoid or end disruptive industrial conflict
- that they will be generally co-operative in the conciliation process.

To be effective, conciliators have to gain the confidence of all parties to the dispute and establish good working relations with them. This depends on the personal qualities, knowledge, experience and, most importantly, the neutrality and impartiality of the conciliator.

According to ACAS (1979: 8), 'the process of conciliation is a dynamic one, requiring a continuous assessment of developments as they occur, and the conciliator adapts his conduct of each case accordingly'. The initial stage in collective conciliation is the preliminary briefing meeting. The conciliator's prime objective at this stage is to obtain a clear understanding of the issues in dispute and the attitudes of the parties. This involves collecting information from a variety of sources, including oral evidence, documents, press cuttings and informed observers. It is at this stage that the conciliator has to decide whether it is appropriate to proceed with conciliation or not.

Conciliation normally consists of a series of 'side' meetings with each party separately and joint meetings chaired by the conciliator. Each party is free to choose its own representatives, though the level of seniority and extent of representation is important. The length of meetings varies and, at an appropriate time, the conciliator tries to direct the discussions into developing an accommodation between the parties. If successful, this can result in a settlement. If not, the conciliation process fails.

Side meetings enable each set of participants to speak freely, reduce tensions and adopt a problem-solving approach. Proposals and counter-proposals are examined, with a view to inducing movements towards a position where a settlement is likely. The conciliator moves between the parties in an attempt to bring their positions closer together. Joint meetings provide an opportunity for negotiations to proceed under an impartial and independent chairperson. They can also be the appropriate place for proposals for resolving the dispute. Joint meetings proceed by each side explaining its position, asking questions of the other and being questioned by the conciliator.

During the various meetings, the conciliator constantly looks for signs that the parties are moving to a settlement. If and when agreement has been reached, or appears to be close in side meetings, the parties can be brought together into a concluding joint meeting. This enables the terms of the settlement to be finalised, with the parties indicating their assent. Since conciliators are not party to any agreements reached, they do not sign the agreed document, except possibly as witnesses.

Arbitration

ACAS is also empowered to appoint external arbitrators in trade disputes, under certain preconditions. These are:

- that the specific consent of the parties is obtained
- that the likelihood of the dispute being settled by conciliation is considered
- that generally any agreed procedures have been used and a failure to agree has resulted.

Most arbitration is conducted by a single arbitrator, from a list maintained by ACAS. This is a relatively simple, flexible and quick method of arbitrating. Boards of arbitration are used for major disputes and may be appointed at the request of the parties.

Requests for voluntary arbitration often come in the form of a joint application from the parties, including their names, addresses and agreed terms of reference. ACAS then appoints a suitable arbitrator, which is confirmed as a signed minute of appointment. Each side is allowed time to prepare and exchange statements. Hearings are held on the employer's premises or at an ACAS office. The parties are notified in writing of all the details, with a request to send their written statements to the arbitrator and to exchange them before the hearing, since the submission and exchange of statements is a normal feature of the arbitration process.

Hearings are normally held in private and are conducted informally. The arbitrator usually meets both parties together and asks the claimant party to state its case in the presence of the other, who is then invited to reply. The arbitrator then questions both parties and invites them to make any closing statements. The arbitration award is submitted to ACAS, about two weeks after the hearing, and is binding on both parties. Awards are confidential and are not published, unless the parties agree to this.

Pendulum arbitration

Pendulum arbitration, known as 'final offer arbitration' or 'last offer arbitration' in the USA, is a relatively new process in Britain (Wood 1985). It is

85

an arbitration process particularly associated with new-style collective agreements (see Chapter 7) and normally requires the arbitrator to choose the 'final offer' of the employer or the 'final claim' of the union side in the negotiation process. The rationale for pendulum arbitration derives from the fact that new-style negotiating procedures normally distinguish between conflicts of rights and conflicts of interests. Rights relate to the application or interpretation of agreements, whilst interests relate to matters not covered by agreement (eg new claims on terms and conditions of employment).

In essence, the negotiating procedures and procedures to avoid disputes in new-style agreements are based on the *rights* of the parties, incorporated in the recognition agreement. The intention is normally to reconcile the few remaining conflicts of interest on substantive issues through in-company negotiation. Where differences of interest persist, pendulum arbitration is used. This is claimed to encourage collective bargaining in the last resort, to keep bargaining claims within reasonable limits and to provide a means for resolving impasses (Burrows 1986).

In pendulum arbitration, the management side states its case and its 'final offer' and the union side states its case and its 'final claim' to the arbitrator. The arbitrator might try by persuasion to bring the two sides closer together but eventually has to settle for one side's case or the other's. There is no 'splitting the difference'. One of the benefits of this type of arbitration is that neither side loses face. This is because their original positions are less divergent than in conventional arbitration, with even the losing side ending up not that far from its stated position. Another advantage is claimed to be that whilst one side is entirely satisfied with the arbitrator's award, the other side does not feel that it has lost so much ground as with conventional arbitration.

Mediation

Voluntary mediation in trade disputes is halfway between conciliation and conventional arbitration. Mediators proceed by way of conciliation but are also prepared to make their own formal proposals or recommendations. These may be accepted as they stand or provide the basis for further negotiations leading to a settlement. Since it provides more positive intervention, mediation tends to constrain the parties more than conciliation does. But it is more flexible and less decisive than arbitration.

As with arbitration, in mediation ACAS may appoint a single mediator or a board of mediation. The three preconditions, listed above, need to be observed and the formulation of the terms of reference requires careful drafting. Written statements are exchanged and sent to the mediator, but the conduct of meetings differs from arbitration. Sometimes the mediator meets the parties in joint and separate meetings. In other cases, hearings proceed in the style of arbitration. In other cases, the mediator acts as the chair of a working party, making recommendations on any points that the parties themselves cannot agree. Where a settlement is reached by mediation, the mediator's final report records the terms of the agreement and no further action is required. In other cases, it may be necessary for ACAS conciliation officers to assist the parties further, if required.

UNILATERAL ACTION AND INDUSTRIAL SANCTIONS

Having examined the main voluntary, bilateral and trilateral processes of conflict resolution and accommodation in employee relations, we now turn to unilateral action and industrial sanctions. Unilateral action and industrial sanctions involve management and unions acting alone as discrete parties. Unilateral action by management or unions, and any industrial sanctions imposed by one side on the other, are voluntary and collective processes of conducting employee relations that differ from other processes in two main respects:

- they involve the ultimate application, by management or unions, of one-sided power in determining and applying employee relations rules
- because of this power dimension, British law impinges more closely on these employee relations processes than on other voluntarist ones, such as collective bargaining, joint consultation, conciliation, arbitration and mediation.

The right to manage

The right of management to manage in organisations is at the root of employee relations decision-making and controversy in all market economies, but especially in countries such as Britain, the USA and Japan. The right to manage or unilateral management decision-making – otherwise known as managerial prerogative, managerial rights or managerial functions – provides the interface between management, employees, the trade union function, collective bargaining and the law, insofar as this supports and constrains the right to manage in private and public organisations.

The origins of the right to manage can be traced to the emergence of capitalist business organisations in the nineteenth century and the parallel growth of craft trade unionism. The early capitalist entrepreneurs claimed their right to manage on the basis of property ownership. Since they and their families owned the factories, mines, railway companies, shipbuilding yards and shipping lines, they demanded to direct and control them. It was they alone, they claimed, who should have the right to employ, pay, deploy, discipline and, if necessary, dismiss the hourly paid and salaried 'black-coated' workers employed in their enterprises.

The entrepreneurial class's advocacy and defence of the right to manage, moreover, was reinforced by the demands of the craft unions. The unions wanted to settle the terms and conditions of employment of their members unilaterally – without reference to the employers – enforce pre-entry closed shops on the employers and control the supply of labour into the labour market (Clegg, Fox and Thompson 1964). This right to manage was embodied in the common law duty requiring workers to obey all reasonable and legitimate instructions given to them by their 'masters' or their supervisory agents. It was also incorporated into statute law by making companies solely accountable to corporate shareholders and stockholders and, unlike in Germany and France after World War II, by not providing workers with a collective legal status, through, for example, statutory works councils and enterprise committees (Bercusson 1986).

Today, the right to manage is largely based on different claims for managerial authority (Storey 1980, 1983). In essence, management justifies the right to manage on the grounds of economic efficiency, technical expertise and professional competency. The arguments run along these lines:

- it is management's responsibility to achieve organisational efficiency and success in the interests of those to whom they are accountable
- it is management alone who have the knowledge, skills and abilities to carry out the tasks of effective managing
- it is essential, if the organisation is to remain profitable, viable and cost-effective, that managers have the autonomy and authority to take and implement corporate decisions, including employment ones, without interference from internal or outside parties.

It is these sorts of idea and interest that have encouraged some British employers to resist a statutory minimum wage, the European Community Charter of Fundamental Social Rights for Workers (Commission of the European Communities 1990) and the Social Chapter of the Treaty of Maastricht (see Chapter 9).

Contemporary justification of the right to manage is both an attractive and a flawed concept. It is attractive because it makes economic sense to argue the necessity of management leadership and know-how in creating, administering and co-ordinating effective organisations. It is flawed, however, because the right to manage can never be absolute in enterprises for four main reasons:

- in practice, managerial authority has to be counterbalanced by the consent of those governed even by unilateral management rules
- where employees are organised into trade unions, the right to make unilateral management decisions is constrained by collective bargaining
- the law provides a floor of legal rights for employees (see Chapter 4)
- the right to manage is not a static concept, either organisationally or societally; what was a managerial right yesterday can become a worker's or a union's right today and what are workers' rights today can regress to managerial rights tomorrow – it depends on the balance of power in the employment relationship, as affected by market factors, trade union organisation, public policy and the law.

It is clear that the right to manage and to take management decisions unilaterally is a difficult employee relations process to examine definitively. It is also clear that since the early 1980s the right to manage has been strengthened. Even where employers recognise trade unions, 'right-to-manage' clauses are now being put in recognition and procedural agreements and *status quo* clauses are being omitted. A *status quo* clause provides that actions proposed by management cannot be implemented, if disputed by workers, until agreement has been reached or the procedure for avoiding disputes exhausted. Right-to-manage clauses state, for example, 'that the Union recognises the right of the Company to plan, organise, manage and decide finally upon the operations of the Company'. Another example, in the public sector, states that 'the [employers' federation] and the signatory Unions recognise that it is the right and responsibility of the institutions to manage their domestic affairs in the context of this Agreement' (Polytechnic and Colleges Employers' Forum 1989).

However complex the concept of the right to manage is, unilateral management rules normally take the form of what used to be called 'works rules' but are now normally referred to as 'company rules' or 'management rules'. These are usually included in employee handbooks, along with background information about the employer, other employment matters, personnel policies and employee relations procedures, and they become incorporated into individual contracts of employment (Marks 1978). The right to manage is also closely linked with management use of employee involvement processes, such as briefing groups, quality circles, total quality management (TQM), profit-related pay and employee share ownership (see Chapter 6).

Union rules

Union equivalents of the right to manage are union rules and custom and practice (C and P). Union rules are subsumed in:

- union rulebooks
- union policies determined at their national policy-making conferences
- day-to-day policies determined amongst local union activists.

Unilateral union-made rules are imposed on management where unions are strong and well organised at employer and workplace levels. C and P are unwritten and informal rules regulating employment and work at enterprise level. They are generally unilaterally determined, with management having no say in making them but tacitly accepting them. Some C and P, however, take the form of 'shared understandings' between management and unions, which management accept but are unwilling to legitimise formally.

Formal union rules affecting employee relations at employer and workplace levels, deriving largely from union rulebooks, cover a wide range of working arrangements. They are traditionally associated with craft unions, such as those in the printing, skilled engineering and metal trades. With the relative decline of skilled manual occupations and the craft unions in recent years – largely due to technological change, market pressures on employers and new product markets – unilateral union rules are less important now than they were in the past (see Chapter 5). This has resulted in multiskilling and job flexibility within companies and union mergers externally. However,

89

examples of such union rules cover:

- the training of apprentices
- the closed shop
- job demarcation
- working arrangements
- staffing levels
- working with other unions.

C and P rules are established by trade unionists. This is either where such rules have been traditionally accepted by management without challenge, in order to maintain industrial peace, or where managerial rules – or joint rules – have lapsed and management 'turns a blind eye' to them because it has lost control of them. Examples include:

- 'lax' time-keeping
- special working practices
- workgroup behaviour.

Workers may be required to finish at an agreed time on a Friday afternoon, for example, but C and P dictate that within the last hour of work, workers who have completed their current job tasks may 'job and finish' and leave the employer's premises before the official finishing time. Alternatively, there may be 'washing up' time at the end of a shift, before leaving work.

C and P are used as precedents by trade unionists, either when arguing with management for a solution to conflicts about new employment rules or in applying existing rules to new situations. Workgroups and unions jealously guard C and P rules and management is only likely to challenge them when organisational efficiency is threatened, enterprise effectiveness is at risk and trade union power is weak. This was the case in some organisations in the 1980s and early 1990s.

Industrial action

Both management and unions are prepared, in certain cases, to use industrial sanctions against one another in order to achieve their employee relations goals. These sanctions, known as industrial action, involve disruption of normal working and can take a number of forms. On the employers' side, the lockout is the best known. Other sanctions open to employers include:

- withdrawing union recognition
- withdrawing union facilities
- transferring workers to less pleasant jobs
- tightening workplace discipline
- taking away bonuses
- reducing overtime

- changing working arrangements unilaterally.

On the union side, industrial sanctions include (see also Chapter 10):

- going slow
- working to rule
- banning overtime
- working without enthusiasm
- stoppages of work.

Sanctions are the means of last resort in employee relations, for both sides, since they involve economic and social costs to both parties. Where employers take industrial action against their workers, the economic and social costs may be lost sales revenue or, in the public sector, withdrawn public services and unintended political consequences. The cost to workers is lost pay and benefits and possibly lost job security.

In participating in industrial action, unions, union leaders and employees are constrained by the law. In outline, the law seeks to regulate industrial action in a number of ways. This is done through a combination of:

- judge-made law, both criminal and civil
- legislation
- codes of practice, such as for picketing.

First, trade unions and individuals organising and taking part in industrial action may be liable for certain civil wrongs or 'torts' in circumstances not protected by statutory 'immunities'. There is no legal 'right to strike' in Britain, as there is in most of western Europe, but legal immunities provide protections for unions and individuals taking part in lawful industrial action, provided the acts are done 'in contemplation or furtherance of a trade dispute'. Second, the law seeks to impose limits on physical manifestations of industrial conflict, such as picketing, occupations and sit-ins (Simpson 1986; see also Chapter 4).

Industrial action also affects the legal rights and obligations of employer and employee under the contract of employment. This is because the common law tends to treat all forms of industrial action by employees as breaches of contract, since they violate the employee's central obligation under the contract to work for the employer. This breach of contract is important in two respects. First, it may provide one of the ingredients of the economic torts for which trade unions may be liable. Second, it may entitle the employer to take disciplinary action against individual employees.

In theory at least, employers can respond to industrial action by individual employees in several ways (Mesher and Sutcliffe 1986):

- they may dismiss the employees, though dismissal letters often contain offers of re-engagement provided the workers return to work by a given date

91

- it is common for employers to claim that the employees have dismissed themselves
- it is possible for employers to sue individual employees for damages, as they have repudiated the employment contract, though this is rarely (if ever) done in practice
- where there is a complete stoppage of work, the employer is entitled to stop the employee's pay, but problems may arise where there is partial stoppage, as in 'working to rule'.

LEGAL ENACTMENT

The traditional way of conducting employee relations in Britain is voluntary joint regulation, through collective bargaining between employers and unions, or through voluntary employer regulation, between employer and employee – sometimes mistakenly called 'individual bargaining'. In most other developed countries, the law plays a much more central role in regulating collective bargaining and the individual contract of employment. Until the 1960s, legal enactment or legal regulation played a relatively minor role in employee relations in Britain, with the general thrust of state policy being non-interventionist (see Chapters 4 and 9). It was largely the common law that regulated the contract of employment (Lewis and Sargent 2000). And it was the so-called emancipatory legislation provided by the Trade Union Act 1871, Conspiracy and Protection of Property Act 1875 and Trade Disputes Act 1906 that regulated relations between employers and trade unions, industrial conflict and trade union activity (Lewis 1976). Both employers and unions, unlike in most other industrialised countries, preferred voluntarism and the abstention of the judges and the courts in employee relations to legal interventionism.

The first indications of the growing influence of legal regulation in British employee relations emerged with the Contracts of Employment Act 1963 and Redundancy Payments Act 1965. The Industrial Relations Act 1971, though repealed in 1974, was followed by further employment legislation enacted by Labour governments in the 1970s and by Conservative governments in the 1980s and early 1990s. The main legislation is largely incorporated in:

- Equal Pay Act 1970
- Equal Pay Amendment Regulations 1983
- Health and Safety at Work Act 1974
- Employment Protection Act 1975
- Sex Discrimination Acts 1975 and 1986
- Race Relations Act 1976
- Wages Act 1986
- Trade Union and Labour Relations (Consolidation) Act 1992
- Trade Union Reform and Employment Rights Act 1993
- Disability Discrimination Act 1995

- Employment Protection (Part-Time) Regulations 1995
- Transfer of Undertakings (Protection of Employment) Regulations 1995
- Employment Rights Act 1996
- National Minimum Wage Act 1998
- Working Time Regulations 1998
- Employment Relations Act 1999.

Some of these legal provisions regulate individual employee relations by providing statutory employment protection rights for employees and statutory union membership rights for trade unionists. Others provide statutory rights for trade unions. And others regulate collective employee relations, such as industrial conflict and trade union activities (see Chapters 4, 9 and 10). The main statutory rights are summarised below.

Employment protection rights

Individual employees have a series of statutory rights, subject to some qualifying conditions. These are illustrated in Exhibit 10, which is neither exclusive nor exhaustive.

Exhibit 10 Main employment protection rights

These include the right to:

- join or not join a union
- not be refused employment on the grounds of union membership
- not be dismissed, or have action short of dismissal taken, because of trade union membership
- written particulars of the main terms of the contract of employment
- an itemised pay statement
- not have unlawful deductions made from wages
- guaranteed payments when not provided with work by an employer on a normal work day
- medical suspension payments
- statutory sick pay
- equal treatment in terms and conditions of employment, irrespective of sex
- not be treated less favourably as a part-time worker than a full-time worker
- time off work for ante-natal care, maternity pay and maternity leave for female employees and, after giving birth, to return to work
- parental leave
- time off work to care for dependants
- time off work for public duties
- not be discriminated against on the grounds of sex, marital status, disability or race
- not be dismissed in connection with medical suspension
- minimum periods of notice

- a statutory minimum wage
- be accompanied by a fellow worker or trade union representative at certain disciplinary or grievance hearings
- a redundancy payment when a job disappears
- time off work to look for work in a redundancy situation or to arrange training
- payment from the Secretary of State in the event of employer insolvency
- protection from detriment or dismissal for refusing to sign personal contracts excluding employees from collectively negotiated terms
- prohibit 'waiver clauses' for unfair dismissal in fixed-term contracts
- not be unfairly dismissed
- not be unfairly dismissed during the first eight weeks of lawful industrial action
- a written statement of the reasons for dismissal.

If an employer infringes any of these statutory rights, an employee may make a claim to an employment tribunal (ET). ETs have powers to make awards, including compensation, and enforce certain rights where an employer has acted unlawfully (Lewis and Sargent 2000).

Union membership rights

In addition to their statutory rights as employees, trade union members have a number of rights relating to union membership. These are illustrated in Exhibit 11.

Exhibit 11 **Main membership rights of trade unionists**

These include the right to:

- not be unreasonably excluded or expelled from a union
- compensation for being unreasonably excluded or expelled from a union
- elect union executive committees, union presidents and general secretaries by secret ballot
- secret ballots endorsing official industrial action
- secret postal ballots for union political funds
- not be unjustifiably disciplined by a union for failing to take part in official industrial action
- apply to the High Court for an order that a union has taken industrial action without a ballot
- stop deductions of union subscriptions at source.

Where trade union members claim that any of these rights have been infringed by a union, they may take their complaint to one of the following agencies, depending on the nature of the complaint: an employment tribunal or the Certification Officer.

Trade union rights

Independent trade unions recognised by employers, the officials of independent recognised unions and members of recognised independent unions all
have a series of statutory rights (Farnham 1990). These are illustrated in
Exhibit 12.

Exhibit 12 **Rights of independent, recognised trade unions and time-off
provisions**

These include the right to:

- appoint safety representatives and to establish safety committees at work
- consultation on pensions in firms contracted out of the state earnings related pension
  scheme
- consultation on collective redundancies involving 20-99 employees in one establishment,
  within 90 days, where the consultation must take place at least 30 days before the first
  redundancy, and those involving 100 or more employees within 90 days or less, where
  consultation must take place at least 90 days before the first redundancy
- information and consultation in business transfers including their reasons, timing and
  implications and the measures that the employer proposes taking in relation to employees
- disclosure of information for collective bargaining purposes requested by trade union
  representatives
- secret ballots for industrial action, union elections and related matters
- time off with pay for officials undertaking trade union duties and training
- time off with pay for safety representatives and training
- time off without pay for union members undertaking trade union activities and
  representing the union.

WORKER PARTICIPATION IN WESTERN EUROPE

Employee relations in western Europe have two main characteristics distinguishing them from those of Britain. First, there are frequently multiple systems of employee representation. These include collective bargaining,
employee representatives on company boards and plant-based works councils. The second feature of European employee relations is its far greater
reliance on legal enactment in regulating both collective relations between
employers and unions and individual relations between employers and
employees than is the case in Britain (Ferner and Hyman 1998).

Co-determination at corporate level

Worker participation with management in corporate decision-making at
board level takes place, in an advanced form, in Germany. The form of
co-determination in Germany depends upon company size, the legal structure of the company and the industry in which it is located. In essence,

board-level worker participation is facilitated through two-tier boards. These consist of a supervisory board (*Aufsichtsrat*) and a management board (*Vorstand*). The supervisory board is legally charged with appointing the management board, or its managing directors, and with overseeing its activities. Employee representatives sitting on the supervisory board have the same rights and duties as shareholder representatives. This is expected to lead to entrepreneurial decisions that serve the joint aspirations of both shareholder and employee interests. Employee representatives may request information from the management board on all aspects of the business, including proposed corporate policies, profitability and sales. The management board is the legal employer, represents the company legally and is responsible for conducting the organisation's business operations.

In companies employing over 1,000 employees in the coal, steel and iron industries, supervisory boards consist of equal numbers of employee and shareholder representatives, though this is a declining sector of employment. Under the Works Constitution Act 1952, companies with over 500 employees but less than 2,000 are required to have a supervisory board, a third of whose members are employee representatives.

In organisations with over 2,000 employees (whether joint stock companies, limited liability companies or limited partnerships based on share capital), supervisory boards consist of equal numbers of employee and shareholder representatives. The size of the supervisory board varies according to company size, but some seats are reserved for trade unions that have members in the organisation, and for managerial employees. This means that 'workers', as a group, do not have full parity of representation on the supervisory board. In smaller firms, employee groups directly elect employee representatives and in larger companies, with up to 8,000 employees, there are electoral colleges. The most important roles of the supervisory board are to appoint the management board and supervise management (Berghahn and Karsten 1987).

In Sweden, by comparison, the approach to co-determination is based on collective bargaining rights. Its source is the Employee Participation in Decision-Making Act (MBL) 1977. It is an expansion of earlier rights of trade unions to negotiate with employers. Employers are obliged to take the initiative in negotiating with trade unions at company level before decisions on major issues are made. These include closure, reorganisation and expansion of operations. The Act also requires employers to keep local unions informed about how company operations are progressing and about the guidelines for company personnel policy.

The MBL also presumes and encourages the signing of collective agreements on co-determination. The so-called 'residual right' to industrial action means that unions are entitled to resort to industrial action if their requests for co-determination agreements, presented in connection with pay negotiations, are not met. The law also gives the unions priority of interpretation in most types of disputes. This is a major strengthening of employee influence, since most disputes of interpretation do not result in negotiations, and the unions have immediate enforcement of their interpretation. It is management that has to request negotiations in these circumstances, with negotiations being referred to national level if necessary or the unions being sued by the employer in the Labour Court (Forsebaick 1980).

Works councils at plant level

Works councils are widespread in Europe. They are prominent in France, Germany and the Netherlands. Basically, a works council is a body, established in law, normally organised at enterprise level, consisting of elected employee representatives with certain rights and responsibilities in their dealings with management and the employer.

In France, there is a multiplicity of representative bodies that have been set up in response to specific social and political pressures, at particular times. Employee delegates (*délégués du personnel*), which were instituted by the Popular Front in 1936, deal with individual employee grievances covering wages, conditions of employment and legal agreements. They are elected by the whole workforce in organisations that employ more than 10 employees. This is done by a system of proportional representation, though in practice most of them are elected on a union slate. Workplace union branches (*sections syndicales*), established in 1968, can appoint their own stewards, collect dues, use noticeboards and organise monthly meetings. In some firms, these branches have offices and other facilities.

Works committees in France (*comités d'entreprise*), set up in 1945, deal with workplace consultation. They can be established in all firms employing at least 50 employees. They have the legal right to be informed and consulted on issues such as the number and organisation of employees, their hours of work and employment conditions. Management have to submit an annual written report to the works committee covering the business's activities, profits or losses, allocation of profits, investments and salaries. Agreement by the works committee is required on arrangements for profit-sharing and changes in individual working hours. Works councils may create subcommittees to examine specific problems and, in companies with at least 50 employees, health, safety and improvement of working conditions committees are compulsory. Firms with at least 350 employees have to set up an employment-training committee and those with at least 1,000 have to set up an economic committee (Goetschy and Rojot 1987).

In Germany, the workforce at establishment level directly elects works councils, though in multi-plant companies a central works council can be formed by delegation from individual works councils. They may be elected in any establishment with at least five employees and must be recognised by the employer. White-collar workers, blue-collar workers and trainees are eligible for election, but executive employees, who have their own employee representative committees, are excluded. The size of the works council increases with size of establishment, and representation of employee groups is in proportion to their numbers in the establishment. The members of the works councils are released with pay for their council activities, are entitled to relevant training for their roles and are protected by law against dismissal by the employer. Works councils in Germany have a wide range of functions (Berghahn and Karsten 1987). Basically, works councils exist to protect the interests of workers in the plant. At the same time, works councils and the employers are expected to work together in a spirit of mutual trust and in co-operation with the trade unions and employers' associations, for the good of the employees and the plant. Under Article 37 of the Works Constitution Act 1972, works councils have 'to see that effect is given to Acts, ordinances, safety regulations, collective agreements and plant agreements for the benefit of employees'. They make 'recommendations to the employer for action benefiting the plant and staff' (Berghahn and Karsten 1987: 108). Works councils in German companies have the right to co-determination in matters outlined in Exhibit 13.

Exhibit 13 **The rights and responsibilities of works councils in Germany**

These cover:

- the conduct of employees in the plant
- daily working times and distribution of working hours
- the reduction or extension of hours normally worked
- the time, place and form of payment of remuneration
- establishing the general principles of leave arrangements and preparing of leave schedules
- introducing and using technical devices designed to monitor the behaviour or performance of employees
- preventing workplace accidents and occupational diseases
- the form, structure and administration of social services in the plant, company or combine
- assigning and vacating accommodation rented to employees
- establishing the principles of remuneration and introducing new remuneration methods
- the fixing of job and bonus rates and comparable performance-related remuneration
- the principles for suggestion schemes in the plant.

Where agreement is not reached on these matters, a conciliation panel takes the decision and its award replaces agreement between the works council and the employer. Employers have to gain the consent of works councils for individual measures of personnel policy, such as staff grading or re-grading, and vocational training. Works councils also have to be heard where employees are dismissed for the dismissal not to be void in law.

European works councils

Since the early 1970s, there have been a series of initiatives within the EU to legislate for more systematic employee participation structures within the corporate sector. The draft European Works Council (EWC) Directive, published by the Commission of the European Communities in January

1991, was one in a line of controversial proposals for employee participation measures in companies operating within European member states over the last 20 years (Commission of the European Communities 1991). Up until then, only those measures requiring information disclosure and consultation on specific issues by employers had been adopted by the Council of Ministers. These included the Directive on Collective Redundancies 1975, the Directive on Transfers of Undertakings 1977 and the Framework Directive on Health and Safety 1989.

Proposals for Euro-legislation on a draft European company statute in the early 1970s, on company law reform from the early 1970s until the early 1980s and on the Vredeling measures in the early 1980s, have been continually blocked within the EU's decision-making institutions because of disagreement between the 'Social Partners' on its proposals for employee participation. This legal provision would allow companies operating in two or more member states to do so under a single set of company laws, based on European law, not national law. In May 1997, an expert body set up by the European Commission recommended that employee participation at company level should be set up on a case-by-case basis through negotiation. Management would be required to negotiate with a special negotiating body but if no agreement were reached within a three-month period, then a set of 'reference rules' would apply. Management and the special negotiating body would agree on information, consultation and board-level participation but, to date, no draft directive has been issued and the matter continues to be subject to controversy and is resisted by employer groups.

The draft 1991 European Works Council Directive was adopted by all member states of the EU, except the UK, together with Iceland, Norway and Liechtenstein, under the Social Policy Agreement of the Treaty on the European Union at Maastricht 1991. Under the European Works Council Directive 1994, European-level information and consultation systems are required to be set up in all companies with 1,000 or more employees in member states employing more than 150 employees in each of two or more countries. A EWC, or an alternative system, must be agreed with central management and a 'special negotiating body' of employee representatives. These provide the EWC with the right to meet central management at least once per year for information and consultation about the progress and prospects of the company, and to request extra consultation meetings before certain major decisions are taken affecting more than one member state.

Until the UK 'opt-in' to the Social Chapter (see Chapter 9), under the Labour Government elected in May 1997, British and other foreign companies in the UK only had to comply with the Directive if their operations in member states other than the UK met the thresholds. In practice, most large UK and foreign companies covered by the legal requirements in other member states included UK representatives in their EWCs, along with employee representatives from other countries, even though they were not legally required to do so. Companies with agreed trans-European information and consultation systems already in place before the end of September 1996 were exempt from these requirements.

EWCs have the right to meet central management annually and be informed of the undertaking's or group's progress and prospects. They also have the right to be consulted on management proposals likely to have serious consequences for the interests of employees. These matters include mergers, closures, relocations, organisational change and new working or production methods. For these purposes, the EWCs are able to request an additional meeting with management, if necessary.

EWCs have a maximum of 30 members, drawn from existing employee representatives, or specially elected ones where none exists. The undertaking or group meets the operating expenses of the EWCs. The original Directive provides that members of the EWC do not have to reveal any information of a confidential nature and that information can be withheld where it would substantially damage the interests of the undertakings or groups concerned.

Hall (1992) argues, on the issue of the legal compulsion underpinning the establishment of EWCs, that the approach was inconsistent with the then-government's emphasis on minimising employers' legal obligations in their dealings with employees and unions. Britain would therefore have been required to fill in the gaps left by the existing reliance on voluntary trade union recognition by employers. A fear of the employers is that mandatory EWCs could potentially be the vehicle for developing European-level collective bargaining within multinational companies. Indeed, it can be expected that collective bargaining strategies in the UK will be influenced by the provision of European-level corporate information.

From the union point of view, the EWC Directive presents, on the one hand, a valuable opportunity for those unions seeking employer recognition. On the other hand, alternative channels of employee representation might have emerged that could inhibit union organisation (Trades Union Congress 1991). It is also likely, since mandatory EWCs are relatively small bodies, that trade unions might have problems agreeing representatives in multi-union situations and where they represent more than one establishment or company.

ASSIGNMENTS

(a) Why has there been a shift to personal contracts of employment in some organisations? Examine the pros and cons of personal contracts for employers and management.
(b) Identify the bargaining level(s), for a named bargaining unit, at which collective bargaining takes place in your organisation. Explain the likely influences on why collective bargaining takes place at the level(s) identified. What other bargaining units, if any, are there in the organisation? Identify the bargaining agents in each case and outline the bargaining scope, in terms of procedural and substantive agreements, for each bargaining group.
(c) Make a presentation describing and analysing the procedural agreements between management and the unions in your organisation.

(d) Read Marchington (1988) and make sure that you fully understand his four models of joint consultation. Using his framework, describe and analyse the joint consultative arrangements in your organisation. How are they linked, if at all, with the collective bargaining machinery in the organisation/industry?

(e) Your organisation's annual pay negotiations with the unions representing manual workers have broken down. Examine the circumstances in which the management side would resort to: (i) conciliation, (ii) arbitration, (iii) mediation, (iv) industrial sanctions. Indicate the pros and cons of using each of these processes.

(f) Read Lewis (1986: 3–43). To what extent have British employee relations become juridified in recent years? Give reasons for your conclusion.

(g) Argue the case for introducing a (non-statutory) 'works council' in the establishment where you work. Provide a draft constitution for such a body and indicate the sorts of issues that would have to be addressed if the council was to operate effectively.

(h) Read Hall (1992). (i) Identify and analyse the developments and pressures that have shaped the current directive on EWCs. (ii) Examine the reasons why the British Government and some employers have been opposed to the directive. What would have been the consequences for British transnational companies, operating in Britain, Germany and the Netherlands, if, say, the European Works Council Directive had been adopted, using the 'qualified majority' principle?

REFERENCES

ADVISORY, CONCILIATION AND ARBITRATION SERVICE (1979) *The ACAS Role in Conciliation, Arbitration and Mediation.* London, ACAS.

ADVISORY, CONCILIATION AND ARBITRATION SERVICE (1983) *Collective Bargaining in Britain: Its extent and scope.* London, ACAS.

BERCUSSON B. (1986) 'Workers, corporate enterprise and the law', in R. Lewis (ed.), *Labour Law in Britain*, Oxford, Blackwell.

BERGHAHN V. *and* KARSTEN D. (1987) *Industrial Relations in West Germany.* Oxford, Berg.

BURROWS G. (1986) *No-Strike Agreements and Pendulum Arbitration.* London, Institute of Personnel Management.

CLEGG H. (1976) 'Pluralism in industrial relations'. *British Journal of Industrial Relations.* XIII (3).

CLEGG H., FOX A. *and* THOMPSON A. (1964) *A History of British Trade Unions since 1889: Volume I 1889–1910.* Oxford, Oxford University Press.

COMMISSION OF THE EUROPEAN COMMUNITIES (1990) *Community Charter of the Fundamental Social Rights of Workers.* Luxembourg, Office of Official Publications of the European Communities.

COMMISSION OF THE EUROPEAN COMMUNITIES (1991) *Amended Proposals for a Council Directive on the Establishment of European Works Councils in*

Community-Scale Undertakings or Groups of Undertakings for the Purposes of Informing and Consulting Employees. Luxembourg, Council of Ministers.

CULLY M., WOODLAND S., O'REILLY A. and DIX G. (1999) *Britain at Work*. London, Routledge.

FARNHAM D. (1990) *Personnel in Context*. London, Institute of Personnel Management.

FARNHAM D. and HORTON S. (EDS) (1996a) *Managing the New Public Services*. Basingstoke, Macmillan.

FARNHAM D. and HORTON S. (EDS) (1996b) *Managing People in the Public Services*. Basingstoke, Macmillan.

FERNER A. and HYMAN R. (EDS) (1998) *Changing Industrial Relations in Europe*. Oxford, Blackwell.

FLANDERS A. (1964) *The Fawley Productivity Agreements*. London, Faber & Faber.

FORSEBAICK L. (1980) *Industrial Relations and Employment in Sweden*. Uppsala, Swedish Institute.

GOETSCHY J. and ROJOT J. (1987) 'France', in G. Bamber and R. Lansbury, *International and Comparative Industrial Relations*, London, Allen & Unwin.

GUNNIGLE P. and FLOOD P. (1990) *Personnel Management in Ireland*. Dublin, Gill & Macmillan.

HALL M. (1992) 'Legislating for employee participation: a case study of the European Works Councils Directive'. *Warwick Papers in Industrial Relations*. Number 39.

INCOMES DATA SERVICES (1991) *Industrial Relations*. London, Institute of Personnel Management.

KOCHAN T., KATZ H. and MCKERSIE R. (1986) *The Transformation of American Industrial Relations*. New York, Basic.

LEWIS D. and SARGENT M. (2000) *Essentials of Employment Law*. 6th edition. London, Institute of Personnel and Development.

LEWIS R. (1976) 'The historical development of labour law'. *British Journal of Industrial Relations*. March.

LEWIS R. (ED.) (1986) *Labour Law in Britain*. Oxford, Blackwell.

MCCARTHY W. (1966) *The Role of the Shop Steward in British Industrial Relations. (Royal Commission Research Paper 1)*. London, HMSO.

MARCHINGTON M. (1988) 'The four faces of consultation'. *Personnel Management*. July.

MARCHINGTON M. (1989) 'Joint consultation in practice', in K. Sisson (ed.), *Personnel Management in Britain*, Oxford, Blackwell.

MARGINSON P., EDWARDS P., MARTIN R., SISSON K. and PURCELL J. (1988) *Beyond the Workplace: Managing industrial relations in multi-establishment enterprises*. Oxford, Blackwell.

MARKS W. (1978) *Preparing an Employee Handbook*. London, Institute of Personnel Management.

MARSDEN D. (1999) *A Theory of Employment Systems*. Oxford, Blackwell.

MESHER J. and SUTCLIFFE F. (1986) 'Industrial action and the individual', in R. Lewis (ed.), *Labour Law in Britain*, Oxford, Blackwell.

MILLWARD N. *and* STEVENS M. (1986) *British Workplace Industrial Relations 1980–84.* Aldershot, Gower.

MILLWARD N., STEVENS M., SMART D. *and* HAWES W. (1992) *Workplace Industrial Relations in Transition.* Aldershot, Dartmouth.

PALMER S. (1990) *Determining Pay.* London, Institute of Personnel Management.

PARKER P., HAWES W. *and* LUMB A. (1971) *The Reform of Collective Bargaining at Plant and Company Level.* London, HMSO.

POLYTECHNIC AND COLLEGES EMPLOYERS' FORUM (1989) *Recognition and Procedure Agreement creating the Polytechnics and Colleges National Negotiating Committee.* London, PCEF.

PORTSMOUTH AND SOUTH EAST HAMPSHIRE HEALTH AUTHORITY (1991) *Contract for Senior Managers.* Portsmouth, PSEHHA.

RICO L. (1987) 'The new industrial relations: British electricians' new-style agreements'. *Industrial and Labor Relations Review.* 41(1), October.

SHIRAI T. (1983) *Contemporary Industrial Relations in Japan.* Wisconsin, University of Wisconsin Press.

SIMPSON B. (1986) 'Trade union immunities', in R. Lewis (ed.), *Labour Law in Britain,* Oxford, Blackwell.

STOREY J. (1980) *The Challenge to Management Control.* London, Kogan Page.

STOREY J. (1983) *Management Prerogative and the Question of Control.* London, Routledge & Kegan Paul.

TRADES UNION CONGRESS (1991) *Unions and Europe in the 1990s.* London, TUC.

WEBB S. *and* WEBB B. (1913) *Industrial Democracy.* New York, Longmans.

WOOD J. (1985) 'Last offer arbitration'. *British Journal of Industrial Relations.* XXIII (3), November.

4 Economic and legal policy

The roles of the state, its government agencies and the law are crucial in influencing the structures, patterns and processes of employee relations at firm and sector levels. The government's economic policies and its legal policies on trade unions, the regulation of industrial conflict and employment protection rights have major implications for employee relations (see Chapters 1 and 9). Where economic policy focuses on creating the economic conditions necessary for full employment (Keynesianism), it strengthens union bargaining power in the labour market and the workplace, whilst weakening that of management. Where economic policy focuses on containing price inflation, this strengthens employers and management in their market relations with trade unions and their managerial relations with employees. The prime economic instruments used to do this are reducing public expenditure, encouraging free market forces and using changes in interest rates to influence economic activity (monetarism and supply-side economics).

Economic management is the actions taken by government to influence economic performance within the macro- and microeconomy. With the demise of classical *laissez-faire* economic policy in the mid-nineteenth century, governments became steadily more interventionist in economic affairs – but not in employee relations, which were dominated by the values of voluntarism and legal abstention. This was in response to a series of political, social and democratic pressures. Political interventions in economic affairs by the state were also influenced by significant events, such as World War I and II. These marked a discontinuity with the past in terms of increased levels of government expenditure, but also pointed to the future in terms of more government involvement and intervention in the economy. During both wars government expenditure rose rapidly, both absolutely and relatively, only to decrease again when hostilities had ceased, but not to pre-war levels (Farnham and Horton 1993, Horton and Farnham 1999). These incremental increases in government intervention in the economy were paralleled by searches for appropriate methods of economic management to accompany them.

Economic management in Britain since the end of World War II, in 1945, can be divided broadly into two periods. First, there was the era of Keynesianism, which was the dominant economic orthodoxy supported by successive governments between 1945 and the mid-1970s. Second, there is the period of monetarism and supply-side economics, which has dominated government economic policy since the mid-1970s. Both approaches to economic management have implications for the parties to employee relations, the processes of employee relations and their outcomes. To what extent the Blair administration, post-1997, represents a 'new' set of economic policy initiatives, a 'new' approach to economic management and a 'third' way to solving the UK's economic problems is, to date, an open question.

Similarly, where there is an 'abstentionist' legal policy supportive of trade union organisation, which encourages collectivist approaches to employment policy on the part of employers, the role of trade unions in employee relations is both legitimised and reinforced and limitations are placed on the right to manage. Where legal policy is 'restrictionist' and is aimed at weakening trade unions and encouraging individualism in employee relations, the power of management is strengthened and that of employees, collectively and individually, is weakened. Again, the years from 1945 until the mid-1970s were a period when the law generally abstained from intervention in the employment relationship. Since then, however, the law has become more interventionist, especially in the regulation of the individual employment relationship, and it has been largely restrictionist in the regulation of collective employee relations.

KEYNESIANISM

The economic ideas associated with John Maynard Keynes (1936), most commonly referred to as Keynesianism, emerged out of the experiences of industrial depression, high unemployment and social deprivation during the 1930s. In the years immediately following World War II, Keynesian economic policies became the new conventional wisdom of both academic economists and social democratic politicians in Britain and western Europe.

Until Keynes's writings, economic theory was mainly concerned with the determinants of the general price level. Keynes, instead, focused on the determinants of the level of output in the economy, stressing the importance of aggregate demand. It is aggregate demand, he argued, that determines the level of employment, with a given population and existing technology. This contrasted with the prevailing economic orthodoxy of the time – classical economic theory – which attributed high unemployment to excessive real wages and high interest rates. According to classical theory, if money wages were reduced, and interest rates were cut, employment would increase because firms would employ more labour – at lower wage rates – and because increased savings would lead to greater investment spending.

In Keynes's General Theory, he argues that far from increasing employment, wage cuts, by depressing aggregate demand, reduce it. This is because the level of employment is determined not by the level of wages, but by the level of aggregate demand. This, in turn, depends on the level of consumption, investment and government expenditure in the economy. He also argues that full employment occurs at a unique level of investment and unless there is some mechanism to ensure the 'correct' level of investment, full employment does not occur spontaneously. The orthodox view, in contrast, was that investment adjusts to the full employment level automatically, via the interest rate. But in Keynes's analysis, there is no automatic adjustment mechanism through the interest rate, so there is no certainty of creating full employment. In Keynes's system, the equality of savings and investment in the economy is achieved not by changes in the interest rate, but by changes in the level of aggregate demand. It is government intervention in the economy, largely through its fiscal policy, which results in full employment, if current demand, including investment spending, fails to produce it.

Fiscal policy

The Keynesian emphasis in economic management is on creating the economic conditions necessary for achieving four policy objectives. These are:

- full employment
- price stability
- balance of payments equilibrium
- economic growth.

The aim underpinning Keynesian policy is that of achieving the level of aggregate demand commensurate with full employment. The policy instruments used by government for this purpose are largely fiscal (Donaldson and Farquhar 1988). This means that when unemployment is rising, due to falls in consumption or in investment spending, fiscal policy is used to inject spending power into the economy by cutting taxes and/or raising public expenditure. The latter is achieved by increasing the public sector borrowing requirement (PSBR), which is the amount by which government revenue falls short of government expenditure in a given expenditure cycle. These 'counter-cyclical' fiscal measures aim to increase aggregate demand and, in consequence, lead to a higher demand for labour by employers, thus reducing unemployment.

One problem of full employment is that it results in increased collective bargaining power by the trade unions in the labour market (Robinson 1937). In the private sector, unless unions restrain their wage bargaining claims, or employers resist them, this leads to rising money wages, not necessarily matched by rises in labour productivity or falls in unit labour costs. These wage rises contribute to a wages–prices spiral. This is caused by companies that have conceded 'unearned' wage increases to their workforces, raising the prices of their products in 'soft' product markets. Other bargaining groups seek higher wages for themselves in 'soft' labour markets and these companies, in turn, pass on the cost of their wage increases to their customers.

In the public sector, wage rises achieved in private industry act as benchmarks for trade union negotiators. This puts pressure on public-sector employers to provide comparable wage levels to those in the corporate sector. These can only come out of increases in productivity, taxes or the PSBR. Tax increases are unpopular with government and the electorate, whilst unions and their members may resist productivity increases. The effects of increases in public borrowing are likely to be inflationary, especially where financing the PSBR takes the form of injecting new currency into circulation from the banking sector. Further, public-sector borrowing raises interest rates through the increased sales of bonds, thus making borrowing by companies more expensive, with possible adverse effects on private investment.

Governments using Keynesian demand-management techniques have two possible policy prescriptions to deal with these economic pressures. One is to deflate the economy through fiscal measures, by cutting back purchasing power through raising taxes and/or cutting public spending. This raises unemployment, strengthens the hands of management negotiators at the wage bargaining table and weakens trade union bargaining power. But it can also result in trade union militancy, slow economic growth and reductions in exports. The result is a 'stop-go' economic cycle, relieved only by the reversal of government economic measures when unemployment and economic recession have brought stabilising pressures to bear on prices and the balance of payments. Reflation, in turn, leads to increases in public spending, renewed growth, falling unemployment, rising wages and rising prices and, eventually, to further attempts at deflation and price stability, thus completing the stop-go economic cycle once more.

Incomes policy

The second policy prescription available to governments pursuing Keynesian economic measures is an 'incomes policy', to complement fiscal policy. An incomes policy is where the government attempts to control wage inflation by intervening in the pay bargaining process between employers and trade unions (Panitch 1976). There are three main types of incomes policy:

- pay freezes
- statutory norms
- voluntary norms.

Pay freezes were used for short periods in Britain on a number of occasions after World War II. They prohibited the implementation of pay settlements during the period of the freeze. They therefore disrupted established internal pay differentials, and external pay relativities, between those who had implemented a settlement immediately before the freeze and those who had been constrained by it.

A statutory pay norm traditionally followed a pay freeze. This defers the re-establishing of traditional wage differentials and relativities, as well as contributing its own distortions to the wages structure. A statutory pay norm normally imposes a zero increase, or a small ceiling, on all wage settlements. Settlements in excess of the statutory norm are usually permitted only where one of a number of criteria for exceptional treatment is satisfied. These may include:

- to reward work groups for rises in productivity
- to help employers respond to labour shortages
- to help the low paid
- to restructure distorted pay differentials.

Statutory pay norms are also accompanied by a restriction on the number of pay settlements that any single negotiating group can achieve in a year, normally only one every 12 months. Statutory norms may be specified in terms of either a percentage pay increase or some absolute money sum to be added to existing pay levels. In practice, pay norms have come to be regarded as the 'going rate' or target rate of increase for most negotiating groups. Where the sum specified has been an absolute money sum, this resulted in a narrowing of percentage wage differentials. The specification of the norm in absolute terms in a succession of incomes policies in Britain in the early 1970s was a main reason for the substantial erosion of occupational wage relativities at that time.

Voluntary pay norms usually involve specifying a maximum permissible level of wage settlements but, unlike statutory policies, they do not have legal force. For this reason, there has normally been less compliance with them. Such policies are effective only where government can exert its own direct control over wage levels, as among public sector groups.

Incomes policies have suffered from a number of shortcomings. First, it is suggested that they merely defer rather than cancel large wage increases, because once the policy is off, employee groups try to catch up lost ground. Second, where the norm relates to basic wage rates, earnings drift (or rises in weekly earnings in excess of negotiated wage increases) emerges to compensate for this, causing resentment among those who remain constrained by wage policy norms. Third, incomes policies tend to ossify the wages structure, preventing differential rates of change in money wages amongst competing job sectors. Fourth, there is the issue of policing incomes policies. In Sweden, in the 1960s and 1970s, both management and unions policed incomes policy voluntarily, without government intervention. In Britain, in contrast, state agencies such as the National Board for Prices and Incomes and the Pay Board were used in the late 1960s and early 1970s, but with varying degrees of success.

The new Keynesianism

After the election of the first Thatcher government in Britain in June 1979, and the first Reagan administration in the USA in November 1980, Keynesian approaches to economic management were largely rejected by both the British and American governments. They were replaced by neo-liberal, market-centred policies, associated with monetarism and supply-side economics (see below). Neo-liberals emphasise the centrality of rational individuals pursuing their own self-interest in the market place as the basis of economic policy. There is a minimum of government intervention supported by sound monetary policy to control inflation and economic measures aimed at improving the ability of producers to supply goods and services to the market efficiently and cost-effectively. The market-liberal critiques of Keynesianism in Britain were fuelled by the onset of 'stagflation' – that is, rising inflation and rising unemployment – and by the failures of successive incomes policies in the 1960s and 1970s.

The economic experiences of the 1970s and 1980s have therefore modified Keynesian thinking (Shaw 1988). First, few Keynesians would still argue that unemployment always represents a problem solely of effective demand without taking account of the supply side of the economy. Second, few Keynesians would argue today that an overall increase in public spending would continue to reduce the level of unemployment, without conceding that the problem is not just one of demand but also of training in human capital. Keynesians are now aware of the need to target public expenditure, by using it, for example, to produce a better-trained workforce, able to produce goods and services to meet consumer demand in the market place. Third, Keynesians are also aware of regional variations in unemployment, of unemployment in the inner cities and of the long-term unemployed. They argue that structural unemployment, for example, is due to declining industries, economic change, new technology and global competition. All these problems require different solutions.

Keynesians now also accept that increasing aggregate demand in the classical Keynesian way will not deal with the problems of unemployed ethnic minorities, of women entering the labour market when there are no childcare facilities or of the unskilled, lacking training, qualifications and work experience. Unlike some market liberals who see these problems in microeconomic terms, Keynesians still see them as a macro concern, justifying a more interventionist approach by government in economic management.

MONETARISM AND SUPPLY-SIDE ECONOMICS

The mid-1970s marked a watershed in economic policy in Britain, as the decade ended in a break with the post-war settlement of full employment, Keynesianism and the welfare state. The wider economic contexts of the 1970s also provided new challenges for government policy-makers. First, there was the replacement of fixed exchange rates, agreed at Bretton Woods in 1944, by countries floating their own domestic currencies in 1973. Second, the spirit of policy co-operation internationally was replaced by foreign competition and freer markets, as countries used the mechanism of interest rates to deal with the dual problems of inflation and balance of payments deficits. Third, rises in oil prices in the early 1970s and late 1970s produced very difficult challenges in economic management for governments of the major industrial countries (Keegan 1984).

Keynesian economics had become associated with interventionism and big government, while monetarism and supply-side economics were becoming associated with rational individualism, the market and 'smaller' government. Mullard (1992: 248) relates the demise of Keynesianism in Britain 'to the failure of UK governments to establish both a Keynesian economic and political agenda similar to that established elsewhere in Europe'. It is monetarism and supply-side economics that have dominated British, North American and Australasian economic management since the mid-1970s.

Monetarism

Monetary policy is concerned with the measures taken by government to influence the price and supply of money in the economy, through changes in the rate of interest. Clearly, in a free, deregulated money market, government can attempt to control either the supply (quantity) of money in circulation or its price, but not both. The growth in importance of monetary policy as an instrument of macroeconomic management is explained to a large extent by the apparent failure of fiscal policy in the 1970s to resolve the problem of stagflation. Monetarist economists explain this failure in terms of excessive government spending, financed by spiralling budget deficits, not only through borrowing – from the banking and non-banking sectors – but also increasingly as a result of printing new money (Friedman and Schwarz 1963, Friedman 1991). Both of these lead to increases in the money supply in excess of the amount needed to finance the transactions arising from growth in the physical output of the economy.

Monetarists argue that if the money supply is allowed to grow faster than the economy's output, then firms and households find themselves holding larger money balances than they want. This surplus of money balances is then spent on goods and services, leading to an increase in aggregate demand that it is beyond the capacity of the economy to supply. According to monetarists, this results in a general rise in prices. Additionally, any upward pressure on prices also fuels expectations of future inflation. This results in higher wage demands from trade union negotiators and an ensuing wages–prices inflationary spiral. A related consequence of excessive monetary growth, it is argued, is unemployment, as the competitiveness of firms declines and workers 'price themselves out of jobs'. In monetarist analysis, unemployment falls, in the longer term, only if the productive efficiency of the economy is increased and inflationary expectations are reduced.

The monetarist analysis of the role of money in the economy is based on the quantity theory of money. This relates monetary growth to the rate of inflation. The monetarist prescription is to allow the money supply to grow at a constant rate approximately equal to the growth in national output (the money supply rule). Money supply in excess of this, it is believed, is likely to result in inflation. Monetarists also believe that there are strong links between changes in the money supply and changes in interest rates, when interest rates (or the price of money) are determined in a free market. This is based on the assumption that people's willingness to hold assets in the form of money balances is relatively sensitive to the rate of interest.

Monetarists also argue that the rate of interest is a main determinant of investment decisions. The reasoning is that a fall in interest rates makes some investments profitable, which were previously unprofitable, and therefore aggregate investment should increase. Conversely, when interest rates rise, aggregate investment should fall. Aggregate investment, therefore, is inversely related to the rate of interest.

In the 1980s, monetary policy in Britain reflected the predominance given by governments to the importance of money in determining economic performance. In March 1980, the newly elected Conservative Government, led by Margaret Thatcher, unveiled its anti-inflation policy, with the announcement of its first medium-term financial strategy. Sterling M3 (broadly defined as notes, coins, current and deposit accounts in UK banks, and private-sector holdings of sterling bank certificates of deposit) was the targeted money supply. However, achieving the desired growth in M3 in the following years proved problematic to achieve (Smith 1987). In 1987, the Chancellor of the Exchequer quietly announced the end of targeting broad money in the Budget that year. This decision came after more than a decade of unsuccessful targeting. The main reason for this policy failure was the dramatic deregulation of the financial services sector in the 1980s, with the consequent acceleration in the rate of financial innovation in money markets.

With the abolition of exchange controls and with financial deregulation in Britain, governments felt it necessary to fall back on interest rate policy to restrain the rise of credit in the economy. But high interest rates, in turn, proved difficult to sustain over long periods for economic and political reasons. Moreover, from the mid-1980s, interest rates appeared to be set more with a view to influencing the level of the exchange rate rather than with a view to constraining growth in the money stock. Interest rates alone seem to be inadequate in restricting monetary growth sufficiently to squeeze out inflation. As such, their use is viewed as a blunt policy instrument.

It is further argued that monetarist measures to reduce inflationary pressures are likely to have a number of negative consequences for businesses (Ellis and Parker 1990). First, high interest rates, since they attract foreign currency into the economy, and cause the external value of the currency to rise, tend to hit exporters. Similarly, as the value of domestic currency rises, domestic producers suffer as imported goods gain a price-competitive advantage over home-produced ones. Second, high interest rates, coupled with a high exchange rate, tend to decrease aggregate demand for domestically produced goods. This is likely to squeeze profits, increase stocks of unsold goods and result in more borrowing to finance this. Third, firms may not be able to survive a combination of high interest rates and a high exchange rate, since these have implications for employment, investment and the productive capacity of the economy.

Supply-side economics

Keynesian and monetarist macroeconomic policies are both concerned with influencing the level of aggregate demand in the economy. Keynesian economics operates primarily through fiscal measures, while monetarist economic policy seeks to control growth in the supply of money and interest rates. The branch of economics focusing on the microeconomic factors that determine aggregate supply is 'supply-side' economics. The aggregate supply of an economy consists of the amount of total real output that producers are willing and able to produce at various prices in the short term.

Supply-side economists argue that the key to reducing unemployment and inflation lies in improving the ability of the economy to supply goods and services to the market efficiently and cost-effectively. In practice, most supply-siders also favour a sound monetary policy to keep down inflation so as to provide a favourable economic climate for employment and production. Recent supply-side economics differs from earlier attempts at dirigiste industrial policy in its emphasis on creating an economic environment conducive to private enterprise and free markets, rather than state planning, government intervention and investment subsidies. Supply-side measures are therefore aimed at creating an economic environment in which there are incentives for individuals to work and for firms to invest, produce goods or services and employ workers. The role of government is not to plan industry and manage demand but to liberalise markets, reduce taxes and public spending and deregulate the labour market.

The primary objective of supply-side policies is to create the economic conditions necessary for fast growth, low inflation and full employment. In essence, supply-side economics is concerned with increasing aggregate supply so that more demand can be accommodated, without inflation. The supply-side measures pursued by successive Conservative governments in Britain between 1979 and 1997 involved:

- reducing direct taxation and creating incentives to work and invest
- privatising public industries
- using the law to restrict union power in the labour market.

Improving economic incentives

After 1979, successive Conservative governments introduced a number of major tax changes to act as incentives to work, invest and encourage private enterprise. These are illustrated in Exhibit 14. The unanswered questions remaining are whether pre-1979 taxes in fact damaged the British economy and whether the changes introduced since then have improved incentives to work, invest and save and encouraged economic growth or not.

Exhibit 14 **Major tax incentives, 1979–97**

These included:

- reductions in the marginal rate of income tax on high earned incomes
- introduction of a uniform rate of tax on earned and unearned incomes
- reductions in the basic rate of income tax
- reductions in the rates of corporation tax on profits
- increases in income tax thresholds, taking more people out of paying tax
- technical changes to taxation legislation, to alleviate the impact of capital gains tax
- tax exemptions and other incentives for investment in plant, buildings, enterprise zones, share options and personal equity plans.

Privatisation and deregulation

These measures involved:

- selling off state monopolies to private shareholders
- introducing market competition into the remaining public services
- introducing more competition into the private sector.

Underpinning them was the assumption that market competition is the key to higher productivity, wider consumer choice and lower prices. First, a wide range of public industries was sold off and denationalised by government after 1979, starting with Associated British Ports, British Aerospace, Enterprise Oil and Jaguar Cars (Farnham and Horton 1993). Second, more competition was introduced into the civil service, local government and National Health Service (NHS) through compulsory competitive tendering. This required these sectors to compete with external contractors for the provision of certain services, such as cleaning, catering and some professional services. Third, more competition was introduced into the private sector through reforming some monopolies and removing restrictive practices, such as in the Stock Market, legal services and supply of spectacles.

Improving labour market flexibility

Another supply-side policy goal of Conservative governments in the 1980s and 1990s was to make the labour market more competitive in the expectation that wages would find their free-market levels. The Thatcher and Major governments believed that real wages were not responsive enough to labour market factors and saw the unions as a prime cause of this. They were convinced that unions destroyed jobs by raising wages above levels that employers could afford to pay. They therefore enacted measures attempting to curb trade unions and their bargaining power through a series of trade union

Figure 7 **Principal legal sources of the TULRCA 1992**

Conspiracy and Protection of Property Act 1875
Trade Union Act 1913
Industrial Courts Act 1919
Trade Union (Amalgamations, etc) Act 1964
Industrial Relations Act 1971
Trade Union and Labour Relations Act 1974
Employment Protection Act 1975
Trade Union and Labour Relations (Amendment) Act 1976
Employment Protection (Consolidation) Act 1978
Employment Act 1980
Employment Act 1982
Trade Union Act 1984
Employment Act 1988
Employment Act 1989
Employment Act 1990

laws: the Employment Acts of 1980, 1982, 1988, 1989, 1990 and the Trade Union Act 1984 (TUA 1984). This legislation was subsequently consolidated, with other trade union legislation, as outlined in Figure 7, into the Trade Union and Labour Relations (Consolidation) Act 1992 (TULRCA 1992).

Another of the Conservative governments' aims was to reduce 'involuntary' unemployment by making the labour market more flexible, thus enabling all those seeking employment to be in work. It was also felt that the structure of employment and levels of social security benefits distorted the labour market. Governments therefore attempted to make the trade-off between receiving social security payments and working less favourable to remaining unemployed. These measures included:

- indexing benefits to retail prices, rather than to earnings
- reforming social security payments
- making the obtaining of benefits more difficult for school-leavers
- abolishing earnings-related supplements, based on the previous level of earnings at work.

NEW LABOUR: A THIRD WAY?

With the election to political power of a 'New' Labour Government, led by Tony Blair, in May 1997, there was much speculation about the possible implications for the UK having its first Labour administration for 18 years and the impact that this would have on economic and employment policy. In economic terms, Labour is continuing the Conservative legacy by being fiscally cautious. It did not increase public spending during its first two years of office and one of the Chancellor of the Exchequer's first actions was to give the Bank of England full independence in monetary matters and freedom to raise interest rates independently of government and the Treasury. This subsequently resulted in four rises in interest rates in the first 100 days of New Labour's administration. Similarly, the Chancellor's first post-election Budget contained few surprises: a windfall tax on the public utilities to fund training for the young unemployed; rises in duties on alcohol, tobacco and petrol; and no income tax rises. The new government's overall objective was to provide the conditions for continuing the steady growth of the economy, already apparent under the previous Conservative administration, promote long-term investment, keep a tight target for inflation and not undermine business confidence.

The overriding economic goals of the new Labour Government were stated in its election manifesto (Labour Party 1997): 'low inflation, rising living standards and high and stable levels of employment'. With economic stability seen to be the essential platform for sustained growth within a global economy, Labour's economic priority was stable, low inflation conditions for long-term growth. To these purposes, Labour claimed that by spending wisely and taxing fairly government could help tackle the country's central economic problems. Its main policy proposals included:

- ensuring that public money was used better, underpinned by a partnership with the private sector
- promoting fair taxes to encourage work and reward effort
- making monetary policy more effective, open, accountable and free from short-term political manipulation
- maintaining strict rules for government borrowing by enforcing the 'golden rule' of public spending – borrowing only for investment, not to fund current public expenditure
- sticking to planned public spending for the government's first two years of office
- switching public spending to investment by using resources better and eliminating public-sector waste
- promoting saving and investment
- reforming competition law to facilitate competition wherever possible
- reinvigorating the private finance initiative
- promoting local economic growth and small businesses
- strengthening the UK's capability in science, technology and design
- taking action on long-term unemployment, through initiatives involving government, businesses and local authorities
- promoting new 'green' technologies.

It was also Labour's stated objective 'for Britain to be a high-quality, high-added-value economy, supported by sustained long-term investment, social cohesion and an ethos of democratic participation and citizenship' (Labour Party 1997: 1). To these ends, Labour believes that to sustain economic opportunity and prosperity in a global economy, government needs, as outlined above, to provide a supportive environment for the business sector. This includes a stable currency, adequate level of public investment, fair tax regime and promotion of fair competition among businesses in the market place. In parallel with its concern for promoting the conditions necessary for steady economic expansion and business confidence, the Labour Government also believes that, to be economically successful, the UK needs to use the talents of its workforce fully. It recognises that competitive success is best achieved through partnership between employers and employees, rather than confrontation. This requires, in its view, leading-edge companies recognising that high business performance is directly associated with maximising the potential of all of its employees in the workplace. In Labour's view, 'the way to achieve this is through trust, consultation, team working and offering people real security.'

The challenge for the Labour Government, in its opinion, is how to create both opportunity for businesses in the modern, rapidly changing, globalised economy – especially in terms of market opportunities, technology and patterns of working – and security for workers. Its prognosis is that companies and individuals need both the capability and flexibility to succeed in this 'new world' of fierce competition, constant innovation and continuous change. Accordingly, there are three principles underlying Labour's approach in trying to balance the creative tensions between economic efficiency, employment flexibility and fairness at work:

- every person at work should be entitled to a basic minimum of standards of fairness, properly enforced
- rigidity should be avoided in labour market regulation to promote the flexibility required
- the best route to job security in the long term is a highly educated and skilled workforce able to succeed in the labour market.

These standards are based on the notion of individual rights, but New Labour accepts that some of them may be best realised through membership of a union. However, Labour's overall purpose is to provide a 'new deal' for people at work, by giving them a decent minimum threshold of fair treatment, while recognising that social partnership is at the heart of successful businesses.

Its starting point in terms of its employment policy is that the modern labour market is changing:

- jobs are changing, with around a third of them classified as professional, managerial and technical
- firms are changing, with a growing proportion of the workforce employed in small to medium-sized businesses
- there are more atypical workers, not employed on full-time, permanent contracts
- more women are working, making up about half of the total workforce
- there is less job security and more individuals are experiencing periods of unemployment

Figure 8 **The law and employee relations**

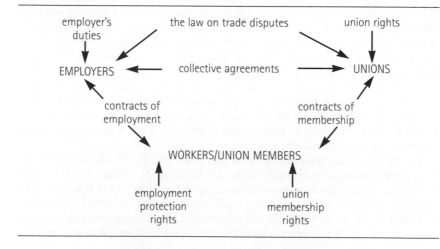

- there is growing inequality and widening pay relativities
- under 50 per cent of the workforce are covered by collective agreements, compared with 75 per cent in the mid-1970s
- only one in three workers is unionised, compared with more than one in two in the mid-1970s.

Labour accepts that this new labour market can bring new opportunities for people, but the market can also bring abuses and unfairness (Farnham 1996). And, since the UK has amongst the fewest basic legal standards to protect working conditions in the developed world, the Government's objective is to establish a framework of minimum standards in the labour market and workplace. This is aimed to support flexibility, on the one hand, and provide protection against unfair treatment by less scrupulous employers on the other.

New Labour's policies for setting basic standards at work should, in its view, be regarded as being part of an individual's citizenship rights. 'They should be regarded as natural as the rule of law and the protection against the abuse of power', at whatever level (Labour Party 1997: 3). The extent to which New Labour's economic, employment and labour-market policy initiatives represent a break with the harsher New Right approach to economic management and supply-side economics – and represents a 'third way' in managing the economy, combining economic efficiency with social fairness – has yet to be effectively demonstrated.

LEGAL POLICY

The state and the law are never neutral in employee relations. The state, through the application of the law, is the ultimate source of authority and power in society and employee relations are not excluded from its influence. Figure 8 illustrates how the law regulates relations between the primary parties to the pay–work bargain, through the contract of employment and employment protection rights. It also shows how the law regulates relations between unions and their members (through the contract of membership and union membership rights) and between the secondary parties (through voluntary collective agreements, trade union rights and the law on trade disputes).

The key to understanding the role of the law in employee relations is identifying its emphasis and impact at particular times. These include:

- whether the law focuses on legal rights or legal freedoms for the parties to employee relations
- whether it is abstentionist, interventionist or restrictive in employee relations processes
- whether it prioritises individual or collective patterns of employee relations
- whether it affects the balance of bargaining power between employers and employees and between management and unions in the labour market

- whether it seeks to regulate intra- and inter-union affairs
- whether the law counterbalances management power by supporting union and employee interests or reinforces this power.

The law is a dynamic and iterative process and its outcomes depend on the legal sources regulating employee relations, the decisions of the courts and which political party in Parliament enacts the law.

The main sources of English employment or labour law are:

- legislation
- codes of practice
- the common law.

Legislation or statute law is determined by Parliament, while delegated legislation is put into action through statutory instruments, which are normally subject to approval from Parliament or from the European Commission and Council of Ministers. Codes of practice, such as those from ACAS, the Health and Safety Commission and the Equal Opportunities Commission, are guidelines to good employment practice, similar to those of the Highway Code for road users. The common law or case law is based on judicial decisions in the courts, which form binding precedents on lower courts. These legal decisions are based on certain legal principles identified by the judges.

THE EMPLOYMENT CONTRACT AND STATUTORY EMPLOYMENT PROTECTION RIGHTS

The individual legal relationship between employer and employee, embodied in the contract of employment, is the cornerstone of British employee relations. The contract of employment originated in the common law and the law of 'master' and 'servant' in early capitalism. Today, the contract of employment is still largely regulated by the common law and the rules of contract built up by the judges. In theory, the contract of employment, made orally or in writing, is determined between two equal parties, employer and employee. As a legal relationship, it is one whereby the employer agrees to provide employment, wages and conditions to the individual employee who, in return, provides effort and skills in carrying out the job's tasks. In undertaking these tasks, the employee is expected to take reasonable care in fulfilling the duties of employment and accepts the legal constraints of employment, such as not acting in conflict with the commercial interests of the employer.

In practice, the legal equality between an employer, normally a corporate body, and an employee, who is an individual, is a fiction. This is because once employed, employees put themselves under a common-law obligation to obey all reasonable and lawful instructions given to them by the employer in carrying out their work tasks. This in reality is an act of subordination. As Kahn-Freund (1977: 7) comments:

> There can be no employment relationship without a power to command and a duty to obey, that is without this element of subordination in which lawyers rightly see the hallmark of the 'contract of employment'.

An element of co-operation can be built into the employment relationship, and the power to command and the duty to obey can be ameliorated, but the ultimate power of command by management remains. A crucial legal issue is how far the courts interpret the contract in order to preserve the employer's power to command and management's right to manage.

A complementary legal issue is how far statute law, enacted by Parliament, offsets employer and managerial power under common law, by providing a series of workers' or employment protection rights for employees. In this way, statute can redress to some degree at least the inherent economic, social and common-law imbalances in the relationship between individuals and their employer. The majority of these statutory rights are not incorporated into the contract of employment itself. The statutory right not to be unfairly dismissed, for example, is separate from the employee's common-law contractual rights to wages, work and co-operation from the employer. The right not to be unfairly dismissed, along with other statutory employment rights, does not become part of the contract. As Wedderburn (1986: 5) points out, there are certain common-law rights enshrined in the employment contract and enforceable by civil actions in the ordinary courts. There are also, on the other hand, 'a separate, minimum "floor of rights" for individual workers gradually added to over recent years by statutes and enforced largely by civil claims in the industrial [sic] tribunals'. Claims for 'wrongful' dismissal – sacking without notice or payment in lieu of notice – used to go to the ordinary courts, while claims for 'unfair' dismissal, for unfair reasons and carried out in an unreasonable way, which are based on employment protection legislation, were settled in industrial tribunals (ITs). Now both types of claim are determined by employment tribunals (ETs).

The statutory floor of employment protection rights extends into many areas of employment law, including:

- unfair dismissal
- redundancy payments
- protection against discrimination on the grounds of gender, ethnic origin, nationality and disability
- union membership
- maternity pay and maternity leave
- minimum periods of notice
- security of earnings.

This floor of legal rights was created in Parliament by governments sympathetic to the view that there should be a basic level of employment protection, below which no employee should fall. It was a level, moreover, over and above which trade unions could negotiate superior conditions through collective bargaining.

In the 1960s and 1970s, statute law sought to weaken employer power and strengthen that of employees by extending the floor of employment protection rights, underpinned by a system of what were then called industrial tribunals (but are now known as ETs) with legal remedies for those claiming that their rights had been infringed by law-breaking employers. Although it must not be overstated, since the 1980s the law tended to strengthen employer power and weaken the legal position of employees by making adjustments to the statutory floor of employment protection rights. Both unfair dismissal and maternity rights were restricted, especially for workers in small businesses. In 1980, the qualifying period for unfair dismissal claims by employees was increased from six months' continuous service to one year. In 1985, it was further extended to two years for newly appointed employees. Guarantee payments in cases of short-time working were reduced, limitations were placed on social security payments – by phasing out earnings-related benefits – and deductions were made from the supplementary benefit payments to families of striking workers. This is because Conservative governments between 1979 and 1997 believed in using market forces and competition to contain inflation and achieve prosperity, with changes in employment law mirroring these economic policy changes.

It may be inferred, therefore, that the content of the contract of employment has changed significantly since the 1970s, largely because of the new framework of statutory rights provided for employees by Parliament. These rights complement rather than replace the common-law contract. As Napier (1986) argues, the role of the common law is twofold. First, it acts as a legal backcloth and provides a set of rules in those situations unregulated by specific statutory measures or where the legal remedies that exist are inadequate or restricted in their application. Second, common law plays a crucial role in the operation of the statutory floor of employment rights themselves, because Parliament has used certain contractual terms and concepts in defining the statutory rights of employees in the workplace.

STATUTORY UNION MEMBERSHIP RIGHTS

A statutory floor of rights for trade union members has been enacted and extended in recent years. Some of these statutory rights, enacted under Labour governments, provide a set of positive rights for individuals to associate into unions, to be active within them and not to be dismissed on the grounds of union membership or for taking part in trade union activities. Others, enacted by Conservative governments since the 1980s, provide negative rights to abstain from union membership, or the right to dissociate. A third set, also enacted since the 1980s, provides positive rights for union members to participate in or restrain union decision-making on specific issues (see Chapter 3).

The right to associate

Traditionally, there was no legal right for individuals to join trade unions in Britain, unlike in most other countries in western Europe. This was because of the philosophy of legal abstention or voluntarism in British employee relations. This specifically excluded the law from intervening in relations between employers and unions, in trade disputes and in supporting or preventing individuals joining trade unions.

The Donovan Commission (1968) put the case for legal protection of the positive right to associate, largely in terms of the reform and extension of collective bargaining. If, as Donovan concluded, voluntary collective bargaining was the best method of conducting employee relations, then a necessary condition for this was effective trade union organisation among the workforce. The Commission therefore recommended that any condition in a contract of employment prohibiting union membership should be void in law and that dismissal for union membership should be deemed to be unfair. After the repeal of the Industrial Relations Act 1971 by the Trade Union and Labour Relations Act 1974, statutory rights to time off work for trade union lay officers and safety representatives were established. Other rights included rights not to be dismissed, or subject to action short of dismissal, because of union membership or union activity.

The right to dissociate

The right for individuals to dissociate from union membership is related to opposition to the practice of the closed shop. A closed shop is any agreement or arrangement between an employer and union(s) requiring employees to be union members as a condition of employment. Pre-entry closed shops limit jobs to those who are members of a specified trade union; post-entry closed shops require those recruited by an employer to join an approved, recognised union within a set period after starting employment.

In the Employment Act (EA) 1980, protections were given for the first time to individuals against dismissal for non-union membership in a closed shop in the case of strongly held personal convictions. This derived from the Government's objections to the closed shop in principle. As the Department of Employment (1981: 66) stated:

> The Government's view of the closed shop is clear: it is opposed to the principles underlying it. That people should be required to join a union as a condition of getting or holding a job runs contrary to the general traditions of personal liberty in this country. It is acceptable for a union to seek to increase its membership by voluntary means. What is objectionable, however, is to enforce membership by means of a closed shop as a condition of employment.

Subsequent legislation first increased the protection and compensation of employees if they were dismissed because of a closed shop, under the EA 1982. The EA 1988 then made post-entry closed shops unenforceable, removed trade union immunity from any industrial action taken to enforce a closed shop and provided legal protection against dismissal for non-union membership, by making dismissal or discrimination against employees refusing to join a union automatically unfair. Under the EA 1990, pre-entry closed shops became void in law, thus effectively making all forms of closed-shop arrangement unlawful.

Another example of the right to dissociate was incorporated in the EA 1988. The TULRCA 1992 now provides protection for union members against what the law describes as 'unjustifiable discipline' by their unions. This upholds the right of individual trade members not to participate in a lawful trade dispute, even where the action has previously been legitimised in a properly conducted industrial action ballot. Also, they cannot be disciplined by their union for failing to take part in the industrial action with which they disagree.

Intra-union rights

Membership participation in the internal affairs of trade unions has traditionally been provided under the union rulebook and, where the rulebook was infringed, there was the right to seek its enforcement through the courts. In the 1980s, governments increasingly held the view that the law needed to be changed in order to democratise the trade unions and make them more accountable to their members. A government Green Paper (Department of Employment 1983: 37) stated that there was much public concern about the need for trade unions to become more democratic and more responsive to the wishes of their members. It argued that 'society, including individual trade unionists themselves, is entitled to ensure that union power is exercised more responsibly, more accountably and more in accordance with the views of their members.'

It was this analysis that led to the passing of the TUA 1984. Its provisions, now incorporated in the TULRCA 1992, are:

- the right for union members to have the opportunity to participate in regular ballots to decide whether or not their union should undertake political activity, through union political funds and the political levy, at least once every 10 years
- the right for trade union members to elect all voting members of their union's executive by secret ballot, at least once every five years
- the right to participate in secret ballots before a union takes organised industrial action against an employer.

A further Green Paper (Department of Employment 1987: 2) went on to argue that there was more to be done, stating:

> It is the view of the Government that, having embarked on the process of giving proper and effective rights to union members, it should ensure that those rights are fully developed so that they provide the ordinary member with the effective protection that he or she is entitled to enjoy in a free society.

Accordingly, the EA 1988, also now incorporated in the TULRCA 1992, extended the rights of union members:

- to elect all the principal union officers by secret postal ballot
- to take part in political fund review ballots by secret postal ballot
- to restrain their union from calling on them to take part in industrial action not supported by a properly conducted secret ballot
- to not be unjustifiably disciplined by their union
- to inspect their union's accounting records.

The office of the Commissioner for the Rights of Trade Union Members (CRTUM), created by the 1988 Act, and that of the Commissioner for Protection Against Unlawful Industrial Action (CPAUIA), were created with power to support individual union members, by giving them advice and paying their costs, when making complaints against their union. But both these bodies have been abolished by the Employment Relations Act (ERA) 1999.

THE LAW AND TRADE DISPUTES

Whether over substantive or procedural issues, employees who are organised into trade unions are likely to take collective industrial action or industrial sanctions against their employer when alternative forms of conflict resolution, such as collective bargaining, conciliation or arbitration, have failed to resolve the differences between the parties. Employee industrial action involves a range of possible activities taken unilaterally by unions and their members against an employer. These include working to rule, banning overtime and stoppages of work, with concomitant legal implications (see Chapters 1, 3 and 8).

Breach of contract

A central legal issue arising from most forms of industrial action taken by employees is that they commonly breach their contracts of employment, by violating the employee's common-law obligation to work for the employer under the terms of the contract. But the law is complex in this respect and there are areas of legal uncertainty. Where, for example, working to rule focuses on working strictly in accordance with the terms of the contract of employment, this is not normally taken to be a breach of contract. Where working to rule refers to the employer's works rules, this too is unlikely to involve a breach of contract in the first instance, since this is within the implied terms of individual contracts. Where overtime is not normally a contractual requirement, a union ban on overtime would also not normally be taken to be a breach of contract by individual employees.

Where, however, an employer unilaterally changes the works rules, employees would normally be expected to conform to them, in all circumstances, since they become incorporated into individual contracts of employment as implied terms. Where working to rule refers to the union rulebook, this too is likely to be in breach of contract, since the terms of the contract are likely to be ignored by employees working in this manner. Similarly, where overtime is contractually required, an overtime ban would be in breach of contract. It is in the cases of stoppages of work that the law is most clear-cut, since such actions are obviously in breach of the employee's common-law obligation to work for the employer and not to impede the employer's business.

All forms of industrial action have profound legal implications for individual employees, since the judges tend to see any industrial action as a challenge to the legitimate authority of the employer to employ labour and deploy it, as embodied in the contract of employment. The employer's capacity to coerce through its economic power is not seen as problematic by the courts but as a legitimate property right. As outlined above, under common law, all industrial action is treated in essentially the same way, as a breach of contract by employees.

This means, first, that breach of contract may provide one of the ingredients of the economic torts (see below) for which trade unions may be liable. Second, it may entitle the employer to take disciplinary action against individual employees. Third, although continuity of employment is not broken by employees taking strike action, any such period does not count towards continuous service for the purposes of claiming employment protection rights.

Economic torts

A second legal issue arising from industrial sanctions taken by unions and their members against employers is that of 'economic torts'. Because the economic interests of employers and other organisations are damaged by collective industrial action, certain torts (civil law 'wrongs') may be committed in the process of conducting strikes, overtime bans and works to rule. The most common economic tort is that of inducing breach of contract.

The inducement may be direct or indirect. Direct inducement takes place when an outsider to the contract persuades one of the contracting parties to break the contract. The necessary elements of the tort are that the party inducing it must act intentionally, there must be evidence of inducement and that party must know or have the means of knowing of the existence of the contract, although it need not know its actual terms. An example of direct inducement would be where a union official persuades union members to go slow or refuse to work mandatory overtime. The official would then have induced a breach of the employment contract. The employer could obtain an injunction to end or prevent the inducement and/or obtain damages relating to any commercial loss it has suffered as a result of the breach of contract. The employer could sue both the official and the union itself.

Indirect inducement is more complicated. This occurs whenever a person (A) persuades a second person (B) to act unlawfully, with the intention of inducing a third person (C) to break a contract entered into with a fourth person (D). Because the inducement is indirect there is a further key requirement that the inducement must be obtained by unlawful means. For example, a union official (A) may persuade members (B) to break their employment contracts with their employer (C), to prevent it supplying goods under a commercial contract with (D). The means of achieving the intended breach between (C) and (D) involves inducing a breach of the employment contract between (B) and (C) – in other words, the commission of an unlawful act. All the key requirements are present and the fourth party (D) may bring an action for damages and/or seek an injunction against both the official and the union.

The tort of intimidation differs from inducing breach of contract in that it is concerned with threats rather than action itself. Intimidation occurs whenever there is a threat to commit unlawful action. 'Unlawful' has been widely defined and it includes, as well as criminal acts, tortious acts and breaches of contract. So a threat by a union official that members will strike in breach of contract unless wages are increased would amount to intimidation. As with inducing breach, there may be direct or indirect intimidation. Both intimidation and inducement can occur in the same dispute. First there may be a threat of unlawful action such as strike (intimidation) followed by the strike action itself (inducement).

Legal immunities

A third legal issue arising from industrial action is the common-law liabilities of those organising or participating in industrial action and the statutory protections, or legal immunities, provided during stoppages of work and other sanctions. Unlike in other western European countries, there is no legal right for workers or their unions to take industrial action in the UK. The situation differs in countries like France, for example, where the Constitution guarantees the individual worker the right to strike, and in Germany, where strikes are lawful, provided that they are in furtherance of improvements in working conditions and do not break a collective agreement (Department of Employment 1981). This means that in these countries workers and their unions are legally authorised, through systems of positive legal rights, to take industrial action against employers, subject to certain statutory conditions and qualifications.

In Britain, the law has followed a quite different path from that in other countries (Wedderburn 1986). Here the law governing industrial action and trade disputes starts with the common law. This provides the basic legal principles underlying subsequent statute law. The statutes governing strikes and other forms of industrial action have defined a system of 'legal immunities'. These protect those organising and taking part in industrial action from the civil (and possible criminal) liability arising from the imposition of industrial sanctions on employers. Without legal immunities, most industrial action would be illegal. This means that trade unions, their officials and their members would be liable to civil actions for damages, and even criminal prosecution, every time they were involved in a strike, unless due notice, under the terms of the contract of employment, were given by the employees to the employer.

Legal immunities do not abolish civil wrongs (or 'torts'), or criminal liability, but they suspend liability in the circumstances of a trade dispute. Where these immunities are reduced, the common-law liabilities are restored. Where they are extended, the common-law liabilities relapse. If there were no immunities, then unions and individuals would be at risk of legal action by employers every time they organised a strike. The history of trade union law in Britain over the past 30 years broadly reflects the differing views of Labour and Conservative governments about the role and scope of immunities in regulating industrial conflict. In general, Labour governments have strengthened immunities and Conservative ones reduced them.

To be protected in law, industrial action by unions and their members must: (1) fall within the legal definition of a 'trade dispute'; and (2) take place 'in contemplation of furtherance of a trade dispute' – the so-called 'golden formula'. It is the golden formula that provides the basis for legal immunities. A trade dispute is now defined in law by section 218 of the TULRCA 1992 as any dispute between 'workers and their employer' that relates 'wholly or mainly to':

- terms and conditions of employment
- engagement or non-engagement of workers or termination or suspension of employment
- allocation of work or the duties of employment
- matters of discipline
- membership or non-membership of a trade union
- facilities for trade union officials
- machinery for negotiation, consultation or other procedures, including trade union recognition.

In contrast to earlier legislation, secondary disputes (between workers and employers other than their own), inter-union disputes and political disputes are no longer incorporated within the statutory definition outlined above.

Legal immunities, as provided by section 219 of the TULRCA 1992, were incrementally limited during the 1980s by amendments to the law through the Employment Acts 1980, 1982, 1988, 1990 and Trade Union Act 1984. In outline, immunity in law is now provided only where:

- industrial action is between an employer and its direct employees, with all secondary or sympathy action being unlawful
- a properly conducted industrial action ballot has been conducted by the union, authorising or endorsing the action
- peaceful picketing is limited to the workers' own place of work.

Immunity is specifically removed where industrial action is taken to impose or enforce a closed shop or where the action is unofficial and not repudiated, in writing, by the union. Where the 'golden formula' does not apply, it is relatively easy for an employer to show that one of the economic torts is being committed and to obtain an interlocutory injunction on that basis. Moreover, since the EA 1982, trade unions are now treated as ordinary persons. This means that they can be sued if responsible for unlawful industrial action (see Chapters 9 and 10). It is significant that the Blair administration made no changes to the law affecting immunities after it came to office in 1997.

ASSIGNMENTS

(a) Consider the situation where unemployment has risen to 3 million and inflation to 4 per cent. What would be a Keynesian economic response to this and how would this affect wage bargaining in your organisation? What would be a supply-side economic response to this situation and how would this affect wage bargaining in your organisation?

(b) Examine the reasons for introducing incomes policies, the forms they take and the conditions necessary for them to be effective. Compare and contrast how (i) a named public-sector organisation might respond to a wages freeze; (ii) a multi-plant manufacturing company negotiating with trade unions might respond; and (iii) a small non-union company with 25 employees might respond. Provide a rationale for your answer in each case.

(c) Present a report summarising what 'unfair dismissal' is and the legal remedies available to those whose claim for unfair dismissal is upheld by an industrial tribunal.

(d) Union membership agreements are now unlawful. What action would you take, as a newly recruited personnel manager, if the chief executive of your company asked you to continue enforcing, on behalf of the company, an informal, closed-shop arrangement with the unions?

(e) Read Simpson (1986: 161–92) and outline the development of trade union immunities in Britain and how the law on immunities has changed since 1980.

REFERENCES

DEPARTMENT OF EMPLOYMENT (1981) *Trade Union Immunities*. London, HMSO.

DEPARTMENT OF EMPLOYMENT (1983) *Democracy in Trade Unions*. London, HMSO.

DEPARTMENT OF EMPLOYMENT (1987) *Trade Unions and Their Members*. London, HMSO.

DONALDSON P. *and* FARQUHAR J. (1988) *Understanding the British Economy*. Harmondsworth, Penguin.

DONOVAN, Lord (1968) *Royal Commission on Trade Unions and Employers' Associations 1965–1968: Report*. London, HMSO.

ELLIS J. *and* PARKER D. (1990) *The Essence of the Economy*. Hemel Hempstead, Prentice Hall.

FARNHAM D. (1996) 'New Labour, the new unions and the new labour market'. *Parliamentary Affairs*. 49(4), October.

FARNHAM D. *and* HORTON S. (EDS) (1993) *Managing the New Public Services*. Basingstoke, Macmillan.

FRIEDMAN M. (1991) *Monetarist Economics*. Oxford, Blackwell.

FRIEDMAN M. *and* SCHWARZ A. (1963) *A Monetary History of the United States*. Princeton, Princeton University Press.

HORTON S. *and* FARNHAM D. (EDS) (1999) *Public Management in Britain*. London, Macmillan.

KAHN-FREUND O. (1977) *Labour and the Law*. London, Stevens.

KEEGAN W. (1984) *Mrs Thatcher's Economic Experiment*. Harmondsworth, Penguin.

KEYNES J. M. (1936) *The General Theory of Employment, Interest and Money*. London, Macmillan.

LABOUR PARTY (1997) *Road to the Manifesto*. London.

MULLARD M. (1992) *Understanding Economic Policy*. London, Routledge.

NAPIER B. (1986) 'The contract of employment', in R. Lewis (ed.), *Labour Law in Britain*, Oxford, Blackwell.

PANITCH L. (1976) *Social Democracy and Industrial Militancy: The Labour Party, the Trades Union and Incomes Policy 1945–74*. Cambridge, Cambridge University Press.

ROBINSON J. (1937) *Essays in the Theory of Employment*. London, Macmillan.

SHAW G. (1988) *Keynesian Economics: The permanent revolution*. Aldershot, Elgar.

SIMPSON B. (1986) 'Trade union immunities', in R. Lewis (ed.), *Labour Law in Britain*, Oxford, Blackwell.

SMITH D. (1987) *The Rise and Fall of Monetarism*. Harmondsworth, Penguin.

WEDDERBURN, Lord (1986) *The Worker and the Law*. Harmondsworth, Penguin.

5 The changing contexts of employee relations

Sylvia Horton

Change is endemic in all societies and social organisations, but the rate of change in the last half of the twentieth century was more rapid and fundamental than in any previous period. This chapter explores the nature of the changes in the economic, technological, social and political spheres, which collectively make up the main contexts within which employee relations are managed.

THE ECONOMIC CONTEXT

Britain was the first industrial nation and had a world lead in economic performance, international trade and wealth creation in 1900. One hundred years later she is still in the league of 'First World' advanced industrial societies but no longer at the top. With a gross national product (GNP), at market prices, of £837 billion in 1998, Britain ranked twelfth in terms of GNP per capita in the 15 member states of the EU, and nineteenth out of the top 25 high-income economies in the Organisation for Economic Co-operation and Development (OECD). These rankings reflect a declining relative world economic position, although Britain's wealth generation is the highest in its history. During the last four decades, dramatic changes have occurred in both international and domestic economies. First, there has been a major restructuring of international markets, with third-world countries developing their own manufacturing industries and becoming important exporters of manufactured and semi-manufactured products to the economies of Europe, North America and Australasia. Second, first-world economies have been de-industrialising and developing their service sectors. The international flow of goods, patterns of trade and capital movements are in a continual state of flux. Third, the collapse of the former communist regimes in eastern Europe and Russia, between 1989 and 1991, and their movement towards open market economies, have extended the scope of the international economy by opening up new opportunities for trade. Fourth, international organisations, such as the World Trade Organisation (WTO), have been trying to liberalise the world economy by removing tariff barriers and encouraging free trade. The British economy has been affected by these international trends and by changes in its domestic patterns of production and consumption.

Table 2 Changing sector distribution of employment in the UK for selected years, 1971–98

	1971	%	1979	%	1981	%	1986	%	1992	%	1998	%
Manufacturing	8,065	(36.4)	7,253	(31.3)	6,222	(28.4)	5,227	(24.44)	4,793	(21.5)	3,970	(17.6)
Services	11,627	(52.5)	13,580	(58.6)	13,468	(61.5)	14,297	(66.9)	15,654	(71.9)	17,200	(76)
Other	2,447	(11.1)	2,340	(10.1)	2,203	(10.1)	1,863	(8.7)	1,524	(7.0)	900,000	(7.9)
All	22,139		23,173		21,893		21,387		21,757		22,600	

Source: *Social Trends 22* 1992 and Office of National Statistics 1999

Britain's annual rate of economic growth has been on average around 2.5 per cent per annum over the last century, but this has been lower than that of its major competitors. Major changes have occurred in the structure and geographical location of industry and in methods and patterns of work. There has been a long-term shift from primary to service industries, as agriculture and traditional industries like coal, shipbuilding, iron and steel and textiles have contracted. The most significant change, in recent years, has been a major decline in the proportion of the labour force employed in manufacturing industries and an increase in the service sector. As Table 2 shows, between 1971 and 1998, the numbers employed in manufacturing fell from 8.0 million to 3.9 million – a fall of more than 50 per cent – whilst those in service industries rose from 11.6 to 17.2 million – an increase of nearly 50 per cent. The service sector now accounts for 76 per cent of the labour force.

Changes in employment have not been smooth and throughout the last three decades there have been fluctuating and relatively high levels of unemployment, as shown in Figure 9. The numbers unemployed rose above 1 million in 1976, 2 million in 1981 and passed 3 million in 1985, peaking at 3.2 million in July 1986. After falling sharply to 1.5 million in early 1990, they rose again to over 3 million at the beginning of 1993 but fell back to 1.6 million in 1999, their lowest level since 1979. In the late 1990s the unemployment rate in the UK was one of the lowest in the EU – in contrast

Figure 9 Unemployment in the UK, 1971–99

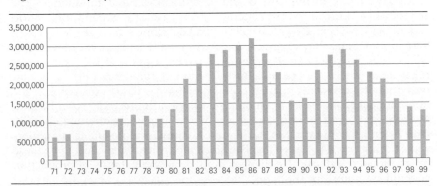

Source: *Annual Abstract of Statistics*, Earnings and Employment Division, ONS

to the early 1980s, when it was the highest. The official unemployment rate is always disputed, as it is based on numbers of claimants rather than those looking for work. The independent Unemployment Unit estimated that in 1997 around 5.4 million people were in fact looking for work, a much higher figure than the official rate recorded by government.

A significant trend throughout the 1980s and 1990s was the number of long-term unemployed – that is, those out of work for more than one year. The long-term unemployed are most likely to be unskilled manual and skilled craft workers, older men over 50, the young between 16 and 25, and some ethnic minorities. Unemployment is actually highest among the young. The Labour Government, elected in May 1997, is committed to tackling long-term unemployment with its 'Welfare to Work' programmes. Initially focused on the under-25s, the programme aims to reduce the number of long-term unemployed in this age group by 250,000 by 2002. It is also targeting over-25s that are out of work for over a year, lone parents and, since April 2000, the over-50s. The Government claims that its policy is working, as unemployment continues to fall, but there is some evidence that only one in 10 under-25s complete their training programmes and only 8 per cent of young people on 'workfare' find permanent employment. It is likely that falling unemployment levels have more to do with a buoyant economy than government schemes.

Changes in the structure of industry have been accompanied by changes in the spatial distribution of economic activity within Britain. As extractive and manufacturing industries have contracted, the traditional industrial regions of Scotland, Wales, the North-East, Lancashire and the Midlands have lost jobs. A census published in 1987 showed that 94 per cent of the jobs lost in manufacturing between 1979 and 1984 had been lost in the North, but the Midlands was particularly badly hit in the late 1980s by the collapse of the car industry. Although expansion of new industries is not confined to the South, the latter has gained most from the rise of new industrial sectors, particularly high-tech and growth in the services. There is something of an inverse relationship between de-industrialisation and tertiarisation and, as a result, inequalities between British regions have tended to increase. The highest levels of unemployment in 1999 were in Cleveland (13 per cent), Tyneside (11 per cent) and South Yorkshire (9 per cent), while the lowest was in Surrey (1.8 per cent).

Changes in the structure of the economy are also reflected in the occupational distribution of the labour force. The working population grew from 25 million in 1971 to a peak of 28.2 million in spring 1999. The increase in the labour force is accounted for mainly by the entry of over 3 million women workers. In 1999, there were 12.3 million economically active women, representing 45 per cent of the workforce, compared with 15.7 million men (55 per cent). There is an increasing convergence in the economic activity rates of men and women, which now stand at 85 and 71 per cent respectively.

Between 1971 and 1999, there was a major expansion of white-collar and professional jobs and a decline in blue-collar ones. In 1999 over half of men and more than two-thirds of women were in non-manual occupations. Only 23 per cent of men were employed in manufacturing, and the fastest-growing areas of employment were managerial and professional occupations, which accounted for 39 per cent of men and 20 per cent of women. Gender segregation continues to be a major feature of employment, with women concentrated in clerical and administration, public services such as teaching, nursing and social work, and the retail and sales sector, while men dominate in construction, engineering, transport, craft industries and as plant and machine operatives. There is also horizontal gender segregation with twice as many male managers and administrators as women, even in those organisations occupied mainly by women workers, such as education and the NHS.

De-industrialisation has resulted in many job losses, but it has been accompanied by increases in productivity and output. Between 1980 and 1998, manufacturing productivity grew at an annual average rate of 5 per cent owing to increased investment, the introduction of new technology and changes in the patterns and structure of the work process. Employers have sought to increase flexibility in their organisational structures and processes through delayering and process re-engineering. They have also adopted a variety of employment modes to control labour costs and resorted to de-skilling, re-skilling and multiskilling to increase the flexibility of their workforces. Part-time employment has increased significantly since the 1970s.

Although women fill most part-time jobs (86 per cent), the fastest rate of growth has been among men. In 1998, 1.3 million out of 14.8 million men and 5.4 million out of 12 million women in employment worked part-time. Among both men and women, it is the youngest and oldest workers who are most likely to be in part-time work. The high rate among the young is because of the number of students who take part-time work and, amongst older age groups, there are a disproportionate number of men who have taken early retirement. In the 25 to 45 age range, almost all part-time jobs are held by women with children under 16. Part-time working is most common in public administration and the distributive industries, where 34 and 44 per cent respectively are part-time jobs. Most people who work part-time do not want to work full-time and this is particularly true of women, because of their dual role – at work and in the home. However, 40 per cent of men in part-time work are there because they cannot find full-time work.

Another feature of the labour market in recent years has been the increase in temporary employment. Some 7 per cent of people in work (1.6 million) are in temporary posts and again there is a higher percentage of women (7.6 per cent) than men (6.3 per cent). This figure is low compared with most other EU countries; only Austria and Belgium have lower rates, while Spain peaks at 35 per cent (*Social Trends* 1997).

THEORIES OF ECONOMIC CHANGE

There is widespread agreement amongst academics and practitioners about the changes in the international and British economies in the last quarter of the twentieth century, including:

- growth in service industries
- revolutionary modes of communication technology
- rapid and radical changes in industrial organisation and production technology
- major restructuring of world markets
- changes in the policies of economic management at the international, national and regional levels.

There is less agreement about how to explain what is happening, as Britain passes from being an industrial to a post-industrial society. The main competing theories can be grouped under a number of headings, including 'neo-Fordism and post-Fordism', 'the information society', 'post-modernism' and 'globalisation'. They all overlap, and many themes are common to all or some of the theories, but what distinguishes them is the framework they use within which to examine these common themes and ideas.

Fordism

Fordism is a term used to describe both an epoch and a form of production that dominated that epoch. During the early twentieth century, a series of innovations in manufacturing led to large-scale mass production of commodities, using highly specialised machinery, extensive division of labour and assembly line processes. Labour was highly fragmented, generally semi-skilled or unskilled, and located primarily in factories. Factories produced long runs of standardised products, at relatively low unit cost. Fordism is also associated with scientific management. Frederick Winslow Taylor (1947), father of scientific management, demonstrated that where employers adopted a rational scientific approach to production, they could maximise productivity, output and efficiency. This entailed separation of planning, organising and controlling from the activities of executing and producing. It was the job of management to plan production scientifically, including the work process, and the job of workers to execute and carry out the work assigned to them. Through time and motion studies, and a careful analysis of the tasks involved in completing an activity, the 'one best way' of doing it could be identified. These ideas, extended to labour, led to scientific approaches to recruitment and training to ensure management had the right quantity and quality of labour to do the job. The result was not only standardisation and bureaucratisation within organisations, but also the emergence of an 'expert' managerial cadre claiming managerial prerogative and the right to manage within the workplace (Rose 1988).

Fordism is also linked to a particular pattern of consumption. Mass production requires mass consumption if it is to be sustained. It also requires market stability. This can be achieved only if purchasing power is sufficient to consume all that is produced. Mature Fordism came to be identified with a period of government regulation known as Keynesianism, where governments sought, through macroeconomic policies, to manage the level of aggregate demand and maintain high levels of employment (see Chapter 4).

The Fordist system of work was also reflected in particular social and economic patterns of employment. Full-time male employment was the norm, with workers' families dependent on a single income and a 'social wage' provided by the state. The nuclear family consumed standardised commodities produced in the private sector and standardised collective goods and services provided by a bureaucratic state (Jessop 1989a). Political processes within industry and at national political level resolved conflicts over the industrial and social wage respectively. In Britain, trade unions sought to increase their members' wages and improve employee relations through collective bargaining, while the major political parties (Conservative and Labour) used parliamentary democracy to resolve conflicts over the size and distribution of the social wage (see Chapter 9).

Challenges to Fordism

Fordism did not characterise the whole of industry, but between 1945 and the late 1970s it was the dominant mode of production in Britain. It provided the basis for the full employment, economic growth and rising living standards of the post-war era, as well as expansion of the welfare state. Several writers (Hobsbawn 1968, Weiner 1981, Jessop 1989a) point out, however, that the prosperity of the period concealed underlying weaknesses of the British economy and its relative decline internationally. The changes that occurred in the British economy after the 1970s are seen, by Fordist writers, as a movement from traditional or classic Fordism to 'neo-Fordism' or 'post-Fordism'. This transformation, they argue, is the consequence of a structural crisis of Fordism. First, Fordism is unable to constantly deliver rising productivity, economic growth and prosperity. It appears to have reached its economic and productive limits, as constantly rising returns to scale have been frustrated by the failure of demand to keep pace with supply. Saturated markets combined with changes in tastes and fluctuating purchasing power have all contributed to a decline in production. Latter-day Fordism was also plagued by employee relations problems, absenteeism and alienated workforces stemming from the mass production labour process, the highly bureaucratised method of control and centralised monitoring systems.

Allied to these domestic factors were the instability of world markets, the increase in global competition, the breakdown of international price-fixing and the emergence of globalised free markets for products, raw materials and finance. Political instability in the Middle East, which led to the oil crisis in 1974, is seen as a turning point in the fortunes of classical Fordism. There are those who argue that the response has been pragmatic and reformist and old Fordism has been 'modernised' and transformed into 'neo-Fordism'. Others argue there has been a fundamental break with Fordism and Britain has entered a post-Fordist period.

Neo-Fordism

Neo-Fordists focus on the introduction of new technologies, increased automation and new modes of employment and working practices that have transformed the labour process. Technological innovations, such as computer-integrated manufacturing systems and electronic offices, have led to reductions in the labour force, employment of more multiskilled technicians, greater flexibility in production methods and diversification in types of product. At the same time, new working practices and introduction of participative working groups, such as quality circles, have introduced flexibility into socio-technical systems in the workplace. These new technologies and working practices have not only increased flexibility in production, but have also led to both domestic and international geographical decentralisation. As Allen *et al* (1992) have pointed out, the neo-Fordist scenario is one in which traditional Fordism is being exported to third-world countries with cheap labour supplies and new potential markets. At home, use of new technologies and increased automation have led to a new, highly skilled technical elite and a de-skilled, peripheral workforce. But mass production is still widespread, employee relations are still rooted in the capitalist dynamics of conflicts of interest and scientific management has revived.

Post-Fordists

In contrast, post-Fordists argue that there is a qualitative shift taking place in the economic system, which is transforming a mass production, mass consumption system into one of flexible specialisation and fragmented consumption. Across sectors of the economy, there have been changes in product life and product innovation (with shorter, flexible runs and a wider range of products on offer), in stock control, (using 'just-in-time' management processes), and in design and marketing, in response to increasingly diverse patterns of demand (Murray 1989). While neo-Fordists stress job de-skilling and increased centralisation of management control, post-Fordists highlight re-skilling and multiskilling and less hierarchical work environments that extend employee involvement and employee control of the work process.

Both neo- and post-Fordists share a common emphasis on the role of flexible manufacturing systems to provide for speedy responses to market demand and to ensure high-quality products. They also emphasise the demise of Keynesianism and the emergence of neo-liberal economic strategies designed to deregulate markets, encourage free enterprise and free trade (Jessop 1989b; Sabel 1982). Further, they both emphasise the globalisation of markets. The differences between them lie mainly in how they perceive technology. Neo-Fordists see technology as being used primarily to save labour and improve productivity and argue that although task structures and modes of management may deviate from conventional Taylorism, they are not significantly different. Neo-Fordism is capitalism's response to the effects of overproduction and saturated domestic markets and the falling rate of profit. It is exploiting new product and labour markets and reconstructing itself, but the classic characteristics of Fordism are still in evidence.

Post-Fordists, in contrast, perceive technology as the trigger not only for the production of new products but also the basis for the transformation of the production process itself (Coombes and Jones 1988). At the heart of post-Fordism is the concept of flexible specialisation, which focuses on the movement away from mass production to batch production and the manufacture of a wide and changing array of customised products, using flexible, general-purpose machinery and skilled, adaptable workers (Hirst and Zeitlin 1991). Changes in taste (which break up mass-market demand) and competition from third-world producers force manufacturers to look for new and diverse products and new technology facilitates a reactive response to complex and niche markets in organising production. The advent of flexible specialisation sees not only the re-emergence of the small firm and craft production but also greater involvement and enhanced work satisfaction of the workers, as it depends on the collaboration between all grades of workers (Piore and Sable 1984).

Hirst and Zeitlin (1991) draw attention to two other features of flexible specialisation. First, it is a system of network production in which firms are aware that they do not know precisely what they have to produce and must count on collaboration of workers and subcontractors in meeting the market's eventual demand. Second, and linked to this, it creates a complex set of practices at company level, involving relationships with subcontractors, other firms and the sectoral and district institutions supporting and sustaining the system of production. Networking becomes essential to successful businesses. Flexible specialisation can also take a number of forms, including numerical flexibility, functional or internal flexibility and pay flexibility (Atkinson 1985, Wood 1989, Thompson 1989). This tends to result in dual labour markets in which a core group of workers benefits from flexible specialisation, with its multiskilling and employee involvement practices, whilst a peripheral group of part-time, subcontracted labour is de-skilled and without secure employment.

Another theory, which is encompassed within the neo-Fordist camp, is regulation theory. Regulation theorists (Aglietta 1979, Boyer 1990, Liepitz 1985, 1988, 1992) are mainly European sociologists who adopt a very broad concept of Fordism and offer a more radical analysis of contemporary economic change than other Fordist writers. For them, Fordism is more than a production system and a particular labour process; it is a specific regime of capital accumulation, or a paradigm of production and consumption, in which the economy is regulated in a particular way. It is the *form* of regulation that is the key to understanding economic activity, stability and change. The mode of regulation acts as a support system for the economy and pulls together and directs the wide variety of actions taken by firms, banks, retailers, workers and state employees. It takes place at two levels – the national and international. The mechanisms within each national economy regulate labour and capital, on the one hand, and different types of capital on the other. These controls include the system of management, the labour process, the system of wage payments, the role of market forces in determining prices and wages and the policies of the state towards incomes control and welfare provision (Harris 1988). At international level, it is the international monetary system that is the key regulator.

Regulationists see the breakdown of both internal and international regulators in the 1970s as the turning point for the economies of the West generally and for Britain in particular. Keynesianism, the mode of regulation compatible with Fordism, failed to cope with the crisis of capitalism in the 1970s. Regulationists trace the structural crisis of Fordism, first, to the Fordist labour process and the inability of mass production methods, for both technical and social reasons, to realise further productivity gains. In addition, insufficient demand for everything that was or could be produced resulted in a fall in profits. The second cause was a change in the global level of demand and an increase in world competition. Capital had to search for new sources of profit and so structural reorganisation became necessary. For regulationists, explanation for changes in the economy lie in the inherent contradictions of capitalism and its tendency towards a falling rate of profit. At the present time, capitalism is in the process of being reconstructed and there are elements of the old and the new coexisting together. For this reason, they argue, both neo- and post-Fordist theories have explanatory power and plausibility. Capitalism's response to the current crisis is to establish a global system on the one hand – which bears the hallmark of classic Fordism with its mass production and mass consumption patterns – along with flexible forms of small batch production in flexible smaller units of production responding to changing tastes and markets in mainly the first post-industrial societies (Kumar 1995). Regulation at international level is also being reconstructed, although an appropriate regulatory system has not yet been formalised.

Post-industrialism and the information society

It was Daniel Bell (1973) who first identified what he thought were the characteristics of a new emergent economic system, which he called the 'post-industrial society'. These were:

- the change from a goods-producing to a service economy
- the emergence of a new professional and technical class
- the central role of theoretical knowledge as the source of innovation
- the creation of new information-based technologies.

Bell described post-industrial society as one in which most people would be employed in service industries and white-collar and professional workers would become a new occupational elite. It would be dominated by information and information technologies, which would transform organisational structures and processes as well as the location and content of work. Information would become the key commodity and it would be an 'information society'. The generation of knowledge and information and new information technologies would be the motors of economic growth rather than profit and production which had been the motivating force – the 'axial principle' – underlying the dynamics of change for the industrial society. Bell was optimistic about the liberating effects of information technologies

137

that would lead to the increasing automation of work processes and to high productivity. He predicted that people would work less and enjoy more leisure time and that the information society would guarantee sufficient wealth to raise standards of living for all and reduce the class conflicts endemic in the industrial era. There would be an 'end of ideology' as all societies moved to the post-industrial stage of development, although he did not envisage the end of ideology as coinciding with the end of the Cold War.

Alvin Toffler's (1980) analysis is more wide-ranging than Bell's. He describes the post-industrial society as a 'third wave' after the 'first wave' agricultural and 'second wave' industrial societies. New sciences, knowledge and technologies would transform the economy structurally, geographically and socially. The new 'information society' is characterised by desynchronisation, decentralisation, matrix structures, multiple command structures, networking, new lifestyles and 'prosumers' (producers and consumers). While second-wave industrial societies sought out predictability and principles compatible with mechanical causality, third-wave societies would be governed by a perception of things as inherently and unavoidably unpredictable. In this type of society, order emerges out of chaos and chance dominates change. Toffler, like Bell, was optimistic about post-industrial society and predicted that information and communication would be the means of integrating society and societies and empowering the individual. He also saw the information society as one in which knowledge would replace labour as the main source of value. However, he went further than Bell in predicting changes not only in the 'techno-sphere' and the 'info-sphere' but also in the 'socio-sphere', the 'bio-sphere' and the 'psycho-sphere'.

A less optimistic view of post-industrial, information society is presented by the French theorist Alain Touraine (1974), who described the emerging society as a programmed society in which knowledge and information and 'technocracy' dominate. Unlike Bell, Touraine did not envisage an end of ideology and social conflict but a new class conflict between those who control information, and its uses, and those who do not. The root of conflict between social classes would no longer be ownership and control of property, but access to information and its uses.

Two further writers, Castells (1989) and Gorz (1982), both in the Marxist tradition, are often grouped together with Bell and Toffler, although they distance themselves from the post-industrial emphasis. Castells argues that the new information-based society is no more post-industrial than the industrial society was post-agrarian. It represents a further stage in the evolution of capitalism, in which new technologies have enabled companies to operate in new ways. In particular, new information technologies now traverse continents, space and time, shrinking the world and markets and enabling flexible and fragmented multinational corporations to emerge. Similarly, within organisations, core 'information workers' now function alongside a peripheral workforce of low-skilled workers, thus segmenting the organisation and polarising the 'knowledge elite' and the supportive mass. Gorz, like Castells, sees new information technologies altering the structure of work and producing a core of secure, well-paid workers, on the one hand,

and a peripheral workforce, which is poorly paid and lacking any job security, on the other. In addition, increased automation creates 'jobless growth' and a rising pool of unemployed. Gorz describes the new class structure as consisting of a securely employed professional class, a 'servile' working class, increasingly alienated and totally instrumental in their attitude to work, and a swelling underclass of unemployed. For Gorz and Castells, the 'new information society' is characterised by growing inequalities.

The common theme among these post-industrial theorists is that knowledge, information and communication technologies are both enabling and driving socio-economic transformation. The result is a changing social and power elite, with old class structures giving way to new social formations. Bell and Toffler are optimistic about the outcomes of change, while Castells, Gorz and Touraine point to the differential benefits within a new class formation.

Post-modernism

'Like post-industrialism and post-Fordism, post-modernism is a "contrast-concept" . . . the initial meaning of *post modernism* is that it is not modernism' (Kumar 1995: 66). But this begs the question, 'what is modernism?' Modernism, like most sociological concepts, is a disputed one and even the point in time which divides modernism from pre-modernism is not agreed. There is some agreement, however, that modernity refers to a variety of social, political, economic and cultural transformations that separated the Middle Ages from the modern period and that modernism is rooted in several key ideas associated with the Enlightenment. The first is that history is a record of humankind's achievements as well as its failures and that it is not predetermined or predestined. Second, reason is the source of all knowledge and understanding of the world and reason, therefore, is the source of human progress and the mastering of nature. Third, social problems can be resolved through the application of reason, while science and empiricism are the means to human understanding. Laws of nature and the order of things can be exposed through scientific endeavour. Out of this paradigm emerged the dominant characteristics of modernism, namely capitalism, scientism, bureaucracy, technocracy, liberalism, democracy and socialism, along with social scientific theories of society, economy and psychology. As Kumar observes (1995: 84): 'History and progress, truth and freedom, reason and revolution, science and industrialism . . . are all the main terms of the "grand narratives" of modernity that post-modernists wish to consign to the dustbin of history.'

Post-modernism and post-modernity arouse highly charged reactions. Some writers refer to it as a period extending from the 1970s to the late 1980s when the impact of new-right ideas and neo-liberal economic policies took hold. Others see it as a contemporary phenomenon in which continuous reflection on current social conditions seeks to extend our understanding of the limitations of modernity. A third, more radical, view is that post-modernity is a form of life beyond modernity and represents a reconstruction of Utopian thought (Giddens 1996). In the latter sense, post-modernism represents a radical assault on all those traditions of modernism. It rejects the belief that reason and the scientific method can 'discover' the reality of the physical and social worlds. It rejects objectivism and claims there are no facts, only interpretations, and no objective truths, only constructs of various individuals and groups. In other words, our perception of the world is relative to time and space and experience. One person's reality is as 'real' as any other and should give way to intuition, sentiment and free play of the imagination. Post-modern culture rejects the Protestant ethic, order and discipline for nihilism, hedonism and experientialism.

Foucault (1970, 1980), a key exponent of post-modernist thought, illustrates rejection of the equation of reason, emancipation and progress, arguing that an interface between modern forms of knowledge and power have created types of domination as irrational as those of the earlier pre-modern age. Like many other post-modernists, Foucault believes that modern rationality is a coercive force rather than a liberating or emancipatory one and that modernism entails its own systems of subordination and domination. He proclaims difference, fragmentation, relativism and chaos as antidotes to the repressive features of modernism. He also insists that no single analytic framework can encompass the complexity of the modern world and advocates eclecticism. It is the irreducible plurality and diversity of contemporary society, and the impossibility of controlling and directing its shape and meaning, which is the key feature of post-modernity.

There are many schools of post-modernist writers identified by Best and Kellner (1991), Kumar (1995) and Turner (1990). There arc also many overlaps between theories of post-modernism, post-industrialism and post-Fordism, with some writers, such as Bell (1980, 1987) and Jameson (1992), featuring in more than one. Along a continuum there are those at one end who see the present period as representing a post-modern rupture in history (Baudrillard 1988, Foucault 1970) and at the other end writers who see elements of continuity between the present age and the period of modernity (Jameson 1992, Laclau 1990). Jameson, for example, adopting a Marxist perspective, links post-modernism to late capitalism. For him the cultural shifts associated with post-modernism are resulting in a cultural style congruent with the latest stage of capitalist development. Each stage of capitalism has its own cultural style and realism; modernism and post-modernism are corresponding cultures to market capitalism and monopoly and multinational capitalism. For Jameson, post-modernism is simply a stage in the development of capitalism.

Globalisation

In the mid-1980s, ideas about globalisation came to the fore and it was the dominant concept of the 1990s, having superseded post-modernism. It is a far less contested concept than Fordism or post-modernism, because most observers agree about the changes that are taking place throughout the world. Although the spread of capitalism and Western culture has been going on for hundreds of years, it is the rate of acceleration of this process and popular awareness of its happening that distinguishes this era from the past. Globalisation is described by Water (1995: 2) as 'a social process in which the constraints of geography on social and cultural arrangements recede and in which people become increasingly aware that they are receding'. Globalisation is occurring in all three spheres of social activity: the economy, the polity and culture and, together with a revolution in global communications, is creating a 'global village'.

Again, there are a number of theories attempting to explain this phenomenon. The first is modernisation theory, which asserts that as societies become industrialised they evolve very similar economic, political and social structures. A pattern of social differentiation emerges in which production and consumption are separated, specialist organisations provide for the educational, health and support needs of society, and mass media becomes the means of enculturating people into a new set of values, beliefs and symbols. Those values are ones of rationalism, individualism, universalism and secularism. This transformation amounts to modernisation. Paradoxically, processes of integration also parallel the process of differentiation, so that modernisation also leads to greater interdependence and to greater centralisation of decision-making because of the need to co-ordinate and control diversity and specialisation. Modernisation results in economic growth and brings material benefits. Therefore it is attractive to non-modernised societies, which seek to emulate wealthier, stronger ones. Societies converge through the process of modernisation because the means to modernisation is the adoption of technologies, which are universal. Thus common socio-technical systems become globalised.

A second theory that explains the phenomenon of globalisation is 'world capitalism'. Here capitalism is seen as the major globalising dynamic, because it is driven towards constantly increasing scales of production and consumption. This is resulting in the emergence of world markets and multinational and international corporations that come to control the economy and divide the world between them. This also explains the inter-societal stratification found in the global economy and the existence of first-, second- and third-world societies, which refer both to stages of development and power relationships. The economic changes identified with advanced capitalism are also the driving forces leading to the transformation of both the political and cultural spheres. The nation state, once the appropriate regulatory system within which industrial capitalism thrived, is being supplanted by regional political organisations, such as the European Union, to support developments in monopoly capitalism. And all parts of the world are being incorporated into a new global system based upon international bodies such as the United Nations (UN), the World Bank, the WTO and the International Monetary Fund (IMF). Furthermore, integration is taking place at transnational level as non-governmental relationships are cementing the global economy and as mass communication systems promote modern consumerist and materialist cultures. Popular culture, 'macdonald-isation' and the World-Wide Web are compressing time and space, as well

141

as creating similar social formations and social relationships across geo-graphical boundaries.

A third school of globalisation theorists (Giddens 1985, Robertson 1992), who challenge the capitalist view as too simplistic, place great emphasis on the importance of international relations and see globalisation as occurring independently of the internal dynamics of individual societies. Globalisation has its roots in the emergence of the culturally homogeneous nation state. Nation states, competing for resources, markets and territory, develop polit-ical, economic, military, administrative and diplomatic systems for exchanges with other states, which are both co-operative and conflictual. As nation states multiply and the nation state becomes universal, so interna-tional relations have to accommodate this. The world comes to be concep-tualised as a whole and new systems evolve to make it more unified – but this does not mean it becomes more integrated or less conflictual, only more conscious of its oneness.

Giddens (1985) explains the process as one in which the first European nation states successfully married industrial production to military action and succeeded in colonising tribal societies and dismembering earlier empires. Their rational-bureaucratic systems enabled them to harness resources to industrial development and modernisation and to manage rela-tions with other states. The destabilisation of international relations caused by the total wars of the twentieth century led to the burgeoning of interna-tional organisations that offer more security, institutionalise the sovereignty of the nation state and provide an environment within which new nation states can emerge.

Four dimensions of modernity – namely capitalism, surveillance, military order and industrialism – are driving globalisation. First, the world is emerg-ing as a universal capitalist system, with the nation state providing the institutional framework for internal surveillance and control. Second, development of international information systems and sharing of knowledge and information across national boundaries enhance this. Third, war has been globalised, and a system of alliances since the end of the Cold War, revolving around the military dominance of the USA, means that only local and peripheral conflicts occur, although that depends on the stability of international alliances. Finally, industrialisation of the world has eroded Western economic dominance but has resulted in commodification of ser-vices and information and the globalisation of culture, which Giddens (1990) describes as the 'axial' determinant of the whole process. For both Giddens and Robertson, and other writers such as Lash and Urry (1987), globalisation is multifaceted and multicausal, but all agree that whilst it appears to be inexorable it is an uneven process of development.

Taken together these theories and others, which can be found in Water (1995), assert that globalisation is a process of economic systematisation, of international relations between nation states and an emerging global culture and consciousness. Globalisation is resulting in the phenomenological elim-ination of space and generalisation of time. Global communication systems are enabling split-second contact between people, governments, firms, consumers and suppliers, creating networks that intensify worldwide social relationships. Thus the local and the international become fused, with each influenced and constrained by the other. Some see this as an inexorable process towards a global economy, a world political system and a cosmopolitan culture of great diversity. Others reject it is a linear process, but see it rather as a journey to the unknown as different countries are developing along different pathways in response to the dynamic forces that make up the global environment.

Overview

This brief summary of the main theories describing and explaining economic and industrial change over the last few decades points to important environmental factors that are influencing organisations and their production, marketing and employee relations strategies. These are:

- the changing industrial structures, modes of production and movement to flexible specialisation
- the globalisation of markets, spread of multinational corporations and geographical relocation
- the emergence of new occupations, the dual labour market and changes in the class structure
- the demise of Keynesianism and its associated patterns of internal and external regulation and the emergence of neo-liberal economic policies and state regulation
- the transition from mechanical and electronic technologies to new information technologies
- the challenge to generalised, rational, scientific-rooted world views by relativist, intuitive forms of expressionism
- the phenomenon of the global village, in which space and time are dissolved in common simultaneous experiences, common cultural symbols and common values, ideas and beliefs.

It is impossible to separate out the interacting forces and to identify a single causal factor, but the rapid changes occurring at the end of the twentieth century appear to be linked to technology.

TECHNOLOGY

Technology is the application of knowledge to aid human production. There are many types of technology and it is advances in technology that have generally accompanied major waves of economic change. Toffler (1980) points to the fact that in all societies the energy system, production system and distribution system are interrelated parts of a 'techno-sphere', which has its characteristic form at each stage of social development. Fossil fuels provided the energy for industrial societies and a new technology spawned, first, steam-driven and, later, electro-mechanically-driven machines. These were then brought together into interconnected systems to create factories, mass production and Fordist structures.

The new technologies, which are energising post-industrial societies, are rooted in 'information technology' (IT). IT in its strictest sense is the science of collecting, storing, processing and transmitting information (Forester 1985). It is itself the result of a convergence of three separate technologies – electronics, computing and communications, and the invention of the silicon chip. Discoveries of the transistor (1947), integrated circuit (1957), planar process (1959) and microprocessor (1971) converged to constitute a new scientific paradigm. In the past, technology transformed processes rather than produced goods or services. The new IT is not only transforming processes, but is also producing information as an output. It has become a commodity in itself. IT is also pervasive as it is not confined to the economic sphere of production but is fundamentally changing the social, cultural and political spheres of society at an accelerating rate, through a fundamental technological revolution.

Applications

IT and computers are now used in homes, schools, hospitals, offices, shops, factories, aircraft and trains. Microchips control domestic appliances, library catalogues, programmed learning, machinery, banking cashpoints and currency transfers, telephones, aeroplanes and satellites. No commercial, service or public organisation has been left untouched. Although the pace of change varies between sectors and organisations, the changes over the last 25 years have revolutionised every aspect of life. In particular, there has been an exponential growth in telecommunications. Microelectronics has made possible the digital network, satellite communications, cable TV, cellular radio and videotext. All of these are transforming the way people work, where they work, how they receive entertainment, how they shop, how they conduct their financial relationships, how they are educated and how they communicate with others. With increased ownership of personal computers, fixed and mobile phones, the majority of the population is now accessible and can access the new networks.

Another dimension of the IT revolution is the international consequences of communication satellites. These make possible the creation of the 'global village'. The international financial market can be accessed from any financial centre in the world. Trader dealings take place continuously and simultaneously throughout a 24-hour period and a financial movement in any one country can send shock waves around the globe, as it did on 'Black Friday' in 1987. Satellites also make possible the exporting of jobs and fragmentation of the production process. Component parts can be produced in one area of the world, where labour is cheap, and transported for assembly into a finished product nearer to the main market. Multinational corporations can have their headquarters in one country and their production units spread throughout the world and communicate on a daily basis via the Internet, e-mail and fax. Meetings are held in airport lounges, as managers fly in from all corners of the globe, or by video-conferencing. Thus modern communication systems facilitate organisational flexibility and 'virtual' organisations.

IT also facilitates development of global supply chains where orders can be input in one part of the world, based on information about production schedules, dedicated consignments, lead times on packaging and distribution in manufacturing units supplied through the communication network. These orders in turn reverberate throughout the system and automatic adjustments are made to the system memory. Instant recall means timeless communication. Most recent developments in the Internet and World-Wide Web are transforming not only methods, means and frequency of communication throughout the world, but also patterns of marketing, advertising, selling and purchasing, and types of consumer products. The Internet – described by Naughton (1999), its most recent historian, as the most revolutionary information distribution system to be developed since printing and the most remarkable thing humans have ever built – is certain to be one of the key drivers to further change. With about 150 million people currently using the Internet and a world population estimated at 6 billion in 2000, its potential is phenomenal.

Effects

Historically, new technology has always met with resistance because it threatens traditional occupations and skills. The reality is that new technology, in the past, has resulted in the creation of jobs, increased production and wealth, and higher standards of living. There is, however, always a social cost to new technology and in the short term there will be winners and losers.

What are some of the effects of the new technology on employment patterns and work processes today? The first stage of the transformation from an industrial to an information society has seen the application of new technology to existing work processes and the emergence of new industries, including a computer hardware and software industry. The latter has set the pace of the IT revolution, as it makes possible new ways of doing things and new things to do. Computers are being used to restructure organisations as 'informatisation' is developed. In particular, computers make it possible to dispense with clerical and paper systems and create electronic offices. They are replacing brainpower by storing, retrieving, sorting and transforming data into information at phenomenal speeds. In medicine and the law, 'expert systems' are replacing people in taking decisions, whilst biotechnology is extending human control over the body and making new medical interventions possible.

In education computers are supplementing teachers and in libraries they are replacing books; access to knowledge is becoming limitless. Within the public sector, during the 1980s and 1990s, IT facilitated the emergence of 'the automated state' (Snellen 1994, Margetts 1997). Part of New Labour's 'Modernising Government' (Cmn 4310 1999) programme is 'electronic government' in which all government departments and agencies will be accessible by the Internet and e-mail. 'One stop' shops will enable citizens to make one contact to obtain information on all services to which they are entitled.

Nilles (1985: 202) draws a comparison between the microcomputer and the car and the telephone line and the highway. In industrial society, cars transported workers via the highway to factories and offices. Today it is information that is transported instead of the worker. 'In principle the telecommuter has access to anyone with a computer and with near-zero transit time.' As a result, work styles are being changed significantly through telework and telecommuting, and social communication is being transformed through telephones, e-mail, video and the Internet. However, while telecommuting may facilitate geographical mobility, offer flexible patterns of work and solve the problem of urban congestion, it may erode employee loyalty, corporate identity and corporate integration and produce the sweatshops of the twenty-first century. Equally, modern social communication enables more frequent and broader contact but holds dangers of social isolation and underdevelopment of interpersonal social skills and a sense of community.

IT is clearly offering scope for:

- relieving the boredom of repetitive assembly-line work
- job enrichment and job enlargement
- new forms of work organisation with flatter hierarchies
- transforming old-style employee relations
- involving workers directly in the decision-making process
- transferring the work base from the office to the home.

These opportunities are being grasped and are resulting in major changes in organisational structures and work processes identified earlier. There is also evidence, however, of the other side of the new technology, which includes: de-skilling of white-collar and professional workers; creation of routine, repetitive jobs in call centres; flatter, lean organisational structures that are more easily controlled; new-style employee relations that are individualised and dominated by managerial prerogative; notional employee participation through tell-and-sell management reporting; and changed employment contracts with an increase in part-time, short-term and temporary employment.

Although there are some technological determinists, the dominant view is that technology is socially constructed and shaped by the economic, technical, political, gender and social circumstances in which it is designed, developed and utilised (Preece 1999: 247). It is clear that not all countries are as advanced as others in using IT, although there is an international trend. The application of IT is speeding up value change, which, in turn, is facilitating further applications of IT. Multinational corporations generally are making the most advanced use of IT and exporting it throughout the world, while multinational communications companies in particular are exporting and promoting the technology. Change in the future is likely to be gradual, disjointed, incremental, pragmatic and unpredictable but shaped by 'technology push' and 'technology pull' factors (Miles *et al* 1988). New knowledge and innovations always provide the potential for change but are not all used. There has to be an awareness of them and they have to be perceived to be relevant and appropriate. Whether they are or are not used depends on management strategies, market conditions and public policies. Equally, a demand for new technology and ways of solving social problems stimulates technological innovation, but the take-up again depends on political will and social acceptability. Technology push and technology pull are not exclusive. They feed on each other, but both depend on the structural context of organisations and markets.

It is difficult, therefore, to predict or forecast the effects of technological change on the British economy and British society. The following developments seem plausible, but IT is likely to:

- be increasingly applied to transform processes of production in all sectors of the economy
- provide growing competitive advantage for firms
- facilitate the re-engineering of organisations and the transformation of their management systems
- link operations over long distances and accelerate the transformation of world markets
- facilitate e-commerce
- be used for scenario-building and to improve decision-making
- be continually adapted to new functions, applications, commodities and services
- ensure that IT management is the key organisational function
- continue to revolutionise the leisure activities of individuals, the way they communicate and their lifestyles
- promote the self-service society
- transform education, health, legal and personal services as it enables individuals to access knowledge and information in the home, at resource centres and at terminals in public places and become their own experts
- facilitate 'e-government'
- enable the electorate and public-service users to be consulted directly and their preferences electronically recorded; direct democracy will become a practical rather than a theoretical idea.

The 'bright' scenario predicts increased freedom, choice and empowerment, more communication and better services, particularly for the sick, the elderly and the disabled. The crucial issues are whether the twenty-first century information society will lead to more integrated and socially equal communities, as predicted by Toffler and Bell, or to new forms of inequality, inequity and the domination by a knowledge elite, as predicted by Touraine.

THE SOCIAL CONTEXT

British society has changed more rapidly during the last half-century than at any time in its past. There have been significant changes in its population, social structures, the role of women, social attitudes, culture and the dominant ideas influencing its politics. These are linked to changes in the economic system and in technology, but are themselves variables in the total equation of change.

Demography

Britain's population was estimated to be 59.2 million in 1998, the eighteenth largest in the world. It grew quite quickly in the first half of the twentieth century, but more slowly after 1951 and slow growth is expected to continue until 2030 (65 million), after which it is projected to fall. There were 29.1 million males and 30.1 million females in 1998. Changes in birth and death rates are important in demographic trends. The overall fertility rate of 1.8 per woman in the childbearing age range (16 to 45) indicates that the population is not replacing itself, although there are differential birth rates amongst its ethnic groups. The highest birth rates are among the Pakistani and Bangladeshi communities, although these are falling towards the national norm. A significant recent trend has been the percentage of births outside marriage, which increased from 8 per cent in 1971 to over 35 per cent in 1999. Another trend is the change in the fertility rates among different age groups. While women between 25 and 29 are the most likely to give birth, there have been increases in the fertility rates among women in their 30s and 40s and a decrease in the 20 to 24 age group, as women are choosing to have babies later. Fluctuations in birth and death rates are reflected in the age structure of the population, as indicated in Table 3, which is also affected by migration.

The declining birth rate has resulted in a fall in the 0–16 age group from over 25 per cent of total population in 1961 to 21 per cent in 1998. At the other end of the age structure, the number of people over 65 is growing both absolutely and relatively. They accounted for one in six of the population in 1999 compared to one in 20 in 1901. This group is expected to increase to 14.5 million, 24 per cent of the population, by 2031 – a rise of nearly 40 per cent over 1990 (*Social Trends* 1993, 2000). The over-80s will grow fastest of all. Historically, the ageing of the population has been due to lower mortality rates, attributed to better nutrition and public health, and advances in medical science. Today, it is lifestyle and advances in medical science that are the major factors in increasing life expectancy, currently 76 for men and 83 for women.

The labour force is traditionally drawn from the 16–64 age group and consists of those who are economically active, ie willing and able to work. It has been rising over the last 40 years, although during periods of recession numbers tend to fall. In 1998, approximately 78 per cent of the age group 16–64 were economically active. The total available for work was 26.1 million, but 1.6 million were unemployed (Office of National Statistics 1999). These are official figures and do not include those working unofficially in the black labour market nor those who are unemployed but not registered as claimants. Both numbers employed and unemployed are likely to be considerably higher. As stated above, the size and composition of the labour force varies between men and women, but since 1971 women's participation rate has been continually rising. In 1971 women made up 38 per cent of the labour force and men 62 per cent. In 1999 the ratio was 48 per cent to 52 per cent, with 71 per cent of women of working age economically active compared to 85 per cent of men.

Because of the ageing profile of the population in general, there is a shift towards higher age groups in the workforce. By 2001 only one in six of the labour force will be under 24 and over one-third of the working population will be over 45. Another trend is an increase in the number of workers above pensionable age who are economically active. These changes in demographic structure, especially the ageing of the population, are likely to have serious consequences for public policies, such as education, health care and pensions, while they will also affect the pensions and health insurance provided by private organisations (Northcott 1999). It is likely that the retirement age will be raised in the near future.

There are officially 3.3 million members of ethnic minorities in the UK, who make up about 6 per cent of the population. An ethnic minority describes a social group sharing social characteristics, including language, religion, nationality, culture and common origin. Ethnicity is a relational concept that depends on how people see themselves, as well as how others see them (Horton 1999). In 1991, the census asked respondents to classify themselves in ethnic terms for the first time. Eight ethnic groups were identified. The largest minority groups are Indian (30 per cent), Black Caribbean (21 per cent) and Pakistani (16 per cent), with smaller communities from Bangladesh, Black Africa, Black Other, and Chinese, each constituting about 5 per cent. According to the Department for Education and

Table 3 Age structure of the UK population for selected years, 1961–2031

	Under 16	16–34	35–54	55–64	65–74	75 & over	All Ages (=100%)
	%	%	%	%	%	%	(millions)
Estimates							
1961	25	24	27	12	8	4	52.8
1971	25	26	24	12	9	5	55.9
1981	22	29	23	11	9	6	56.4
1991	20	29	25	10	9	7	57.8
1998	21.3	26.5	27.5	9.9	8.5	8.4	59.2
Projections							
2001	20	25	29	10	8	7	59.5
2011	18	24	29	12	9	7	60.1
2021	18	23	26	14	11	8	61.1
2031	17	22	25	13	13	11	60.7

Source: *Social Trends* 1997, 2000

Employment Labour Force Survey in 1996, over 50 per cent of ethnic minority members were born inside the UK. There are significant differences in the age structures of ethnic minorities, with Pakistani and Bangladeshi groups having 75 per cent under 35, and 43 per cent under 16 in 1998–99, compared with approximately 25 per cent and 20 per cent of the indigenous white population respectively. Diversity amongst ethnic groups is reflected in family size, employment patterns, health and education, and there are as many differences between ethnic groups as between them and the majority white ethnic group. Intermarriage is making the concept of ethnicity very fluid, as the UK is becoming a multiracial society. Ethnic minorities, however, are not distributed evenly throughout the country but are concentrated in large cities. They also tend to be found in the lowest-paid jobs and are more likely to be unemployed than white people (Peach 2000).

Almost 90 per cent of people in the UK live in urban areas and 84 per cent live in England. There was a slow but continual migration of population from the North to the South throughout the last century, with Scotland experiencing an absolute population decline since 1961. The overall pattern is one of net migration from Scotland, Northern Ireland, Wales and the north of England to the south-east of England. Since the late 1980s, however, the major growth areas have been East Anglia and the South-West. Other significant trends have been sub-urbanisation, with people moving out of metropolitan areas to smaller towns and with the growth of retirement centres concentrated mainly in coastal areas. Geographical mobility is also an increasing social feature of the UK, especially among the young and retired.

Social structure

The period between 1945 and the late 1970s was one of relative affluence and social progress throughout the UK. A post-war consensus among the major political parties on welfare-Keynesianism, an expanded public sector and high levels of employment and consumption led to rising standards of living for all. There was increased immigration and women entered the labour market to meet labour shortages. New occupations and new professions emerged, especially in the growing welfare state. These changes resulted in a more pluralistic society and complex social structure. Distinctions and boundaries between classes were blurred as the working class became more affluent and white-collar jobs increased. There was greater social mobility and lifestyles merged along with patterns of consumption. Finally, income and wealth became more evenly distributed.

Class and occupation

Class has traditionally been linked to occupation and income, as this is clearly important in affecting lifestyles of people and their life chances. A simple tripartite model of the class structure has focused on: working class – associated with blue-collar, manual occupations; middle class – white-collar workers, professions and the self-employed; and upper class, which

150

includes the aristocracy, wealthy industrialists, landowners and financiers, and the nouveau riche. In 1951, about two-thirds of the population and their families were in manual occupations, under one-third made up a heterogeneous middle class and about 5 per cent constituted an upper class. Between the 1971 and 1981 censuses, the proportion of employed people in manual work fell from 62 per cent to 56 per cent for men and from 43 per cent to 36 per cent for women (Halsey 1988). By 1999, less than 30 per cent of the labour force had manual jobs and an increasing proportion of those were females and members of ethnic minorities. The traditional working class is therefore smaller than it was and its composition has changed as a result of:

- a contraction of the industries in which manual workers were traditionally found, ie shipbuilding, coal, iron and steel, docks, transport and textiles
- loss of jobs due to restructuring, automation and the introduction of new technology in industries such as printing and car manufacturing
- transfer of production to countries with cheaper labour and the closure or contraction of British plants.

In contrast the middle class has grown dramatically and now constitutes the largest group. It is predicted to grow between 10 per cent and 14 per cent over the next decade (*Social Trends* 1997). The middle class is very heterogeneous and consists of three elements:

- an upper middle class, which includes the higher professions, senior civil servants, senior managers and those holding senior technical positions
- a middle middle class, which includes the lower professions, middle management and technical grades and the old middle class of small business owners and farmers
- a lower middle class of those in clerical and supervisory positions, minor professionals, para-professionals and white-collar shopworkers.

The upper class remains the smallest class, but it too has changed. It consists of a small number of interconnected families that own a disproportionate amount of wealth, control and own large parts of industry, land and commerce, and hold top positions in business, politics and other institutions, thus making up the 'Establishment'. It includes chief executives and directors of the FT100 group, large multinational corporations, finance houses and banks in the City. 'The core of the class consists of those who are actively involved in the strategic control of the major units of capital of which the modern economy is formed' (Scott 1982: 114). Dahrendorf (1987), however, distinguishes between the old and the new upper class. It is the latter that is increasing and old money that is declining.

These changes have led to claims that the old class system is coming to an end, as boundaries between the classes are increasingly open and fluid. Pop stars, inventors, successful business people who are millionaires, ministers and members of the House of Lords with working class origins, aristocrats and landowners all now constitute an increasingly heterogeneous upper class. A 'new working class', which is more skilled, educated and affluent than the 'old working class', has lifestyles and consumption patterns in common with the professional middle classes. The combination of increased social mobility and the higher status attached to new occupations, it is argued, is also levelling the distinctions and blurring the differences. Are we all middle class now?

A closer analysis, however, gives rise to an alternative perspective that views class as not only a function of an individual's market situation but also his or her work situation. The market situation consists of income, degree of job security and opportunity for upward mobility. The work situation refers to 'the set of social relationships in which the individual is involved at work by virtue of his position in the division of labour' (Lockwood 1958: 15). The latter is reflected in the degree of autonomy, independence and control that an individual has over work and the skills that the work requires. The working class is distinguishable not only by the market situation workers occupy but also by their work situation, where they have little control and no autonomy over the work process. Though there continue to be differences between the working and middle classes based upon income and types of work, status and qualifications, the changing nature of the work process in many clerical, managerial and professional occupations is leading to a loss of autonomy and job control that is blurring class distinctions. Many white-collar, para-professional and lower professionals are effectively being proletarianised and this is reflected in their more instrumental attitude towards work.

Another significant factor is that many clerical jobs have become feminised and this has led to a relative decline in the rewards and status of office work. From this perspective it appears there is a downward merging of the classes and an enlargement of the working class rather than upward mobility. Furthermore, the movement to more flexible employment patterns is removing the greater security associated with middle-class jobs and much of the autonomy.

Class, income and wealth

Class is more than a group of people with similar jobs or market position. Class is associated with common lifestyles, culture, consumption patterns and command over resources that gives power, status and freedom of choice. Thus the class structure reflects the distribution of power within society, differential access to resources and relative life chances. Mobility between the classes enables people to change their status and their life chances (Heath and Payne 2000). Between 1945 and 1975, there was some evidence of an increase in equality of personal income. The Royal Commission on the Distribution of Income and Wealth (1979) showed there had been some marginal change, with the share of the top 10 per cent falling from 29.4 per cent of total income in 1959 to 26.6 per cent in 1974–75. Over the same period, the share of the top 1 per cent had fallen from 8.4 per cent to 6.2 per cent. However, the bottom 50 per cent only increased their share from 23.1 per cent to 24.2 per cent. So although there was redistribution among the top third of income earners, income distribution in general remained relatively stable. Personal income after tax showed a small degree of equalisation, due mainly to progressive taxation and welfare-state redistributive social policies.

This trend was reversed after 1979 and the gap between the richest 10 per cent and the poorest 10 per cent more than doubled between 1979 and 1995 (Atkinson 2000). The richest tenth saw their incomes rise by 65 per cent, while the poorest tenth saw their incomes fall by 13 per cent in real terms, creating a 78 per cent gap between the richest and the poorest (Labour Research Department 1997). The United Nations Human Development Report (1996), using the ratio of the top 20 per cent to the bottom 20 per cent of income, placed Britain with the greatest increase in inequality of income of the top 13 European countries.

The most conspicuous consequence of the increase in income inequality has been growth in numbers in poverty. The poverty threshold adopted by the Government today is 60 per cent of median disposable income, but in the past it has been 50 per cent. In 1979 some 25 per cent of households were in relative poverty (Townsend 1979). By the mid-1990s, this had risen to 30 per cent, or some 14 million people, including one in four children. Using the Labour Government's new threshold, in 1998 18 per cent of the population lived in poverty (below 60 per cent of median income), including 3.2 million children. Labour claims to have removed 1.2 million children from poverty and to have got 800,000 into work. It is committed to ending child poverty over the next 20 years.

Among this stratum of poor, there is a group described as a new 'underclass' (Dahrendorf 1987). It is distinct from the traditional working class, because it is not just poor but economically and politically marginalised and socially excluded. They are not only on low incomes but also experience poverty of education, health and environment. Those in the underclass tend to be apathetic and fatalistic and include a criminal subculture, functioning outside the norms and institutions of society. The growth in the underclass is, in part, a consequence of the economic changes taking place in Britain, in particular falling demand for manual workers, creation of the dual labour market with low-paid peripheral workers and the economic decline of inner cities that are characterised by multiple deprivation. Government policies of rolling back the welfare state and reducing social benefits and welfare support have also contributed. A more controversial explanation of the underclass is found in the writings of Charles Murray (1994), who argues that the 'dependency culture' fostered by the welfare state is the major cause.

Reasons for growing inequality of income since 1979 are complex, but the main factors are changes in the structure of the economy, high levels of unemployment and in particular long-term unemployment, deregulation of the labour market and movement to more flexible modes of employment. Part-time and temporary contracts, abolition of wages councils and freedom of top executives to pay themselves what they want and to inflate their salaries explain these shifts. Another factor increasing inequality is changes in the social security system introduced by Conservative governments. Some benefits have been cut and others pegged to cost of living rather than average wage increases. With low levels of inflation, pensioners have seen their incomes fall relative to those in employment since 1983. The complicated systems for claiming means-related benefits have discouraged claimants and it is estimated that up to 32 per cent of those eligible do not apply. Finally, changes in taxation have fuelled growing inequality. Between 1979 and 1997, governments reformed the tax system and reduced its progressive effect with the result that lower income groups pay higher levels of tax and higher income groups pay less (Northcott 1999). A report of the Office of National Statistics in April 2000 stated that inequality was still increasing, especially for the lowest 10 per cent, under the Labour Government. However, the effects of its latest policies to redress inequality of income, including the minimum wage and working family tax credits, had not been taken into account.

Distribution of wealth in the UK changed quite significantly during the post-war period, but it was essentially a redistribution among the top 50 per cent of the population, who still own over 90 per cent of disposable wealth. The top 1 per cent now owns 19 per cent, the top 5 per cent owns 39 per cent, and the top 50 per cent owns 93 per cent of marketable wealth, compared with the bottom 50 per cent, who owns only 7 per cent (*Social Trends* 2000). The distribution does not change significantly when the value of dwellings is excluded, but does change marginally when occupational and state pensions are included. Then the most wealthy 1 per cent owns only 11 per cent, while the least wealthy 50 per cent owns 17 per cent. Wealth continues to be very unevenly distributed, even more so than income, with the gap continuing to widen. In a survey of household savings in 1998, 50 per cent of households had less than £1,500 savings and 30 per cent had no savings at all.

Class and consumption

Class based upon occupation, income and wealth is an objective perception, but people's own subjective perceptions and how they assign themselves is often very different. Self-assignment is more often based on patterns of consumption and lifestyle than on market or job position. It is this that has led some writers to suggest that class rooted in production relationships is no longer the most significant social division. They argue it is changing consumption patterns that explain contemporary political alignments, not economic class (Dunleavy 1980, Hamnett 1989, Saunders 1978, 1984).

Saunders distinguishes between 'collective consumption' and 'private consumption'. The former refers to those goods and services provided by the state and available to the public as a citizenship right. Private consumption refers to the purchase of goods and services, by individuals, through the market. There was a great increase in collective consumption after 1945, with the spread of the welfare state. Collective provision of health, education, housing and other community services was associated with rising standards of living for all and was an important factor in the *embourgeoisement* of the working classes. From the 1960s, greater personal affluence enabled the working class to consider home ownership and consumer durables similar to those enjoyed by the middle class and there was a convergence of material lifestyles. However, there was little private consumption of merit goods, such as health and education, except among the upper class. Both the middle and working classes received universal services from the state.

Since 1979, there has been a notable shift within both the working and middle classes towards private consumption. Conservative governments between 1979 and 1997 encouraged this, with the sale of council housing and tax incentives to take out private health insurance, educational covenants and private pensions. Changes in public expenditure and restructuring of public services also persuaded people to look more to the market and to privatised consumption. These changes had consequences, particularly for those whose market position was weak. Consumption was becoming every bit as important as occupational class in understanding patterns of power, privilege and inequality, in explaining the kaleidoscopic nature of modern social structure, and in accounting for the changing political alignments that occurred during the years of Conservative market-centred governments.

The present class structure is less clear than in the past. At every level – upper, middle and lower – it consists of heterogeneous elements. An upper class still tops the social strata, upheld by institutions like the monarchy, House of Lords, aristocracy and honours system. But it is divided between the traditional aristocracy and gentry and the nouveaux riches who have made their money in the market place and are 'entryists'. The power and functions of the upper class remain the same, since they combine ownership of property and wealth with strategic control of industry and other major institutions. They are, however, becoming increasingly invisible and globalised and part of a new transnational capitalist class.

The enlarged middle classes are the fastest-growing and most heterogeneous group. They range from the traditional higher professions and salariat of managers and administrators to the new professions and technocrats who have acquired status and strengthened their market position through exclusionary practices. At the lower level of the middle class are the paraprofessionals, shopkeepers and self-employed. The reconstituted working class consists of manual and low-level clerical and technical workers who are distinct from both the apathetic underclass and the middle class. Those in the new working class are affluent but not bourgeois, are less class-conscious and politically committed to the trade union and labour movement than the old working class, are more instrumental in their attitudes towards work, unions and politics, and are more privatised in their social lives. They prefer to amass material things, own their own homes and spend time with their families. In the work situation, however, they have little control, are the most vulnerable to economic change, are affected by de-skilling and have the weakest market position. Technological change often downgrades some of these workers and relegates them to the status of a proletarian working class, whilst upgrading others who gain access to a higher class. The new working class lacks homogeneity but is less heterogeneous than the 'new' middle class.

Gender

Class is not the only basis of inequality in Britain. Another social division cutting across class is gender. Gender differences are socially constructed and reflect different social expectations and roles, which are attached to men and women in society. Just as changes taking place within the economy are affecting the class structure, so they are affecting gender relationships, especially, but not exclusively, at work. In 1901, women accounted for only 29 per cent of the workforce and most were confined to unpaid domestic work within the home. Two world wars saw women called in as a reserve army of labour to do jobs left by the men mobilised into the armed forces. Most women returned to the home after 1918, but in 1945 the welfare state opened up many new jobs for women and, since then, they have formed an increasingly important part of the labour market. The pattern of women's employment is different from that of men in a number of ways since, first, women are concentrated in four main areas of employment. These are: clerical and administrative work; catering, cleaning and hairdressing; retailing; and the caring services, including nursing, teaching and social work.

Women's opportunities for work have depended on the growth and expansion of these sectors. After 1945, expansion of the welfare state and, in the 1970s and 1980s, growth of service industries, provided millions of jobs for women. Their employment base has been widening in the last two decades, but horizontal segregation still persists.

Second, there is also vertical segregation. Women's jobs tend to be concentrated in the lower levels of the occupational hierarchy, with fewer women than men found in managerial positions. The number of women in management is increasing, but they still only represent 33 per cent in the wider economy and this falls to 5 per cent at boardroom level. Their position has improved mostly in the public sector, where they sometimes represent half of the managerial workforce, as in local government (Local Government Management Board 1997). Black women, however, are the most underrepresented.

Third, in addition to occupational segregation, women are also found disproportionately in part-time jobs. Part-time paid work, virtually unknown before 1939, is now an increasingly important feature of the labour market. The increase of women in work over the last 25 years has been almost entirely accounted for by part-time employment. In 1971, there were 5.5 million full-time and 2.8 million part-time female workers. By 1998 the figures were 6.6 million and 5.4 million respectively. Full-time female workers are more likely to be women without children, without dependent children, or professional women. Part-time workers are more likely to be married

156

women with dependent children. 'Part-time employment is particularly appropriate for married women because it enables them to continue to shoulder their dual role – caring for their families and adding to the family income – without radically disturbing the gender divisions of labour within the home' (McDowell 1989: 165). Women also account for 40 per cent of temporary full-time work.

Women's position in the labour market is reflected in their earnings. Not only is there a difference between gross hourly earnings of around 25 per cent, but women's take-home pay is only around 70 per cent of the average male income, due to both horizontal and vertical segregation. Women are more likely to be in low-paid, low-status, part-time jobs with low levels of responsibility. This has a significant effect on women's career structures and career development.

The reason for this position of women in the labour market is partly a result of social expectations and early socialisation, but is largely a consequence of the structure of the family and structure of employment itself. Traditionally, the structure and organisation of employment have been based upon male working and career patterns, which take no account of women's role in childbearing and child rearing. A continuous working day, week, year and work life are incompatible with the dual role of women in society. Consequently, if women wish to return to work after the birth of a child, they tend to look for part-time employment. An interrupted career inevitably limits opportunities for promotion and career advancement and results in the smaller number of women in managerial levels or at the top of the professions. Operating in a patriarchy has also meant endemic discrimination against women in all spheres of social activity. Women are under-represented not only in the higher positions of employment but also in politics, the churches, the media and all other major social institutions (Randall 1987, Rees 1992, Witz 1992).

Since the 1970s, equal opportunities legislation and policies have paved the way for changes in the status of women and improved their economic, political and social conditions. There are now a growing number of women in the professions, they constitute 50 per cent of graduates and are breaking into the male bastions of the higher civil service, academia, police, media and politics. Women are returning to employment more quickly after childbirth and many more employers are providing crèches, flexitime, annual hours and termtime-only contracts to both attract and retain women. A major event was the election of 116 women MPs in the 1997 election, 101 of these MPs representing Labour. This is the largest number of women ever to enter the House of Commons and was the result of positive action by the Labour Party in selecting women candidates in their most winnable seats.

In stark contrast to these positive actions, in the dual labour market – which is emerging as a feature of economic reconstruction – women provide the majority of the peripheral workforce. They are also in those clerical occupations which Gorz (1982) and others see as being proletarianised, and constitute a reserve army of labour which enables employers to adopt numerical flexibility strategies. Contraction of the welfare state and occupations traditionally associated with the social services affect women disproportionately. When service industries shed labour during periods of recession, it is women who are most affected. Women have traditionally been reluctant to join trade unions and are therefore more receptive to calls for individualised systems of employee relations. While the changing economic situation offers women employment opportunities, it also exposes women's generally weaker market situation. In addition, women are faced with pressures resulting from changes in gender roles in the family and society generally. Recent changes in the law that confer rights to parental leave, extend maternity rights, guarantee nursery places and offer a New Deal in getting back to work have the potential to both assist and penalise women.

Culture and change

National culture consists of the ideas, values, attitudes and beliefs that influence the way that people perceive the world and themselves in it. It fashions their behaviour, how they relate to others and how they interpret and understand their experiences. Socialisation during childhood, through the primary agencies of family, kinship and school, has a major influence on the formation of perceptions, attitudes and beliefs. Halsey (1986: 97) describes the nuclear family of parents and dependent children as 'the reproductive social cell of class, status and of culture'. However, socialisation continues throughout life and secondary agencies such as workplace, trade unions, churches, the army, peer groups and the media may reinforce or challenge earlier influences. People change as a result of their own experiences and observations of their changing environment.

Social change

Society is constantly changing but there is normally a cultural lag. People are often resistant to change, because it threatens their security, understanding of the world and status within it. Change is accompanied by uncertainty and threats, although it can also offer opportunities. Older people are usually the most resistant to change, because they have invested so much in the past. Younger people find change easier to cope with, if only because they lack the reference points of older generations. Also, a rejection of traditional values is seen by the young as a necessary step in asserting their independence.

Britain has experienced rapid change over the last half-century. Halsey (1986) paints a picture of pre-1945 Britain as consisting of a classic industrial economy, a family-centred social structure and a centralised democratic polity. This was the essential triangle within the social order. Men worked and women ran the homes, the economy produced and the family reproduced, and the state protected and administered. After 1945, the social order changed as the state assumed many of the responsibilities of the family in education, health and care of the elderly, whilst it supplemented family incomes with benefits and supported the old and unemployed. The family changed as contraception enabled women to control their fertility, fewer children were born and more women, especially married ones, entered paid employment. Marriage itself became less stable, as women enjoyed greater economic independence, secular values replaced religious ones and changes in the law made divorce easier. More men became economically inactive, whether by retirement or unemployment, and began to assume domestic responsibilities. This challenged conventional gender roles. More people continued their education beyond school-leaving age and a more educated population emerged. Changes in the economy led to changes in occupations and a larger GNP led to higher personal incomes. People worked less, consumed more and had more leisure time. State expenditure on the welfare state increased, resulting in a rising social wage, more public-sector employment and a larger proportion of GNP being spent by government.

From the mid-1970s, the social order began to change again, coinciding with the economic transformation identified earlier in this chapter (Halsey and Webb 1999). The last quarter of the twentieth century was one of economic instability, political turbulence and social disruption. In particular, family relationships with the state and the economy have changed. The family today is both a production and a consumption unit. As women increasingly work, men have assumed domestic roles of parenting and home working, and work and leisure have become intertwined as people 'do-it-themselves'. Most unpaid work within the family, however, is still performed by women. Divorce rates have risen to the highest in western Europe, with one in two marriages now destined to end in divorce. Serial monogamy has increased and complex networks of unconventional extended families have emerged at the same time that conventional kinship networks are weakened by social and geographical mobility. Further changes in the family have arisen from child-centred, hedonistic approaches to child raising. Traditional authority relationships have given way as 'familial controls over upbringing were attenuated'. Halsey (1986: 113) describes a situation in which traditional culture has been weakened by these multiple forces of change and, among the younger generation, fashionability, hedonism and a desperate individualism serve as substitutes for a securely held morality. The state is withdrawing from its provider role in some areas and families are having to resume responsibility, either voluntarily or compulsorily.

Education has come to the fore both as the vehicle for social mobility and changing the nature of the workforce by training people in new skills. Education is no longer restricted to the young, although the participation rate of the 18–21 cohort in further and higher education has risen dramatically (*Social Trends* 2000). Adult education and training are being used increasingly as means of changing attitudes towards an enterprise culture. Education has been at the forefront of government policy throughout the 1980s and 1990s and was given top priority in New Labour's election manifesto in 1997.

Social attitudes

Britain's immediate history, like its past, is characterised by both continuity and change. Continuity is usually associated with stability, tradition and consensus, while change is associated with instability, conflict and dissent. How far changes in the last quarter of the twentieth century have affected social beliefs, values and culture is difficult to assess. One way to monitor people's attitudes is through regular surveys over time. This has been done since 1983 by Social and Community Planning Research (SCPR), which carries out an annual British Social Attitudes Survey (BSAS). This provides a moving picture, portraying how British people see their world and themselves, and through their eyes how society itself is changing. During the 1990s, these surveys have focused on people's attitudes towards: the economy; public spending and the role of government; changes in the family; and moral climate. The evidence is that public attitudes have changed and, when plotted against class, gender and age, the results provide a picture of where cultural transformation is accompanying economic change and where traditional attitudes are persisting.

The eighth BSAS (Jowell et al 1991) revealed that Britain was divided, although on most issues attitudes were not polarised. Class provided the social roots of economic convictions, although disagreements within each class were as common as between the classes. Polarisation, where it existed, tended to occur on moral issues, such as gender roles and homosexuality, but these posed no threat to social stability. The most recent surveys (Jowell et al 1996, 1998) indicate some narrowing of the divide found in earlier surveys. This largely reflects the changing economic geography of the country and narrowing of the gap between north and south. Although unemployment is still higher in the North than in the South, people's perceptions of the differences between the regions have changed. A significant difference in attitudes is evident in people's economic ideology. Although, in general, those living in the south of England are most likely to adopt a pro-free-market/right-wing stance and those living in Scotland are more likely to take a more anti-free-market/left-wing position, differences in the rest of the country are quite small. These converging attitudes were reflected in voting behaviour in the 1997 general election.

In spite of attacks on the welfare state throughout the period since 1979, there is still a widespread public attachment to it. Throughout the 1980s, 98 per cent of BSAS respondents supported government provision of health care and 97 per cent supported a decent standard of living for the elderly. Although attitudes towards the unemployed were more divided, two-thirds thought the government should provide jobs for those wanting them (Jowell et al 1991). Support for public provision has not abated during the 1990s and there is still near-universal agreement that health, education and basic old-age pensions should be the responsibility of the state and that government should create jobs and ensure job protection. In the 1997 election campaign, voters and parties rated unemployment as the most important issue, followed by health and education. Although there is often an inconsistency in people's attitudes towards social policy and taxation, the vast majority appears willing to pay more tax for health, education and social benefits, whilst a declining number wish to keep taxes the same or to reduce them. In 1983, 63 per cent favoured stable or reduced taxes compared with

36 per cent in 1995. Notably, almost 75 per cent opted for more spending on pensions. There is clearly still a widespread consensus on the welfare state and on a positive role for government in dealing with unemployment.

There are different interests among the classes reflected in the survey. Working-class people are especially likely to regard the provision of jobs, unemployment benefits and housing for poorer groups as essential government responsibilities, to name social security as a priority for extra spending, and to criticise unemployment benefit as being too low. The middle classes, in contrast, favour expenditure on universal services. They are fortunate in having all-class support for those services, such as health, education and pensions, of which they make the most use. There is no evidence, however, that rich people are less in sympathy than poorer ones with increases in public spending, even if they are asked to pay a higher share of the tax burden to finance them (Brook et al 1996).

Strong support for the welfare state is also matched by positive support for a narrowing of income and wealth inequality. In 1983, 72 per cent thought that the gap between high and low incomes was too large. This has risen consistently throughout the period and stood at 87 per cent in 1995. An analysis of responses by social group and income reveals that concern about inequality has increased the most among social groups 1 and 2, who are now in line with the general consensus. The only areas that remain outside the national consensus are benefits for single parents and unemployment benefits, which are still not widely supported.

There is evidence of acceptance and agreement across the sexes, generations and classes on changed family and gender roles (Scott 1998). Cohabitation is endorsed by 64 per cent of the respondents and 85 per cent of under-25s, while only 57 per cent think people who want children should get married (a drop of 13 per cent since 1988). Attitudes have become less pro-child and divorce is widely supported (85 per cent) when relationships break down. Attitudes have also changed on working mothers and gender roles. The majority (63 per cent) thinks working mothers can have good relationships with their children and 60 per cent agree men and women should share household chores, even though traditional gender roles persist. There are systematic attitudinal differences linked to age, which gives rise to a generational effect. Men differ far less in their attitudes to gender roles than women, but there is a class difference – graduates and middle-class men tend to adopt more liberal views.

The one area where there has been a significant change in attitudes during the 1990s has been on the European Union. There were steady increases in British public acceptance of EU membership from the early 1980s until 1991, when 77 per cent of those surveyed supported membership of the EU, but this had fallen to 55 per cent by 1997. This decline has been linked to withdrawal from the ERM, the BSE crisis and most recently the euro. All of these have been projected very negatively in the media and the high levels of public ignorance about the EU makes it 'susceptible to the more hostile of the anti-European campaigning that has emerged in recent years' (Evans 1998: 179). Euro-scepticism is now widespread and a growing minority is supporting exit from the EU. Opinions, however, cut across class and gender and are equally divided between those who want Europe to be only a trading bloc and those who want closer political and economic union.

THE POLITICAL CONTEXT

Changes within society stemming from economic, technological and social forces give rise to conflicts. It is these conflicts that are at the root of politics. Politics is the process by which societies resolve and manage conflicts and disagreements about the allocation of resources, distribution of power and the making of the rules, which regulate social behaviour. It is about who decides the rules, how the rules are made, and what the rules will be. Not all social behaviour comes within the ambit of politics and there is both a private and public domain. That divide, however, is not fixed but is itself politically determined. The boundary between the public and the private domain became a major political issue in the 1980s and significant changes took place in the last two decades of the century.

The British political system is primarily concerned with making and implementing public policies and rules that govern society. In contrast to the market, where individuals themselves take decisions about what to produce and consume, politics is about the collective, authoritative allocation of resources whereby representatives of the people take decisions on their behalf. These decisions are binding and can be enforced by the legitimate exercise of power by state agencies, the police and courts. The power to take authoritative decisions is distributed between levels of government, although ultimately power rests with the central government at Westminster. Power was devolved to a new Scottish Parliament and Welsh Assembly in 1999. The Scottish Parliament has more powers than the Welsh Assembly, but both bodies can determine policy in the areas prescribed and have control over their own expenditure (Scotland Act 1998, Government of Wales Act 1998). They both choose an executive which is accountable to their elected 'assemblies' between elections. A Northern Ireland Assembly and Executive were also created in 1999. After a short-lived start, they were suspended for three months owing to the failure to implement the Good Friday Agreement. They resumed operation again in June 2000, but their future looked uncertain because of an absence of consensus amongst the political parties in the coalition government.

In May 2000 a new Regional London Council and Mayor were elected but with a limited range of powers relating mainly to transport and economic planning and development. Finally, throughout the whole of the UK, there are elected local authorities that have both mandatory and permissive powers to provide important public services, such as education, social services, roads, planning, economic development and leisure within their areas. These are essentially administrative bodies, with limited tax-raising powers.

All these governing bodies are directly elected every four or five years when political parties compete for power offering the electorate manifestos and policies from which they can choose. The constitution and the law as to what they can and cannot do and the ways in which they can exercise their authority circumscribe all governments. They are also constrained by the need to maintain support within the elected body, to whom they are accountable, between elections. They need to ensure acceptance of their policies by those who have to implement them and their freedom of choice will always be constrained by the availability of resources. All levels of government are increasingly constrained by international organisations, such as the EU, the UN and the WTO, and by transnational and multinational corporations over which they have no control. And they must retain the support of the electorate if they are to be returned to office.

Political change

One of the main characteristics of the British political system throughout the twentieth century was its dominance by two main political parties. In the first part of the century, the dominant parties were the Liberal and Conservative Parties, and in the second half the Conservative and Labour Parties. In all general elections between 1945 and 1974, it was the Conservative and Labour Parties who between them never won less than 87 per cent of the vote and since 1945 one or other of the parties has been in government. However, as Table 4 shows, there have been significant changes in support for the two main parties and a realignment of the electorate since 1974. At national level, third parties have taken approximately 25 per cent of the vote and in the 1999 Scottish and Welsh elections, this was more pronounced. In both cases national parties came second to Labour and joined with Labour to form coalition governments (see Table 5). One explanation for these results was that the assemblies were elected under a new system of proportional representation. Each elector had two votes, one to cast in the first-past-the-post constituency contests and the second for regional party lists from which top-up seats were allocated according to percentage share of the votes. The new Scottish Parliament has 129 members, 73 elected directly for the Westminster constituencies in Scotland and 56 from party lists. The new Welsh Assembly has 60 members, 40 elected by constituency votes and 20 from party-list votes. In contrast, the Westminster Parliament has 651 seats, all elected on a constituency basis by simple plurality. It is clear that proportional representation influences the results of elections and the way that people vote. Proportional representation is now used for all but local elections in England, Wales and Scotland and the national Parliament. It is likely to be extended to those arenas in the future.

Along with some party de-alignment, another significant trend in the last quarter of the century has been a fall in the electoral turnout at all elections. The lowest turnouts are recorded at the local government and European elections, which rarely exceed 40 per cent, but only 46 per cent and 59 per cent turned out in the Welsh Assembly and Scottish Parliament elections respectively in 1999. These changes in the political system have coincided with changes in the economic and social structures identified above.

Table 4 UK electoral statistics, 1945–97

	Electoral Turnout %	Conservatives % votes	seats	Labour % votes	seats	Liberals[1] % votes	seats	Welsh & Scottish Nat. % votes	seats	Other % votes	seats
1945	73.3	39.8	– 213	48.3	– 393	9.1	– 12	0.2	–	2.5	– 22
1950	84.0	43.5	– 299	46.1	– 315	9.1	– 9	0.1		1.2	– 2
1951	82.5	48.0	– 321	48.8	– 295	2.5	– 6	0.1	–	0.6	– 3
1955	76.8	49.7	– 345	46.4	– 277	2.7	– 6	0.2	–	0.9	– 2
1959	78.7	49.4	– 365	43.8	– 258	5.9	– 6	0.4	–	0.6	– 1
1964	77.1	43.4	– 304	44.1	– 317	11.2	– 9	0.5	–	0.8	– 0
1966	75.8	41.9	– 253	47.9	– 363	8.5	– 12	0.7	–	0.9	– 2
1970	72.0	46.4	– 330	43.0	– 288	7.5	– 6	1.3	– 1	1.8	– 5
1974 Feb	78.1	37.8	– 297	37.1	– 301	19.3	– 14	2.6	– 9	3.2	– 14
1974 Oct	72.8	35.8	– 277	39.2	– 319	18.3	– 13	3.5	– 14	3.2	– 12
1979	76.0	43.9	– 339	37.0	– 269	13.8	– 11	2.0	– 4	3.3	– 12
1983	72.7	42.4	– 397	27.6	– 209	58.4	– 23	1.5	– 4	3.5	– 17
1987	75.3	42.3	– 376	30.8	– 229	22.6	– 22	1.7	– 6	2.8	– 17
1992	77.7	41.9	– 336	34.4	– 271	17.8	– 20	2.3	– 7	3.5	– 17
1997	71.4	31.5	– 165	44.4	– 419	17.2	– 46	2.5	– 10	4.4	– 19

[1] 1945–1979 Liberals; 1983–7 Lib-SDP Alliance; 1992 Liberal Democrats
Source: Butler, D. and Kavanagh, D. *The British General Election of 1992, Labour Research 1997 June*

Historically, class appeared to be the dominant factor in the way people voted throughout the twentieth century. The Labour Party, created by the trade unions in 1900 to represent working-class interests in Parliament, attracted the majority of the enfranchised working-class votes, although never all of them. The Conservative Party, seen as the party of the privileged, propertied and business classes, attracted the votes of the upper and middle classes and some working class 'deferential' voters. The two main parties tended to present issues in class terms, although they also claimed to be acting in the national interest. Although class voting was the norm, throughout most of the century substantial minorities – both of the middle and working classes – have voted against their supposedly natural class interests. Indeed, about one-third of the working class regularly voted Conservative and about 20 per cent of the middle class voted Labour in the post-1945 period (Nordlinger 1967, McKenzie and Silver 1968). The Liberal Party and nationalist parties have always attracted voters from all classes.

In the last 25 years, the electorate appears to have fragmented politically along unfamiliar lines and political scientists have sought to explain this partisan de-alignment. One view, before the 1997 election, was that there was a shrinking working class and this explained the decline in Labour voting (Heath *et al* 1985). Another view was that voters are more discriminating now and vote for the party they think will run the economy most efficiently (Crewe 1984). A third view was that party ideologies were changing and media projections of those ideologies were attracting or repelling secular voters (Dunleavy and Husbands 1985). The main beneficiaries of the changes in voting patterns since 1974 have been centrist and nationalist parties whose images and ideologies are not class-based. Their electoral support has not been able to break the mould of British politics at the

Table 5 Elections in Scotland and Wales, 1999

Scotland

Party	First % vote	Second % vote	Seats contested	Top-up	Total
Labour	38.8	33.8	53	3	56
Scottish Nationalist	28.7	27.0	7	28	35
Conservative	15.6	15.4	0	18	18
Liberal Democrat	14.2	12.5	12	5	17
Others	2.7	11.4	1	2	3

Turnout = 59 per cent

Wales

	First % vote	Second % vote	Seats contested	Top-up	Total
Labour	37.6	35.4	27	1	28
Plaid Cymru	28.4	30.5	9	8	17
Conservative	15.9	16.5	1	8	9
Liberal Democrat	13.4	12.6	3	3	6
Others	4.7	5.1	0	0	0

Turnout = 46 per cent

Source: *Keesings Archives* 1999

national level because of the non-proportional electoral system. However, the mould does appear to be breaking at regional level, with the aid of proportional representation. In retrospect, devolution may well prove to be the most significant change in British politics in the last 50 years. It may herald not only the break-up of the unitary state but also the end of the two-party system, which still seemed strong in 1997 when, after 18 years of Conservative governments, a Labour government was returned with a massive, landslide majority.

The post-war settlement

Evidence from the BSA Surveys since 1983 suggest that major changes in the ideologies and policies of the main political parties have been responses to the economic and social changes occurring within society itself. Although there were ideological differences between the major parties after World War II, there was also a broad political consensus on the role of government. All governments elected between 1945 and 1979 were broadly agreed on policy objectives, although there were differences of emphasis on means and priorities. They all supported:

- a mixed economy, incorporating Keynesian demand management
- a welfare state with universal services, including health, education, housing, social insurance and old-age pensions
- a social democratic state within which people had both civil and social entitlements and rights
- corporatism, whereby major interests were incorporated into the policy-making process and industry and labour, represented by the Confederation

of British Industry (CBI) and the Trades Union Congress (TUC), joined with government to form a tripartite structure for discussing economic policy.

This post-war consensus provided a political context compatible with the economic and social systems based on Fordist principles of mass production and mass consumption. All governments were committed to the four economic goals of full employment, economic growth, low inflation and a stable currency. Use of Keynesian economic techniques and state welfarism ensured a high and constant level of aggregate demand and the transfer of many of the social costs of capital accumulation to public agencies (see Chapter 9). As a result, public expenditure increased, the public sector expanded and large public bureaucracies became the monopoly suppliers of social services and public utilities. Initially this was funded by the constantly rising GNP, but by the 1970s the state was consuming almost 50 per cent of GNP and accounted for almost 30 per cent of the labour force.

In the 1970s, cracks began appearing in the political consensus, largely because Keynesian demand management of the economy, which had worked in the 1950s and 1960s, was no longer working. Growth was slowing down, unemployment was rising, inflation was proving difficult to control and there were recurrent balance-of-payments crises. Britain was rapidly losing its share of world markets, while import penetration by its main competitors was encroaching on domestic markets. Keynesianism, as an economic strategy, came under attack, as did the welfare state. High public expenditure on the welfare state was seen as a root cause of Britain's economic problems, because high taxation, high borrowing and high interest rates sustained it. All of these, it was claimed, discouraged investment, choked off consumption, reduced Britain's competitiveness and led to economic stagnation.

The new right

Critics and critiques of the post-war settlement came from both the left and the right of the political spectrum but it was the 'new right' that came to the fore advocating the primacy of the market over politics. This was both as a means of producing and distributing goods and services in society and as an institutional arrangement for providing social organisation and social control. They argued that markets offer freedom of choice, result in the most efficient use of resources and give opportunities for inventiveness, creativity and enterprise. Politics, or state control, in contrast, restricts, constrains, denies choice and results in inefficiency and a misallocation of resources. The new right also argued that the welfare state had created dependency, weakened individual responsibility, denied people freedom of choice and empowered professional interests. These ideas and this ideology came to dominate the Conservative Party, especially under the leadership of Margaret Thatcher, and they were evident in the policies pursued by consecutive Conservative governments following the elections of 1979, 1983, 1987 and 1992. They found a receptive audience among those who had lost confidence in the ability of governments to manage the changing economy. Conservative governments claimed they would reverse Britain's relative economic decline, improve the efficiency of the economy, create new conditions for continual economic prosperity, re-assert Britain's role in the world and 'destroy socialism', which they saw as the root cause of Britain's decline. The strategies they adopted were to 'roll back the state', reduce public expenditure, cut taxation and state borrowing, privatise the nationalised industries and other parts of the public sector and deregulate the economy, including the labour market.

Quasi-markets and new management systems were introduced into the public sector aimed at increasing economy, efficiency, effectiveness and value for money of public organisations. Monetarism and supply-side economics replaced Keynesianism and the major economic priority of government became controlling inflation. There were concerted efforts to change public expectations and wean people from supporting the welfare state to supporting 'popular capitalism' and an 'enterprise culture'. A property-owning democracy was engineered by the forced sale of council houses, privatisation of public industries and encouraging share-ownership schemes and profit-sharing in the private sector. Compulsory competitive tendering (CCT) in local government, the NHS and civil service broke down the barriers between the public and private sectors and deregulation afforded opportunities for businesses, old and new, to compete in public transport, telecommunications, hospitals, residential nursing homes and ophthalmic services. Gradually CCT, or market testing, was extended throughout the whole of the public sector. Labour market deregulation was accompanied by attacks on the trade unions. A programme of legislation curbing the powers of trade unions sought not only to free up the labour market but also to undermine collectivism in favour of individualism at work (see Chapter 9).

For 18 years successive Conservative governments pursued their objectives, taking it as axiomatic that market decision-making was inherently superior to political decision-making, and that free markets, free enterprise and free trade were the panaceas for Britain's economic problems. They consistently sought to bring inflation down in the belief that a stable medium of exchange and store of value is essential for the market to function efficiently. They achieved low inflation and Britain's competitive position in international trade improved but at the cost of high unemployment rates and growing inequality. Income tax fell, although overall taxes increased. Financial, product and labour markets were deregulated, which resulted in increased competition and economic activity but the success rate of new businesses was low, less than 60 per cent surviving more than one year. Governments failed to reduce public expenditure, which was the same proportion of GNP in 1997 as it had been in 1979, and neither did they consistently reduce the public-sector borrowing requirement, which in 1997 was higher than at any time since 1945. Failure to meet people's expectations about key welfare services undoubtedly contributed to their eventual defeat in the 1997 election.

New Labour

During this long period of Conservative domination of British politics, the Labour Party undertook a major review of its own ideology. After its fourth electoral defeat in 1992, 'New' Labour emerged under a new leadership, with a new set of ideas aimed at getting the party into power at the next general election. The reforms had started back in the late 1980s under the leadership of Neil Kinnock, but gained momentum in the 1990s. Between 1987 and 1997, the party moved incrementally to the centre of British politics and it effectively ceased to be a democratic socialist party. First, it reformed its internal structures and procedures, weakening its close links with the trade unions and expelling the more extreme socialist elements within it. Second, it abandoned its Clause IV commitment to the 'common ownership' of the means of production, distribution and exchange. Third, it elected a new leader, Tony Blair, who was committed to creating a 'New', modernised Labour Party capable of winning the next election. He adopted a strategy of embracing many of the changes introduced by successive Conservative governments since 1979 but offering a fairer and more just distribution of resources. Focusing on people's concerns about unemployment, education and health services, New Labour made an appeal to voters from all sections of society and all classes. In doing this, it moved to the centre of the political spectrum offering a 'Third Way' between traditional Labour statism and new right neo-liberalism (Mandelson and Liddle 1996; Horton and Farnham 1999).

Differences between Old and New Labour were spelt out in the Labour Party's election manifesto (1997: *passim*):

> The old left would have sought state control of industry. The Conservative right is content to leave all to the market. Government and industry must work together to achieve key objectives aimed at enhancing the dynamism of the market not undermining it.
>
> We have rewritten our constitution, the new Clause IV, to put a commitment to enterprise alongside the commitment to justice . . . in the utility industries we will promote competition [and] . . . pursue tough, efficient regulation...which is fair both to consumers and shareholders and at the same time provides incentives to managers to innovate and improve efficiency.
>
> We have put our relations with the trade unions on a modern footing where they accept they can get fairness but no favours from a Labour government . . . In industrial relations there will be no return to flying pickets, secondary action, strikes without ballots or trade union law of the 1970s. There will instead be basic minimum rights for the individual at the workplace, where our aim is partnership not conflict between employers and employees.
>
> We will give Britain the leadership in Europe which Britain and Europe need . . . [but on the single currency] there are three conditions that would have to be satisfied before Britain could join during the next Parliament: first the Cabinet would have to agree; then Parliament; and finally the people would have to say 'Yes' in a referendum.
>
> We will be the party of welfare reform . . . we will design a modern welfare state based on rights and duties going together . . . get the unemployed from

welfare to work . . . save the NHS . . . be tough on crime and causes of crime
. . . strengthen family life . . . help get more out of life . . . the best way to
tackle poverty is to get people into jobs – real jobs . . . we will stop the growth
of an 'underclass'.

It was on the basis of this new ideology and 10 commitments covering a
range of policy pledges that New Labour was elected with a landslide majority of 146 seats over all other parties on 1 May 1997.

New Labour has followed through most of its manifesto commitments
and claims after three years in office to show that the 'third way' works. It
has placed far more emphasis on political reforms than market reforms and
sought to bring about greater democracy and citizen participation. The new
Scottish and Welsh assemblies, London Government and reforms of local
government are designed to bring government closer to the people and
encourage more participation in the managing of their own affairs.
Participation is also being encouraged through the use of people forums in
all major government organisations and in the 'Service First' strategy to
encourage the production of charters setting down customer and user rights
and requiring satisfaction surveys and appeals mechanisms to be put in
place. Combined with a new Freedom of Information Act (1999) and
Human Rights Act (2000), government is to become more open and accessible. The third way is also based on ideas of partnership and stakeholder
democracy. Partnership between the public and private sector is being pursued through Private Partnership Schemes, Private Financial Initiative and
Community Development Programmes funded by Regeneration Funds
from central government and the EU.

To overcome the fragmented organisational and administrative structures
created by the Conservative governments in their pursuit of competition,
New Labour has promoted both vertical and horizontal co-operation
between government bodies, the voluntary sector and private businesses.
Examples of this strategy are the Employment, Education and Health
Action Zones, which bring together public and private organisations in tackling local problems. This emphasis on co-ordination, integration and bringing together is best illustrated by the Government's 'joined-up government'
policy. By 2002, 25 per cent of all government transactions will be dealt with
electronically and members of the public will be able to use 'one-stop' centres to deal with all government services. E-government will be paralleling
the developments in e-commerce as the government invests heavily in information and communication technology. Government on the Internet is the
future.

It appears that political parties do make a difference to how a country is
governed, although the external constraints within which they operate limit
the choices they can make. The new right Conservative Party under Margaret
Thatcher and John Major and New Labour under Tony Blair have both
responded to changes in the economic and social structures of the UK by
rethinking their ideological frameworks and developing policies that reflect
those values and beliefs. There clearly are differences between the two parties,

but there are also similarities that point to the constraining forces of the external context of globalisation, increased international interdependence, transnational and multinational capitalism and the power of the media in creating and transmitting images that are the basis of popular culture. A new consensus appears to have emerged based upon commitment to:

- a predominantly market economy regulated by the state
- a contract state in which the boundary between public and private domains is fluid
- a residual welfare state based upon selectivity
- a corporatist system based on stakeholders incorporated into state organisational policy-making structures
- a managed public and private sector in which managers are the key to the efficient and effective use of national resources
- globalisation and increased international co-operation.

As in the past, there are differences of emphasis and priorities between the parties, but faced with an economy and society in the process of transformation from an industrial to a post-industrial information one, their prescriptions are remarkably alike.

ASSIGNMENTS

(a) What are the major changes that have occurred in the British economy since 1976?

(b) Read the latest edition of *Social Trends* and identify three major features that could be having an effect upon employee relations in your organisation.

(c) What are the main characteristics of pre-industrial, industrial and post-industrial societies? What causes a change from one to another?

(d) Read Murray (1989) and argue the case for a new model of political economy.

(e) Divide into groups and examine one of the four theoretical perspectives of social and economic change in Britain – Fordism, post-industrialism, post-modernism and globalisation. Discuss the similarities and differences between them and their implications for employee relations management.

(f) Consider the major differences between the old technologies and IT.

(g) Within groups, discuss whether class is still the major division in British society.

(h) What are the most significant observations of the latest British Social Attitudes Survey?

(i) What are some of the implications of the changing role of women, both within society and the work organisation?

(j) Read Allen *et al* (1992: 357–68) and examine the 'modernist dilemma'.

(k) What light do theories of flexibility shed on the major transformation in the gender composition of the workforce?

(l) Read Chapter 7 of Miles *et al* (1988). Debate the optimistic and pessimistic scenarios of the future effects of technology in the UK. How relevant are they 10 years on?
(m) What are the implications of the Internet for commerce, the public services and democratic participation?
(n) What do you consider to be the main economic, social, technological and political factors affecting the management of employee relations in recent years?
(o) What evidence is there that the human resources control strategies that management adopt are changing in line with changes in the structure and organisation of work?
(p) How would you categorise your organisation's current patterns of employee relations management?
(q) What difference, if any, is the 'New' Labour Government having on employee relations?

REFERENCES

AGLIETTA M. (1979) *A Theory of Capitalist Regulation: The US experience.* London, Verso.

ALLEN J., BRAHAM P. *and* LEWIS P. (1992) *Political and Economic Forms of Modernity.* Oxford, Polity Press.

ATKINSON A. (2000) 'Distribution of income and wealth', in A. Halsey and J. Webb (eds), *Twentieth Century British Social Trends*, London, Macmillan.

ATKINSON J. (1985) 'Flexibility: planning for an uncertain future'. *Manpower Policy and Practice.* 1, Summer.

BAUDRILLARD J. (1988) *Selected Readings.* Ed. Poster, M. Cambridge, Polity Press.

BELL D. (1973) *The Coming of Post-Industrial Society.* New York, Basic Books.

BELL D. (1980) 'Beyond modernism. Beyond self'. *Sociological Journeys: Essays 1960–1980.* London, Heinemann.

BELL D. (1987) 'The World and the United States in 2013'. *Daedalus.* 116.

BEST S. *and* KELLNER D. (1991) *Postmodern Theory.* London, Macmillan.

BOYER R. (1990) *The Regulation School: A critical introduction.* New York, Columbia University Press.

BROOK L., HALL J. *and* PRESTON I. (1996) 'Public spending and taxation', in R. Jowell *et al*, *British Social Attitudes: The 13th Report*, Aldershot, SCPR/Dartmouth Publishing.

CASTELLS M. (1989) *The Informational City.* Oxford, Blackwell.

CMN 4310 (1999) *Modernising Government.* London, The Stationery Office.

COOMBES R. *and* JONES B. (1988) 'Alternative successors to Fordism'. Paper presented at the Conference on Society, Information and Space, Swiss Federal Institute of Technology, Zurich. Mimeo, UMIST and Bath University.

CREWE I. (1984) 'The electorate: partisan dealignment 10 years on', in H. Berrington (ed.), *Change in British Politics*, London, Frank Cass.

DAHRENDORF R. (1987) 'The erosion of citizenship and its consequences for us all'. *New Statesman*. 12 June.

DEPARTMENT FOR EDUCATION AND EMPLOYMENT (1996) *Labour Force Survey*. London, HMSO.

DUNLEAVY P. (1980) *Urban Political Analysis: The politics of collective consumption*. London, Macmillan.

DUNLEAVY P. and HUSBANDS C. (1985) *British Democracy at the Crossroads*. London, Allen & Unwin.

EVANS G. (1998) 'How Britain Views the EU', in R. Jowell *et al*, *British Social Attitudes: How Britain differs (15th Report)*, Aldershot, Ashgate.

FOUCAULT M. (1970) *The Order of Things: An archaeology of the human sciences*. London, Tavistock Publications.

FOUCAULT M. (1980) *Power/Knowledge*. London, Tavistock.

FORESTER T. (ED.) (1985) *The Information Technology Revolution*. Oxford, Blackwell.

GIDDENS A. (1985) *The Nation State and Violence*. Cambridge, Polity Press.

GIDDENS A. (1990) *The Consequences of Modernity*. Cambridge, Polity Press.

GIDDENS A. (1996) *In Defence of Sociology*. Cambridge, Polity Press.

GORZ A. (1982) *Farewell to the Working Class*. London, Pluto Press.

HALSEY A. (1986) *Change in British Society*. Oxford, Oxford University Press.

HALSEY A. (1988) *British Social Trends 1900–1986*. Basingstoke, Macmillan.

HALSEY A. and WEBB J. (1999) *Twentieth Century British Social Trends*. London, Macmillan.

HAMNETT C. (1989) 'Consumption and class in contemporary Britain', in C. Hamnett, L. McDowell and P. Sarre (eds), *The Changing Social Structure*, London, Sage.

HARRIS L. (1988) 'The UK economy at a crossroads', in J. Allen and D. Massey (eds), *The Economy in Question*, London, Sage and the Open University.

HEATH A., JOWELL R. and CURTICE J. (1985) *How Britain Votes*. Oxford, Pergamon.

HEATH A. and PAYNE C. (2000) 'Social mobility', in A. Halsey and J. Webb (eds), *Twentieth Century British Social Trends*, London, Macmillan.

HIRST P. and ZEITLIN J. (1991) 'Flexible specialisation versus post-Fordism: theory, evidence and policy implications'. *Economy and Society*. 20(1), February.

HOBSBAWN E. (1968) *Industry and Empire*. New York, Weidenfeld & Nicolson.

HORTON S. (1999) 'Social Structure', in D. Farnham, *Managing in a Business Context*, London, Institute of Personnel and Development.

HORTON S. and FARNHAM D. (1999) *Public Management in Britain*. Basingstoke, Macmillan.

JAMESON F. (1992) *Postmodernism or The Cultural Logic of Late Capitalism*. London, Verso.

JESSOP B. (1989a) *Thatcherism: The British road to post-Fordism*. Essex Papers in Politics and Government No. 68. Department of Government, University of Essex.

JESSOP B. (1989b) 'Conservative regimes and the transition to post-Fordism: the cases of Britain and West Germany', in M. Gottdiner and N. Komninos (eds), *Capitalist Development and Crisis Theory: Accumulation, regulation and spatial restructuring*, London, Macmillan.

JOWELL R., BROOK L. and TAYLOR B. (EDS) (1991) *British Social Attitudes: The 8th Report*. Aldershot, Dartmouth.

JOWELL R., CURTICE J., PARK A., BROOK L. AND THOMSON K. (1996) *British Social Attitudes. (13th Report)*. Aldershot, Dartmouth.

JOWELL R., CURTICE J., PARK A., BROOK L., THOMSON K. and BRYSON C. (1998) *British Social Attitudes: How Britain Differs (15th Report)*. Aldershot, Ashgate.

KEESINGS ARCHIVE (1999) *Results of Elections to the Scottish Assembly and the Welsh Council 1999*. Harlow, Longman.

KUMAR K. (1995) *From Post-Industrial to Post-Modern Society*. Oxford, Blackwell.

LABOUR PARTY MANIFESTO (1997) *New Labour: Because Britain deserves better*. London, Labour Party.

LABOUR RESEARCH DEPARTMENT (1997) 'Editorial'. *Labour Research*. May. Vol. 86, No. 5.

LACLAU E. (1990) *New Reflections on the Revolution of our Times*. London, Verso.

LASH S. and URRY J. (1987) *The End of Organised Capitalism*. Oxford, Polity.

LIEPITZ A. (1985) *The Enchanted World: Money, finance and the world crisis*. London, Verso.

LIEPITZ A. (1988) *Mirages and Miracles: The crisis of global Fordism*. London, Verso.

LIEPITZ A. (1992) *Towards a New Economic Order*. Oxford, Polity.

LOCAL GOVERNMENT MANAGEMENT BOARD (1997) *Flexible Working in Local Authorities*. Luton, LGMB.

LOCKWOOD D. (1958) *The Blackcoated Worker*. London, Allen & Unwin.

MCDOWELL L. (1989) 'Gender divisions', in C. Hamnett, L. McDowell and P. Sarre (eds), *The Changing Social Structure*, London, Sage.

MCKENZIE R. and SILVER A. (1968) *Angels in Marble*. London, Heinemann.

MANDELSON P. and LIDDLE R. (1996) *The Blair Revolution: Can New Labour deliver?* London, Faber & Faber.

MARGETTS H. (1997) 'The automated state', in A. Massey (ed.), *Globalization and Marketization of Government Services*, Basingstoke, Macmillan.

MILES I., RUSH M., TURNER K. and BESSANT J. (1988) *Information Horizons: The long-term implications of new information technologies*. Aldershot, Edward Elgar.

MURRAY C. (1994) *The Underclass: The crisis deepens*. London, Institute of Economic Affairs.

MURRAY R. (1989) 'Fordism and post-Fordism', in S. Hall and M. Jaques (eds), *New Times*, London, Lawrence & Wishart.

173

NAUGHTON J. (1999) *A Brief History of the Future*. London, Weidenfeld & Nicolson.

NILLES J. (1985) 'Teleworking from home', in T. Forester (ed.), *The Information Technology Revolution*. Oxford, Blackwell.

NORDLINGER E. (1967) *Working-Class Tories*. London, MacGibbon & Kee.

NORTHCOTT J. (1999) *Britain's Future: Issues and choices*. London, Policy Studies Institute.

OFFICE OF NATIONAL STATISTICS (1999) *Annual Abstract of Statistics 1999*. London, Office of National Statistics.

OFFICE OF NATIONAL STATISTICS (2000) *Comparisons of Income Data Between Family Expenditure and Family Resources Survey*. London, The Stationery Office.

PEACH C. (2000) 'Immigration and ethnicity', in A. Halsey and J. Webb (eds), *Twentieth Century Social Trends*, London, Macmillan.

PIORE M. *and* SABEL C. (1984) *The Second Industrial Divide*. New York, Basic Books.

PREECE D. (1999) 'Technology', in D. Farnham, *Managing in a Business Context*, London, Institute of Personnel and Development.

RANDALL V. (1987) *Women and Politics*. London, Macmillan.

REES T. (1992) *Women and the Labour Market*. London, Routledge.

ROBERTSON R. (1992) *Globalization: Social theory and global culture*. London, Sage.

ROSE M. (1988) *Industrial Behaviour*. London, Penguin.

ROYAL COMMISSION ON THE DISTRIBUTION OF INCOME AND WEALTH (1979) *An A to Z of Income and Wealth*. London, HMSO.

SABEL C. (1982) *Work and Politics: The division of labour in industry*. Cambridge, Cambridge University Press.

SAUNDERS P. (1978) 'Domestic property and social class'. *International Journal of Urban and Regional Research*. 2.

SAUNDERS P. (1984) 'Beyond housing classes'. *International Journal of Urban and Regional Research*. 8.

SCOTT J. (1982) *The Upper Classes: Property and privilege in Britain*. London, Macmillan.

SCOTT J. (1998) 'Partner, parent, worker: family and gender roles', in R. Jowell *et al*, *British Social Attitudes: How Britain Differs (15th Report)*, Aldershot, Ashgate.

SNELLEN I. (1994) 'ICT: a revolutionizing force in public administration'. *Information and the Public Sector*. Vol. 3. No. 3/4.

Social Trends 22 (1992) London, HMSO.

Social Trends 23 (1993) London, HMSO.

Social Trends 27 (1997) London, HMSO.

Social Trends 30 (2000) London, Office of National Statistics.

TAYLOR F. W. (1947) *The Principles of Scientific Management*. New York, Harper & Row.

THOMPSON G. (1989) 'Strategies for socialists'. *Economy and Society*. 18(4), November.

TOFFLER A. (1980) *The Third Wave*. New York, Bantam Books.

TOURAINE A. (1974) *The Post-Industrial Society: Tomorrow's social history*. London, Wildwood House.

TOWNSEND P. (1979) *Poverty in the United Kingdom*. Harmondsworth, Penguin.

TURNER B. (ED.) (1990) *Theories of Modernity and Post Modernity*. London, Sage.

UNITED NATIONS (1996) *United Nations Human Development Report*. New York, United Nations.

WATER M. (1995) *Globalization*. London, Routledge.

WEINER M. (1981) *English Culture and the Decline of the Industrial Spirit 1850–1980*. Cambridge, Cambridge University Press.

WITZ A. (1992) *Professions and Patriarchy*. London, Routledge.

WOOD S. (ED.) (1989) *The Transformation of Work*. London, Unwin Hyman.

Part 2
EMPLOYEE RELATIONS IN PRACTICE

6 Non-union firms, employee involvement and communications at work

As outlined in Chapter 2, management has four policy choices in the ways in which it manages the wage–work bargain with employees and these are based on degrees of 'individualism' and 'collectivism' in the workplace. The traditional approach in large parts of the private and public sectors was 'high' on collectivism and 'low' on individualism and used collective bargaining and joint consultation as the dominant employee relations processes (see Chapters 3, 7 and 8). As employee relations strategies, collective bargaining and joint consultation are based on a policy of 'union incorporation' in employment decision-making with managers. It is a joint approach to employee relations and depends on employees being organised into independent trade unions, the unions being recognised by the employer for negotiating purposes and a fair balance of power existing between the two sides in the bargaining and consultative relationship.

In the Workplace Employee Relations Survey 1998 (WERS 1998), it was estimated that union presence at workplace level in Britain had fallen from 73 per cent of all workplaces employing over 25 employees in 1980 and 1984 to 64 per cent in 1990 and 54 per cent in 1998. Second, union membership density fell from 65 per cent in 1980 to 58 per cent in 1984 and to 47 per cent in 1990, while by 1998 it was down to only 36 per cent. Third, 'after remaining stable in the early 1980s at roughly 65 per cent, the proportion of workplaces with recognised trade unions declined substantially from 1984 to 1990'. This trend continued to 1998, with union recognition falling from 53 per cent of workplaces in 1990 to 42 per cent eight years later (Cully et al 1999: 238). Furthermore, union recognition at a workplace does not imply that all employees working there are directly affected by collective bargaining. Indeed, research has indicated that coverage of collective bargaining in Britain fell from 70 per cent in 1984 to 54 per cent in 1990, falling further to 41 per cent of employees in 1998. Thus by 1998, a majority of workplaces did not recognise trade unions and did not engage in collective bargaining with their employees.

This means that individualist, human resources management (HRM) approaches to managing people and the employment relationship have become more commonplace and have grown in importance and scope in recent years (Millward et al 1992). These are often based on 'union-free' environments, though in some workplaces HRM approaches operate in parallel with trade unionism. These approaches to managing the wage–work bargain tend to be employer driven, are unitary in their frames of reference and are:

- based on high levels of individualism and low levels of collectivism in the workplace
- focused on task-based or job-centred types of employee involvement
- aimed at employees as individuals
- predicated on a management policy of 'employee commitment' in the workplace.

In other cases, managing the wage–work bargain in non-union firms is based on a policy of 'worker subordination'. This is commonly rooted in authoritarian or paternalistic styles of management and low levels of both collectivism and individualism – a situation that is more common in smaller business enterprises than larger ones. Indeed, as the WERS 1998 concluded, 'overall, small businesses – especially those with working owners – had a *less* formal approach than small multiples to the regulation of the employment relationship.' They were less likely to have significant personnel expertise in-house or sophisticated personnel systems. 'Owner-managers generally took the view that they were there to take decisions, and this was reflected in the ways they ran their businesses' (Cully *et al* 1999: 273).

An alternative, pluralistic but still non-union approach to involving and communicating with employees in their organisations was the attempt to set up experiments in worker participation in the late 1970s. These engaged employee representatives in strategic decision-taking with senior management at corporate level in the public sector in Britain, with varying degrees of success (Ferner 1988). Unlike in western Europe, where employees frequently have legal rights to representation on company boards, such as in Denmark, Germany and the Netherlands, and in works councils or works committees (Incomes Data Services 1991, Ferner and Hyman 1998), in Britain there is no statutory provision for worker participation in management. Indeed, worker participation remains a controversial and contentious issue among companies, employers and managers in Britain. This is exemplified by continued employer hostility to the planned introduction of European-style works councils in Britain for all enterprises employing over 25 employees.

NON-UNION FIRMS

Guest and Hoque (1994) have argued that changing patterns of employee relations since 1980 have awakened interest in non-union establishments. Even by the time of the third Workplace Industrial Relations Survey (WIRS) in 1990, it was widely recognised that the majority of private-sector establishments employing more than 25 employees were non-union ones (Millward *et al* 1992). Further, the same survey revealed that well over two-thirds of establishments set up since 1980 were non-union organisations, indicating that non-union firms were increasingly becoming the norm. Accordingly, as non-union firms have become more common, Guest and Hoque have proposed a way of classifying new, non-union establishments, which recognises their diversity. This is necessary since in practice, 'it seems unlikely that non-union establishments are either all good or all bad' (*ibid*: 1) as had been argued by some observers.

Their classification of non-union firms was based on two dimensions: the first was whether or not firms had a human resources strategy and the second was the nature of their human resources policies and practices. Using these two dimensions, they identified four possible types of non-union establishments:

- *Good establishments*. These had clear human resources strategies and made extensive use of a range of HRM practices. They reflected high-involvement and high-commitment approaches and could be classified as a full utilisation, high-involvement model of non-unionism.
- *Lucky establishments*. Though these establishments did not have clear HRM strategies, they still appeared to have adopted a large number of innovative HRM practices – more by luck than by judgement. Guest and Hoque suggested that such establishments might have stumbled upon best HRM practices by guidance from others, copying others or following current fads and fashions.
- *Bad establishments*. These had no HRM strategies, low uptakes of HRM practices and represented the 'bad face' of non-unionism.
- *Ugly establishments*. These establishments had clear strategies but made little use of HRM practices, in that they provided minimum levels of workers' rights, appeared 'to be bleak environments in which to work' (*ibid*: 3) and were perceived as 'an efficiency-driven model' of non-unionism.

Based on their sample of 94 non-union enterprises, Guest and Hoque identified a range of independent variables as potential predictors of non-union type including size, national ownership, sector, regional location and degree of independence. They concluded that 'good' establishments were British owned, rather than American or German owned, and were parts of larger organisations in the non-financial services sector. 'Lucky' establishments were distinguishable as only employing more than 100 staff. 'Bad' establishments were smaller, German rather than British owned and more likely to be single independent establishments. 'Ugly' establishments had no distinguishing features, since there were only eight in their sample. Examples of the 'managerial outcomes' of different types of non-union establishment categorised by Guest and Hoque are set out in Figure 10, subdivided into 'HRM outcomes', 'employee relations outcomes' and 'performance outcomes'.

Guest and Hoque made three general points regarding HRM outcomes in non-union firms: good establishments reported the most positive HRM outcomes; ugly establishments reported (surprisingly) positive results with respect to quality and flexibility; and bad establishments, without a strategy and with low use of HRM practices, consistently emerged as having poor HRM outcomes. In terms of employee relations outcomes, good establishments had the best patterns of results and ugly establishments the worst, with the type of strategy making a difference rather than just having a strategy. In terms of performance, good establishments claimed the best outcomes, with all other categories emerging as significantly worse on at least one item. In summarising their findings, the authors highlighted the differences that they had observed in the range of outcomes across non-union establishments (*ibid*: 11):

> The good, those with a strategic approach to HRM which involve[d] extensive use of a range of HRM practices, consistently report[ed] the best results for HRM, employee relations and performance outcomes. In contrast, the bad establishments, those with no strategy and a low take up of HRM practices, consistently report[ed] the poorest outcomes. The ugly reveal[ed] a mixed pattern with some positive outcomes but distinct problems with employee relations . . . Perhaps most importantly, the results demonstrate[d] that strategic HRM [paid] off. The good, with their full utilisation strategy reflected in extensive use of HRM practices, report[ed] better results on all three sets of outcomes. Equally important, the bad, those without a strategy and with a low take up of HRM practices, report[ed] the worst outcomes . . . it appear[ed] that in new establishments . . . HRM [was] a feasible and sensible strategy to pursue.

Figure 10 **Managerial outcomes for new, non-union establishments**

HRM outcomes

- commitment of lower grade staff
- quality of staff employed
- quality of work of lower grade staff
- quality of HR policies and practices
- flexibility of staff
- ability to move between jobs
- line manager enthusiasm for HR policies

Employee relations outcomes

- labour turnover
- absenteeism

Performance outcomes

- quality targets obtained
- weathering recession
- productivity benchmarked against UK
- quality benchmarked against UK
- productivity benchmarked against world
- quality benchmarked against world

Source: Guest and Hoque 1994

In summary, then, a managerial strategy of non-unionism is a distinctive and growing phenomenon in the private, market sector of the economy, especially among 'new' or recently established enterprises in 'high-tech' greenfield site industries. It is a strategic choice based on a policy either of employee commitment or of worker subordination and is rooted in the belief that union presence in the company is detrimental to efficient performance and freedom to manage. Some more sophisticated, 'blue chip' employers go on to argue that the union role is unnecessary for employee 'voice' or protection, as their organisations provide terms, conditions and employee benefits in excess of those provided by unionised companies. It needs to be recognised, however, that the non-union firm does not necessarily equate with the use by employers of high employee involvement strategies.

EMPLOYEE INVOLVEMENT

Marchington and his colleagues (1992: 7) have defined employee involvement as practices 'initiated principally by management, [that] are designed to increase employee information about, and commitment to, the organisation'. Companies in Britain with over 250 employees are required to state in their annual reports, as a result of the Employment Act (EA) 1982, now incorporated within the Trade Union and Labour Relations (Consolidation) Act 1992 (TULRCA 1992), what action they have taken to promote 'employee involvement' practices within their organisations. They have to describe what steps they have taken to introduce, maintain or develop employee involvement arrangements in the following areas:

- information and communication between management and employees
- economic awareness of their businesses
- financial participation by employees in the companies employing them
- consultative arrangements.

Information and communication systems are the essential means by which employers provide systematic information on matters of concern to employees. Economic awareness schemes are aimed at achieving a common understanding by employees of the economic and financial factors affecting the performance of the company employing them. Financial participation is aimed at encouraging the involvement of employees in their company's financial performance, through employee share schemes or other means. Consultation, in the sense that it is used here, normally refers to 'informal consultative arrangements'. These are the processes through which employers provide regular channels of communication, between management and individuals or with small groups of employees, so that the views of employees can be taken into account by management when it takes decisions likely to affect employee interests at work.

Employee commitment

Employee commitment is at the heart of employee involvement programmes. Although 'commitment' and 'involvement' are different concepts, they are closely linked, since both are concerned with how employers can encourage employees to identify with a company's business interests through a variety of communication processes, employee relations activities and corporate policies. Employee commitment, in outline, is the extent to which employees identify with the organisation's work ethic, co-operate with its goals and objectives and contribute to corporate performance. Employee involvement, in contrast, is the term normally used to denote the processes set up within an organisation to enable its employees to become involved in decisions largely affecting the ways in which their work is done.

The argument, from the employer's point of view, for trying to win a high level of employee commitment to work, jobs and the company, in contrast with merely seeking instrumental compliance by employees to management decisions, is based on a number of assumptions. These include the claims that committed employees:

- devote their energies to working for the employer rather than for their own private interests
- favour the company in which they are employed rather than other companies
- give additional time and effort to the company when they are needed
- give priority to corporate values and employer interests when these seem to be in conflict with those of external bodies such as trade unions or professional associations.

The degree to which employees are committed to their work, job and employer can be inferred from their feelings, attitudes, behaviour and actions whilst at work. According to an early study by White (1987), employee commitment denotes three kinds of feelings or behaviour relating to the company in which an individual is employed. First, employees believe in and accept the goals, values and ethos of their employer. Second, employees are willing to work beyond what is normally expected under their contracts of employment: there is an extended 'psychological contract' between employer and employee. Third, there is a desire by employees to maintain membership of the organisation, rather than to leave it. Because commitment is voluntary and personal, management cannot impose it, others cannot initiate it, but those offering it can withdraw it, if they decide to do so.

A number of factors appear to influence the commitment of individual employees in organisations, including:

- gender and marital status of the employee
- educational attainments of the employee
- length of service of the employee
- the employee's personality.

Other factors are the psychological needs of individual employees and the strength or weakness of the work ethic in both the organisation and the wider society. It also seems that underlying employer attempts at increasing employee commitment is the assumption that it improves organisational performance. Employee commitment is claimed to relate to corporate performance in three ways (White 1987: 13). These are:

> First, strong commitment to work in general is likely to result in conscientious and self-directed application to work, regular attendance, minimal disciplinary supervision, and a high level of effort.

> Second,...strong commitment to a specific job will also result in a high level of effort insofar as good performance is related to self-esteem, including ambition and career plans...

> Third, commitment to the organisation...includes the intention to stay, and is associated with turnover. As might be expected, commitment normally also becomes weaker as the event of leaving draws nearer. It is difficult to assess which is cause and which the effect but there is a definite link between a fall in expressed commitment and turnover. This, of course, adds to the costs of production when it necessitates recruitment, training and supervision.

The concept of employee commitment is clearly a complex one and is associated with several objectives, but commitment of employees at work certainly affects a variety of organisational variables, such as absenteeism, turnover, effort and the quality of performance within organisations. It therefore has a number of implications for personnel and corporate policies. These include:

- generating early commitment amongst new employees
- designing strategies for improving commitment
- maintaining the reciprocity between the rewards received and the contribution being made by employees
- reducing turnover by increasing commitment
- developing participative strategies for introducing new technology
- implementing appropriate personnel policies, sometimes in association with employee representatives.

Aims of employee involvement

The term 'employee involvement' first began to appear in management literature in the late 1970s. After its National Conference in 1978, the Confederation of British Industry (CBI) published its first set of guidelines on employee involvement (CBI 1979). These were aimed at promoting the voluntary development of employee involvement practices within companies. What the CBI was talking about, at that time, was an open style of management, operated by managers with the necessary skills, self-confidence and 'pride in their jobs', so as to facilitate appropriate communication and consultation arrangements with employees. This approach, it was believed, would help managers achieve the consent that they needed to put their decisions into action. It would also, it was anticipated, bring about 'collaboration and involvement in the common purpose of the company and the mutual interest which all employees have in the success of the business' (CBI 1979: 4).

The objectives of such a strategy were to achieve a more competitive and efficient British industry through improved employer–employee relationships by ensuring that decision-making took place with the understanding and acceptance of the employees concerned. 'In this way, companies can reduce conflict by fostering co-operation and making the most of the individual employee's contribution' (*ibid*: 6). The CBI suggested that arrangements for involving employees could therefore be directed at:

- promoting understanding of their contribution to wealth creation in their companies
- promoting employee involvement in job content and job purpose
- ensuring employees were aware of the reasons for management decisions
- ensuring employees were aware of the business situation of their enterprise
- informing employees of their company's future objectives and plans.

The CBI went on to say that it was very easy 'to get hung up on words' (CBI 1979: 3). However:

> We have decided to use the word 'involvement' in order to avoid the emotional and political overtones of other words. There has, however, been so much talk and political argument about 'industrial democracy', 'participation', 'consultation' and 'a participative style of management' that we are in danger of missing the woods for the trees.

The CBI's stance, it was claimed, was based on its long-standing policy that employee involvement was best developed voluntarily, not though legislation, and in accordance with the circumstances of the industry and the company concerned. There was no universal blueprint for employee involvement practices.

Other CBI statements on employee involvement build on its earlier position and the experiences of its members. Thus the CBI believes that employee involvement (CBI 1990: 7):

- is a range of processes designed to engage the support, understanding and optimum contribution of all employees in an organisation and their commitment to its objectives
- assists an organisation to give the best possible service to customers and clients in the most cost-effective way
- entails providing employees with the opportunity to influence and, where appropriate, take part in decision-making on matters that affect them

- is an intrinsic part of good management practice and is therefore not confined to relationships with employee representatives
- can be developed only voluntarily and in ways suited to the activities, structure and history of an organisation.

The CBI goes on to argue that employee involvement promotes business success. It does this by: fostering trust and a shared commitment to an organisation's objectives; demonstrating respect for individual employees; and enabling employees to get maximum job satisfaction from their work. There is a range of means for generating management-led employee involvement practices. These include: two-way communications between management and employees; regular consultation; devolving decision-making to the lowest possible levels; training in communication skills; financial participation; harmonising terms and conditions of employment; and seeking individual contributions aimed at 'continuous improvement' in the organisation.

The CBI's position has not altered over the years. In another of its other policy statements, the CBI (1997: 11) continued to emphasise the need for companies to drive business-led improvements in employee involvement and motivation:

> Successful companies need high levels of motivation and commitment. These can only be achieved through high-quality workplace communication and involvement and well designed remuneration policies which give employees a stake in the prosperity of the company.
>
> The approach to these goals must be driven by business in line with individual companies' specific needs. So business opposes legislative imposition of specific forms of employee relations. The challenge is for business to develop and widely adopt best practice adapted to their own particular needs.

INFORMATION PROVISION AND CHANNELS OF COMMUNICATION

Information provision involves any process used by management for communicating with employees on issues affecting the organisation and employee interests at work. The information provided may be passed on in writing, orally or visually, with combinations of these methods normally being used. In the view of the Advisory, Conciliation and Arbitration Service (ACAS 1989: 4), successful workplace communication enables organisations to function effectively and employees to be properly informed about corporate developments. Done effectively, it helps:

- employees perform better and become more committed to their company's success
- managers perform better and make better decisions
- create greater trust between managers, trade unions and employees
- reduce misunderstandings
- increase employees' job satisfaction.

Both the CBI (1977) and the (then) Institute of Personnel Management (IPM) (1981) have supported the view that information provision should focus on the five 'Ps'. These are:

- progress
- profitability
- plans
- policies
- people.

Progress refers to information about the success of the organisation in achieving its corporate goals and targets. It covers three categories of information: markets; costs; and the working environment. The sort of information that can be provided by management in this area is outlined in Exhibit 15.

Exhibit 15 **Examples of information on company progress**

These include:

Markets

- sales
- market share
- trading position
- state of the order book
- contracts gained or lost

Costs

- return on capital
- labour costs per unit of output
- inflation
- raw material and input prices
- productivity
- quality
- waste measures
- number of employees

Working environment

- accident and safety records

The importance of profitability to a company can be demonstrated by its providing relevant financial information to its employees. This can incorporate the company balance sheet, statements of income and expenditure and more specific information relating to 'value added', how the company is financed and how its income is spent. This information needs, as far as possible, to be free from accounting jargon and to encourage greater awareness among employees of the sources of corporate income, investment and expenditure and their impact on business activity and the firm's future prospects.

As far as company plans are concerned, employees are normally most interested in the ones affecting them directly, particularly those relating to expansions, closures, relocations and reorganisations. The information provided here normally includes details on:

- investment
- relocations and reorganisations
- amalgamations and redeployments
- expansion
- training
- human resources issues.

A company's policies, especially on human resourcing, employee relations and training, need to be explained to all employees, along with the reasons for them. These cover areas such as pay, conditions, holidays, sickness benefits, pensions and employee relations procedures. As these policies are updated, they can be disseminated to employees so that they are kept continuously informed on all matters affecting their job and employment interests.

Information about people covers such matters as:

- appointments
- resignations
- retirements
- promotions
- vacancies
- awards.

Other more personal information relating to births, deaths and marriages and to sporting and social events is also sometimes communicated to employees. This is done to facilitate employee awareness of what is happening among colleagues and to encourage group maintenance at the workplace.

Downward communication practices

Downward communication practices are the methods used by managers to communicate directly with employees and can be executed in writing or verbally. There is a wide variety of methods by which management can provide downward information, with the following forms being some of those most commonly used by management in organisations.

Briefing or discussion groups

These have been popularised by a number of organisations and management interest groups, especially the Industrial Society, since the 1970s (Garnett 1983). In essence, a briefing group system seeks to bring down the levels of oral communication, between management and workforce, below those of departmental or unit meetings, into workgroups. There are a variety of types of briefing group, but a 'briefing group system' is defined by the Industrial Society (1970) as:

> A group which is called together regularly and consistently in order that the decisions, policies and the reasons for them, both at company and departmental levels, may be explained to other people. Those briefed communicate in turn to their own briefing group so that information is systematically passed down the management line, in a number of interlocking steps . . . The objective of a briefing group system is to convey understanding of a communication to every employee through face to face contact with his or her supervisor.

The benefits claimed of briefing groups are that they enable supervisors to take on the role of workgroup communicators. They also provide for face-to-face communication among people who know each other well. They are likely, therefore, to be informal and to allow genuine two-way communication to take place within them.

The size of briefing groups varies from about four to 18 members who meet for up to half an hour monthly or bi-monthly, under the leadership of their supervisor. Typically, these groups focus on the five 'Ps' outlined above. The two most important elements in creating and sustaining effective briefing group systems are the commitment of senior management and the training of group leaders. Supervisors, in particular, have to be made aware that operating the briefing group system is part of their job, and not an optional extra to be ignored during periods of pressure. Equally, every effort needs to be made to ensure that briefing group leaders receive appropriate training in running their groups, and in understanding the aims and objectives of the system, so that the groups can operate effectively.

Bulletins and briefing notes

These are used to update employees, especially middle and junior managers, on important matters. They need to be up to date and well-informed, taking account of the latest information and details available from senior management.

Employee handbooks

These are an important and often neglected source of one-off communication from management to employees. Through continuous updating, they allow a lot of basic information to be provided to employees over time. The sorts of information covered include:

- the history and background of the organisation
- the organisation's products or services
- the organisation's objectives, structures and methods of operating
- the main employment conditions and benefits to employees
- the principal rules of the organisation.

Employee reports

It is increasingly common for larger companies to provide an annual report to their employees. The annual report is an ideal place for bringing together all the information provided to employees over the year in an up-to-date form. It normally includes financial information, general information about sales, investment and employment, future trends and other relevant indicators of 'corporate health and wealth'. Annual employee reports need to be attractively presented, free from jargon and readable. In this way, employees are more likely to become aware of how they contribute to organisational performance and effectiveness. They are better able to understand the company's sources of income, investment and expenditure. And, with information presented to employees in a systematic, fair and easily understood manner, greater trust can be engendered between management and its workforce.

House journals

Well-produced house journals, steering a neutral course between employer and employee interests, can provide a useful, regular communication medium within organisations. Unfortunately, they are expensive to produce and distribute, need professional journalistic direction and their content can be so bland that they fail to attract the interest of their potential readership. A well-designed, well-edited and well-produced house journal, however, can be a very effective means for enabling management to provide employees with relevant organisational information and for employees to have their say about in-house matters that concern them.

Letters to employees

These are useful for presenting information on a single, important topic. They can be sent to an employee's home, put in pay packets or circulated internally. Internal memos are a variant of these but they focus on specific issues so that they are not confused with management directives or employer instructions.

Meetings

These include departmental meetings and mass meetings. The departmental meeting represents a step towards the briefing group system. Departmental meetings represent the bottom end of the communication chain and they are the basic means of enabling departmental managers to pass on information to staff from higher management, as well as of taking up points and issues raised by members of their own departments. Such meetings are often fairly informal, although they are likely to have pre-circulated agendas and agreed rules for conducting business. They also tend to be held fairly frequently and therefore may provide a useful forum for enabling departmental heads to meet staff regularly and for staff to put their points of view to management, and the issues of immediate concern to them, as they arise.

Mass meetings are more formal, set-piece occasions. They enable members of senior management to address all staff at a given location, on specific issues. They are not normally held very frequently and the opportunity for interaction between management and employees is more limited than for departmental meetings. However, with skilful use of 'question and answer' sessions, exchanges can take place and the usefulness of the meetings can become enhanced as a result of this. Because of their size, however, such meetings require professional planning if they are to be successful. Speakers need to be sufficiently briefed, well prepared and clearly structured in their presentations, using appropriate visual aids and learning technologies to get their messages across.

Newsletters

Newsletters provide the lower tiers of formal written communications in organisations and are useful means for enabling junior managers to inform their staff of issues relevant to them. They are most successful where they are used as an informal adjunct to the 'company' newspaper or house journal. Means need to be provided for retrieving such information and updating it when necessary.

Noticeboards

These are a cheap and easy way of getting instant, current messages across to employees and can provide information clearly, accurately and positively, although if the noticeboard is in a bad position, no one may read the notices provided. Noticeboards may also get cluttered, information may get lost and it may be presented in an unattractive and unimaginative way. On the other hand, information may be read by one individual and passed on to others orally.

Developments in downward communication

According to the WERS 1998, the most common methods used by managers to communicate downwards with their employees were team briefings (61 per cent of all workplaces) and systematic use of the management chain (60 per cent). These were followed by regular newsletters distributed to all employees (50 per cent) and regular meetings with the entire workforce (48 per cent). Most workplaces reported using a number of these communication methods, with 10 per cent operating all four, and a further 31 per cent had three of these four in place. It was larger workplaces, those part of larger organisations and those in the public sector that were most likely to be using all these methods (Cully *et al* 1999).

Upward communication practices

Another group of communication practices are those where information flows upwards in the workplace. These largely 'interactive' methods of communication normally enable two-way communication to take place within organisations, especially upwards from employees to management. The methods used depend on the size of the group being communicated with, what is being communicated and to whom it is being communicated. Used effectively, these communication practices enable genuine feedback to be generated between management and workforce and trust and openness to be reinforced between them.

Attitude surveys

Structured and regular attitude surveys of staff within organisations provide a systematic means for management to investigate the opinions and views of employees on issues of specific relevance to both employer and workers and to get valuable feedback on them. Attitude surveys are undertaken for various reasons, including:

- diagnosing organisational problems
- assessing the effects of organisational change
- measuring employee attitudes prior to and subsequent to a programme of change
- providing feedback on management policies, actions and plans
- identifying matters of collective concern to employees.

Conferences and seminars

These are meetings of selected or specified employees who come together to study, discuss and examine a particular problem. Emphasis is placed on questioning and group discussion. For example, when major organisational changes are envisaged, full-day conferences or seminars are a useful means of creating communication channels between senior management and those likely to be affected by the changes. Conferences and seminars can be in-house or off-premises, with the latter being particularly useful where management wants to encourage an informal atmosphere. For successful results and outcomes, conferences and seminars need to be organised in accordance with a number of accepted guidelines. These include:

- the meeting should be of manageable size to ensure informality and the flow of ideas
- it should last at least one day
- management presentations should be short, snappy and to the point
- delegates should be encouraged to ask questions, put their views and work collaboratively
- all ideas provided should be followed up, analysed and acted upon.

Health and safety committees

Joint management–worker or management–union health and safety committees provide useful, interactive channels for information and communication between employers and employees at workplace level. Improving health and safety in the workplace is an integrative activity in which both employers and employees have a common concern. Unhealthy working conditions and accidents at work cause considerable hardship to individuals, create additional expense for organisations and damage the reputations of employers. Positive health and safety measures, to which all employees can contribute, are a vital part of management's responsibility. Joint committees on health and safety are a valuable medium for management–worker dialogue and can ensure that the highest standards of health and safety are established and maintained within the enterprise.

Effective joint committees can help to produce healthy and safe working environments by:

- ensuring that there are regular inspections in the workplace
- monitoring health and safety records
- analysing records and statistics
- making sure that appropriate training takes place
- keeping in touch with new developments
- seeing that legislation is implemented
- stimulating health and safety awareness
- providing specialist advice within the workplace.

Where they are active and properly constituted bodies, joint health and safety committees benefit the employer, employees and, where they are recognised, trade unions.

Problem-solving groups

A problem-solving group is a group of people within an organisation who meet together on a regular basis to identify, analyse and solve problems on quality, productivity, performance or other aspects of daily working life, using problem-solving techniques. Membership of such groups, which usually have four to 12 members, is normally voluntary and members are commonly from the same work area or do similar job tasks and activities. The reasons for introducing problem-solving groups into organisations are to develop employees, facilitate communications, improve quality, increase competitiveness, improve performance and make cost savings. Having met together, problem-solving groups then present solutions to management and are usually involved in implementing and monitoring them.

Where problem-solving groups are used effectively, it has been shown that they develop individuals, provide personal progression for members, improve managerial leadership, promote teamwork and contribute to quality and performance improvements (Russell and Dale 1989). Appropriate attitudes, skills and behaviour by managers are essential if problem-solving groups are to succeed, grow and develop. Top management commitment is crucial for the effectiveness of such activities – this means management willingness to listen and respond positively to group presentations, to implement their outcomes and to monitor implementation. Middle and supervisory managers, however, can be obstacles to the success of problem-solving groups where they fear loss of managerial control. One way in which this issue is addressed is by creating such things as group leaders, facilitators and steering groups. But it is also sometimes necessary to establish a 'parallel' organisational structure, one concerned with production and the other with change. In other words, problem-solving groups can exist as parallel structures in organisations, in tandem with the operating hierarchy, and be mainly concerned with facilitating change.

Apart from some misgivings about the membership of problem-solving groups being selected rather than elected, many trade unionists are not opposed to problem-solving groups in principle. One of their main concerns, however, is that management may manipulate groups to undermine the role of trade union representatives in the workplace and they therefore could lead to a weakening of the union function and even to union de-recognition. Yet some groups have workplace representatives as their leaders, whilst one piece of research contended that most of the issues dealt with by quality circles, for example, had few employee relations implications (Bradley and Hill 1987). Another approach used to mitigate trade-union anxieties about problem-solving groups is the creation of a joint management-union steering group at the outset. By involving both parties from the beginning, the initiators of problem-solving approaches can be clear about the intentions, objectives and expectations of the groups from the start. They are then better able to create the conditions conducive to trust and openness amongst management, workers and union representatives.

Suggestion schemes

These are used to encourage employees to put forward ideas about improving methods of working, cutting costs, increasing productivity or modifying any aspect of the work environment that might benefit the organisation and/or its workforce. Financial or other rewards are normally provided to individuals whose ideas are accepted and put into operation by the employer. The employer provides special forms or suggestion boxes and publicity can be given through the house journal, posters and employee pay packets.

Training

Training is an important form of communication. It can help employees understand the information given to them and encourage them to play a fuller part in the ways an employer conducts its affairs. Training is needed because information about corporate performance or management activities sometimes involves specialist terminology and data that are difficult to interpret. Well-designed training courses are a useful way of giving employees factual information about their employment. Training events can provide explanations of what is happening in the organisation, and opportunities for questions to be put to management and answers to be given on issues raised by course members. Training in communication skills is also important for those who have to communicate. It can enable managers to:

- become more aware of the importance of effective workplace communications
- understand their roles and responsibilities as communicators
- improve their ability to communicate.

Such training is particularly important for supervisors who have a critical communication role but may have limited experience in doing it well. Further, the Investors in People standard, which aims to encourage employers to raise organisational performance through the effective development of people, is characterised by 'organised learning'. It requires commitment from the top of the organisation to develop all employees to achieve business objectives, and regular reviews of the training and development of employees. As such it is linked with employee involvement strategies.

Developments in upward communication

Table 6 summarises the main forms of upward communication practices (or direct employee participation practices) identified by the WERS 1998, by sector and industry. The survey showed that problem-solving groups were more likely to be found in workplaces with a personnel specialist, those with an integrated employee development plan and in workplaces with recognised unions. Suggestion schemes were a less formal way for managers to obtain ideas from employees and a little over four-fifths of workplaces used this method. Whereas problem-solving groups were strongly related to workplace size, there was less evidence of this in suggestion schemes. Just under a half of workplaces, in turn, had conducted a survey of employees at least once in the past five years. Workplace surveys were most likely in organisations that were part of a wider organisation and where there was a personnel specialist at workplace or higher level. They were also more likely where there were integrated employee development plans, in workplaces accredited with Investors in People and in workplaces with recognised trade unions (Cully *et al* 1999).

FINANCIAL PARTICIPATION

Financial participation is a form of employee involvement that, like other forms of employee involvement, is employer-driven, unitary in its emphasis and normally centred on individuals. Companies use this approach to encourage employees to identify more closely with their firm's aims and objectives and to promote the idea that their common interest lies in maximising corporate profits. It is hoped that employees will see the advantages

Table 6 Upward communication practices by sector and industry in Britain, 1998

	Employee participation in problem-solving groups	Workplaces with suggestion schemes	Survey of employees during last five years
	% workplaces	*% workplaces*	*% workplaces*
Private sector	35	31	40
Public sector	45	38	56
Manufacturing	43	30	36
Electricity, gas and water	54	46	86
Construction	21	11	14
Wholesale/retail	35	33	53
Hotels/restaurants	28	38	53
Transport and communications	29	40	47
Financial services	53	49	62
Business services	39	24	38
Public administration	38	68	75
Education	54	23	50
Health	29	37	34
Community services	17	27	29
All workplaces	38	33	45

Source: Cully *et al* 1999

of co-operation, flexibility and teamwork and the disutility of conflict and pursuit of unco-ordinated self-interest at work (Ridley 1992). The main types of financial participation schemes used by employers in Britain are profit-sharing, profit-related pay, employee share ownership and gain-sharing, all of which, by definition, are limited to private-sector businesses. This approach to seeking employee commitment has to some extent been encouraged by legislation since the early 1980s. This has arisen, in part at least, because, in the view of successive governments, financial participation breaks down the 'them and us' attitudes between management and employees in the private sector. As such, it is thought likely to bring about a greater identity of interest between the two parties at enterprise level. Table 7 shows the incidence of financial participation in private-sector workplaces from 1980 to 1998. Overall, the WERS 1998 found different forms of financial participation appeared to go hand-in-hand rather than as substitutes for one another. A fifth of private-sector workplaces had both a profit-sharing scheme and an employee share-ownership scheme, though about half had neither (Cully *et al* 1999).

197

Table 7 Profit-sharing and employee share ownership in private-sector workplaces, 1980–98

	1980	1984	1990	1998
	% of workplaces	*% of workplaces*	*% of workplaces*	*% of workplaces*
Profit-sharing schemes	-	19	44	46
Share-ownership schemes	13	22	30	24

Profit-sharing

It is a widespread view that there is an inexorable trend towards profit-sharing in Britain, the EU, Japan and the USA. Yet Japanese bonus payments – which are paid only in larger firms – vary but little over time and increase in line with earnings. In Germany, where almost all employees are covered by financial participation arrangements as a result of the Capital Formation Act, legislation requires employers to make a fixed financial contribution to a form of savings for employees, chosen by them, but not necessarily in their own companies. Even in the USA, regarded by some as the home of profit-sharing, only some 16 per cent of full-time employees are covered by actual profit-sharing arrangements. The vast majority of schemes in the USA provide deferred payments, which are usually invested on behalf of the employees in savings plans for their retirement (Incomes Data Services 1992b).

'Pure' profit-sharing is paid to employees at management's discretion. It is the 'residue' profit allocated for payment to employees, after the company's obligations to its shareholders have been fulfilled. It is left entirely to management to decide:

- the proportion of total profit to be used for profit-sharing
- the amount to be allocated to individual employees (and the rationale for this)
- the frequency of such bonus payments.

Profit-sharing, then, is a periodic bonus paid by an employer, out of corporate profits, which is added to the employee's basic pay. Experience suggests, however, that problems arise for management when they use periodic profit-sharing bonuses as a substitute for a competitive wage. Flanders and his colleagues (1968) found, for example, in their study of the John Lewis Partnership, that there was a much higher level of staff dissatisfaction with basic pay than with profit-sharing. In other words, profit-sharing is only likely to work where employees have reasonable pay levels, good conditions of employment and confidence in management's basic approach to employee relations. It is no remedy for bad employee relations.

A significant feature of profit-sharing is the way in which pay-outs average around 5 to 6 per cent of annual salary over time. According to

Matthews (1989), where profit-sharing bonuses become too large or too small, the company often terminates them and their replacement schemes normally pitch their bonuses at around the 5 per cent level. Difficulties arise where, because of trading difficulties, bonuses fall to zero. Yet the durability of some schemes is surprising. This is normally where there is an ideological commitment to them by the management and owners, who continue to support the scheme, however poorly the company is performing financially.

To some extent, the introduction of profit-sharing is optimised when the market conditions facing companies are tight. Tying profit-sharing arrangements to the overall performance of the company or enterprise carries a strong message of collective responsibility for corporate efficiency during difficult times. There are clear advantages in introducing a scheme when initial costs are low, with the likelihood that payments will improve in the future. On the other hand, problems are created by continually rising payments, especially if the scheme is presented as an incentive. By the very nature of incentives, they fluctuate each year. But if profits are maintained at a constant level, or are on a rising curve, the expectation is that profit-sharing payments will remain as they are or will increase too.

Profit-related pay

There has been a growth in profit-related pay in recent years (Millward et al 1992). The introduction of profit-related pay into the corporate sector was stimulated by the Finance Act 1987. After an initial surge, schemes tailed off, but interest in them revived after the Finance Act 1991. This Act doubled the tax relief on such schemes and model rules were published to help employers implement them. The sudden rush of schemes was also stimulated by the major accountancy firms that provided clients with formula-based schemes to avoid paying tax on elements of basic pay.

Part of government thinking about the introduction of profit-related pay is the assumption that financial participation by employees in the economic success of their firms encourages loyalty to their employer and support for the profit motive. But it is also linked with the aim of getting firms to substitute a variable profit bonus for basic pay. An implication of this is that paying flexible wages encourages firms to retain their employees in difficult economic times and to reward them when times are good.

Employee share ownership

There is also growing interest by both employers and government in employee share ownership (ESO). The main types of ESO are:

- *Approved deferred share trust (ADST) schemes.* In these, profits are put in a trust fund that acquires shares in the employing company for employees. These shares are then allotted to participating employees according to a set formula. Employees must retain the shares for a specified period to avoid tax liability.

- *Save as you earn (SAYE) share-option schemes.* These schemes are where all employees are eligible and employees buy their employer's shares from the proceeds of an SAYE savings contract. Employees then accumulate savings over a five- or seven-year period and use them to purchase shares at a predetermined price. There is no liability to income tax, although capital gains tax is payable.
- *Company share option plans (CSOPs).* These are, by definition, limited to company executives and are aimed at middle managers. They are used both to reward executive employees and reinforce their loyalty to their companies. Under these arrangements, up to £30,000 of options can be contributed over a three-year period. Income tax is payable and National Insurance also, unless the company has shares that are not readily convertible into cash.
- *Enterprise management incentives.* These schemes, introduced by the Labour Government in 2000, allow small, high-risk companies to target share options at up to 10 key employees, comprising a maximum of £100,000 over a three-year period. No income tax or National Insurance is incurred, but the capital gains on the sale of shares is taxable and tax reliefs are greater than under SAYE and CSOP schemes.

Other types of share-ownership scheme are found in partly employee-owned firms like the National Freight Corporation (NFC). NFC, an internationally based company, was formed when the National Freight Consortium was privatised in the early 1980s. It was floated on the Stock Exchange in 1989 and more than 90 per cent of its employees are now shareholders, although they own only about 20 per cent of the company's equity. To protect the principles on which the company was established, employee shareholders have a double vote on all issues. This is provided that they collectively hold more than 10 per cent of the equity. The employee ownership philosophy of the company enables the NFC to use it as a marketing tool. Each individual employee is in contact with customers, which is a good sales pitch. In addition, employee ownership helps maintain a strong corporate identity that might otherwise be lost.

Gain-sharing

The main distinguishing feature of gain-sharing is that it is a group incentive payment linked to productivity, based on a formula that in turn is linked to past performance. Also, unlike some other financial participation schemes, it can involve trade unions in the way it operates. The thinking behind gain-sharing is the desire of management to promote a team philosophy amongst employees by rewarding them collectively for improvements in performance. Gain-sharing is most commonly found in the USA, but a prominent example in Britain is at British Steel. This scheme was developed in the early 1980s and took the form of a quarterly pay bonus, based on the ratio of added value to employment costs, together with more sophisticated measures, such as quality of output and delivery time.

One of the most common gain-sharing schemes is the Scanlon Plan. One version is based on the ratio of labour costs to total production value, with negotiators agreeing on a normal ratio so that any savings are distributed to employees on a monthly basis. Management's profit from the plan is derived from increased sales with no corresponding increases in costs. The plan allows for revisions to be made to the basic formula where there are changes in product prices or increases in basic pay. Schemes can also be revised where capital investment takes place that obviously raises productivity without additional employee effort.

Another approach is that of 'added value', a concept developed by A. W. Rucker, again in the USA. Added value is defined as the difference between sales revenue and the cost of goods and services bought in. It represents, in effect, the 'wealth' created by a company. Rucker showed that labour costs, expressed as a proportion of added value, remain stable over long periods. It can thus provide a measure of productivity. The weakness of the Rucker scheme – and of the Scanlon Plan – is that the ratios used may be affected by factors that have little to do with the productivity of employees. Technological changes, or changes in prices or product mix, may affect sales revenue without affecting wage costs.

Gain-sharing appears to be a better motivator than profit-sharing – although they are not mutually exclusive. It is particularly attractive where labour costs are a high proportion of total costs. And gain-sharing schemes can be geared to improvements in quality, delivery and the cost of waste. They are also more flexible than profit-sharing. On the other hand, gain-sharing can inhibit change, its formulae can be difficult for employees to understand and such schemes require a lot of monitoring and communication on the part of management and supervisors. Gain-sharing also assumes that employees actually influence performance measures, whereas in many organisations they do not.

TOTAL QUALITY MANAGEMENT

Total quality management (TQM) has become a major issue for many companies in Britain in recent years. Yet the term is often used imprecisely, loosely and without defining what 'total quality' actually is. The 'management of quality' in Britain is not a new concept but, with the move away from the traditional role of quality inspection, there has been a tendency to label all approaches to quality management as total quality. This is inaccurate and fails to take account of the complex origins of TQM, the diversity of TQM practices and the links it has with employer attempts to obtain employee commitment and to structure employee involvement initiatives in organisations (Marchington *et al* 1992).

Origins and variations

The origins of TQM can be traced back to the search by Japanese companies for quality improvements in the 1950s. By the 1960s, ideas on quality improvement combined the pioneering works of Deming (1986) and Juran (1989) with the concepts of statistical process control and teamwork. It was around this time that the first quality circles were introduced in Japan. Both Deming and Juran argued that quality control should be conducted as an integral part of management control, with 'continuous improvement' as the ultimate goal. In asserting that 'quality is free', Crosby (1978) argued that in expressing their concerns with quality issues, managements are also dealing with people situations. His approach was closely linked with those of Deming and Juran but stated, in essence, that quality starts with sets of attitudes for which management has the major responsibility. But changing attitudes within organisations, at all levels, takes time and needs to be managed on a long-term, proactive basis. The development of quality control into total quality control (TQC) emerged from these debates, with TQC becoming known as TQM by the late 1980s.

TQM is distinguished from quality circles in a number of ways. According to Wilkinson and his colleagues (1992), quality circles have five main characteristics that contrast with TQM. They are voluntary groups, 'bolted on' to organisations, acting 'bottom-up' and operating at departmental or unit level. Their aim is to improve employee relations. TQM, on the other hand, is compulsory, an integrated quality system, 'top-down' and company-wide. Its underlying purpose is quality improvement. Nevertheless, TQM has implications for employee relations. Employees take greater responsibility for quality, are accountable for its achievement and work in teams. In addition, TQM is supposed to place greater emphasis on employee self-control, personal autonomy and individual creativity. The active co-operation of employees is expected, rather than just their compliance with management policy decisions and the employment contract. However, since TQM comprises both production and employee relations elements, it 'highlights tensions between, on the one hand, following clearly laid-down instructions whilst, on the other, encouraging employee influence over the management process' (Wilkinson *et al* 1992: 6).

The British Quality Association provides three definitions of TQM. The first focuses on its soft, qualitative characteristics: customer orientation, culture excellence, removal of performance barriers, training, competitive edge and employee participation. The second emphasises its hard, operations management aspects: systematically measuring and controlling work, setting performance standards and using statistical control procedures to assess quality. The third definition incorporates a mixture of hard and soft approaches to TQM and consists of three features: an obsession with quality, the need for a scientific approach to total quality and the view that all employees are part of the same team.

In Britain, TQM focuses on variants of the hard and mixed approaches. Oakland (1989), for example, has viewed TQM as improving business effectiveness, flexibility and competitiveness and meeting customer requirements both inside and outside the organisation. He saw TQM as a triangle and a chain – indicating the interdependence of customer–supplier links throughout the organisation – with the three points of the triangle representing management commitment, statistical process control and team working. Dale and Plunkett (1990: 6), while focusing on the statistical and operational characteristics of TQM, also linked it with employee relations, arguing that the 'key features of TQM are employee involvement and development and a teamwork approach to dealing with improvement activities'. Collard (1989) has regarded TQM as a management discipline aimed at preventing problems from occurring in organisations by creating attitudes and controls that make problem-prevention possible. For him, improved quality need not lead to increased costs. Indeed, costs are likely to fall because of a decline in failure rates and reduced costs of detection.

The basic elements of TQM

A useful general definition of TQM has been provided by the Institute of Management Services (1992: 5). It emphasises that TQM is not simply a system for achieving zero defects in the products or services provided by a company, but that it also involves people. In its view, TQM is:

> a strategy for improving business performance through the commitment and involvement of all employees to fully satisfying agreed customer requirements, at the optimum overall cost, through the continuous improvement of the products and services, business processes and people involved.

TQM, in short, is focused on achieving business success through satisfying customer needs. This is facilitated by involving every employee within the organisation in achieving this end and by expecting employees to see others, both internal and external to the organisation, as customers for their services.

There is no blueprint for developing, implementing and evaluating a TQM programme within an organisation. It is contingent upon organisational circumstances, management preferences and the resources available. However, the literature on TQM identifies a number of common elements. These are:

- emphasis on continuous improvement
- the need for commitment from top management
- the issue of attitudinal change
- the impact of TQM on the organisation as a whole.

There are also human resources implications arising from TQM, such as training, development and creation of appropriate organisational structures, which are examined in the next section.

Since the focus of TQM is continuous improvement aimed at satisfying customer needs and providing value for money, at optimum cost to the organisation, this requires that everyone in an organisation that has introduced TQM should become involved. This includes:

- using a defined process of delivering quality
- continuously identifying opportunities for improvement
- delivering improvement through structured problem-solving techniques.

People also have to use error-prevention mechanisms, practise corrective-feedback mechanisms and apply key business processes across the whole organisation, rather than within individual functions alone. The idea of continuous improvement means that people have to understand and identify any quality problems early on, at all levels in the organisation, and accept their responsibility for doing this. Continuous improvement is based on continuous measurement and evaluation, with this taking place both within the organisation and externally with clients or customers.

For TQM to be successful, its proponents argue that it needs effective leadership and long-term commitment by management – with managers acting as role models, leading and empowering change within their organisations. This needs to be supported by a culture of 'learning together', with guidance and support for the learning process being provided by management. TQM also incorporates clearly defined business objectives, communicated by managers and understood and owned by all employees. It is also management's task to encourage and empower every employee to adopt appropriate ownership behaviour (Hakes 1991). This includes ownership of outputs, customer problems and improvement actions. Most importantly, TQM focuses on success through people, which entails the invocation of solutions by consensus, providing education and training opportunities based on user needs, and facilitating teamwork and effective intra-organisational communications.

This means that top management has a major responsibility to continuously reinforce a TQM programme through example as a group. Whether in meetings, newsletters or in-house journals, management has to demonstrate its complete commitment to total quality. In this sense, some writers assert that changing management attitudes is the key to developing successful TQM and that it must start at the very top of an organisation. To show this commitment, it is argued, top management should make sure that everybody, from top to bottom in the enterprise, is clear about its long-term goals and objectives. This affects styles of management, communication systems and the way things are done within the organisation.

The issue of attitude change is critical in introducing, maintaining and implementing TQM programmes. Because of the consequences of TQM, it requires a complete change of attitudes, expectations and the prevailing culture in an organisation. These consequences may include: reductions in staffing, such as amongst inspectors and those administering complaints procedures; lack of staff knowledge of the techniques used in TQM, such as new statistical and control techniques; and anxieties about the implications of change. TQM also involves more participative management styles, with middle management having less control over the supervisory and quality processes. Further, changes in management style, with greater devolution of management responsibilities, are often seen as a threat by middle managers.

The need for attitude change is not confined to managers, however – it is required of the whole workforce – but it applies particularly to management.

As an organisationally-based process, TQM focuses on the best use of resources for the total organisation, organisational flexibility and responsiveness to change. It is also concerned with customer/supplier relationships, embracing not only external and internal customers but also external and internal suppliers. It is concerned, in short, with all those people who are bound together in long-term business relationships inside and outside the organisation. Other aspects of the TQM process include: measuring performance in terms of agreed customer requirements, customer satisfaction and process efficiency; anticipating customer needs; and delivering products and services that 'delight' customers. This requires identifying and adopting best working practices, as well as monitoring continuous improvement.

Human resources implications

There are three main sets of human resources implications arising from the introduction of a TQM programme. These comprise:

- the need for management leadership to stimulate employee motivation
- the training and development implications
- the creation of an appropriate organisational structure to facilitate TQM.

A major feature of introducing TQM in any organisation is the need to change corporate culture into one that is more people-oriented. This entails leadership at all levels, opportunities for employee empowerment and development of relevant skills within the workforce. Managers act as motivators, stimulating employees to accept responsibility for satisfying the agreed needs of their customers, whilst also encouraging employees to become committed to total quality. Meetings need to be run effectively, team-building skills need to be brought out and communication skills need to be developed. Another aspect of motivation is providing recognition, rewards and performance feedback to the employees concerned.

Training for TQM aims to develop self-motivated, self-reliant employees and enable them to achieve both their personal goals and those of the organisation, while satisfying the requirements of their customers. It commonly focuses on:

- top-down cascading of ideas and information
- workgroup training, with managers leading the training of their teams
- relating training content to the team's actual work.

The content of TQM training includes quality delivery, quality improvement and quality management. There is also the need to develop interpersonal skills among people within the workplace, such as team-building, motivating, leadership and communicating skills.

Collard (1989) has been both descriptive and prescriptive about the training needs arising from TQM. He has claimed that a total quality training programme combines three elements:

- management skills training
- training in quality management techniques, such as in the use of appropriate statistical techniques
- corporate culture development.

He has also identified four levels of training involving top management, middle management, task group leaders and facilitators. Development of group leadership, group-working, and communication and presentation skills for managers, for example, is seen as being particularly important. These include competency in chairing meetings, developing the skills of group members and developing appropriate leadership styles. Other behavioural skills that need to be developed include problem-solving techniques, presentation techniques and brainstorming. In Collard's view, organisations need to develop company-specific training programmes, not use off-the-shelf packages. These should incorporate the concept of continuous development, with total quality training 'occurring regularly for all levels, not just at the beginning of the programme. The training should seek to extend and develop understanding of the basic techniques' (*ibid:* 138).

Developing an appropriate organisational structure and a quality function includes a number of measures, such as:

- providing a quality support organisation to help management develop a strategy to implement the total quality process
- co-ordinating the application of quality management
- tracking the cost of quality.

It is also necessary to co-ordinate quality management systems and integrate health, safety and customer considerations into products, services and business processes. This is important in order to ensure effective communication structures and to facilitate employee involvement and co-operation in each case.

WORKER PARTICIPATION IN MANAGEMENT

Throughout this book the emphasis has been on how the potential conflicts arising from the pay–work bargain are managed in an advanced market economy like that of Britain. In addition to a policy of union incorporation (effected through collective bargaining and formal joint consultation in unionised enterprises), there are three other policy choices available to managements in determining their employee relations strategies. These determine pay arrangements, how work relations are structured, how work is organised and what emphasis should be adopted in managing people at work. These three policy choices are (see above and also Chapter 2):

- worker subordination (effected through managerial prerogative in non-union enterprises)
- employee commitment (effected through employee involvement practices in non-union and unionised organisations)
- worker participation (effected through worker directors, board-level representation and enterprise committees).

These management policy thrusts are not necessarily mutually exclusive: they can operate in parallel within the same organisation, with different policies being used for different groups of employees. Traditional management policy in Britain for much of the nineteenth century was worker subordination. During the first three-quarters of the twentieth century, union incorporation was the dominant policy model, particularly when this was supported by the state during the years of the employee relations consensus (see Chapter 9). More recently, since the mid-1980s, with increasing product competition, higher unemployment and growing market deregulation, employee commitment has become a favoured policy choice for increasing numbers of employers. Worker participation, however, has not been either a management policy issue or a major political one in Britain since the late 1970s, when the report of the Bullock Committee of inquiry into industrial democracy was published (Department of Trade 1977). This is largely because of hostility to it by successive governments and the changed balance of power in the labour market and workplace favouring employers and management, whereas in mainland Europe worker participation in management is a long-established and non-political issue.

Approaches to worker participation

Worker participation is any employee relations process enabling employees to share in the making of enterprise or corporate decisions. In Britain, management and managerial organisations generally argue that worker participation is best operated at the 'direct', individual or small group level, rather than through 'indirect', representative participation based on power-sharing. Direct worker participation is most usefully done, it is contended, by providing opportunities for individuals and small groups to 'participate' in the ways their jobs are organised. The methods used include problem-solving groups, quality circles, share ownership and taking some of the profits of the company employing them. Another approach is TQM initiatives at departmental and corporate levels and in communication, information and consultative channels provided by employers. This type of 'worker participation', which is management-defined and employer-centred, can be best described as task work-based direct participation aimed at individual employees. It is low-level participation, soft on power and management-driven, and is essentially a managerial definition of the term 'worker participation'.

In Britain, trade unions, in contrast, generally claim that the best method of advancing worker participation at work is collective bargaining. In this view, collective bargaining becomes less a method of sharing in the making of managerial decisions than a method of promoting 'industrial democracy' in the workplace and at employer level. Democracy, in essence, means providing the opportunity for employees, through their union representatives, to influence the making of decisions that affect the vital interests of employees. The concept of industrial democracy, therefore, envisages employees having the right to exert influence over those decisions most affecting their daily working lives. These include the economic, social and personnel aspects of the workplace and of the enterprise employing them. Industrial democracy, it is argued, calls for real, indirect worker participation in the decision-making process, through the agency of trade unions. Conversely, it implies a sharing of the right to manage in those areas involving employee representatives. In this sense, industrial democracy is high-level, power-centred, and union and worker-driven. It is for this reason that British employers are hostile to such a concept of 'worker participation in management' or what the unions describe as industrial democracy.

It is arguable, however, that industrial democracy goes beyond traditional collective bargaining. Collective bargaining is a power relationship and is a process of interest group representation in limited areas of personnel decision-making. It is an assertion of power, or of countervailing power, in a procedural framework negotiated between management and union representatives. The emphasis is on resolving conflicts of interest between the parties, with the outcomes of collective bargaining being determined by the relative balance of negotiating power between them. Collective bargaining becomes industrial democracy only where the negotiating agenda is widened beyond that of the pay–work bargain – the 'managerial concept' of collective bargaining (see Chapter 7). This is when both parties adopt an integrative or co-operative approach to the management–union relationship.

Marsden (1978) views industrial democracy as a contest over collective control within enterprises. It takes a variety of forms resulting from the struggle for control and from power shifts between the competing parties – employer and employees, and management and unions. The outcomes of this struggle depend on the level and scope of participation exercised and the ways in which effective worker participation is determined. In effect, worker participation takes place at enterprise or corporate level. But since participation at corporate level challenges the right to manage more than it does at enterprise or workgroup level, it is even more strongly resisted by management and management interest groups than at other levels.

There are two routes, in effect, through which industrial democracy/worker participation can be advanced. One is by the 'bottom-up' process of local initiatives driven by workers and their trade unions. This aims to develop participative working relationships with employers and management. In Britain, the voluntary bottom-up route, led by shop stewards, has been the preferred method for trade unions and their members. This strategy is likely to be successful in well-organised enterprises and industries, with strongly based trade unions, in conditions of full employment. It is less likely to achieve results where there is surplus labour supply, hostile employers, worker apathy to union organisation and weak trade unions. Moreover, since the bottom-up model is based on adversarial employee relations, it is difficult to reconcile with the objective of creating consensus within the enterprise and integrative management–union relationships.

The other route to worker participation is the 'top-down' process of supportive public policy, with legal enactment or centrally determined 'framework' collective agreements between employer and trade union confederations. This, in contrast, has been the preferred approach in most of western Europe since the end of World War II. Co-determination at board level, works councils at plant level and other sets of participatory rights for workers have been the product of political struggle and political representation at government level. Unlike the bottom-up model, the top-down model is based on the idea of social partnership between employers and unions and management and workers. It is rooted in providing a set of legal rights and responsibilities for the parties to employee relations, based either on civil law or on legally enforceable collective contracts. This model of worker participation aims to create identity and harmony of interest between management and workers, in order to increase the enterprise's potential for wealth creation and weaken the likelihood of industrial conflict. It also seeks to institutionalise co-operative and trusting working relations between employers and employees, at both the workplace and corporate levels.

Participation in the workplace

Formal systems of worker participation in the workplace are at their most advanced in western Europe. Most EU member states, and some countries in post-communist central and eastern Europe, such as Bulgaria, the Czech Republic and Hungary (Farnham 1997), have some form of statutory provision or agreed systems for facilitating worker participation at workplace level. The precise mechanisms vary according to each country's legal framework for employee relations, the relative strengths of employers and unions, the coherence and unity of the trade union movement and the dominant culture of employee relations (Ferner and Hyman 1998). The Netherlands and Germany, for example, have highly legalistic systems, with extensive and detailed powers for worker representatives. In Denmark and Italy, by contrast, worker participation is built into central collective agreements. It is these that provide broadly defined obligations for employers and employees in determining their participation arrangements.

Legal systems

The most institutionalised system of worker participation at workplace level is to be found in Germany. Here industrial democracy or worker participation is embodied in the concept of co-determination (see Chapter 3). This is based on the principle of co-decision-taking between management and elected worker representatives on a number of issues considered to be vital to each party. At the level of the workplace, this is done through the institution of 'works councils', although since the Works Constitution Act 1972, workers are represented not only at plant level but also at company level. The most important participation rights of German works councils are outlined in Figure 11. These cover a wide range of issues and give German workers some measure of joint control in areas affecting their conditions of employment, working practices and workplace organisation. Assessments of the effectiveness of German works councils vary. Berghahn and Karsten (1989) argue that works councils have strengthened the position of workers in the enterprise. Jacobi and his colleagues (1992: 243), on the other hand, claim that: 'in general, works councils' participation rights are strong in relation to social policy; weaker in the case of personnel issues; and weaker still in financial and economic matters.'

In the Netherlands, the dominant form of worker representation at enterprise level is through the statutory system of works councils. Employers must establish them in any enterprise employing at least 100 employees or at least 35 employees working more than one-third of normal working hours. They are employee-constituted bodies, elected by all the employees within an enterprise who have at least six months' service. The size of the works councils varies according to the size of the enterprise and all employees can stand for election provided they have at least one year's service with the employer. Works councillors have protection against dismissal, time off with pay to attend works councils meetings and time off with pay for relevant training. But they are also bound by the requirements of confidentiality and must not disclose their employer's business or trading secrets, even when their periods of office as works councillors have finished (Incomes Data Services 1992a).

Works councils in the Netherlands are obliged to meet with management at least six times a year. They have rights of information, consultation and veto. Employers, for example, are required to provide works councils with

Figure 11 **Main participation rights of German works councils**

Rights	Social matters	Personnel matters	Economic matters
Co-determination	working time holidays payment system piecework work organisation	staff files selection training	social plan
Veto		recruitment redeployment wage groupings dismissal	
Consultation and information	labour protection accidents	HR planning appeals	plans new plant job content

all the information reasonably required for them to carry out their tasks (Visser 1998). This information includes:

- the legal constitution of the employer
- its annual accounts
- reports on the general conduct of the business
- at least once annually, a report on employment trends in the enterprise and its social policy.

The main issues on which employers are required to consult works councils are:

- transfers of control of the enterprise
- acquisitions and joint ventures
- closures or relocations
- changes in the enterprise's activities
- recruitment of employees
- commissioning of expert advice by the employer.

Agreement of the works council is also required where the employer seeks to amend provisions relating to:

- hours and holidays
- job evaluation schemes
- pensions or profit-sharing
- health and safety at work
- grievance procedures
- rules relating to recruitment, dismissal, promotion, training and appraisal.

Systems of statutory works councils are also established in other European states, such as in Belgium, France, Greece, Portugal and Spain. They vary in their legal and constitutional details (Ferner and Hyman 1998), but they all basically provide sets of legal rights and duties for employers, works councils and elected employee representatives at enterprise level. In some cases, such as in Belgium and France, works councils are paralleled by other representative bodies at enterprise level. In Belgium and France, in addition to statutory works councils there are 'trade union delegations', which are made up of elected trade union representatives and have collective bargaining functions. In Belgium, trade union delegations are not statutory bodies but are established by central collective agreements between employer and union confederations. In France, in contrast, trade union delegations are regulated by law, which provides their members with paid time off work to carry out their duties, with protections against dismissal – during their periods of office – and with consultative and negotiating rights.

In most cases, apart from those of the Netherlands, Italy and Portugal, there is also a statutory duty on employers to establish plant-level health and safety committees. These complement works councils and their main functions are to elect employee safety representatives and ensure that issues relating to the health and safety of employees are discussed regularly with management. They are also legally required to oversee health and safety issues, improve working conditions and ensure that employers comply with relevant health and safety legislation.

Voluntary systems

In Denmark, employee representation at workplace level is based on a voluntary, corporatist approach and is largely through union-based shop stewards and 'co-operation committees' established through centralised, framework collective agreements. There is, for example, a long tradition of shop steward representation of employees in Denmark and agreed provisions for their election, status and role within the workplace. Central and industry-wide agreements define their functions, prescribe their activities and regulate their employee relations duties. In essence, shop stewards are direct links between management and employees on issues relating to workplace terms and conditions. They are also a focal point through which local grievances are articulated, channelled and resolved. In larger organisations with many shop stewards, they establish joint union delegations and union 'clubs' incorporating different unions. Within the authority of framework and national agreements, Danish shop stewards are expected to act with restraint and help maintain good working relations and joint co-operation between management and employees.

The principle of employee relations co-operation in Denmark is extended through the creation of co-operation committees at workplace level. Their aim is to promote industrial harmony, business competitiveness and employee job satisfaction in the workplace. The Co-operation Agreement between the Danish Employers' Confederation and the Federation of Trade Unions stresses the importance of active participation by employees and their union representatives in the arranging and organising of their daily working lives. It also facilitates the setting-up of co-operation committees in enterprises with more than 35 employees. These consist of managers, senior personnel who are not union members, directly elected employees and shop stewards.

The rights and duties of co-operation committees under the Co-operation Agreement are (Incomes Data Services 1992a: 29):

- establishing principles for the work environment and human relations, as well as the principles for the personnel policy pursued by the enterprise
- establishing the principles of training and retraining for employees who are to work with new technology
- establishing principles for the in-house compilation, storage and use of personnel data
- exchanging views and considering proposals for guidelines on the planning of production and work, and the implementation of major changes in the enterprise

- assessing the technical, financial, staffing, educational and environmental consequences of the introduction of new technology and major changes to existing technology
- informing employees about proposals for incentive systems of payment . . . also informing employees about the possibility of setting up funds for educational and social security purposes.

Co-operation committees are not empowered, however, to deal with matters covered by collective bargaining. But employers are required to inform employees of their firm's financial position, its prospects and any major changes likely to occur in the future.

Employee relations in Italy are in a state of considerable fluidity and instability (Ferner and Hyman 1998) but, in workplace relations, employee participation remains based on union organisation, not on works council legislation. Collective agreements remain the principal source of workers' rights to information and consultation, while the Workers' Statute 1970 confers a number of rights on the most representative unions at enterprise level. The principal national agreements, for example, generally include provisions outlining the information and consultation rights of trade unions. At company level, firms with over 200 employees must provide information to trade union representatives on significant changes to the production process or work organisation and on planned large-scale transfers of employees. Where there are over 350 employees, information must be provided about investment and the employment and environmental implications of new working operations or an extension of existing operations.

Under the Workers' Statute 1970, employees have the right to set up representative bodies for dealings with management within the enterprise, provided that such bodies are initiated by the employees, the employer has over 16 employees and the bodies are under the auspices of the most representative trade unions. Trade union representatives have the right to represent members in the workplace and be involved in bargaining. They are entitled to time off work to undertake their duties, to unpaid leave of absence for other union duties and not to be dismissed by the employer, except for serious misconduct.

Board-level participation

Statutory worker participation arrangements providing for employee representation on company boards exist in Denmark, the Netherlands and Germany. This representation is normally facilitated through the device of two-tier board structures, consisting of an upper-tier 'supervisory' board and a lower-tier 'management' board. Supervisory boards determine overall company policy and must be consulted on important corporate decisions, while management boards are concerned with day-to-day operations and issues. Employee representatives sit on the supervisory board.

In Denmark, the law provides for employee representatives on the supervisory boards of all limited liability companies and companies limited by guarantee. They have the same rights and duties as other board members. The supervisory board must ensure that employees are given information about the company's circumstances, including finances, employment and production plans. The arrangements in the Netherlands have existed since 1971. They require all public limited companies with more than 100 workers to establish a supervisory board with employee representatives. The most advanced system of board-level co-determination is in Germany, where there are three models of board-level participation. In joint stock and limited liability companies and limited partnerships with more than 2,000 employees, the supervisory board consists of equal numbers of employee and shareholder representatives, with the size of the board varying according to company size. Enterprises with more than 1,000 employees in the coal, iron and steel industries have supervisory boards consisting of an equal number of employee and shareholder representatives. In companies with between 500 and 2,000 employees, one-third of the members of the supervisory board must be employee representatives. As in the other countries, employee board members have the same rights and duties as shareholder members (Lane 1989).

In France, there is no statutory system of employee representation at board level. However, under a decree of October 1986, companies may provide for a number of employee representatives on the board of directors, with renewable periods of office of up to six years. Additionally, the Auroux laws provide rights for employees to express their views on the content, conditions and organisation of work. These rights are essentially collective and the legislation stipulates that agreements on employees' rights should be concluded between employers and unions where companies employ 50 or more employees and have trade union delegates. Nevertheless, individuals may go straight to members of management with opinions or problems, without having to go through the normal employee representation channels (Goetschy 1998).

ASSIGNMENTS

(a) By what criteria would you assess whether or not your organisation operates an 'employee commitment' strategy? You might consider your analysis under headings – which are neither exclusive nor exhaustive – such as: jobs; workgroups; departments; other units of organisation; products/services; type of organisation; functional roles within the organisation; corporate values; or work in general.
(b) Identify and critically evaluate the methods of information provision used by management in your organisation.
(c) Read Cully et al (1999: 48–83) and summarise the major trends in the ways that managers manage employees, as highlighted by the WERS 1998 survey.
(d) As head of department, provide a draft agenda for your next departmental meeting. What sort of preparation will you have to do to make the meeting a success?

(e) Prepare a position paper for your chief executive outlining the case for introducing (or revising) a briefing group system in your organisation.

(f) Present a report on the structure, operation and effectiveness of either the quality management system or problem-solving groups in your organisation.

(g) What would be the pros and cons of introducing a profit-sharing scheme in your company?

(h) Read Marchington and his colleagues (1992: 33–42). Report on the impact of employee involvement practices on employees, managers and trade union representatives, as outlined in this research.

(i) Read either Collard (1989), or Dale and Plunkett (1990), or Hakes (1991), or Oakland (1989) and make a presentation on the elements of TQM as examined by one of these authors.

(j) To what extent has 'total quality' been introduced in your organisation? Report on the issues, problems and human resource implications arising from this.

(k) Read Ferner and Hyman (1998) and provide a report on one European system of industrial relations analysed in this book. Indicate how this system differs from that of Britain.

(l) What are the cases for and against employee representation on company boards as happens in other parts of the EU? On what grounds do British employer groups oppose this type of worker participation?

(m) Read Lane (1989: 224–48) and provide a comparison of the patterns of industrial democracy in Germany, France and Britain.

REFERENCES

ADVISORY, CONCILIATION AND ARBITRATION SERVICE (1989) *Workplace Communication*. London, ACAS.

BERGHAHN V. *and* KARSTEN D. (1989) *Industrial Relations in West Germany*. London, Berg.

BRADLEY K. *and* HILL S. (1987) 'Quality circles and management interests'. *Industrial Relations Journal*. 26(1), Winter.

COLLARD R. (1989) *Total Quality: Success through people*. London, Institute of Personnel Management.

CONFEDERATION OF BRITISH INDUSTRY (1977) *Communication with People at Work*. London, CBI.

CONFEDERATION OF BRITISH INDUSTRY (1979) *Guidelines for Action on Employee Involvement*. London, CBI.

CONFEDERATION OF BRITISH INDUSTRY (1990) *Employee Involvement – Shaping the Future*. London, CBI.

CONFEDERATION OF BRITISH INDUSTRY (1997) *Prospering in the Global Economy*. London, CBI.

CROSBY P. (1978) *Quality is Free*. New York, McGraw-Hill.

CULLY M., WOODLAND S., O'REILLY A. *and* DIX G. (1999) *Britain at Work*. London, Routledge.

DALE B. *and* PLUNKETT J. (1990) *Managing Quality*. London, Allen.

DEMING W. (1986) *Out of Crisis*. Cambridge, Mass., MIT.

DEPARTMENT OF TRADE (1977) *Report of the Committee of Inquiry on Industrial Democracy*. London, HMSO.

FARNHAM D. (1997) 'The role of trade unions in economic and social transition in central and eastern Europe since 1989: a review and assessment', in L. Montanheiro and N. Nevenska (eds), *Private and Public Partnership: Learning for growth*, Sheffield, PRU.

FERNER A. (1988) *Governments, Managers and Industrial Relations*. Oxford, Blackwell.

FERNER A. *and* HYMAN R. (EDS) (1998) *Changing Industrial Relations in Europe*. Oxford, Blackwell.

FLANDERS A., WOODWOOD J. *and* POMERANTZ R. (1968) *Experiment in Industrial Democracy*. London, Faber.

GARNETT J. (1983) *The Manager's Responsibility for Communication*. London, Industrial Society.

GOETSCHY J. (1998) 'France: the limits of reform', in A. Ferner and R. Hyman (eds), *Changing Industrial Relations in Europe*, Oxford, Blackwell.

GUEST D. *and* HOQUE K. (1994) 'The good, the bad and the ugly: employment relations in new non-union workplaces'. *Human Resources Management Journal*. 5 (1).

HAKES C. (ED.) (1991) *Total Quality Management*. London, Chapman & Hall.

INCOMES DATA SERVICES (1991) *Industrial Relations in Western Europe*. London, Institute of Personnel Management.

INCOMES DATA SERVICES (1992a) *Industrial Relations*. London, Institute of Personnel Management.

INCOMES DATA SERVICES (1992b) *IDS Focus: Sharing Profits*. 64, September.

INDUSTRIAL SOCIETY (1970) *Systematic Communication by Briefing Groups*. London, Industrial Society.

INSTITUTE OF MANAGEMENT SERVICES (1992) *Members' Handbook*. London, IMS.

INSTITUTE OF PERSONNEL MANAGEMENT (1981) *Communication in Practice*. London, IPM.

JACOBI I., KELLER B. *and* MUELLER-JENTSCH W. (1992) 'Germany: co-determining the future?' in A. Ferner and R. Hyman (eds), *Industrial Relations in the New Europe*, Oxford, Blackwell.

JURAN J. (1989) *Juran on Leadership for Quality*. New York, Free Press.

LANE C. (1989) *Management and Labour in Europe*. Aldershot, Edward Elgar.

MARCHINGTON M., GOODMAN J., WILKINSON A. *and* ACKERS P. (1992) *New Developments in Employee Involvement*. London, Employment Department.

MARSDEN D. (1978) *Industrial Democracy and Industrial Control in West Germany, France and Great Britain*. London, Department of Employment.

MATTHEWS D. (1989) 'The British experience of profit sharing'. *Economic History Review*. November.

MILLWARD N., STEVENS M., SMART D. *and* HAWES W. (1992) *Workplace Industrial Relations in Transition*. Aldershot, Dartmouth.

OAKLAND J. (1989) *Total Quality Management*. London, Heinemann.

RIDLEY T. (1992) *Motivating and Rewarding Employees – Some Aspects of Theory and Practice: Work Research Paper 51*. London, ACAS.

RUSSELL S. *and* DALE B. (1989) *Quality Circles – a Broader Perspective: Work Research Unit Occasional Paper 43*. London, ACAS.

VISSER J. (1998) 'The Netherlands: the return of responsive corporatism', in A. Ferner and R. Hyman (eds), *Changing Industrial Relations in Europe*, Oxford, Blackwell.

WHITE G. (1987) *Employee Commitment: Work Research Unit Occasional Paper 38*. London, ACAS.

WILKINSON A., MARCHINGTON M., GOODMAN J. *and* ACKERS P. (1992) 'Total quality management and employee involvement'. *Human Resource Management Journal*. 2(4).

7 Collective bargaining and joint consultation

In 1981, the International Labour Office (ILO 1986: 1–2) adopted Convention 154, which provided an operational definition of collective bargaining. This defined it as all negotiations between employers (or employers' organisations) and workers' organisations for the purposes of determining terms and conditions of employment and/or regulating relations between them. The ILO added that 'not the least important objective of collective bargaining is that of avoiding violence as a means of resolving problems [between employers and employees].' Voluntary collective bargaining between employer and trade union representatives remains an important employee relations process in contemporary Britain, albeit a declining one (see Chapters 1, 3 and 9). As a managerial strategy for managing the wage–work bargain, collective bargaining covered 41 per cent of all employees in the 1998 Workplace Employee Relations Survey (WERS), compared with 70 per cent in 1984 and 54 per cent in 1990. It was predominantly a public-sector phenomenon in 1998, covering 63 per cent of all public-sector employees though even here coverage had fallen from 80 per cent in 1990. This was largely because pay review bodies had replaced joint regulation for some major public-sector occupational groups, such as schoolteachers, nurses and midwives, and the professions allied to medicine. Coverage of collective bargaining in private manufacturing fell from 51 per cent to 46 per cent between 1990 and 1998, while coverage in private-sector services fell even more proportionally from 33 per cent to 22 per cent (Cully *et al* 1999).

As an employee relations process, collective bargaining in Britain determines, by voluntary negotiations between representatives of employers and trade unions, the market and managerial relations between employers and employees. In other countries, such as in Europe and the USA, it is legally regulated and collective agreements are legally enforceable between the parties. Collective bargaining is the major method used by trade unions in pursuing the employment goals of their members (see Chapter 8), but positive managerial attitudes to collective bargaining and trade union representation are vital for its stability and effectiveness. It is interesting to note in this context that, according to the WERS 1998, average union density was higher where workplace management was more favourable or encouraging to trade union membership. 'In workplaces without any union members, the vast majority of managers were either opposed or, at best, neutral to union membership' (*ibid:* 80).

There are a number of different models of joint consultation (see Chapter 3) and it too is a voluntary process and, where unions are recognised, normally involves managerial and union representatives. By seeking to exclude matters subject to negotiation, 'adjunct' joint consultation complements collective bargaining, rather than replaces it, by focusing on the common interests of the parties at workplace and/or employer levels, not their divergent ones. In this way, it provides a joint forum where management and unions can freely exchange views on matters of mutual concern, such as health and safety, welfare, training, efficiency, quality and information. Unlike collective bargaining, joint consultation is not a power relationship but an information and communication exchange channel, where management can brief the unions and employees about matters not subject to negotiation or about other issues prior to negotiation. Similarly, unions can raise issues on which they wish to be informed by management. While taking account of union and employee views on these matters, however, management retains the power and authority to take the final decision on any issues under discussion. In this way, management protects the right to manage on non-negotiable matters and the unions are disassociated from unpopular decisions opposed by them. Like collective bargaining, joint consultation is predominantly a public-sector phenomenon, with 81 per cent of public-sector organisations having some kind of joint consultative committee in 1998, compared with only 42 per cent of private-sector organisations (Cully *et al* 1999).

THE ELEMENTARY ECONOMICS OF COLLECTIVE BARGAINING

In free labour markets, the price or wage of labour is established, in the short term, when the market between buyers and sellers is in equilibrium (see Chapter 1). This is the market wage where the amount of labour demanded by the employers is equal to the amount supplied by workers. In practice, the characteristics of the real-life labour market are inconsistent with the perfectly competitive, free market model. This is because of (Adnett 1989):

- heterogeneity of workers and jobs, resulting in persistent wage differentials among the workforce
- imperfect and costly information, making it difficult for firms and workers to be fully aware of labour market conditions
- high costs involved in labour turnover for firms and job changes for workers
- the existence of imperfectly competitive product markets
- the behaviour of trade unions as wage bargainers with employers.

There is also the debate about 'segmented' labour markets. Those using this analysis argue that open labour markets are found only in the secondary labour market, characterised by labour-intensive, low-technology, low-paid industries. In the primary labour market, which is characterised by well-paid, high-status, secure jobs, firms operate structured internal labour markets (ILMs) that are often non-unionised. These structured ILMs are largely independent of competitive forces in the wider labour market. This requires firms to finance their own internal training programmes, partly because of the technological demands of jobs, thus encouraging them to reduce their labour turnover (Doeringer and Piore 1971). Because of these factors, the wages structure reflects custom and practice, rather than worker productivity or external market forces. It is social cohesion, rather than efficiency, which underlies the relative wage rigidity and seniority-determined pay scales of ILMs (Doeringer 1986).

What, then, is the function of trade unions in the labour market? Basically, it is to offset the relative disadvantage in market bargaining power that workers have as individuals when negotiating wages and conditions of employment with employers. The employer is in a strong labour market position if it negotiates separate wages deals with each of its workers individually because it can undercut wages, especially in conditions of less than full employment. The employer does this by recruiting only those workers willing to take the wages offered; workers are normally 'wage-takers', not wage negotiators. By joining the union, employees try to even up the wage bargaining disparity between themselves and the employer, through collective power and organisation, thus remedying their labour market disadvantages.

Once it is recognised as a wage bargaining agent by the employer, the union aims to gain improvements in its members' terms and conditions of employment. It does this through its wages claims. Union wage claims are based on one or more of the following grounds:

- the rate of inflation
- the profitability of the enterprise
- increases in the labour productivity of its members
- inter-occupational wage comparisons
- labour market shortages.

One way in which the union can achieve its wages objectives is by restricting the supply of labour to those who either are union members or who join the union once they are employed. If the employer can hire cheaper non-union labour, then the union can find it difficult to protect existing wage levels and conditions of work of its members. The classic method used by unions was to restrict labour supply through 'the device of the restriction of numbers' (the apprenticeship system) and the closed shop (Dunn and Gennard 1984). Current legislation, however, makes it very difficult for employers and unions to negotiate closed-shop agreements – whether of the pre-entry or post-entry type. Indeed, the WERS 1998 estimated that only 2 per cent of workplaces had arrangements requiring employees to be union members to get or keep their jobs (Cully et al 1999), compared with 23 per cent of all employees in 1980 and 18 per cent in 1984 (Millward and Stevens 1986).

Figure 12 The union effect on wage rates and employment

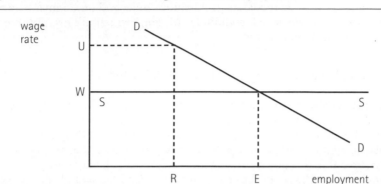

The union effect on wage rates and employment through collective bargaining is outlined in Figure 12. In the absence of a union, the firm, operating in a free labour market, faces a downward-sloping labour demand curve DD and a horizontal labour supply curve SS, since labour supply is fixed in the short term. This results in a market wage of W and an employment level of E. By restricting labour supply to the firm to amount R, the union can increase the market wage to U, thus trading off lower employment for higher wages for its members. How far the union goes in this direction depends on the preferences and tastes of the union leadership and its members. It can try to maximise either the per capita income of those in employment or the total income of its members. What its wages policy is depends on the distribution of power and the structure of decision-making within the union.

Union wage bargaining power varies across firms and industries. In addition, the more inflexible labour demand is, in a firm or an industry, the larger is the wage differential for the workers. Since the demand for labour is a derived demand, which depends on the demand for a firm's output, there are differences in the wage rewards between firms and industries operating in different product markets. In industries in 'soft' markets, with little domestic or foreign competition, firms are likely to make substantial profits in buoyant market conditions, with the unions and their members benefiting from this.

In highly competitive industries with 'hard' markets, by contrast, if the union raises wages above the market level, firms will be driven out of business. It is possible to raise wages above the market level only where the union organises the whole industry. The result of this will be that firms will pass on wage increases, negotiated by the union for its members, to consumers in the form of higher product prices.

Union wage differentials can also arise from unpleasant conditions of work. Thus where unions operate in firms and industries with rising productivity due to management-led changes in working practices, and this results in unpleasant working conditions, they try to negotiate compensating wage increases for their members. Consequently, the employer obtains higher productivity, shareholders gain higher profits and union members are compensated for worsened conditions of employment. This practice is called productivity bargaining.

THE NATURE OF COLLECTIVE BARGAINING

It was the Webbs (1913) who provided the first detailed analysis of collective bargaining when they identified it as one method by which unions enforce the common rules of the trade (see Chapter 8). They put forward the classic view of trade unions as primarily wage bargaining agents, whose role is to offset the power inequalities of individual bargaining between employers and workers in the labour market. For Flanders (1968), collective bargaining was a power-centred rather than an economic process, with unions using their power to penetrate the management function by acting as institutions of 'job regulation' on any matters affecting the employment interests of their members (see Chapter 8). Dubin (1954), a sociologist, saw collective bargaining primarily as the industrial counterpart to political democracy, which provides a source of social stability, social order and social change in industry and society.

Kahn-Freund's (1954) penetrating analysis of collective bargaining, from a socio-legal perspective, argued that it is associated with the evolution of social norms to regulate social conflict in industry. The emergence of collective bargaining depends on the extent and forms of legal intervention by the state. For Marxists, collective bargaining is the process by which the working class, through experiencing industrial action, trade union militancy and employer exploitation, becomes politicised. Unions are the means not only of protecting the employment interests of their members but also of furthering the class struggle between the wage earning 'proletariat' and profit-seeking capitalists (Hyman 1975).

Bargaining: contract, law and governance

Chamberlain and Kuhn (1965) have provided one of the most comprehensive and persuasive analyses of collective bargaining, by identifying three views of the process. These are 'the marketing concept', 'the governmental concept' and 'the industrial relations concept'. In outline, in the marketing concept, collective agreements act as a 'contract' between the parties to employee relations. In the governmental concept, they are a system of 'law-making', applied and adjudicated through collective bargaining. And in the industrial relations concept, collective agreements provide a method of 'industrial governance', whereby corporate decision-making focuses on 'jointly decided directives'.

The wage–work bargain

The marketing concept views collective bargaining as an exchange relationship. It is a means of contracting for the sale of labour, between employer and employee, through the agency of the union. The collective agreement acts as a contract for the buying and selling process, which is strictly and definably limited for a specified period. This view of collective bargaining is equivalent to that of the Webbs and is based on the assumption that the bargaining inequality in the labour market, between corporate employer and individual employee, oppresses individual workers and needs to be remedied. Whether or not the substantive agreements arrived at establish an equality of bargaining power is irrelevant. What is important is the strict interpretation and application of the collective agreement. Its terms represent the bargain struck and its clauses are to be honoured for the period that it runs. In disputes over the contractual obligations of the parties, recourse may be made to the relevant procedural arrangements between the parties.

Industrial jurisprudence

The governmental concept of collective bargaining views it as a constitutional system in industry and the workplace. It is a political relationship, in which the union shares industrial sovereignty with management over the workers and, as their representative, uses that power in their interests. The industrial constitution, written by management and union representatives, has legislative, executive and judicial elements. The legislative branch consists of joint management–union committees that make and interpret agreements. Executive authority and the right to initiate decisions are vested in management but within the framework of the industrial 'legislation' determined by the parties. Management has the right to manage, plan product development, change working methods and create personnel policy, but it must act within established 'rules'. Where differences between the parties cannot be resolved by negotiation, the judicial element of the industrial constitution is used. This involves using procedures to settle differences between the parties and, ultimately, the intervention of third parties to determine the issue, if necessary.

According to Chamberlain and Kuhn (1965), the ethical principle underlying the governmental approach to collective bargaining is 'the sharing of industrial sovereignty', which has two facets (*ibid*: 124):

> In the first place, it involves a sharing by management with the union of power over those who are governed, the employees. In the second place, it involves a joint defense of the autonomy of the government established to exercise such power, a defense primarily against interference by the state. Both stem from a desire to control one's own affairs.

The sharing of power between management and union means that only rules of employment that are mutually acceptable, and have the consent of employees, can be legitimised and enforced. Sovereignty is held jointly by management and unions in the collective bargaining process, resulting in participation by the union in job control. On the other side, sovereignty is also concerned with limiting the control of those, outside the employee relations constitution, who might wish to interfere in the autonomous collective bargaining process.

Chamberlain and Kuhn went on to distinguish between the 'constitutional law of industry' and its 'common law'. In the former, the collective agreement establishes the terms of the employer–employee relationship and individual cases are governed by these terms. In the firm's common law, developed through joint procedures for settling grievances and differences of interpretation of agreements, there are no written standards of control. 'It is the mutual recognition of the requirements of morality and the needs of operation which provides the basis of decision and ultimately the norms of action' (*ibid*: 128). These are often rooted in the social customs and unwritten conventions of the enterprise.

Industrial governance

The third concept of collective bargaining, the industrial relations concept, is a functional relationship. It is where the union joins with company officials in reaching decisions on matters in which both have vital interests. A system of industrial governance follows out of a system of industrial jurisprudence. The presence of the union allows workers, through their representatives, to participate in the determination of policies guiding and ruling their working lives. Indeed, 'collective bargaining by its very nature involves union representatives in decision-making roles' (*ibid*: 130). Since the nature of the bargaining process is appropriate to its own industrial or sectoral setting, collective bargaining is a method of conducting industrial relations, using procedures for making joint decisions on all matters affecting labour.

The ethical principle underlying the concept of collective bargaining as a process of industrial governance is that those who are integral to the conduct of an enterprise should have a voice in making those decisions of most concern to them. This is the 'principle of mutuality' and is a correlate of political democracy. According to Brandeis (1934):

> collective bargaining is today the means of establishing industrial democracy –
> the means of providing for workers in industry the sense of work, of freedom,
> and of participation that democratic government promises them as citizens.

This view of collective bargaining implies that authority over workers requires their consent. And defining authority within the enterprise involves areas of joint decision-making through collective agreement. As conceptions of the corporate decisions affecting worker interests expand, so does the area of joint agreement. 'And as the area of joint concern expands, so too does the participation of the union in the management of the enterprise' (*ibid*: 135). Ultimately, collective bargaining becomes a system of management.

Bargaining as an evolutionary process

These three views of collective bargaining are not mutually exclusive. They can be seen as stages in the development and evolution of the collective bargaining process and of the bargaining relationship between employer and union. As the scope of collective bargaining extends, there is a shift along the spectrum from the marketing, the jurisprudential and the industrial governance concepts. Similarly, as the scope of collective bargaining shrinks, there is a shift back towards the marketing concept.

These three approaches to collective bargaining represent different conceptions of what the bargaining process is about and they express normative judgements about it. Each stresses a different guiding principle and each influences the actions taken by the parties. For example, under the marketing concept, withholding data or distorting facts may be a legitimate negotiating tactic by the parties. Under the governmental concept, it may be difficult to determine whether specific data should be accessible to both parties or confidential to only one. Under the industrial relations concept, all relevant data become necessary to make informed, joint decisions.

The distinctions among these three approaches are not just academic but are also practical. The marketing approach emphasises the existence of alternative choices in any employer–union relationship, however limited these are. The governmental and industrial relations approaches emphasise the continuity of a given relationship and regard collective bargaining as a continuous process. Which approach is stressed is determined by the views adopted by the parties as to the nature of the bargaining process, the importance they place on particular bargaining outcomes and the balance of bargaining power between them.

NEGOTIATING BEHAVIOUR

Walton and McKersie (1965) have provided a seminal but complex analysis of negotiating behaviour in the collective bargaining process. They distinguished four subprocesses of negotiating activity, each with its own function for the parties to negotiation, its own patterns of behaviour and its own instrumental tactics. These subprocesses are: distributive bargaining; integrative bargaining; attitudinal structuring; and intra-organisational bargaining. The originality of their study lies in its synthesis of the interaction and interrelationship among these four subprocesses.

The distributive bargaining model

Distributive bargaining is a conflict-resolving process, involving competitive bargaining behaviour between negotiators. It is aimed at influencing the division of limited resources between them. It is central to management–union negotiations and is usually regarded as the dominant activity in their relationship. Distributive bargaining involves a 'win–lose' situation for the two parties. In a wage negotiation, for example, what the management side wins, the union side loses. And what the management side concedes, the union side gains. In game theory, it is a 'fixed-sum' pay-off, with each side giving up something to achieve a compromise agreement for itself.

225

In distributive bargaining, the collective bargaining agenda consists of 'issues' or areas of common concern in which the objectives of the parties are in conflict. Since distributive bargaining is the process by which each party attempts to maximise its own share of fixed, limited resources, the following sorts of issues are determined by it:

- wage levels
- conditions of employment
- working arrangements
- staffing levels
- union security
- employee job rights
- discipline
- lay-offs.

But there is also a degree of mutual dependency between the parties, because settling conflict between them enables each side to benefit from the relationship. Both sides need to continue their relationship, rather than terminate it.

The bargaining range of the parties is bounded by upper and lower limits. At some upper limit of wage costs, the employer is forced to cease trading. At some lower limit, it loses the ability to retain its workforce. For any particular settlement point chosen by the negotiators, within this bargaining range, there are two possible outcomes. The parties may agree or disagree. Yet what negotiators demand, and what they actually expect, depends on their preferences or 'subjective utilities' for possible settlements. These also depend on their preferences or 'subjective disutilities' for avoiding strikes – and the potential costs of these to each of them. Negotiators have to evaluate various possible settlements by assigning probabilities to them. Their target and resistance points, in the bargaining range, reflect assessments of these utilities, probabilities and expected outcomes.

The integrative bargaining model

Integrative bargaining is a problem-solving process in which negotiators seek a solution to a common employee relations problem. It takes place when the nature of the problem permits solutions that benefit both parties, or at least do not require equal sacrifices by both of them. It is the process by which the parties attempt to increase the size of the joint gain between them, without regard to division of resources. The resolution of the problem, by negotiation, represents a 'win–win' situation for the parties. In productivity bargaining, for example, where management and the union try to get lower unit costs of production, through more-efficient working practices, the gains in cost savings are shared between them. This results in more profits for the company, higher wages for the workforce and lower prices for customers. In game theory, this is a 'positive sum' game, with benefits to both sets of negotiators.

The integrative collective bargaining agenda focuses on 'problems', rather than issues. These contain possibilities of greater or lesser amounts of value to both parties. Walton and McKersie have argued that integrative bargaining potential is more normally found in qualitative rather than monetary employee relations issues. These include:

- providing individual job security, while increasing management flexibility
- preserving jobs, while raising enterprise efficiency
- expanding employment benefits, while limiting the employer's costs
- facilitating union security, while providing management control through institutions such as closed shop or 'agency' shop agreements.

The integrative bargaining model comprises four main stages: identifying the problem; searching for alternative solutions and their consequences; ordering preferential solutions; and selecting a course of action. The conditions facilitating collective bargaining problem-solving depend on a number of factors, including:

- motivation of the parties
- access to information by the parties
- their having the communication skills to exchange this information
- a supportive and trusting climate between them.

The tactics used by negotiators for optimising integrative bargaining outcomes focus on developing and inducing these conditions between the parties.

Mixed bargaining

It is rare, in practice, for the collective bargaining agenda not to include items that can be pursued only through some combination of distributive and integrative bargaining. Management–union negotiations present few pure-conflict situations and few problems allowing the parties total mutual gain. This results in 'mixed bargaining', which is a complex combination of the two processes, involving a variable sum, variable pay-off structure. Distributive bargaining assumes little or no variability in the sum available to the parties, whilst integrative bargaining assumes no difficulty in allocating shares between them. Mixed bargaining confronts both these possibilities simultaneously, recognising that they are interdependent. It involves complex bargaining strategies and presents the parties with difficulties in identifying the preferred strategy. As Walton and McKersie have written (*ibid:* 179):

> The point . . . is that as bargaining comes to a showdown, what is purely integrative bargaining or what is beginning to move toward distributive bargaining becomes difficult to separate. Both sides are trying to converge on a point, but at the same time they are trying to protect their own self-interests.

The attitudinal structuring model

According to Walton and McKersie, an additional function of negotiating is influencing relationships between the parties. These attitudes include friendliness or hostility, trust, respect, the motivational orientation towards each other – especially regarding competition or co-operation between them – and beliefs about each other's legitimacy. Negotiators take account of personal interaction in negotiations to produce attitudinal changes between them. Attitudinal structuring is a socio-emotional process used by negotiators to attain desired relationship patterns between themselves and to change attitudes during negotiations.

Walton and McKersie constructed a model of the social-psychological forces affecting bargaining relationships. These include:

- the structural determinants of behaviour
- attitudinal structuring activities
- emergent relationship patterns
- the consequences of these patterns.

They then developed a model of the attitudinal change process using two theories: cognitive balance theory and reinforcement theory.

The essence of cognitive balance theory is that individuals prefer consistency or balance among their cognitions, rather than dissonance. There is a psychological cost in holding discrepant cognitions. By introducing a discrepant cognition into another's awareness, the negotiator creates forces aimed at modifying existing cognitions, inducing a change in the target attitude and producing a change in negotiating behaviour.

Reinforcement theory assumes that people behave in ways that are rewarded, whilst avoiding behaviour that is punished. Negotiators therefore use rewards and punishments to shape the other party's behaviour. Where that party adopts co-operative patterns of behaviour, which are rewarded by his or her opposite number, it tends to develop more positive attitudes consistent with the new behaviour. In this case, a change in the target behaviour results in changes in negotiating attitudes.

The intra-organisational bargaining model

Intra-organisational bargaining is the process that takes place within the management side and union side prior to and during negotiations. It seeks to resolve conflicts over objectives, strategies and tactics within each bargaining organisation and to achieve internal consensus within them. Walton and McKersie analysed these conflicts in terms of the relationships between the chief negotiators and the groups they represent.

In examining the nature of internal conflict within bargaining organisations, Walton and McKersie focused on 'boundary role conflict' and 'factional conflict'. Boundary conflict results from: the forces pulling chief negotiators in opposite directions; those forces arising from the internal expectations of their own groups; and those arising from the other side's expectations during negotiations. Factional conflict arises from differences over negotiating objectives or the means of achieving them. The conditions under which internal conflict is likely to be most pronounced are where there are different preferences and feasibility estimates within the bargaining organisation. These, in turn, arise out of differences in underlying motivations, perceptual factors and the emotional states of its constituents.

In response to boundary and factional conflicts, chief negotiators use a variety of behavioural techniques aimed at bringing the expectations of their constituent groups into line with their own. The problem arises from gaps between the expectations of the negotiators' groups and the negotiators' projections about the outcome and their judgements about the best way to bargain. 'The problem is resolved if expectations are brought into alignment with achievement, either before the fact of settlement or afterward, or if perceived achievement is brought into alignment with expectations' (Walton and McKersie 1965: 303).

Chief negotiators have to make strategic choices about whether to modify, ignore or comply with the substantive and behavioural expectations of their groups, applying appropriate 'tactical assignments' to them. They may do this by:

- attempting to modify the aspirations of their group by ignoring their behavioural expectations, which is the most active strategy for achieving intra-organisational consensus
- trying to modify their group's aspirations, but less directly, by managing to comply with their behavioural expectations, which is a moderately active strategy
- ignoring, rather than changing, their group's aspirations, whilst complying with their behavioural expectations, which is a passive strategy.

Synthesising the subprocesses

In synthesising the four subprocesses of negotiation, Walton and McKersie identified the 'commitment pattern' as the key aspect of distributive bargaining: 'openness in communication' in integrative bargaining; 'trust' in attitudinal structuring; and 'internal control' within the bargaining organisation in intra-organisational bargaining. Strategic and tactical issues arise, however, in the synthesising process. For example, whilst an 'early and firm commitment strategy' is preferable in distributive bargaining, it frustrates integrative bargaining, is likely to be negative for attitudinal structuring and could frustrate the other party's aim of achieving internal consensus in his or her bargaining organisation.

Similarly, a high degree of open communication is preferable for integrative bargaining and is consistent with efforts aimed at improving relationships between the parties. However, anything but openness is required for distributive bargaining. It can also be problematic for intra-organisational bargaining, where negotiators often keep their organisations in the dark about bargaining developments or exaggerate their bargaining achievements.

Trust is a key element affecting attitudinal structuring. It plays a limited but essential role in distributive bargaining, has a more central role in integrative bargaining and facilitates intra-organisational bargaining. 'The fact is that trust appears to be an unmixed asset in [all] negotiations' (Walton and McKersie 1965: 358). There is little to commend a policy of distrust in any respect. The amount of 'internal control' influences how negotiators attempt to resolve intra-organisational bargaining within the bargaining organisation: the more the control, the more the chief negotiator is able to persuade the group to adopt his or her views. However, although control is important for purposive attitudinal structuring, it has advantages and disadvantages for the processes of both distributive and integrative bargaining.

BARGAINING POWER

Bargaining power is a central and important concept in collective bargaining. As Fox and Flanders (1969: 250) have commented: 'Power is the crucial variable determining the outcome [of collective bargaining]...[though] only when the group is able to mobilise sufficient power...does [employee relations] conflict become manifest.' Various theories have been proposed to explain bargaining power and its impact on negotiating outcomes.

One group of theories analyses how bargaining power is generated or created by the participants. The writers examining the 'causes' of bargaining power include Hoxie (1921), Pen (1952), Hicks (1932) and Dunlop (1950). Hoxie, for example, discussed the factors giving unions bargaining strength. Pen suggested a model of bargaining that incorporates the relative satisfactions of the parties in the bargaining process. He also considered how time brings about changes in the balance of power as economic conditions and public opinion shift. Hicks, an economist, saw wage bargaining power in terms of the levels of sacrifice made by the parties, to achieve specific advantage for themselves and those they represent. For Dunlop, bargaining power is determined primarily by the preferences of employers and workers, market conditions, negotiating skills and the ability to coerce the other party.

Atkinson (1980) argued that certain propositions can be derived from what these theorists have hypothesised about the generation of bargaining power:

- What creates bargaining power can be appraised in terms of subjective assessments by individuals involved in the bargaining process.
- Each side can guess the bargaining preferences and bargaining power of the other side.
- There are normally a number of elements creating bargaining power.
- The volatile elements in creating bargaining power may be positive or negative: positive elements provide inducements to adopt certain bargaining positions, while negative elements are the costs or disadvantages likely to be incurred by negotiators in not adopting certain bargaining positions.
- Bargaining power is dynamic and not static.

The second group of theories analysing bargaining power examines the consequences or the 'effects' of that power in bargaining relationships. Phelps Brown (1966: 331), for example, estimated the differences made by collective bargaining to wage movements and identified 'a positive association between those movements and collective bargaining'. Schelling (1963) suggested that bargaining power is, in the last analysis, the strength of the negotiator's position in the 'non-bluff' situation. Stevens (1963: 81) defined bargaining power as either 'power which is fully inherent in the original (pretactical play) pay-off matrix' or power which 'is (in part) tactically contrived by "moves" which rig the game'.

According to Atkinson (1980: 11), the propositions following from these analyses of the effects of bargaining power are as follows:

- The scarcer the resource in contention – and the greater the desire of the parties to possess it – the greater the importance of the strengths of the positions from which they make their demands.
- Bargaining power determines the position that can be adopted by each party after all bluff has failed.
- The credibility of a negotiating position depends on whether the other side perceives that power to be real and that it will be used in support of a bargaining commitment.
- It is not total bargaining power that is important in the negotiating process but the 'area of imbalance' between the two sides in the bargaining relationship.

Assessing bargaining power

A useful model for assessing bargaining power is provided by Atkinson. He has linked the definition of bargaining power provided by Chamberlain and Kuhn (1965: 170) with the bargaining model of Levinson (1966). Chamberlain and Kuhn defined bargaining power as the ability to secure another's agreement on one's own terms. A union's bargaining power, for example, is management's willingness to agree to the union's terms, with that willingness, in turn, depending 'on the cost of disagreeing with the union terms, relative to the cost of agreeing to them'. This definition assumes that negotiators adopt the course of action least likely to hurt them and the side they represent.

Your party's 'bargaining power', according to Atkinson, is indicated by the *disadvantages to your opponent of disagreeing with your proposal* relative to the *disadvantages to your opponent of agreeing with your proposal*. Conversely, their bargaining power is indicated by the *disadvantages to you of disagreeing with their proposal* relative to the *disadvantages to you of agreeing with their proposal*.

Both the disadvantages of disagreement and the disadvantages of agreement need to be examined in terms of the costs of the disadvantages to the party and the *likelihood* of the *costs*' being incurred. Atkinson has suggested that the costs for each element representing a disadvantage may be rated

231

from 1 (a very low cost) to 10 (a very high cost). Similarly, the likelihood of the cost's being incurred for each element may range from 0.1 (where the element has little chance of becoming a cost) to 1.0 (where the element is certain of becoming a cost).

Combining the costs and likelihoods for each element gives a total weighting for the disadvantages of disagreeing and of agreeing with a bargaining proposal. Where agreement with the proposal incurs more weighting (costs) than disagreement does, bargaining power rests with *the party to whom that proposal is made* (for that proposal alone). Where agreement with the proposal incurs *less* weighting (costs) than disagreement does, bargaining power rests with *the party making the proposal*.

Applying the bargaining power model: an example

A hypothetical example of how the above model can be used to assess bargaining power is shown in Figure 13. In this case, the model is being used to provide guidance to the management negotiators in determining their immediate response to the annual wage claim made by the unions representing the manual workers in their company. The basic question facing management is where bargaining power rests and why.

Consider a situation where the unions are claiming an across-the-board wage increase of 7 per cent and a shortening of the working week from 37.5 hours to 35 hours. The factors to be taken into account by management in making their response include: inflation is 4 per cent and falling; the going rate for local wage increases is 2–3 per cent; unemployment locally is low but rising; and demand for the company's products is rising. The unions have balloted, and received support, for a 'work to rule' if the wage claim is not satisfied.

Figure 13 **An illustrative use of the bargaining power model**

Disadvantages to management of disagreeing with the unions' claim			
Element	Cost	Likelihood	Total
work to rule	8	1.0	8.0
lost orders	8	0.9	7.2
some workers might leave the firm	7	0.4	2.8
			18.0
Disadvantages to management of agreeing with the unions' claim			
Element	Cost	Likelihood	Total
increased unit costs of production	10	1.0	10.0
settlement higher than 'going rate'	7	1.0	7.0
could set a precedent	8	0.5	4.0
			21.0

In this example, agreement by management with the unions' bargaining proposal is likely to incur more weighting (or costs) to management than disagreement, thus indicating that bargaining power rests with management for this proposal. In this case, however, the balance of power is relatively marginal. This illustrates both the strengths and weaknesses of this approach to assessing bargaining power. On the one hand, when individuals make such assessments:

- they are clearly subjective
- reassessments are necessary as bargaining proceeds, in the light of new information
- it is difficult to quantify 'bargaining power'.

On the other hand, this approach:

- identifies the elements contributing to bargaining power in different situations
- provides a basis for analysing a bargaining position
- helps formulate a bargaining strategy and prepare a case.

EMPLOYER PAY BARGAINING STRATEGY

In deciding to recognise trade unions for collective bargaining purposes, employers also have to determine a strategy regarding the bargaining level at which they negotiate with the union(s) (see Chapter 8). The most important aspect of collective bargaining from the managerial viewpoint is pay negotiations, since control and prediction of employment costs are major imperatives acting on both public- and private-sector employers (see Chapter 1). Post-recognition, a reassessment of bargaining levels may also be necessary. A number of strategic choices of bargaining levels is available: multi-employer, single-employer and workplace bargaining, or a combination of these levels (see Chapter 3 and below). The level or levels at which collective bargaining takes place, particularly on pay, is a vital management task and a crucial element of an employer's bargaining strategy. As Towers (1992: iii) has concluded, it has implications for the process of bargaining and the distribution of power between the parties. 'It affects the content of collective agreements and has important "knock-on" effects for the role and status of the personnel function and trade unions.' In addition to controlling employer labour costs, bargaining level can also be important for achieving national economic policy objectives.

Bargaining trends

Collective bargaining at multi-employer level has tended to be the most important one for pay determination in the public sector, for both manual and non-manual bargaining groups over the post-war period. A corresponding decline in multi-employer pay bargaining in the private sector is part of a long-term trend that can be traced back to the 1950s and is one that accelerated in the early 1980s (Confederation of British Industry 1988). The trend towards decentralised pay bargaining within private-sector organisations accelerated from the late 1970s. Indeed, a CBI survey in 1986 reported that nearly 90 per cent of all employees in establishments with collective bargaining had their basic pay negotiated at company or workplace level. However, the situation was complicated by the fact that some employers sought an optimum balance between centralised and decentralised bargaining arrangements (Kinnie 1987), whilst others retained central or corporate control within which local pay bargainers operated (Marginson 1986).

By 1990, single-employer pay bargaining was the major feature of private-sector services, for both manual and non-manual employees. Correspondingly, between 1984 and 1990, the importance of single-employer pay bargaining had declined in private manufacturing. This was accompanied by growth in importance of workplace pay bargaining for manual employees in private manufacturing between 1984 and 1990 and by the relatively high proportion of non-manual employees in this sector who were covered by workplace pay agreements in both 1984 and 1990 (Millward et al 1992). All this suggests that enormous diversity in the extent and patterns of recognition and levels of pay bargaining remain the norm among different parts of the private sector, but that the public sector continues to be characterised by much greater uniformity and homogeneity (Farnham and Horton 1996).

Table 8 indicates the main pay-bargaining levels for non-managerial employees by sector in 1998, including pay determination set by management unilaterally, either at workplace or higher levels. Indeed, 63 per cent of non-managerial employees in the private sector, but only 10 per cent in the public sector, had their pay determined by management alone and were not covered by any collective bargaining arrangements, and this represented just under half of all workplaces at that time. Interestingly too, 22 per cent of private-sector workplaces had a mixture of pay determination methods, as did 37 per cent of public-sector ones. By 1998, collective bargaining as the main method of pay determination in the private sector covered only 9 per cent of all non-managerial employees, compared with 33 per cent in the public sector. It was single-employer bargaining that was the most common pattern of collective bargaining for private-sector non-managerial employees, covering about 66 per cent of those employees whose pay remained collectively determined, compared with 22 per cent covered at multi-employer and 11 per cent at workplace levels. In the public sector, in contrast, single-employer bargaining covered only 33 per cent of all non-managerial employees whose pay was determined by collective bargaining, with 66 per cent of them being covered by multi-employer bargaining (Cully et al 1999).

Towers (1992) has highlighted a number of factors explaining the trend towards decentralised pay-bargaining levels, particularly in the private sector. These included:

Table 8 Main pay-bargaining levels for non-managerial employees in Britain by sector, 1998

	Private sector	Public sector	All workplaces
	% of workplaces	*% of workplaces*	*% of workplaces*
Method of pay determination			
Multi-employer level	2	22	7
Single-employer level	6	11	7
Workplace level	1	0	1
Set by management at higher level	32	9	25
Set by management at workplace level	31	1	23
Individual negotiation	3	0	3
Some other method	3	20	8
Mixture of methods	22	37	26
All workplaces	100	100	100

Source: Cully *et al* 1999

- trade union weakness
- corporate decentralisation preceding decentralised bargaining
- growth of performance-related pay
- pressures for employers to link worker productivity with appropriate pay increases.

Palmer (1990: 27) has suggested that the shift towards pay decentralisation has been heavily influenced by the need to recruit, motivate and retain employees of the right calibre to ensure business success. Employers also seem to want the freedom not only to determine pay rates and pay increases locally but also to introduce new pay strategies – including profit-sharing, merit pay, performance pay and pay bonuses – more suited to their own business strategies. 'For many organisations, pay policy has become a critical element of their strategic business planning.'

Multi-employer bargaining

Multi-employer bargaining, sometimes called industry-wide or national bargaining, is where minimum terms of employment are negotiated for all employers that are party to the 'national agreement'. Multi-employer bargaining normally requires the constituent employers to belong to the appropriate employers' association (see Chapter 2). The advantages and disadvantages to employers of multi-employer bargaining are outlined in Exhibits 16 and 17 below.

Exhibit 16 **Advantages of multi-employer bargaining**

Multi-employer bargaining:

- concentrates employer and union employee relations resources
- leaves local management to concentrate on other business issues
- provides equitable treatment of employees by all employers in the sector, covered by national bargaining
- prevents employers playing each other off in the wage-bargaining process.

Exhibit 17 **Disadvantages of multi-employer bargaining**

Multi-employer bargaining:

- reduces the ability of individual employers to negotiate according to local circumstances
- leads employers to pay something for nothing locally
- forces some employers to pay more than they can afford
- can lead to employees' expecting that national pay increases will be applied to local pay rates, irrespective of effort, whilst some employers will want to pay less than what is negotiated nationally
- ignores local labour markets, worker productivity and employee performance
- concentrates union bargaining power and negotiating skills.

Single-employer bargaining

Single-employer or company bargaining is where all pay and conditions are negotiated at employer level, in either single-site or multisite organisations. The advantages and disadvantages of single-employer bargaining to employers are outlined in Exhibits 18 and 19.

Exhibit 18 **Advantages of single-employer bargaining**

Single-employer bargaining:

- provides uniform terms and conditions across the company for similar jobs
- provides stable pay differentials amongst different bargaining groups within the company
- provides a common approach for handling grievances and resolving disputes in the company
- concentrates the bargaining power of management and the negotiating skills of management
- provides greater predictability of labour costs for management
- avoids wage 'leapfrogging' and minimises wage parity claims across the company.

Exhibit 19 **Disadvantages of single-employer bargaining**

Single-employer bargaining:

- is inflexible and makes it difficult to accommodate differences in production systems, product markets, labour markets and technologies within a centralised bargaining system
- raises the level of management decision-making, reducing local management and employee commitment to these decisions
- requires very effective in-company communications
- can lead to overformalisation of employee relations, be slow to respond to change and be too inflexible
- can be expensive because of the need to maintain a centralised employee relations system
- may make it difficult to integrate new businesses within the employee relations system.

Workplace bargaining

Workplace or plant bargaining is where terms and conditions are negotiated between management and union representatives locally, not at corporate level. Workplace bargaining is either autonomous or co-ordinated. Autonomous workplace bargaining is where each plant has the authority to settle all terms and conditions locally. Co-ordinated workplace bargaining is where negotiations are conducted at plant level within limits set by the centre. The advantages and disadvantages of workplace bargaining to employers are outlined in Exhibits 20 and 21.

Exhibit 20 **Advantages of workplace bargaining**

Workplace bargaining:

- provides shorter lines of communication and speeds the resolution of disputes
- increases the authority of local management by providing clear responsibility for employee relations
- increases management ability to respond flexibly to employee relations by introducing pay, conditions and incentives geared to local conditions
- increases the commitment of employees through locally determined agreements
- dissociates union bargaining power.

Exhibit 21 **Disadvantages of workplace bargaining**

Workplace bargaining:

- requires management planning and negotiating skills that may not exist at plant level
- increases the danger of claims for 'wages parity' by the unions
- requires total pay decentralisation, otherwise it is difficult to maintain differentials
- complicates labour cost control.

Multilevel bargaining

Multilevel bargaining is where some elements of the reward package are determined at one level whilst others are determined at another, lower level. In some cases, multi-employer agreements settle minimum pay rates or minimum earnings nationally and company agreements supplement them by providing the means for determining actual earnings, including pay flexibility, at employer level. In this way, employers combine the stability of framework agreements at industry level with maximum flexibility for individual employers, who are party to national agreements, at corporate level. Such arrangements are claimed to stabilise wage costs at industry level, while remaining sensitive to variations in regional and local labour markets.

In other cases, multilevel bargaining takes place within single-employer bargaining arrangements. Here basic conditions of employment can be settled at corporate centre, with pay – especially performance pay – being determined at workplace or plant level. This enables employers to obtain the best of two worlds. Even where decentralised bargaining takes place, co-ordination at corporate level may be retained through 'the budgetary control mechanism, where labour cost targets are often specified in line with broader targets or rates of return on sales and capital employed' (Purcell 1987: 55).

Factors affecting bargaining levels

Determining the appropriate bargaining level is a complex task for employers and management, especially those with multi-plant operations and complex business structures. An old study by the Advisory, Conciliation and Arbitration Service (ACAS 1983) suggested that certain structural and organisational factors were key determinants of an organisation's collective bargaining structure, especially bargaining levels. These factors included: the firm's product market; its forms of work organisation; the technology used; its geographic location; its business structure; the union structure; and the payment system.

An analysis by Palmer (1990), which sought to help employers identify the type of bargaining structure best suited to their own needs, examined the internal factors, external factors and bargaining topics likely to affect an employer's decision in determining the optimum bargaining level. The internal factors included:

- company organisation (such as decision-making levels, degrees of diversity and plans for expansion)
- management style and management strengths
- plant characteristics (such as size, technology and degrees of interdependence)
- job categories and relationships (such as wage policy, payment systems and bargaining reference groups).

The external factors were:

- union organisation (such as representation, power and membership levels)
- industry structure (such as market competition, national collective agreements and trading relationships).

The bargaining topics likely to affect decisions on bargaining levels included: the terms and conditions that were negotiable; the procedural agreements that existed; and whether arbitration was used for resolving disputes between the employer and the unions.

General indicators of multi-employer bargaining being preferred by employers are industries having: a large number of small companies; competitive product markets; high levels of trade union membership; high labour costs relative to other costs; and geographical concentration of the sector. Single-employer bargaining is likely in companies with: single-product businesses; stable product markets; a centralised corporate structure; and strong trade union organisation. Workplace bargaining is likely in companies with: multiproduct businesses; unstable product markets; multidivisional structures; and weak trade union organisation locally.

THE NEGOTIATING PROCESS

John Dunlop, a major theoretician of employee relations and an outstanding mediator, has argued that there have been two main approved institutional arrangements for resolving conflicts of interest among groups and organisations in Western societies for over 200 years. These are 'the give and take of the market place and government regulatory mechanisms established by the political process' (Dunlop 1984: 3). He sees negotiating as a positive, alternative mode of conflict resolution between competing groups, such as employers and unions, which has made inroads into both the market and governmental distributive processes. Negotiating provides benefits to both sides, involves compromise, avoids uncertainty and is flexible in its approach. Moreover, even if collective bargaining does not entirely displace market forces, he has argued, the differences between negotiators in 'pure bargaining skills and power' may 'result in somewhat different terms and conditions of employment over time than would arise through markets or under governmental dictation' (*ibid*: 6).

Based on his own experiences and research, Dunlop has provided a 10-point basic framework for analysing the negotiating process:

- it takes agreement within each negotiating group to reach a settlement between them
- initial proposals are typically large, compared with eventual settlements
- both sides need to make concessions in order to move towards agreement

239

- a deadline is an essential feature of most negotiating
- the end stages of negotiating are particularly delicate, with private discussions often being used to close the gap between the parties
- negotiating is influenced by whether it involves the final, intermediate or first stages of the conflict-resolution process
- negotiating and overt conflict may take place simultaneously, with the conflict serving as a tool for getting agreement
- getting agreement does not flourish in public
- negotiated settlements need procedures to administer or interpret final agreement
- personalities and their interactions affect negotiating outcomes.

An overview

The purpose of employee relations negotiations is to resolve any conflicts of interest or conflicts of right between employers and trade unions, through both sides modifying their original demands to achieve mutually acceptable compromises between them. The issues may relate to terms and conditions of employment, non-wage matters or combinations of these. A number of stages are discernible in the negotiating process: objective-setting; preparing; bargaining; and implementing.

Objective-setting

To enable movement to take place between the bargaining parties in the negotiating process, each side has to establish a realistic spectrum or set of bargaining objectives. As shown in Figure 14, these consist of an 'ideal settlement point' (ISP), a 'realistic settlement point' (RSP) and a 'fall-back point' (FBP). The ISP is what the negotiators would ideally *like to achieve* through negotiation, if possible. The RSP is what they *intend to achieve*, while the FBP is what they *must achieve* at the very minimum, and without which no settlement can result. The bargaining range of each side lies between its ISP and its FBP, with final settlement taking place between each of the parties' FBPs. Where the FBPs of the two sides do not overlap, there is a 'bargaining gap' and, unless there is a modification of their bargaining objectives, no negotiated compromise is possible.

Figure 14 **Hypothetical wage-bargaining objectives for management and unions**

Management side	ISP *		RSP *		FBP *				
	3	4 *	5	6 *	7	8 *	9	per cent wage rise	
Union side		FBP		RSP		ISP			

Preparing

Identifying, collecting and deciding how to use relevant information across the bargaining table are key elements in preparing for negotiating. Information relates to a number of areas, including: facts, precedents, personalities, power and issues. Decisions have to be taken by the bargaining teams about what information is to be disclosed to the other side, when it is to be disclosed and what is to be withheld. In this sense, 'knowledge' or information is power and it can provide a cutting edge in the negotiating process if used tactically and authoritatively by either or both sides. Information is normally provided to support and justify the propositions made by each party, as well as to challenge each other's propositions. Bargaining conventions dictate that initial negotiating propositions focus on each party's ISP, with neither side revealing its full strength initially.

Preparing also involves each team deciding who is to be lead negotiator, who is to take records at the meetings and who is to observe. The leader's role is to conduct the negotiation for the bargaining team. The leader does most of the talking, makes proposals, trades concessions and calls adjournments. Recorders take notes, ask questions, summarise situations and generally keep negotiations on track, especially when the going gets tough. Recorders support the lead negotiator but never 'take over' the main negotiating role. Observers 'read' negotiations. They do not normally say much but analyse the negotiations, pick up the subtleties and moods of the participants and provide inputs of new information and ideas during adjournments, as appropriate.

Bargaining

Bargaining involves a number of phases, which are described in detail below. Atkinson (1980) has identified four phases: clarifying the other side's position; structuring the expectations of the other side; getting movement; and closure. Kennedy and his colleagues (1984) have proposed three similar phases to Atkinson, once the parties have determined their bargaining objectives: 'arguing'; 'proposing'; and 'exchanging and agreeing'. They have also identified three sub-phases. These are: 'signalling' within the arguing phase; 'packaging' within the proposing phase; and 'closing' within the exchanging and agreeing phase. What differentiates each phase from the other is the skills and activities appropriate to them. However these phases are defined and delineated, they provide a 'negotiating landscape' within which negotiators direct their resources, skills and knowledge, structure their behaviour and act out their roles, according to the situations facing them.

Implementing

This is the process by which both parties are responsible for carrying out the decisions and outcomes jointly determined by the parties. Final decisions need to be recorded, put in writing and signed by both sides. This avoids further conflict over interpreting what has actually been agreed between the negotiators.

Arguing

In this initial phase of bargaining, each side makes its opening statements and the arguments underpinning them. Both parties normally reveal only their ISPs and are reluctant to concede anything to the other side in terms of information or clues to their real negotiating objectives. The underlying aim of the negotiators is to justify the positions of their own sides, maximise the information obtained about the other side's RSP and reveal the minimum information about their own. There is intense listening on both sides, questioning for clarification and challenging the other side to justify its negotiating stance. Each side remains non-committal about the other party's proposals, while testing its commitment to its case. There is mutual seeking of information but little exchanging takes place at this phase. This is because arguments cannot be negotiated; they only set the contexts and parameters of each side's opening positions.

The process of 'signalling', identified by Kennedy and his colleagues (1984: 62), is where qualifications are 'placed on a statement of a position'. The initial statements of the parties are absolute ones. For example, 'We'll never agree to that'; 'Your offer is totally unacceptable to our members'; or 'Your proposal is nonsense.' Signalling provides the parties with the opportunity to move towards each other in the early stages of negotiation, after the initial stonewalling responses of both sides. Examples of signalling by one of the parties could be: 'Well, we could discuss that point' (meaning that it is negotiable). Or, 'We would find it very difficult to agree to that' (meaning that it is not impossible to do so). Skilled negotiators reward signalling behaviour where possible. It moves the parties away from their opening gambits and creates possibilities for concessions later. To be productive, signalling needs to be reciprocated. It is important to reward signals, not obstinacy. This is done by responding positively to the other side with phrases such as: 'We're always prepared to consider reasonable proposals.'

Proposing

A proposition in the negotiating process is an offer, or a claim, made by one of the parties to the other, moving it away from its original position. Initial proposals tend to be tentative and non-committal. They aim at reassuring the other party and at marking out the parameters within which exchanges can take place between them and agreement can be reached. Proposals become more specific as negotiations proceed, thus providing a means for moving towards real bargaining or concrete exchanges between the parties later. Propositions are conditional, never absolute. They are stated in the following way: 'If you are prepared to do "A", then we will consider doing "B".' Generally, negotiators open with unrealistic proposals and move only slowly towards each other. Choosing the opening position therefore is crucial.

242

Propositions are normally firm on generalities, such as: 'We are determined to settle this issue quickly.' But they are flexible on specifics, such as: 'We propose an offer of X.' The party receiving a proposal needs to listen to it carefully and not reject it out of hand, so that it can respond and provide a counter-proposal. Opening conditions are normally large, whilst opening concessions are normally small. However, since negotiators learn their craft through experience, and about each other through observation, these influence the ways in which they structure their proposals, respond to initiatives and act out their negotiating roles.

'Packaging' is the term used by Kennedy and his colleagues to describe the bridging that is made between the opening movements of the parties and their shifting into final agreement. 'It is, effectively, the activity which draws up the agenda for the bargaining session' (Kennedy *et al* 1984: 89). Packaging aims to facilitate convergence between the parties, from where they are, after the arguing and proposing phases have taken place, to where they can finally agree a settlement. This entails:

- identifying the other party's reservations about coming to an agreement, its negotiating objectives and its bargaining priorities
- considering its possible 'signalled' concessions
- each side's reviewing its own negotiating objectives, bearing in mind its ISP, RSP and FBP, and those of the other side.

This enables each side to determine whether there is enough movement between them to produce a package and how it can modify it or adapt it to meet some of the other side's reservations.

Each side has to consider:

- the concessions it wants
- the room it has for manoeuvre
- the concessions it is prepared to signal in the package
- what it wants in return.

So doing enables each party to tell the other what package is on offer, thus providing a negotiating platform, including readiness to trade concessions, which prepares the ground for exchanges between them. These exchanges of concessions follow the general rule of not giving anything away without getting something back in return. The pattern is: 'If you move on that issue, then we will move on this one.' In trading concessions, each party needs to value them in terms of their perceived value to the other party. This means evaluating the worth of a concession to the other party, its cost to your side and what is wanted in exchange for it.

Exchanging and agreeing

This is the most crucial phase of the bargaining process. Unless the parties are able to make final exchanges and concessions between them, bargaining reaches an impasse and a failure to agree is recorded. The key to reaching a successful agreement is for each party to come up with positive propositions, which remain linked but are conditional on movement by the other side. The sorts of statements made by the parties are: 'If your side agrees to A, then we will agree to B.' By continuing to put conditions on what they are prepared to exchange, negotiators ensure that they do not concede anything without getting something back in return.

Linking all the issues ensures that both sides list every item in the package, which means that when either party raises an issue, it can be dealt with in the context of the package as a whole. This provides the negotiators with some degree of flexibility and leverage. They also have the opportunity to link each concession to corresponding concessions on other items, as they move towards final agreement. All the items are negotiated conditionally upon the package as a whole being agreed. Keeping items linked makes them available for trading and exchange, as bargaining proceeds to its concluding stages. The more items there are to exchange, the stronger the bargaining positions of the negotiators. The process of linking facilitates moves on one issue with trade-offs for something else. In this way, single items in the negotiating package are not picked off in a piecemeal way. And negotiators are provided with more room for manoeuvre, provided that the linking amongst the items is realistic.

Closing a negotiation requires judgement. If the parties are unable to close their bargaining activity, their continued negotiating can result in further concessions that collectively may be costly to each side. One way of closing is for one side to make a 'final' concession to the other, preferably on a minor issue. A second way is by summarising what has been agreed to date, stressing the concessions that have been made and emphasising the benefits of agreeing to what is on offer. A third way is through an adjournment. This enables the other side to have time to consider what is on 'final' offer. Fourth, one side can present the other with an ultimatum. This states, in effect, that unless what is on offer is accepted, a failure to agree will result. Finally, the choice of alternatives may be given to the other side. This enables it to consider which alternative is preferable, while not changing what is actually on offer.

Once final agreement has been reached, it must be listed in detail and recorded in writing. Both sides must be absolutely clear what has been agreed, with all relevant points being listed, clarified and explained as necessary. Where there is any disagreement on any item, negotiations must continue until agreement is reached. In short, what has been agreed has to be clearly summarised, accurately recorded and finally signed by both parties.

COLLECTIVE AGREEMENTS

Collective agreements are the outcome of collective bargaining between employer and union representatives. Being bilateral employment rules, they differ from company rules and employer policy statements, which are unilateral in origin. The collective nature of these rules is also reflected in the fact that the terms and conditions of employment, and employee relations procedures, incorporated in collective agreements, apply to groups of workers covered by them. Substantive agreements cover any kind of payments and a wide range of working conditions. Procedural agreements spell out the steps by which employee relations processes are to be carried out. These include: machinery for negotiation, consultation and arbitration; negotiating, handling grievances and resolving disputes; discipline and dismissal; and facilities for trade union representatives.

Good practice suggests that formal, written collective agreements are the norm in employee relations. Over-formality is not conducive to good employee relations, but employers and unions prefer written agreements for a number of reasons:

- They focus attention on problem areas and lead to joint policies bringing about agreed solutions.
- Written agreements create order in employee relations and facilitate change. They overcome, for example, the problems involved where either management or union negotiators move on for one reason or another.
- They provide continuity in employee relations, enabling decisions to be determined in the light of past practice, precedent and accepted norms.

In some cases, management drafts agreements, with the final details being considered and agreed by the parties jointly. In other cases, unions take the initiative and management responds to what is proposed. In other cases, the development of agreements is best handled by a joint working party.

The legal status of collective agreements

A collective agreement is defined in law as any agreement or arrangement made by or on behalf of one or more trade unions and one or more employers or employers' associations, relating to one or more of the matters listed in the Trade Union and Labour Relations (Consolidation) Act 1992 (TULRCA 1992). These are (section 178):

(a) terms and conditions of employment, or the physical conditions in which any workers are required to work;
(b) engagement or non-engagement, or termination or suspension of employment or the duties of employment, of one or more workers;
(c) allocation of work or the duties of employment between workers or groups of workers;
(d) matters of discipline;
(e) a worker's membership or non-membership of a trade union;
(f) facilities for officials of trade unions; and
(g) machinery for negotiation or consultation, and other procedures, relating to any of the above matters, including the recognition by employers or employers' associations of the right of a trade union to represent workers in such negotiation or consultation or in the carrying out of such procedures.

The distinctive feature of British collective agreements is that they are not legally enforceable between the employers and unions negotiating them. As the TULRCA 1992 states (section 179): 'a collective agreement shall be conclusively presumed not to be a legally enforceable contract', unless it is in writing and contains a provision stating that it is intended to be enforceable. Unlike in many other countries, collective agreements in Britain do not have a 'contractual function' between the parties making them, they are 'binding in honour' only. But they do have a 'normative function'. This means that the terms, conditions and rules determined by them become incorporated into individual contracts of employment, expressly or sometimes by implication.

The non-enforceability of collective agreements was underlined by *Ford Motor Company* v. *AUEF and TGWU* [1969]. The company brought a legal action alleging breach of contract against the unions, on the grounds that they had supported their members' strike action in breach of agreed collective bargaining procedures. The High Court decided that the unions were not liable because their collective agreements with the employer were not intended to be legally enforceable contracts. The Court argued that, as experienced negotiators, management and unions had no intention of creating legal enforceability, so there was no contract between them – only 'an unenforceable gentleman's agreement'. This judgement was not taken to appeal, and although the Industrial Relations Act 1971 presumed all collective agreements to be legally binding unless the parties declared them otherwise, almost every collective agreement between 1971 and 1974 contained a clause stating that 'this is not a legally enforceable agreement' (Weekes *et al* 1975).

The customary way of securing the normative function of collective agreements is to incorporate their provisions into the individual contracts of employment of each worker. Whilst in some countries collective agreements have an automatic effect upon employment contracts, in Britain they do not. The best way for the employment contract to incorporate the collective terms relating to pay, conditions and benefits is to incorporate them expressly. The most useful vehicle for doing this is the written statement of particulars given to employees after starting their employment. A problem with trying to incorporate the terms of a collective agreement as implied terms is that the normal rules of contract law determine that nothing can be implied into a contract affecting any matter covered by an express term. Thus individual contracts of employment cannot be overridden by collective agreements.

Incorporation of procedural clauses of collective agreements into individual contracts is less clear-cut and more problematic. Procedures dealing with individual employee rights, such as those relating to grievances and disciplinary matters, provide little problem. For example, the Employment Rights Act 1996 requires employers to set out matters relating to discipline and grievances in the note accompanying a worker's written particulars in a way that envisages these procedures being incorporated into individual contracts of employment. There is more doubt about procedures concerned with workers' collective action, such as no-strike clauses, restrictions on industrial action until the procedure to avoid disputes is exhausted or other collective procedures.

One problem with these procedures is that they sometimes involve questions of policy. In the case of *British Leyland* v. *McQuilken* [1978], for example, the employer had made an agreement with the union that, in closing down a department, all employees would be interviewed for retraining or redundancy. McQuilken was not interviewed because management changed its policy, but he was told he could transfer to another place or be retrained. He claimed a redundancy payment and went to an employment tribunal. The tribunal declared the refusal to implement the agreement to be constructive dismissal. On appeal, the Employment Appeal Tribunal (EAT) rejected this on the grounds that the terms of the agreement between the employer and the union did not alter McQuilken's individual contract of employment. 'That agreement was a long-term plan, dealing with policy rather than with the rights of individual employees.'

Types of collective agreement

There are a variety of types of collective agreements, since collective bargaining is an infinitely flexible process of employee relations and the format of collective agreements reflects this. So far, earlier discussions have focused primarily on what may be described as standard approaches to the content of substantive and procedural agreement (see Chapter 3). This section is more penetrating in its approach and focuses on some of the newer, less common forms of collective agreement, such as 'partnership agreements', 'new-style agreements', 'technology agreements', 'flexibility agreements' and 'workforce agreements'.

Partnership agreements

Partnership collective agreements between employers and trade unions are often negotiated in reaction to crisis or radical changes facing the parties to employee relations, such as competitive pressures and economic uncertainty facing firms. The central focus of partnership at work is unity of purpose between the parties, and partnership agreements normally incorporate common approaches to problem-solving and working together at company and workplace levels. Though there is no model template of partnership agreements, they tend to emphasise elements such as:

- co-operation between management and union(s) as an obligation within the partnership arrangements
- establishment of single status for all employees
- development of mutually acceptable pay review formulae.

The mutuality and co-operation expected between management and union(s) in partnership agreements is normally set out in the general principles of their procedural arrangements. A good example of this was provided in an early partnership agreement negotiated between Welsh Water and its 'Signatory Unions' (1991: 15). This stated that both the company and the recognised unions agreed that it was in the best interests of employees and the company to maintain constructive and co-operative relationships at all times. The principles underpinning this agreement were:

- Promoting openness on problems and issues of mutual concern.
- Valuing good communications both to employees and trade unions.
- Consulting and involving employees and their representatives at an early stage of formulating proposals for change.
- Ensuring that the focal point of dealing with employee issues is as near to the workplace as possible, and that any problems are resolved wherever possible through informal discussion at the lowest possible organisational level.
- Conducting formal consultation and negotiations on a joint basis covering all employees, wherever it is practical and relevant to do so.
- Devoting formal consultative meetings to matters of concern and relevance to all employees and the business.

The institutional arrangement for facilitating the partnership approach to employee relations and partnership agreements is often a company council. This is a representative body consisting of employer and union representatives, which has a number of functions. These normally include: acting as a negotiating forum; acting as a consultative forum; establishing subcommittees and working parties; facilitating the resolution of grievances and disputes; and promoting the agreed principles of employee relations between the employer and the union(s).

Single status for all employees in partnership agreements is commonly rooted in three main principles:

- employees should all have good terms and conditions of employment, since all of them contribute to customer or client satisfaction
- change is best introduced through discussion and agreement with all those involved
- additional costs, because of single status, can be offset by improved customer provision.

Single status typically incorporates the following sorts of procedural and substantive provisions within partnership agreements: single-table negotiating and consultative arrangements; standard working hours; monthly pay; an integrated pay structure; expectations about productivity improvements and job flexibility; and job security arrangements, sometimes including a 'no compulsory redundancy' agreement.

Pay review formulae in partnership agreements can incorporate a number of elements. These include changes in the retail price index, the employer's position in relevant pay markets and the employer's financial and operational performance. They can also provide a profit-related pay element in the pay package. The main features of pay review formulae are that they are open, rational and mutually agreed in advance by the employer and union(s), normally for an agreed period. This enables all parties – including employees – to understand the principles and standards upon which pay is based.

Union commitment to partnership at work was reflected in a successful motion, proposed by USDAW, a strong advocate of partnership at work, at the TUC's annual congress in 1999. It concluded by saying (Trades Union Congress 1999: 8):

> Congress, therefore, urges the General Council to continue to stress to Government that improved competitiveness and real partnership are best delivered through independent trade union recognition and organisation; to do everything possible to ensure that any and all funding made available for the training of employee representatives in the principles and practices of part-nership is dedicated to the training of independent trade union representatives; and to ensure that availability of funding and training for partnership is widely publicised and promoted amongst affiliates.

New-style agreements

New-style agreements (NSAs) contain a number of procedural elements distinguishing them from standardised, more traditional procedural arrangements, but they also have some common features with partnership and flexibility agreements. As Burrows (1986) indicates, a major feature of NSAs is that their negotiating and disputes procedures are based on the mutually accepted 'rights' of the parties, expressed in the recognition agree-ment. The intention is to resolve any differences of interest on substantive issues between the parties by negotiation, with pendulum arbitration pro-viding a resolution of these issues where differences persist. Exhibit 22 sets out the main features of NSAs.

Exhibit 22 **Main features of new-style collective agreements**

SINGLE-UNION RECOGNITION

- only one bargaining agent
- 'open' shop
- other unrecognised unions with members

SINGLE STATUS

- harmonisation of terms and conditions
- annual salaries
- one canteen for all staff
- no reserved car parking
- first names used in the company
- identical uniforms

LABOUR FLEXIBILITY

- few job gradings
- no job descriptions
- pay geared to skills
- employment security
- training and retraining

COMPANY COUNCILS

- negotiating and consultative forum
- advice, information and consultation
- employee representatives
- discussion of business plans, investment and efficiency

NO-STRIKE OR PEACE CLAUSES

- interest issues resolved without recourse to industrial action
- reflecting of complementary relationship between the parties
- not legally enforceable: binding in honour only

PENDULUM (FINAL OFFER) ARBITRATION

- conciliation on interest issues
- arbitrator to select 'final offer' of either party
- no compromise solution
- decision of arbitrator final

NSAs aim to reinforce harmony of interests between company, signatory union and its employees. Employees are not required to join the union but are encouraged to do so. NSAs frequently stress the need for quality, teamwork and flexibility in the work process, for avoiding unnecessary industrial action that disrupts production and for open and direct communications between the company and its employees. Only one union is recognised for the purposes of negotiation, consultation and information-giving to staff. All of these processes are normally carried on within a 'company council' consisting of management and employee representatives. Employee representatives are elected by a secret ballot of the entire workforce, with the balloting process being supervised by the local full-time union officer. Company and union often provide joint training for representatives to enable them to carry out their duties satisfactorily and effectively.

The negotiating procedure for determining new substantive issues within NSAs normally incorporates two underlying principles. The first is that during negotiations – and during conciliation and arbitration – there is to be no recourse to industrial action. Second, management and the union often affirm their commitment to resolving issues within the company, but where there are any remaining differences between them, if they fail to agree, these are resolved through binding conciliation or arbitration. Arbitrators are required to make a decision, based on the 'final offer' of one or other of the sides. There is no 'split' decision. Pendulum arbitration of this sort, it is argued, not only encourages realistic bargaining positions by each party but also provides a means of peacefully resolving persisting disputes of interest between the company and its workforce.

Individual grievances and collective issues of 'rights', in contrast, are resolved through the grievance procedure and procedure to avoid disputes respectively. The latter states that there is to be no industrial action while the issue is in procedure. Where such matters are not resolved in-house, they may be referred to ACAS or another third party who may conciliate or arbitrate, with the terms of reference being agreed by the parties, within the time limits set for determining the issue.

Procedures also exist for ensuring the fullest use of human resources and labour flexibility in the single-union company. These include agreed changes in working practices likely to affect productivity and staffing levels, and can involve the use of appropriate industrial engineering and human resource planning techniques. Finally, to ensure labour flexibility and organisational change, provisions are made for training and retraining the workforce for future human resources requirements.

Technology agreements

Technological change is endemic to the work process (see Chapter 5). Since the 1980s especially, microelectronics and related information technologies have been continuously applied to a range of industries, occupations and sectors, with non-manual employment being particularly affected by these changes. Although research shows that it is common for these changes to be imposed unilaterally by management, largely without consultation with staff (Daniel 1987), in some cases attempts have been made to negotiate the introduction of 'new technology' and new working methods between management and unions. This is done to facilitate the introduction of new equipment, train people in using it and reduce the anxieties associated with change, thus providing benefits to the employer and to employees in conditions of uncertainty. Such agreements are sometimes referred to as 'technology agreements'.

A number of negotiating issues arise with the introduction of new technology, each of which has procedural and substantive implications for employee relations. The negotiating issues include: job contraction; job content; job control; and health and safety at work (Winterton and Winterton 1985). Job contraction is synonymous with new technology, and potential job losses account for many of the fears felt amongst employees when new technology is being introduced into organisations. Job content, too, can be adversely affected by either de-skilling the work of employees or dehumanising it, as a result of technological change. The impact of new technology on individual job control is twofold. First, it can result in workers having less discretion in the ways in which their jobs are performed. Second, where technology creates less-skilled work, job control shifts from workers to management, since these operations are easier for management to direct. Also, although new technology reduces some physical hazards at work, it also has potentially damaging effects where it results in irregular shift work, social isolation or physical strain, such as repetitive strain injury.

The procedural issues arising from the introduction of new technology include its impact on: existing procedures and bargaining arrangements; employee training; and the monitoring and operation of new technology. Existing procedures likely to be affected by technological innovation are: union recognition; grievances and disputes; discipline; redeployment and redundancy; and the level at which collective bargaining takes place. This is because technological innovation impacts on employee relations locally. Employee training is an important aspect of introducing new technology, and procedures need to be determined regarding both the job training needs of employees and the employee relations training needs of union representatives. Two main procedural mechanisms are used to monitor new technology: either joint management–union study teams or outside consultants.

The substantive issues arising from the introduction of new technology arrangements cover a number of matters. These include: how the savings generated from productivity increases are to be shared between management and workers; how any job losses are to be managed; the impact of changes on terms and conditions of employment; and their impact on health and safety. The benefits of increased productivity can be shared in a number of ways, including higher wages, shorter working periods, early retirement and additional leave. Where job losses result, they can be achieved by a variety of means. These include natural wastage, redeployment, voluntary redundancy or compulsory redundancy, with the relevant terms being negotiated and agreed between management and unions.

Procedural provisions may need to be made to improve the quality of working life after the introduction of new technology. These can take the form of additional breaks, job rotation, job enrichment and job redesign. The problems associated with the health and safety hazards connected with new technology need to be addressed. Such provisions can cover such matters as eye strain, shift working, the implications of robotics and any psychological hazards arising from the work environment. Introducing new technology can also affect equality of opportunity at work in matters such as job grading, promotion, patterns of work and job retraining. Procedural adjustments need to be made here too.

Flexibility agreements

Collective agreements aimed at changing entrenched working practices – and removing job demarcations – by introducing labour flexibility in firms have been a common feature of employee relations since the 1980s. In its assessment of the scope and nature of some early flexibility agreements, Industrial Relations Review and Report (1992a, 1992b) concluded that there were limits to the usefulness of such agreements in introducing flexible working practices. While the companies investigated no longer faced 'who does what' disputes, the research questioned the extent to which total interchangeability of labour was desirable. Further, in technologically sophisticated environments, in particular, it appeared to be uneconomic to train the whole workforce in complex skills, which are used by only small numbers of employees.

Of the four organisations examined at that time, two – Mobil Coryton and Babcock Energy – changed working practices at times of financial difficulty. The other two – Toshiba Consumer Products and the Co-operative Wholesale Society (CWS) at Deeside – introduced new working practices on greenfield sites but also against a background of economic difficulties. These studies focused on six aspects of flexibility deals: flexibility developments; flexibility and labour-force size and composition; the extent to which flexibility had progressed; training needs and their implications; the collective bargaining effects; and the impact of flexibility on corporate performance.

The flexibility agreements at Toshiba and Mobil established the principle of a total end to demarcation so that these companies did not feel a need for any substantial changes in working practices subsequently. In the CWS, broad flexibility measures were expanded to a single group of employees who combined both production and maintenance skills. At Babcock, the initial flexibility agreement listed specific changes in required working practices. This was followed by a later agreement on broad flexibility, with further changes focusing on individual issues.

The flexibility deals at Mobil and Babcock contributed to labour-force reductions, with substantial hiving-off of some job activities to subcontractors. Toshiba, in contrast – being a greenfield site operation – did not use much contract labour but, in adapting to product market fluctuations, varied its use of temporary staff to maintain the stability of its permanent workforce.

At Babcock, the principle was established that multiskilled craftworkers would not have the specialist skills required in a complex industry. Its agreement was based on the need to train workers in 'secondary' skills. At Mobil and Toshiba, the flexibility agreements were based on the principle of multiskilling, so reducing the risks of demarcation disputes. In practice, however, some employee specialisation was essential, especially in conditions of technological sophistication. In these companies, production-maintenance flexibility was limited to production workers doing minor maintenance on the plant for which they were responsible. Flexibility seemed to have progressed furthest at the CWS, but even here it was not economic to provide all employees with the full range of skills required within the workplace. In general, it seems that these flexibility deals increased the breadth of workforce skills, but not their depth.

In all four companies, it appeared that flexibility provisions meant that new workers required certain skills training. Both Babcock and Toshiba operated their own apprenticeship schemes, while Mobil had wound its scheme down. This enabled Mobil to direct some of its resources at a skill-training centre in a local town. It also provided opportunity for the work-forces of its subcontractors to become adequately skilled.

At both Toshiba and the CWS, the employee relations structures remained as they had been. Toshiba had one of the earliest single-union agreements and the CWS combined its consultative and collective bargaining machinery. Babcock did not consider that introducing labour flexibility had a great effect on union influence. However, because of contracting out and union mergers, a smaller number of unions was recognised than had been the case some 10 years earlier. At Mobil, on the other hand, culture change was seen as laying the groundwork for targeting employee relations practices at individual employees and their performance. This, it was envisaged, might lead to a change in the role of trade unions in the future.

In terms of the impact of labour flexibility on corporate performance, all four case studies found it difficult to separate the effects of introducing labour flexibility from those of other company innovations. All the companies felt that labour flexibility had contributed to organisational well-being, especially in producing acceptable labour productivity levels. Mobil and the CWS added that an employee relations climate free of demarcation disputes was a direct result of changed working practices.

Workforce agreements

Under the Working Time Regulations 1998 and the Parental Leave Regulations 1999, it is possible for 'relevant' agreements to be reached, enabling employers to agree variations in the regulations directly with their employees or their representatives. Thus where there are no collective agreements, employers can negotiate workforce agreements with employee representatives modifying the regulations, to take account of the specific needs of local working arrangements. In other words, workforce agreements allow employers and employees to agree on how to use the flexibilities permitted in implementing the regulations locally. A workforce agreement exists where:

- it is in writing
- it is for a specified period, not exceeding five years
- it applies to all relevant members of the workforce
- it is signed by representatives of the group.

JOINT CONSULTATION

Joint consultation is a diverse process with a long history that can be traced back at least to the recommendations of the Whitley Committee in 1917–18. Its influence as an employee relations process has fluctuated widely over time, however. The pattern has been: decline in the inter-war years; resurgence during World War II; decline again during the 1950s and 1960s; further resurgence in the 1970s and early 1980s; renewed decline in the late 1980s and early 1990s; and stability since then (Millward and Stevens 1986, Millward *et al* 1992, Cully *et al* 1999).

The WERS 1998 identified four types of joint consultative committee (JCC): workplace committees; workplace and higher-level committees; higher-level committees; and European works councils (EWCs). The survey reported that in 1998 just over half of workplaces in Britain had a JCC operating at one or more of these levels. Incidence of these committees conformed to 'some well-observed patterns', which were: number of workers at workplace and corporate level; workplace employment size; organisation employment size; and trade union presence at the workplace (Cully *et al* 1999: 98). There were also variations in the incidence of JCCs by industry and employment sector, as illustrated in Table 9.

Table 10 shows the presence of workplace JCCs in Britain by sector and union recognition from 1980 to 1998, derived from the WERS 1998. This

Table 9 Joint consultative committees in Britain by sector, organisational status and industry, 1998

	No committee	Workplace committee only	Workplace and higher-level committee	Higher-level committee only
	% of workplaces	*% of workplaces*	*% of workplaces*	*% of workplaces*
All workplaces	47	17	11	25
Private sector	57	16	8	18
Public sector	18	20	19	42
Organisational status				
Stand-alone	78	22	–	–
Part of wider organisation	35	16	15	34
Industry				
Manufacturing	64	25	4	7
Electricity, gas, water	3	15	46	36
Construction	73	11	6	10
Wholesale and retail	48	8	15	28
Hotels and restaurants	54	11	12	33
Transport and communications	34	17	17	33
Financial services	37	6	8	49
Other business services	61	18	4	16
Public administration	11	18	39	31
Education	25	29	11	34
Health	45	11	8	36
Other community services	49	26	5	20

Source: Cully *et al* 1999

showed that there had been no further fall in workplace joint consultation between 1990 and 1998. However, though workplace JCCs became less common in the public sector, falling from 49 per cent in 1990 to 39 per cent in 1998, they became more common in the private sector, rising from 20 per cent to 25 per cent during these years. According to the researchers, 'this slight resurgence in the private sector, following the steady decline in the 1980s, was confined to small and medium-sized workplaces and was more apparent where unions were recognised than where they were not' (Cully *et al* 1999: 244).

Factors influencing the development of joint consultation

Marchington (1989) identified four main factors influencing the development of joint consultative machinery within organisations. These were:

* management philosophy
* union organisation and worker resistance
* trust and co-operative relations
* the external environment.

According to Marchington, it is management that initiates most joint consultative arrangements, therefore the model of consultation that is adopted within an organisation reflects the management's dominant employee relations philosophy and its basic intentions in managing people. The four models of joint consultation identified by Marchington were:

* the non-union model
* the marginal model
* the competitive model
* the adjunct model.

Table 10 Workplace joint consultative committees in Britain by sector and union recognition, 1980–98

	1980	1984	1990	1998
	% of workplaces	*% of workplaces*	*% of workplaces*	*% of workplaces*
Private sector	30	26	20	25
Public sector	43	48	49	39
All workplaces	34	34	29	29
Union recognition (private sector)				
Yes	40	32	23	32
No	20	21	18	22

Source: Cully *et al* 1999

Management's underlying purpose in supporting the non-union, marginal and competitive models of joint consultation, for example, is to weaken trade unions and maintain power by opposing or even confronting the unions. In contrast, in adopting the adjunct model of joint consultation, management does so with the expectation that this will result in co-operation with the unions and their incorporation into the employee relations process, rather than in conflict and discord with them.

Related to this is the strength of union organisation and willingness of workers to resist management plans for setting up and running joint consultative arrangements on management's terms alone. Again the non-union, marginal and competitive models are more likely to be established where unionism is weak or where worker organisation is channelled into staff associations, 'house' unions or company-based 'works councils'. Where joint consultation is used to undermine trade unionism or to bypass it, unless this is resisted by the unions and their members, union representatives are in effect marginalised or excluded from the consultative process. As Cressey and MacInnes (1984) have pointed out, with the power balance favouring managements, it is management that determines what items to take to joint consultative committees, the form of discussion within them and the outcomes arising from them.

In adjunct joint consultation, union representatives are more likely to have joint ownership of the consultative machinery and the right to refer issues to the negotiating machinery. This increases their commitment to the consultative process. Moreover, as Marchington and Armstrong (1983) have indicated, where workplace representatives are well organised, they value joint consultation. But where they are poorly organised, they are generally neutral or negative about it.

It has also been argued that high trust between management and union representatives is an important ingredient in 'good industrial relations' (Purcell 1981). High trust is more likely to be part of adjunct joint consultation than it is in other consultative arrangements. However, high trust, where it exists, is more common in soft product market conditions than in hard ones. As Marchington (1989: 397) has concluded: 'If employers are attempting to prevent or marginalise unions, a tight economic climate makes consultation less necessary since the unions are further weakened, and the time for involvement is less available.' Conversely, where the adjunct model is adopted, economic recession might well induce both sides to continue maintaining good working relationships together, within both the consultative and the negotiating machinery. This is likely to ensure that high trust is sustained between the parties, even in difficult external circumstances.

Finally, the level of decision-making within an organisation also has an impact on the efficacy of joint consultation. Where management decision-making is largely centralised, this is unlikely to give much authority to local, workplace JCCs. This fits the marginal or competitive models of joint consultation. In contrast, where management decision-making is devolved, or at different levels within an organisation, this is more likely to provide the consultative process with added authority. This fits the adjunct model of joint consultation, especially where the consultative machinery is linked hierarchically throughout the organisation.

Constitutional arrangements

The constitutional arrangements for setting up and operating JCCs vary widely. Where joint consultation is entirely management driven, such as in the non-union, marginal and competitive models, the constitutional arrangements for JCCs are obviously determined by management decision alone. Management decides the terms of reference, membership, structures, frequency of meetings and the agenda of such committees. The underlying purpose of such committees is to keep them firmly under management control, either by excluding the union presence (the non-union model) or by weakening union influence (the competitive and marginal models). The terms of reference of these types of JCCs are normally unitary in purpose, while membership on the 'staff' side is usually drawn from employee representatives, rather than from union representatives. Sometimes their constituents elect employee representatives; in other cases management appoints them. These JCCs are located largely at workplace level and rarely have links higher up the organisation. Frequency of meetings varies but is likely to lie within the range of monthly, quarterly or half-yearly meetings. The agenda of these sorts of JCCs is likely to be 'soft', with management using them largely as downward information-providing bodies, rather than as opportunities for asking employees about their views on workplace matters and listening to them before taking decisions.

Adjunct JCCs are formally constituted bodies, at workplace and/or corporate level and are established through negotiations between management and union representatives. They are normally the result of formal joint consultation agreements. It is the joint responsibility of both management and unions to ensure that the consultative arrangements, established within the procedure, comply with their terms of reference and the constitution embodied within the agreement.

Adjunct consultation

Joint consultation is at its most advanced when it is of the adjunct variety. The sorts of arrangements set out for adjunct JCCs are outlined below.

Aims

The underlying purpose of adjunct joint consultation is to establish arrangements that involve the signatory unions in the consultative process between management and the employees covered by the joint consultation agreement and to participate with them in the interests of good employee relations. In this sense, adjunct consultation is normally concerned with those matters of mutual concern to management and employees that are not covered by the negotiating procedures. Matters may be discussed within the consultative machinery, prior to negotiation, and be referred to the negotiating machinery subsequently. Adjunct consultation is a problem-solving, two-way information-exchange process between the parties rather than a bargaining or a 'top-down' process.

Adjunct consultation enables management, employees and the unions to consider and, as far as is practicable, to resolve the problems facing them. In this sense it may be considered as an integrative process. Joint consultation thereby increases the effectiveness of the organisation's operations to the mutual benefit of both employer and employees. JCC systems of this type are thus ways of improving staff morale, reducing tensions between management and employees, increasing job satisfaction and raising employee productivity.

Perkins (1986: 44) sees the underpinning aims of effective joint consultation as being fourfold:

- Joint consultation ensures continuity of structure, enabling it to be used as a method of communication on all matters of concern to management and employees.
- Used correctly, it reinforces the trust and goodwill existing between management, employees and unions.
- It provides problem-solving procedures between management and employee representatives, although these are only meaningful if they precede final decisions.
- It allows employees to raise their own issues and grievances, to receive management's views and to instigate action where appropriate.

Effectively constituted and properly managed joint consultation, in short, enables employees, through their union representatives, to discuss and consider matters of mutual concern to them and management, thus allowing them to influence management proposals before final decisions are taken.

Functions

The primary function of adjunct JCCs at workplace level is to provide regular and recognised opportunities for the joint consideration, by management and employee representatives, of all issues affecting them that are not covered by joint negotiating machinery. They are also recognised channels of communication between the parties to any matter put on the JCC agenda by either management or employee representatives. Examples of the functions of JCCs are provided in Exhibit 23, but these are neither exclusive nor exhaustive and some JCCs have much narrower functions than those listed.

Exhibit 23 **Functions of joint consultative committees**

These can include discussions about:

- recruitment and selection
- productivity, efficiency and quality
- staffing or human resources planning
- safety at work
- education and training
- working conditions, such as leave, holiday arrangements, working hours, absenteeism, meal breaks, transport and catering facilities
- systems of payment
- performance appraisals
- equal opportunities
- handling grievances
- health and welfare of employees
- new equipment
- welfare of retired employees.

Membership, structure and rules

Adjunct JCCs are based on the principle that workplace union representatives speak on behalf of employees within the consultative system. Such representatives, however, act on behalf of all their constituents, regardless of whether or not they are union members. The number of union representatives usually takes account of the number and types of employees working in the plant, site or workplace. Senior management selects management representatives, in turn, again in accordance with the joint consultation agreement.

Many JCCs only operate locally at workplace level, but in multi-plant or multisite organisations, arrangements are sometimes made to co-ordinate the consultative machinery throughout the organisation, by means of vertically linked consultative committees. JCCs at organisational level have union members drawn from locally based consultative committees. But these trade unionists are not usually elected directly by the employees within the plants. They are drawn from among workplace union representatives on lower-level committees. In some cases, full-time union officers take on the role of representatives at corporate level. Management representatives are appointed to such committees by senior management, as indicated above.

The rules of JCCs are found in the constitutions determined by the joint consultation agreement. Terms of reference are essential to establish what subjects are matters for consultation and what subjects are negotiable. Guidance is given on the objectives of the consultative procedure and the means by which these are to be effected. Examples of JCC rules are illustrated in Exhibit 24.

Exhibit 24 **Examples of joint consultative committee rules**

These include:

- title of the JCC
- parties to the agreement
- preamble
- aims of the JCC
- means of achieving the aims
- functions
- definitions
- membership
- retirement of members
- casual members
- substitutes
- co-options
- periods of office
- secretariat
- meetings
- quorum
- decisions and recommendations
- agenda
- minutes
- variation or termination of the agreement.

The agenda is often the most important part of JCC meetings and its contents reflect whether or not the committee is really working. Agendas and other relevant papers must be circulated well in advance – except where meetings are held at short notice – if the JCC is to operate effectively. It is the nature of joint consultation meetings that agendas tend to reflect management topics, especially at workplace level, so every effort must be made to get employee representatives to submit their own items for discussion.

Resolving conflicts

It is normally the right of a signatory union, or of a group of signatory unions, or of management, to require a matter to be dealt with through the negotiating procedure, rather than the consultative machinery, where it thinks this is appropriate. Further, if a JCC fails to resolve any disagreement on a matter on which it is competent to take a decision, this matter is normally dealt with in the formal negotiating procedure. Finally, where a JCC exercises its advisory or consultative functions in ways likely to affect any other JCC within an organisation, it usually transmits its recommendation on that matter to the JCC concerned.

ASSIGNMENTS

(a) What are the advantages and disadvantages to employers of collective bargaining as a method of determining terms and conditions of employment and for regulating relations between employers and employees?

(b) What is the case for and against legally enforceable collective agreements? What are the main implications for employers, unions and employees where 'collective contracts' are negotiated?

(c) Read Adnett (1989: Chapter 2). What are the main features of the neoclassical model of the labour market and that of the structural model? How do these models relate to the labour markets in which your organisation operates?

(d) Read Kahn-Freund (1954) in Flanders (1969: 59–85). Comment on his analysis of how 'intergroup' conflicts between employers and unions are regulated through collective bargaining in Britain, Europe and the United States. How does he account for the differences amongst the bargaining systems?

(e) Read Chamberlain and Kuhn (1965: 162–90). How do they conceptualise bargaining power? How useful is their analysis for practical bargaining purposes?

(f) Read Walton and McKersie (1965: 222–80). Examine the nature of 'attitudinal structuring' and why it is an important subprocess in collective bargaining. What tactics can be used by negotiators to change the attitudes of their opposite numbers in the bargaining process, applying the concepts of either 'balance theory' or 'reinforcement theory'?

(g) Use the bargaining power model to assess the relative balance of power in your organisation, when either the union presented its last wage and conditions claim to your employer or management made its last wage proposal to the union. Did the bargaining outcome fit with your analysis?

(h) Read Towers (1992: 7–11). What does he identify as the reasons for employers withdrawing from multi-employer bargaining, what are the experiences of decentralised bargaining for employers and what are the wider organisational effects of it?

(i) Identify the organisational conditions – such as product markets, labour markets, technology, business structure and so on – where (i) multi-employer, (ii) single-employer, and (iii) workplace bargaining is most favourable to employer interests.

(j) What are the advantages and disadvantages to unions of (i) multi-employer level bargaining? (ii) single-employer level bargaining? (iii) workplace-level bargaining? Under what conditions are each of the above levels most favourable to union negotiators?

(k) The unions representing white-collar staff in your organisation have presented management with their annual pay claim. This is for a 5 per cent across-the-board wage increase, a reduction in weekly hours of 20 minutes and improved sickness benefits for their members. Identify the sort of information that management would need to collect in this situation, where it might be collected and how it might be used in the negotiating process.

(l) Read Atkinson (1980: 137–54). What are some of the main tactics used by negotiators to get movement by their opponents in the latter stages of negotiating? Alternatively, what are some of the tactics used to get closure (*ibid*: 155–80)?

(m) Bring in a set of procedural and/or substantive collective agreements of your organisation to the group you are studying with and make a presentation of the main content and features of these agreements.

(n) Read Burrows (1986: 72–92) and comment on the content and practicalities of the single-union deal signed by Nissan (UK) and the AEU.

(o) Read *Industrial Relations Services Employment Trends No. 505* (Industrial Relations Review and Report, February 1992: 11–15). Analyse and report on the flexibility package concluded at Rolls-Royce Motor Cars.

(p) Provide a report on the joint consultative arrangements in your organisation. How effective are they from a management point of view? What is a typical list of agenda items?

(q) Draft a constitution for a JCC.

(r) Read Cully *et al* (1999: 98–102, 244) and identify and comment on the incidence and changes in joint consultation in Britain since 1990.

REFERENCES

ADNETT J. (1989) *Labour Market Policy*. London, Longman.

ADVISORY, CONCILIATION AND ARBITRATION SERVICE (1983) *Collective Bargaining in Britain: Its extent and scope*. London, ACAS.

ATKINSON G. (1980) *The Effective Negotiator*. Newbury, Negotiating Systems Publications.

BRANDEIS L. (1934) *The Curse of Bigness*, quoted in N. Chamberlain and J. Kuhn, 1965, *Collective Bargaining*, New York, McGraw-Hill.

British Leyland UK Ltd v. *McQuilken* [1978] IRLR 245.

BURROWS G. (1986) *No-Strike Agreements and Pendulum Arbitration*. London, Institute of Personnel Management.

CHAMBERLAIN N. *and* KUHN J. (1965) *Collective Bargaining*. New York, McGraw-Hill.

CONFEDERATION OF BRITISH INDUSTRY (1988) *The Structure and Processes of Pay Determination in the Private Sector: 1979–1986*. London, CBI.

CRESSEY P. *and* MACINNES J. (1984) *The Relationship between Economic Recession and Industrial Democracy*. Glasgow, Centre for Research in Industrial Democracy and Participation, University of Glasgow.

CULLY M., WOODLAND S., O'REILLY A. *and* DIX G. (1999) *Britain at Work*. London, Routledge.

DANIEL W. (1987) *Workplace Industrial Relations and Technical Change*. London, Pinter.

DOERINGER P. (1986) 'Internal labor markets and non-competing groups'. *American Economic Review*. 76 (2).

DOERINGER P. *and* PIORE M. (1971) *Internal Labor Markets and Manpower Analysis*. Massachusetts, Lexington.

DUBIN R. (1954) 'Constructive aspects of industrial conflict', in A. Kornhauser, R. Dubin and A. Ross (eds), *Industrial Conflict*, New York, McGraw-Hill.

DUNLOP J. (1950) *Wage Determination under Collective Bargaining*. New York, Macmillan.

DUNLOP J. (1984) *Dispute Resolution*. London, Auburn.

DUNN S. *and* GENNARD J. (1984) *The Closed Shop in British Industry*. London, Macmillan.

FARNHAM D. *and* HORTON S. (1996) *Managing People in the Public Services*. London, Macmillan.

FLANDERS A. (1968) 'Collective bargaining: a theoretical analysis', in A. Flanders, 1970, *Management and Unions*, London, Faber & Faber.

FLANDERS A. (ED.) (1969) *Collective Bargaining: Selected Readings*. London, Penguin.

Ford Motor Co. v. *AUEF and TGWU* [1969] 2 QB 303.

FOX A. *and* FLANDERS A. (1969) 'Collective bargaining: from Donovan to Durkheim', in A. Flanders, 1970, *Management and Unions*, London, Faber & Faber.

HICKS J. (1932) *Theory of Wages*. New York, Macmillan.

HOXIE R. (1921) *Trade Unionism in the United States*. New York, Appleton.

HYMAN R. (1975) *Industrial Relations*. London, Macmillan.

INDUSTRIAL RELATIONS REVIEW AND REPORT (1992a) *Industrial Relations Services Employment Trends*. 505, February.

INDUSTRIAL RELATIONS REVIEW AND REPORT (1992b) *Industrial Relations Services Employment Trends*. 512, May.

INTERNATIONAL LABOUR OFFICE (1986) *Collective Bargaining*. Geneva, ILO.

KAHN-FREUND O. (1954) 'Intergroup conflicts and their settlement'. *British Journal of Sociology*. 5 (3).

KENNEDY G., BENSON J. *and* MCMILLAN J. (1984) *Managing Negotiations*. London, Business Books.

KINNIE N. (1987) 'Bargaining within the enterprise: centralized or decentralized?' *Journal of Management Studies*. 214 (5).

LEVINSON H. (1966) *Wage Determination under Collective Bargaining*. New York, Wiley.

MARCHINGTON M. (1989) 'Joint consultation in practice', in K. Sisson (ed.), *Personnel Management in Britain*, Oxford, Blackwell.

MARCHINGTON M. *and* ARMSTRONG R. (1983) 'Shop steward organisation and joint consultation'. *Personnel Review*. 12 (1).

MARGINSON P. (1986) 'How centralized is the management of industrial relations?' *Personnel Management*. October.

MILLWARD N. *and* STEVENS M. (1986) *British Workplace Industrial Relations 1980–1984*. Aldershot, Gower.

MILLWARD N., STEVENS M., SMART D. *and* HAWES W. (1992) *Workplace Industrial Relations in Transition*. Aldershot, Dartmouth.

PALMER S. (1990) *Determining Pay: A guide to the issues*. London, Institute of Personnel Management.

PEN J. (1952) 'A general theory of bargaining'. *American Economic Review*. 42.

PERKINS G. (ED.) (1986) *Employee Communications in the Public Sector*. London, Institute of Personnel Management.

PHELPS BROWN H. (1966) 'The influence of trade unions and collective bargaining on pay levels and real wages', in W. McCarthy, *Trade Unions: Selected readings*, London, Penguin.

PURCELL J. (1981) *Good Industrial Relations*. London, Macmillan.

PURCELL J. (1987) 'Mapping management styles in employee relations'. *Journal of Management Studies*. 24 (5). September.

PURCELL J. (1989) 'How to manage decentralized bargaining'. *Personnel Management*. May.

SCHELLING T. (1963) *The Strategy of Conflict*. London, University Press.

STEVENS C. (1963) *Strategy and Collective Bargaining Negotiation*. New York, McGraw-Hill.

TOWERS B. (1992) *Issues in People Management No. 2: Choosing Bargaining Levels – UK experience and implications*. London, Institute of Personnel Management.

TRADE UNION AND LABOUR RELATIONS (CONSOLIDATION) ACT 1992.

TRADES UNION CONGRESS (1999) *General Council Report for 1998*. London, TUC.

WALTON R. *and* MCKERSIE R. (1965) *A Behavioral Theory of Labor Negotiations*. New York, McGraw-Hill.

WEBB S. *and* WEBB B. (1913) *Industrial Democracy*. New York, Longman.

WEEKES B., MELLISH M., DICKENS L. *and* LLOYD J. (1975) *Industrial Relations and the Limits of the Law*. Oxford, Blackwell.

WINTERTON J. and WINTERTON R. (1985) *New Technology: The bargaining issues*. Nottingham, Universities of Leeds and Nottingham in association with the Institute of Personnel Management.

8 Management and trade unions

Voluntary collective bargaining between management representatives and trade union representatives on labour market and certain managerial issues remains an important employee relations process in Britain, although the proportion of employees in workplaces covered by collective bargaining has declined significantly over the past 20 years. In the 1984 Workplace Industrial Relations Survey (WIRS), for example, it was estimated that the proportion of employees covered by collective bargaining was 71 per cent. This had fallen to 54 per cent in 1990 (Millward and Stevens 1986, Millward et al 1992) and 41 per cent in 1998, though the pattern of declining coverage varied by sector. Thus in private manufacturing the coverage of collective bargaining fell from 51 per cent to 46 per cent between 1990 and 1998 and in private-sector services from 33 per cent to 22 per cent. Even in the public sector, where collective bargaining has traditionally been most firmly rooted, its coverage had declined from 80 per cent in 1990 to 63 per cent in 1998. Management's willingness to allow trade unions to represent employees in negotiating terms and conditions, in turn, is reflected in its agreement to grant recognition to unions at corporate or workplace level. After remaining stable in the early 1980s at around 65 per cent, the proportion of workplaces with recognised trade unions declined from around 52 per cent to 42 per cent between 1984 and 1998 (Cully et al 1999).

The conditions necessary for effective collective bargaining to take place include:

- freedom of association for workers to organise into independent trade unions
- willingness of workers to join and participate in the activities of independent trade unions
- the ability of the unions to recruit, retain and service their members effectively
- employer recognition
- a fair balance of bargaining power between employers and unions in the bargaining process.

To deal with trade unions effectively, therefore, management needs to understand the nature of trade unions, their employee relations activities, their methods of working and the values and purposes for which they stand. Management also needs to be aware that whilst unions collectively share certain common principles and ideologies, each individual union has its own institutional characteristics, employment policies and responses to employee relations problems.

In Britain, employer recognition of trade unions depends on the ability

266

and voluntary efforts of trade unions in recruiting and retaining members and providing them with effective membership services. It also reflects the level of economic activity and structure of the economy at any one time. The willingness of employers to recognise trade unions is a function of:

- the balance of bargaining power between the parties, when unions demand recognition for the first time
- the perceived benefits of recognition to the employer in each case
- the role of the law in determining union recognition.

With the economy expanding and demand for labour rising, union recognition is more easily achieved by the unions and more likely to be agreed to by management. With the economy in recession and with excess labour supply, union recognition is less easily achieved and more likely to be resisted by management. In these circumstances, union derecognition may be a more attractive option for some employers to adopt. With the prospect of statutory trade recognition under the provisions of the Employment Relations Act 1999 (ERA 1999) (see below), employers are faced with a further constraint on their power to refuse recognition on good grounds. And unions, in turn, are provided with an opportunity of gaining recognition for collective bargaining purposes when faced with obstructive and difficult employers.

DEVELOPMENTS IN TRADE UNIONS

Membership trends

One way of measuring trade union presence is aggregate union membership. In Britain, union membership is a Pareto distribution, where there is a small number of very large unions and a large number of very small ones, with the latter making up over 80 per cent of total union membership. At the beginning of 1998, for example, the Certification Office listed 17 unions each having over 100,000 members, and another 217 unions each with fewer than 100,000 members. The 17 largest unions comprised just over 6 million members and the other 217 unions had only about 1.4 million members distributed among them. This compared with 23 unions with over 100,000 members and a total of 8 million members in 1990, and 264 with under 100,000 members and a total of 1.8 million members (Certification Office 1992 and 1999).

Table 11 shows that in 1960 there were 15 major trade unions in Britain with more than 100,000 members each, comprising a total of over 6 million members. By 1980, there were 26 such unions, totalling over 10 million members. In 1990 this had fallen to 24 unions of this size, including the Police Federation, which is not listed by the Certification Office, with a total of 8 million members. In other words, total union membership in Britain's largest unions in 1990 was about 2 million members fewer than it had been in 1980. This total membership, however, was still some 2 million members higher than amongst similar unions in 1960. In 1997, there were 17 major

Table 11 Union membership in Britain's largest unions in 1960, 1980, 1990 and 1997

				(000s)
	1960	1980	1990	1997
UNISON – the public service union	*	*	*	1355
Transport and General Workers Union (TGWU)	1302	1887	1224	881
Amalgamated Engineering and Electrical Union (AEEU)[1]	973	1166	702	720
GMB[2]	796	916	865	709
National Union of Mineworkers (NUM)	586	370	116	*
Union of Shop Distributive and Allied Workers (USDAW)	355	450	362	293
National Union of Railway Maritime and Transport Workers (NURMTW)[3]	334	167	101	*
National and Local Government Officers Union (NALGO)***	274	782	744	*
National Union of Teachers (NUT)	245	272	218	276
Electrical Electronic Telecommunications and Plumbing Union (EETPU)[4]	243	405	367	*
National Union of Public Employees (NUPE)***	200	699	579	*
Manufacturing Science and Finance Union (MSFU)[5]	*	491	653	416
Union of Construction Allied Trades and Technicians (UCATT)[6]	192	312	207	114
Confederation of Health Service Employees (COHSE)***	*	216	203	*
Communication Workers Union (CWU)[7]	166	203	203	274
Society of Graphical and Allied Trades (SOGAT)[8]	158	200	169	*
Iron and Steel Trades Confederation (ISTC)	117	104	*	*
Civil and Public Services Association (CPSA)[9]	140	216	123	112
Graphical Paper and Media Union (GPMU)	*	*	*	205
Royal College of Nursing (RCN)	*	181	289	312

Banking Insurance and Finance Union (BIFU)	*	141	171	113
Association of Professional Executive Clerical and Computer Staff (APEX)[10]	*	140	*	*
National Communications Union (NCU)[11]	*	131	155	*
National Association of Schoolmasters/ Union of Women Teachers (NAS/UWT)	*	156	169	246
Amalgamated Society of Boilermakers (ASB)[12]	*	124	*	*
Association of Teachers and Lecturers (ATL)	*	*	139	153
National Graphical Association (NGA)[13]	*	116	130	*
Police Federation (PF)	*	112	180	205
Public Services Tax and Commerce Union (PSTCU)[14]	*	109	114	154
British Medical Association (BMA)	*	*	*	104
	6332**	10066	8183	6587

* Not applicable

** This total includes two other unions, the National Union of Agricultural Workers and the National Union of Garment and Tailoring Workers, with 135,000 and 116,000 members respectively in 1960.

*** Merged to form UNISON in 1993.

1. Known as the Amalgamated Union of Engineering Workers in 1980; became the Amalgamated Electrical and Engineering Union in 1992, after a merger with the EETPU.
2. Known as the General and Municipal Workers Union in 1960 and 1980.
3. Known as the National Union of Railwaymen in 1960 and 1980.
4. Known as the Electrical Trades Union in 1960.
5. Known as the Association of Scientific Technical and Managerial Staff in 1980. It merged with the Technical Administrative and Supervisory Section of the AEU to form the MSFU in 1988.
6. Known as the Amalgamated Society of Woodworkers in 1960.
7. Known as the Union of Post Office Workers in 1971. CWU was formed in 1995, following a merger between the Union of Communication Workers and the National Communications Union.
8. Known as the National Union of Printing Bookbinding and Paper Workers in 1960. Became the SOGAT in 1975 and merged with the NGA in 1991 to form the Graphical Paper and Media Union.
9. Known as the Civil Service Clerical Association in 1960.
10. Merged with the GMBU in 1989.
11. Known as the Post Office Engineering Union in 1960 and 1980. See also footnote 7.
12. Merged with the General Municipal Workers Union in 1982.
13. See note 8 above.
14. Known as the Society of Civil and Public Servants in 1980 and then as the National Union of Civil and Public Servants (NUCPS) until 1996.

Source: TUC and Certification Officer *Annual Reports*

unions, each with over 100,000 members, totalling about 6.4 million members, which was about the same total union membership as in 1960.

Table 11 shows that of the 15 largest unions listed in 1960, only three had smaller memberships in 1980. These were the NUM, NURMTW and ISTC. By 1980, these 15 largest unions had been joined by 11 others:

MSFU (then known as ASTMS); COHSE; RCN; BIFU; APEX; NCU; NAS/UWT; ASB; NGA; PF; and NUCPS. The decline in the absolute and relative size of some of the old 'smokestack' unions, such as the NUM, NURMTW and ISTC, and the rise to prominence of 'white-collar' unions in the public and private services by 1980 reflected the changing industrial and employment structures in Britain during the 1960s and 1970s (Bain 1970).

Between 1980 and 1990, as also shown in Table 11, this trend continued. During this decade, there was a decline in the absolute memberships of all the largest unions recruiting manual workers (except the NGA), and even amongst some white-collar unions in the public sector, such as the NUT, NALGO and CPSA. But there were rises in membership in other white-collar unions recruiting professional, technical and administrative workers in parts of the private and public sectors. The large unions gaining members during these years were: MSFU; RCN; BIFU; NCU; NAS/UWT; AMMA; and NUCPS. Some of this growth in the memberships of these unions can be accounted for by union mergers, such as those involving the MSFU. In other cases it arose from expanding recruitment opportunities for unions such as the RCN and BIFU or for the NAS/UWT and AMMA, which were taking members from established organisations in their own sector, such as the NUT. Further evidence of the relative decline of some large private-sector unions during the 1980s is provided by the absence of the ISTC, ASB and APEX from those organisations with over 100,000 members each in 1990. By this time, the membership of the ISTC had fallen to around 40,000, the ASB had merged with the General and Municipal Workers' Union in 1982 to form the GMBU, and APEX, in turn, had merged with the GMBU in 1989.

By 1997, as shown in Table 11, there were 17 large unions, each with over 100,000 members. Between 1990 and 1997, decline in the membership of manual workers' unions continued, except in the AEEU, and in white-collar unions such as MSFU, CPSA and BIFU, except PSTCU which increased by amalgamation and merger. The professional and technical unions that increased their memberships during these years were in the public sector, such as the NUT, RCN, NAS/UWT, ATL and Police Federation, and in the utilities, such as CWU.

It is likely that the trend towards more union amalgamations and mergers will continue in the 2000s. The AEU and EETPU amalgamated in 1992 to create the Amalgamated Engineering and Electrical Union, with over 1 million members. NUPE, NALGO and COHSE also merged, in 1993, to form the largest public-sector union in Britain, UNISON, with some 1.5 million members. In the mid-1990s there was a spate of union transfers of engagements from smaller to larger unions, such as the Scottish Health Visitors' Association to UNISON, the Rossendale Union of Boot, Shoe and Slipper Operatives to the National Union of Knitwear Footwear and Apparel Trades and the Northern Ireland Bakers' and Confectioners' Union to the Bakers' Food and Allied Workers Union (Certification Office 1997). Another major merger took place in the public services, after a series of legal appeals, between the PSTCU and CPSA in 1998, resulting in the creation of the Public and Commercial Services Union with a membership of almost 266,000 members.

Table 12 TUC membership, TUC affiliation and non–TUC membership, 1978–97

Year	Membership of TUC	Numbers of TUC-affiliated unions	Membership of non-TUC unions
1978	11,865,390	112	1,188,206
1979	12,128,078	112	1,084,276
1980	12,172,508	109	1,463,847
1981	11,601,413	108	1,709,821
1982	11,005,984	105	1,738,406
1983	10,510,157	95	1,789,722
1984	10,082,144	89	1,691,809
1985	9,855,204	91	1,963,745
1986	9,580,502	89	1,017,506
1987	9,243,297	87	1,236,853
1988	9,127,278	83	1,259,960
1989	8,652,318	78	1,391,288
1990	8,405,246	78	1,404,773
1991	8,192,664	74	1,296,370
1992	7,786,885	72	1,142,017
1993	7,647,443	70	1,018,501
1994	7,117,436	69	1,113,109
1995	6,894,604	67	1,136,722
1996	6,790,339	73	1,147,874
1997	6,756,544	75	1,044,771

Source: TUC, *Annual Reports* and CO, *Annual Reports*

Another way of examining recent union membership trends is by analysing membership in unions affiliated to the Trades Union Congress (TUC) (see Chapter 2) and unions that are not TUC-affiliated, as shown in Table 12. This shows, first, that total union membership in Britain peaked at an all-time high of 13.2 million members in 1979, comprising 12.1 million members in TUC-affiliated unions and just over 1 million in non-TUC unions. By 1990, the overall level of union membership had fallen to 9.8 million members, consisting of some 8.5 million in TUC-affiliated organisations and some 1.4 million in non-TUC unions. This represented a fall of 26 per cent in overall membership, a fall of 30 per cent in the membership of TUC unions and a rise of 30 per cent in the membership of non-TUC unions for the period 1979–90. Between 1990 and 1997, however, these relative decreases in union membership levelled down, with further falls of 20 per cent in overall union membership, 20 per cent in TUC-affiliated membership and 25 per cent in non-affiliated union membership.

Second, between 1978 and 1997, the number of unions affiliated to the TUC declined from 112 to 75. This reduction in the number of TUC-affiliated unions is largely accounted for by the series of amalgamations and mergers taking place amongst TUC unions after 1980. Yet, though membership in TUC-affiliated unions fell steadily during the 1980s and early 1990s, that in non-TUC unions grew slowly from 1981, after it had fallen dramatically by over 600,000 members between 1979 and 1980. The effect was that between 1981 and 1990, membership in non-TUC unions rose by almost 100 per cent from about 709,000 to 1.4 million. Between 1990 and 1997, however, membership in non-TUC unions fell by some 360,000.

Union density

Another way of measuring trade union presence is union density. This is the percentage of employees in the national economy, sector, organisation or workplace, who are members of a relevant union compared to total potential membership. Successive workplace surveys show that aggregate union density in Britain fell from 65 per cent in 1980, to 58 per cent in 1984, to 47 per cent in 1990 and to 36 per cent in 1998. Cully and his colleagues (1999) have shown that in each major sector of the economy – private manufacturing, private services and the public sector – there was falling aggregate union density up to 1990, followed by further falls from 1990 to 1998. In the earlier period, however, union density fell by about a quarter in private manufacturing and private services, but the decline was much less in the public sector. Since 1990, in contrast, the fall in private services has been much greater than in the other two sectors – over a third compared with about a fifth. In 1998, it was estimated that aggregate union density was 26 per cent in the private manufacturing and private services, compared with 57 per cent in the public sector. Table 13 summarises aggregate union density, by workplace and industry, in 1998.

Table 13 Trade union density in Britain by workplace and industry, 1998

	Workplace average	Aggregate density
Industry		
Manufacturing	19	41
Electricity, gas and water	74	68
Construction	17	30
Wholesale and retail	8	14
Transport and communications	40	54
Financial services	42	32
Other business services	9	8
Public administration	66	63
Education	56	51
Health	34	43
Other community services	17	24
All workplaces	27	36

Source: Cully *et al* 1999

In the private sector, the trend of declining union density during the 1980s accelerated during the 1990s. According to Cully *et al* (1999: 236), 'the rate of decrease moved from 2.7 per cent per year in the late 1980s to 3.5 per cent in the 1990s.' Falls in union density in the private sector affected all sizes of workplace and all sizes of enterprise. Since 1990, however, smaller workplaces have shown a more rapid decline in union density than larger ones, with over 500 employees. 'Similarly it was the smallest enterprises that showed the sharpest falls in recent times.' Further, older workplaces have tended to have higher membership density than younger ones. But whereas in the 1980s union density increased with age of workplace, in 1998 the highest levels of union density were only apparent in the oldest workplaces. 'This suggests that workplaces established since the 1970s, when union membership was at its historical peak, have been less likely to acquire union members than their forerunners' (ibid: 238).

Union structure

Union structure focuses on the recruitment and membership bases of trade unions, which are organised on occupational (or craft), industrial or general lines. Occupational, 'craft' or 'trades' unions are exclusive bodies and were the first type of employee organisation to emerge in Britain (during the nineteenth century). One of their main recruiting devices was the pre-entry closed shop (Gennard 1990). Today, few pure occupational unions exist and those that do are relatively small in size. This is because of changing occupational boundaries, the widening scope of occupational classifications, the de-skilling of craftwork due to technological changes, the growth of multiskilling and the breakdown of traditional craft sectors of employment. Unlike industrial unions that recruit vertically within an industry, occupational unions recruit horizontally across industries.

Current examples of occupational-type unions include the British Actors' Equity Association, British Medical Association, British Airline Pilots' Association and Professional Footballers' Association. The main structural feature of occupational unions such as these is that they recruit members selectively, on a job-by-job basis, irrespective of where they work. It is the worker's occupational status, job skills and qualifications or training that determine whether or not individuals qualify for membership of a particular occupational union, not the industry or the organisation that employs them.

Industrial unions recruit their members selectively, but less exclusively than occupational trade unions. They seek members vertically from amongst all employment grades, normally including both manual and non-manual workers within a single industry. The best examples of industrial unions are in Germany, where there are now 11 such unions, as a result of recent union amalgamations and mergers, with some 8 million members in these organisations. These unions are members of the Deutscher Gerwerkschaftbund (DGB), which is the trade union umbrella organisation that represents the German trade union movement in dealings with governmental authorities at federal state and national levels, political parties and employers' organisations (Jacobi et al 1998). The DGB also works with the European Trade Union Confederation (ETUC) and International Confederation of Free Trade

Unions (ICFTU). The DGB is not directly involved in collective bargaining but co-ordinates joint demands, themes and campaigns for its 11 member unions. The DGB's 11 industrial unions are:

- Construction, Agriculture and Environment
- Mining, Chemicals and Energy
- The German Railwayworkers' Union
- Education and Science
- Commerce, Banking and Insurance
- Media
- Metalworkers
- Food, Beverages and Catering
- Public Services, Transport and Traffic
- Police
- Post Office.

In Britain, in contrast, because of the continually dynamic and constantly evolving structure of industry and commerce, the difficulty of defining industrial boundaries with precision, and the growth of multi-occupational and multi-industry unions, there are very few single-industry unions left. The best remaining examples are the NUM and the ISTC, with the NURMTW and the Broadcasting Entertainment Cinematograph and Theatre Union retaining some features of industrial unionism. Yet even in these cases there are other unions competing for members in these sectors, thus weakening the exclusivity of the industrial union base.

General or 'open' unions, in contrast to occupational and industrial unions, are 'all-comers' organisations with four main membership characteristics. They draw their members:

- non-exclusively from any particular industrial sector
- from among both manual and non-manual workers
- horizontally across industries
- vertically within industries.

For a number of historical and structural reasons, general unions have become the dominant model of British trade unionism.

Because of recent financial pressures on them, substantial membership leakages in the 1980s and 1990s and changes in the economy, British trade unions have had to adapt their recruitment strategies and institutional structures to these circumstances. The essential issues facing British unions in recent years have been employer hostility, financial viability and membership retention. Consequently, most craft unions have opened up their boundaries to less skilled workers; industrial unions have continued to diversify their memberships – sometimes across industrial sectors; and general unions have sought to retain and extend their membership boundaries to maintain their influence and power in the trade union movement.

The net result has been a series of union amalgamations and mergers since the early 1980s. This has strengthened general unionism in Britain at the expense of occupational and industrial unions. These mergers have often been driven by the political allegiances of union leaderships or the search for stronger union membership bases, rather than by the desire to create rational union structures. There are four main consequences of this:

- There has been a shift towards the creation of a few 'super' unions whose membership boundaries overlap, resulting in competitive membership recruitment among them.
- These amalgamations and mergers have not removed the problems associated with multi-unionism at industry, employer and workplace levels and in dealings with employers.
- The role of the TUC has to some degree been weakened, since larger unions feel less need for the services and support of an umbrella organisation at central level like the TUC and are sometimes more critical of its co-ordinating functions.
- At the same time, the TUC (1995: 12) has been forced to become a more crusading body, seeking to be:

A high profile organisation which campaigns successfully for trade union aims and values, assists trade unions to increase membership and effectiveness, cuts out wasteful rivalry and promotes trade union solidarity.

TRADE UNION POLICY

The fundamental principle of trade union policy is to protect the employment interests of union members, as individual workers, by dealing with employers collectively. As Hyman (1975: 64) has written, the central purpose of a trade union 'is to permit workers to exert, collectively, the control over the conditions of employment which they cannot hope to possess as individuals'. They do this largely 'by compelling the employer to take account, in policy- and decision-making, of interests contrary to [its] own'.

Any general analysis of union policy starts by examining their functions and roles as economic and political agents, acting on behalf of employees in their market and in managerial relations with employers. Such an analysis highlights the essential divergences between union policy and employer policy on many employee relations issues. Employer policy is normally aimed at achieving profitability, economic efficiency and management control of working processes and employee behaviour, largely through 'top-down' corporate hierarchies. Union policy, on the other hand, is aimed at achieving 'fair' terms and conditions of employment, participation in corporate decision-making and power-sharing with management, achieved through collective bargaining, other employee relations processes and internal union democracy.

It is these differences in organisational rules and values, stemming from this dichotomy in purpose and method, that give rise to possible conflicts of interest in employee relations between employers and unions, where trade unions are recognised. This dichotomy also explains why some employers resist union organisation and recognition in their workplaces.

The labour market function of trade unions

The Webbs provide the classic analysis of the trade union function. It was they who first described, analysed and evaluated the purposes and methods of trade unions. For the Webbs, unions exist to enforce 'Trade Union Regulations' on employers for the workers they represent. There is no 'Trade Union Rate of Wages' nor 'a Trade Union Working Day' but many different rates and hours of work varying from occupation to occupation (Webb and Webb 1913: 560). The Webbs thus saw unions as bodies defending sectional economic interests, rather than working-class interests as a whole. Whilst all unions have broadly similar purposes, and use largely the same methods to achieve them, each union has its own unique purposes and uses those methods most appropriate to its particular circumstances.

The Webbs identified seven trade union regulations:

- the standard [wage] rate
- the normal [working] day
- sanitation and safety [at work]
- new processes and machinery
- continuity of employment
- the entrance into a trade
- the right to a trade.

At the core of the Webbs' analysis is their conclusion that: 'In the making of the labor contract the isolated individual workman, unprotected by any combination with his fellows, stands in all respects at a disadvantage compared with the capitalist employer' (*ibid*: 658). Whilst workers strive to get the best terms they can from their employers, the employers, in turn, 'are endeavouring, in accordance with business principles, to buy their labor in the cheapest market' (*ibid*: 658 and 184). Workers combine together, therefore, to be better able to enforce the regulations of their trade upon employers.

Unions use two 'economic devices' to do this: 'the Device of the Restriction of Numbers' and 'the Device of the Common Rule' (Part III: Chapter III). The device of the restriction of numbers is concerned with labour supply. It involves unions using apprenticeships, excluding new competitors from the trade and asserting a vested interest in a particular trade in order to influence the labour market. In these ways, unions can make a better bargain with the employers, insisting on adequate wages, better conditions of employment and shorter hours of work for their members.

The device of the common rule is the enforcement of minimum standards of employment on employers below which no employer (or employee) may fall. It is not a maximum standard, since some employers may provide terms and conditions better than the minimum. The Webbs go on to analyse the 'three distinct instruments or levers' used by unions to enforce the regulations of their trades. These are: 'the Method of Mutual Insurance, the Method of Collective Bargaining, and the Method of Legal Enactment' (*ibid*: 150).

Mutual insurance

The method of mutual insurance is the provision of funds by trade unionists, through collective subscriptions, to insure their members' incomes against the economic misfortunes of unemployment, sickness and accidents. According to the Webbs, 'until Collective Bargaining was permitted by the employers, and before Legal Enactment was within the workman's reach, Mutual Insurance was the only method by which Trade Unionists could lawfully attain their end.' The existence of friendly society benefits enabled unions to maintain discipline over members who broke union rules and the power to enforce upon all members the decisions of the majority.

Where differences arise between an employer and its employees, unions using the method of mutual insurance can apply economic pressure on employers, through what the Webbs described as the 'Strike in Detail'. This is the process where, if an employer refuses to conform to the regulations of the trade, union members leave the employer's employment, one by one, and are sustained by 'Out of Work' benefit from the union. But, as the Webbs stated, 'as a deliberate Trade Union policy, the Strike in Detail depends upon the extent to which the union has secured the adhesion of all the component men in the trade' and their capacity to pursue their common ends collectively (*ibid*: 166 and 169).

Collective bargaining

The method of collective bargaining enables joint machinery to be established between employers and unions to settle the employment rules within a trade (Part II: Chapter II). Collective bargaining prevents wage undercutting by both employers and employees, maintains 'industrial peace' and enables distinctions to be made between the negotiating arrangements for concluding new agreements and those for interpreting existing ones. Also (*ibid*: 209):

> When the associated employers in any trade conclude an agreement with the Trade Union, the Common Rule thus arrived at is usually extended by the employers, as a matter of course, to every workman in their establishment, whether or not he is a member of the union.

Determining the common rules of the trade through collective bargaining is a very flexible union method, since agreements can be made at 'shop', 'district' and 'whole industry' level, with 'impartial umpires' or conciliators being available, acceptable to both sides, where collective agreement cannot be reached. For the Webbs (*ibid*: 218), this joint method for settling the terms and conditions of employment, 'neither by the workmen nor by the employers [alone], but by collective agreement', was attracting 'a growing share of public approval' and support at the time. This was because of the compromises and concessions required of the two sides in the negotiating process and the benefits it gave to both sides in adopting it.

Legal enactment

The method of legal enactment enforces the regulations of the trade through Act of Parliament. For the Webbs, legal enactment is a method about which trade unionists are ambivalent. On the one hand, before unions can get a common rule enforced by the state, they must convince the community at large 'that the proposed regulation will prove advantageous to the state as a whole, and not [be] unduly burdensome to the consumers'. Further, what Parliament enacts might not be the full measure asked for. On the other hand, Acts of Parliament apply uniformly to all districts, whether unions are strong or weak, and to all employers. Legal enactment, therefore, is 'the ideal form of Collective Bargaining, a National Agreement made between a Trade Union including every man in the trade, and an Employers' Association from which no firm stands aloof'.

The Webbs saw the TUC as the body to obtain, by Parliamentary action, particular measures desired by its constituent unions. But, as the Webbs warned, once the TUC 'diverges from its narrow Trade Union function, and expresses any opinion, either on general social reforms or party politics, it is bound to alienate whole sections of its constituents' (Part II: Chapter IV).

Summary

For the Webbs (1897: 560), then, all trade union regulations are based on the assumption that in the absence of common rules the determination of terms and conditions of employment are left to the free labour market, placing workers at an economic disadvantage vis-à-vis employers.

> this always means, in practice, that they are arrived at by Individual Bargaining between contracting parties of very unequal economic strength. Such a settlement, it is asserted, invariably tends, for the mass of the workers, towards the worst possible conditions of labor – ultimately, indeed, to the barest subsistence level – whilst even the exceptional few do not permanently gain as much as they otherwise would.

In the Webbs' analysis, the essence of trade union policy is to remedy and offset this imbalance in labour market power, through the use of appropriate economic devices and methods. For everything beyond 'the National Minimum', wage earners must depend on the method of collective bargaining. But for those regulations and rules based on enduring considerations, such as the health and efficiency of workers, legal enactment is to be preferred (*ibid*: 796–806).

The democratic function of trade unions

It was Flanders who took the Webbs' analysis of union policy and the union function a stage further. In his view, the value of a union to its members is less in its economic achievements than in its capacity to protect their dignity. Whilst union members are interested in labour market regulation and how labour is managed, because these define their rights, status and security, they are also interested in making and administering employment rules and having a voice in shaping their own destiny. To secure membership allegiance and support, unions must provide services to their members and 'this is made possible by [union] participation in job regulation'. They do this primarily through collective bargaining. Yet since collective agreements are a body of jointly agreed rules, and the process of negotiation 'is best conceived as a diplomatic use of power, trade unions operate primarily as political, not economic, institutions' (Flanders 1968a: 238–40).

The constant underlying purpose of trade unions, then, is participation in job regulation. 'But participation is not an end in itself, it is a means of enabling workers to gain more control over their working lives' (Flanders 1968b: 42). The issue that concerned Flanders was the slow rate of progress made by trade unions in advancing this social purpose, especially, when he was writing, under conditions of full employment. For him, one of the weaknesses of trade unions was that a lot of their energies are absorbed in the struggle for 'more money' for their members. The struggle for their members' status in the workplace receives far less attention. In his view this is remediable only where unions refuse to accept any final definition of exclusive managerial functions. 'They have recognised that the frontiers of union control are shifting frontiers, that any decision that affects the life and well-being of their members can be their concern' (Flanders 1961: 23). Participation by unions jointly with management in non-wage issues is clearly legitimate where their members' job interests are affected and substantially extends the democratic rights of workers in employment.

TRADE UNION PRACTICE

Trade union practice derives from trade union policy. Given the essential role of trade unions in providing collective representation for employees in their relations with employers, trade union practices are directed towards any area of common concern to their members, employment status or occupational interests. Union practices are reflected in the objectives, means and methods of trade unions. These vary by union and according to the circumstances facing any trade union group at the time. A number of contingent factors affect whether or not these objectives are achieved and whether or not the means and methods used are effective. These include (see also Chapters 5 and 9):

- the state of labour markets
- employer policy
- management style
- the law
- public policy.

Objectives

Because of the sectionalised nature of British trade unionism, it is difficult to provide a definitive set of universal trade union objectives applicable to all unions at all times, and it is significant that neither the Webbs nor Flanders tried to do so. Nevertheless, a prescriptive analysis of the 'permanent objectives' of unions is provided by the TUC in its evidence to the Donovan Commission. The objectives distinguished by the TUC (1966) are of different kinds. Some are substantive, some procedural and others do not concern employment as such. They are seen as being complementary to one another and as providing choice for unions, enabling them to place lesser or greater emphasis on any one or more of them at any given time. The union objectives outlined by the TUC are illustrated in Exhibit 25.

Exhibit 25 The TUC's definition of union objectives

- improved terms of employment
- improved physical environment at work
- security of employment and income
- industrial democracy
- fair shares in national income and wealth
- full employment and national prosperity
- improved social security
- improved public and social services
- a voice in government
- public control and planning of industry

Of these 10 objectives, only the first four are direct employee relations objectives. The next three are macroeconomic and the last four are political objectives. It is some measure of the difficult environment facing trade unions in the early twenty-first century that only the first three of the above objectives are realistically being aimed at by trade unions in Britain currently.

A modified analysis of union objectives was provided by the TUC (1974: 6–7) some years later. It is through trade unions, the TUC argues, that employees set the key objectives for advancing their interests and their rights at work:

- *Establishing terms of employment.* Bargaining with employers about pay, hours and working conditions, including equal pay, allowances, retirement and pensions, redundancy, safety and health, and training, for all workers who are employed, part-time as well as full-time.
- *Fair representation.* Representing members to ensure implementation of all rights flowing from collective agreements and the law – such as maternity pay; safety requirements; protection against unfair disciplinary action or dismissal; protection against race or sex discrimination.
- *Influencing employer decisions.* Working together with employers to ensure the future of the enterprise to safeguard jobs and, to that end, to improve productivity.

Over and above this, however, workers' standards of living depend on actions taken by governments. These include:

- how the government manages the economy
- the priorities given to welfare and public services
- how taxes are raised and used
- what government does to ensure that unions are not at a disadvantage given the enormous power of many modern businesses.

The union role, then, is to protect and advance the standards of living of workers in any appropriate way to this purpose.

The TUC is always updating its approaches to fulfilling this role and protecting workers' interests in employment. Following the continual challenges posed to trade union organisation in the past two decades, and reorganisation within the TUC itself, it 'relaunched' itself in 1994 and made a commitment to turn itself into a high-profile campaigning organisation fighting for trade union goals and values. As its general secretary, John Monks, reported in 1995: 'Our priorities are firmly rooted in the world of work. Full employment remains our central objective. But alongside this we are also campaigning for minimum standards at work.' The TUC's stated purpose regarding its new role is 'to bring workplace relations out of the feudal era and into a new age of industrial enlightenment' (TUC 1995: 8). The chief characteristics of this 'new "campaigning" unionism' are:

- concentrating on priorities on world-of-work issues
- giving voice to the common concerns that people have in the world of work, as well as those specific to union members
- setting out to address new audiences
- taking the TUC's and the unions' arguments to all main political parties
- arguing the benefits of unions' working as social partners at workplace and national levels.

In its 'new' campaigning role, the TUC focused on four key areas: campaigning through task groups, raising current issues, campaigning for equality, and campaigning in Europe. TUC task groups, for example, have specific remits and a clear timetable. Four task groups were initially created:

- representation at work
- full employment
- minimum standards and national minimum wage
- part-time working.

Eight other campaigning initiatives were also raised by the TUC in its 'relaunch':

- top pay, corporate governance and standards in public life
- public services

- benefits and the world of work
- pensions
- training
- repetitive strain injuries
- industry/sector work
- technology and employment.

In its campaign for equality, the TUC identified four immediate areas demanding attention:

- women workers
- uniting against racism
- disability
- lesbian and gay rights.

Campaigning in Europe focused on three main issues:

- economic policy and employment
- social policy
- European works councils (EWCs).

Means and methods

For the TUC (1966: 43), trade union 'means' are interdependent with trade union 'methods'. It is impossible to bargain without anything to bargain with. 'This is the distinction between trade union means and trade union methods.' The choice between means and methods is a practical one, with union practice reflecting the circumstances in which a particular group of workers finds itself. But the basis of trade union effectiveness is 'combination' and this involves a number of means. Exhibit 26 illustrates the union means, listed by the TUC.

Exhibit 26 The TUC's definition of union means

These include:

- organisation
- 100 per cent membership
- national and local co-ordination
- income
- union competence.

Without sound organisation, high levels of membership, responsive leadership – nationally and locally – and sufficient income, a union's ability to perform its representative functions on behalf of employees is seriously impaired.

Union methods, in turn, are related to their objectives and means. The TUC argues that the dividing lines between various union methods are imprecise, they are diverse and their emphasis varies according to circumstances. The union methods that the TUC distinguishes are illustrated in Exhibit 27.

Exhibit 27 The TUC's definition of union methods

These include:

- collective bargaining
- joint consultation
- autonomous job regulation
- services for members
- influencing government
- political action
- international activities.

The challenges to the unions

It is clear that by the early 2000s a number of factors had weakened the 'permanent objectives', means and methods of trade unions. These included labour market factors, the employee relations strategies of some employers and the policy instruments of successive governments. Levels of unemployment, which remained high by immediate post-war standards, obviously affect trade union practice. Union practice is also affected by employers using 'soft' forms of joint consultation or non-union forms of employee involvement (see Chapter 6). Union effectiveness also suffers when government policy is directed towards deregulating the labour market and excluding the unions from the political process. As a result, since the mid-1980s, trade union practice, membership recruitment patterns and membership attitudes have all been adversely affected by a number of contextual and employee relations factors.

Contextual changes

The period since the 1980s has been one of immense economic, technological, social and political change in the Western world, but especially in Britain (see Chapters 4 and 5). There have been significant changes in the social structure, an ageing population, a larger proportion of women workers in the labour market and a weakening of traditional class allegiances. Working methods and working practices, in turn, have been dramatically affected by technological change, while the information technology revolution has left few occupational groups unaffected by its impact on employment, job tasks and the work environment (Daniel 1987).

For almost two decades, there have been persistent and relatively high levels of unemployment and radical changes in the structure of the economy, with shifts in the balance of provision between manufacturing and services, the private and public sectors and the 'old' and 'new' (e-commerce) economies. The international economic environment has been continuously turbulent and unstable. Large flows of finance capital are regularly transferred across national frontiers, with the purpose of gaining the highest possible returns from it, resulting in the weakening of national employment bases and traditional patterns of employment. Further, the move towards a single European market has not always resulted in the economic stability and economic potential expected of it by some British companies.

The election to power of four consecutive Conservative administrations, in 1979, 1983, 1987 and 1992, resulted in employee relations policies that were generally recognised as being unsupportive of and even antagonistic to the trade union function. The result was a set of labour market policies, employment legislation and government strategies that weakened union bargaining power, outlawed inter-union solidarity action and denied the unions any role in influencing public policy (see Chapters 3 and 9).

The election to office of a Labour Government in May 1997, however, is having some positive impacts on the trade union function. This is because, on balance, Labour in power continues to be more favourable to working people's interests, and more receptive to taking account of them, than were previous Conservative administrations in the 1980s and 1990s. This is despite the fact that 'New Labour' is sometimes seen as being too broadly based and too closely connected with big business and some business leaders. Nevertheless, the leader of the Labour Party and Prime Minister, Tony Blair, has argued for 'fairness' for the unions and their members, although he has promised them 'no favours'. Further, Labour's 1997 election manifesto commitment to supporting union recognition, 'where a majority of the relevant workforce vote in a ballot for the union to represent them' (Labour Party 1997: 17), has been subsequently enacted in the ERA 1999. Similarly, both the TUC and Labour Government support the concept of 'partnership at work'. Indeed, the TUC has argued strongly for a 'new approach' being needed in relationships at work based on the development of a world-class workforce, with skills to produce high-quality, high-value-added products and a response to rapid technological change. For the TUC, this new approach 'can best be achieved through a partnership between employers and trade unions', a key element of which is commitment by employers to security of employment (TUC 1994: 5). This mirrors the Labour Party's statement, in its 1997 election manifesto, that the best companies recognise their employees as partners in their enterprises and that many employers and unions are embracing 'partnership in place of conflict' in the workplace, which, in the TUC's view, government should welcome.

In summary, the changes outlined above have not always benefited the unions. Many employment units have become smaller, mass redundancies have resulted in large membership leakages from the unions and recruitment of new members from the 'new' service sector has proved to be problematic for trade unions. The occupational structure, nature of labour markets and job tasks have changed, thus weakening traditional union membership bases and patterns of union recruitment. The impact that the Labour Government's employee relations policies are having on trade union practice is generally favourable, rather than being detrimental to union and membership interests (see Chapter 9).

Employer policies

With private employers facing increasingly competitive open markets, and the public services being privatised or deregulated, there has been a shift towards employment flexibility in both sectors. This has resulted in increased use of short-term contracts, part-time working and changing patterns of shift work. These new working arrangements are generally not conducive to employment stability and membership retention in the trade unions. According to the third Workplace Industrial Relations Survey (WIRS) in 1990, there was little evidence of full union derecognition in Britain at that time, which amounted to 'just over 1 per cent of all workplaces in 1990' (Millward *et al* 1992: 74). But its limited data on the timing of derecognition was suggestive of a growing phenomenon, with a substantial concentration of the practice in 1989. Though this view has not been fully substantiated by later survey evidence, the fourth Workplace Employee Relations Survey (WERS) in 1998 nevertheless concluded that its results showed 'unambiguously that where management are predisposed towards unions, membership and recognition were far stronger than where management were opposed' (Cully *et al* 1999: 94).

The third WIRS also concluded that although new consultative arrangements created by management normally supplemented rather than replaced collective bargaining, there was evidence of management initiatives aimed at increasing employees' involvement at work, which took place with increasing frequency throughout the 1980s (Millward *et al* 1992). In these circumstances, it is possible that some employees saw the union role of participating in job regulation as being less important, especially where management adopted so-called proactive employee relations practices of these sorts. Indeed, the TUC claimed (1988: 6) that union influence was being further challenged in organisations because of trends 'such as the increasing management emphasis on winning the commitment of the individual employee ("human resources management") and the continued decentralisation of collective bargaining'.

The fourth WERS, conducted in 1998, illustrated the continuation of these trends. First, it reported that by 1998 union recognition was disappearing at an accelerating rate, even if not all the indicators of union presence and activity suggested increasing union weakness. This was largely because new workplaces were much less likely to recognise unions than were similar workplaces that they had replaced in the workplace population. Second, a number of alternative, individualist approaches to employee relations were being adopted in different types of workplace and different parts of the economy. WERS described these various and fragmented patterns of employee involvement as 'high commitment management practices', which appeared to be more prevalent in larger workplaces that were part of large organisations in the public sector or in organisations employing personnel specialists at workplace or corporate level. These practices included personality tests, performance tests, flexible working arrangements, off-the-job training, profit-related pay, employee share ownership, single status, autonomous working teams, staff appraisals, team briefings, channels of communication and information, and others (see Chapter 6). Clearly, the evidence pointed to growing interest by employers in introducing and implementing direct methods of employee participation and managerial practices imported from the United States and Japan, rather than tradition-alist union-based ones (Cully *et al* 1999: 82).

Earlier research conducted by the TUC (1994: 6), however, using data from WIRS 1990, concluded that human resources management (HRM) in practice was 'rarely applied as a comprehensive package' and that fragments of high commitment or HRM practices were more likely to be found in unionised rather than non-unionised workplaces. Its findings suggested that:

* multiple channels of communication were more likely to be used in unionised workplaces
* non-union workplaces were characterised by authoritarian and hierarchi-cal management practices
* non-unionised workers had few opportunities to influence their working lives
* workers in unionised companies received more information from their employers than did workers in non-unionised firms
* financial participation was as common in unionised as in non-unionised companies
* the most anti-union employers were least likely to offer financial partici-pation schemes
* single status was found as frequently in unionised as in non-unionised companies
* the more anti-union an employer, the less likely single status applied.

The TUC argued therefore that there was no correlation between anti-unionism and HRM. Indeed, the more anti-union the employer, the less likely it was that HRM techniques were being used. Four years later, in 1998, WERS indicated that use of high commitment management practices was not independent of structure or strategy. But there was 'evidence that a number of the practices consistent with a human resource management approach are well entrenched in many British workplaces' (Cully *et al* 1999: 82).

Inter-union competition

Differences between unions arise from a number of factors, including:

* competition for membership recruitment
* job demarcation
* union recognition and collective bargaining rights
* wages policy
* subscription contribution levels and services to members.

In the majority of inter-union disputes involving TUC affiliates, the TUC is the final arbiter through the device of TUC disputes committees. In the 1980s, the so-called 'Bridlington Principles', which aimed to regulate inter-union membership competition and poaching amongst affiliated unions, came under increasing stress. This was the result of (TUC 1988):

* pressure on unions to recruit new members in competing areas because of membership leakages after 1980
* the multi-occupational and multi-industry structure of British unions
* the emergence of 'single-union agreements' on greenfield sites that excluded other unions with members in the unit from employer recognition
* controversy over the 'no-strike' provisions in some of these agreements.

However, pressures for inter-union competition are likely to become more intense, now that the Trade Union Reform and Employment Rights Act 1993 provides trade union members with a statutory right to decide for themselves which union to join, even in multi-union situations. This effectively removes the Bridlington arrangements for dealing with disputes over membership among TUC unions.

It was the issue of single-union or 'new-style' agreements that caused particular differences among TUC-affiliated unions and led eventually to the expulsion of the EETPU from Congress in September 1988. The decision to expel the EEPTU from the TUC arose from a complaint by the GMB, TGWU and USDAW that the EEPTU had acted in contravention of the TUC's Disputes Principles and Procedures by signing a single-union deal with Christian Salvesen at its Warrington and West Cross depots. The disputes committee decided, on the evidence presented, that the complaining unions should have been consulted by the EEPTU before it entered into a sole negotiating agreement with the company at the two depots. The EEPTU's failure to accept the decision of the committee placed it in direct conflict with Congress, which heard the union's appeal on 5 September, which it lost.

TRADE UNION STRATEGY

Trade union strategy points the ways in which unions adapt their policies and objectives and adjust their means and methods in response to changing economic and social factors, employer initiatives and the framework of public policy (and EU policy) within which employers and unions operate. As voluntary associations promoting the employment interests of their members, trade unions are a mixture of 'movement and organisation' (Flanders 1968b). Members of a movement combine together because they share the same sentiments, values and ideas and want to achieve common goals collectively. To survive as organisations, however, unions must have effective means for translating their goals into practical outcomes for their members. By their very nature, unions have to be organisationally dynamic, while maintaining the values and ideas for which they stand. They 'need organisation for their power and movement for their vitality, but they need both power and vitality to advance their social purpose' (*ibid:* 44). As indicated above, this dual measure of trade union effectiveness has been severely tested in recent years. The main responses of the unions to these challenges are discussed below.

The collective bargaining agenda

Objectives

During the 1990s and early 2000s, trade unions have developed and are developing a number of positive and developmental responses to the economic, technological, social and political challenges facing them and their members. The TUC (1991a: 12–13) initially outlined some of these developments in what it described as the 'New Bargaining Agenda' of trade unions, which it built on subsequently. This agenda provided examples of attempts by some unions to raise the negotiating horizon beyond immediate pay concerns to embrace a 'wide range of longer-term developmental considerations'. The emerging themes, identified by the TUC, at which the unions should aim, are illustrated in Exhibit 28. In the TUC's view, the more the unions talked about employee development issues of this sort, and about devolution of management responsibilities to their members, the more they would find themselves questioning existing management prerogatives.

Exhibit 28 The bargaining agenda for TUC unions since the 1990s

---

- building for the future in terms of job security, job creation, the attainment of full employment and elimination of underemployment

- focusing on job development, training and career prospects to give more workers control over their working lives and to provide them with more satisfying, fulfilling and rewarding jobs

- emphasising 'fair play' policies, such as: improving the jobs, careers, status and pay of low-paid workers; up-valuing the jobs of women; providing equal opportunities for disadvantaged groups; and providing developmental opportunities for those doing part-time, temporary and subcontract work

- giving priority to environmental and quality-of-life objectives and essential working conditions, such as: health and safety; the working environment; leisure; sickness benefit; occupational pensions; and family provisions

---

The GMBU and CWU (1991: 1) suggested a similar 'New Agenda' that Britain's unions should adopt. In their view, it was essential that Britain's unions abandon traditional reactive stances and set an agenda that confronted the issues of the 1990s by taking 'collective bargaining into territory that we have barely explored before'. They argued that unions needed to work together with employers and government to create successful industry, a strong economy and a 'caring, sharing society'. In these unions' analysis, the new circumstances facing employers, unions and government in the 1990s and beyond were:

- the European Union
- rising expectations among consumers and employees
- the role of women in the workforce
- environmental concerns
- restructuring within industry.

The GMBU and CWU argued that this situation should involve a joint response by unions and employers, with government support, aimed at matching productivity levels abroad. It should also aim at negotiating ways of working which ensured that new skills and new plant were brought to bear on the productivity gap separating Britain from its foreign rivals.

In response to these challenges, the GMBU and CWU wanted unions to talk to Britain's employers about how to achieve quality performance, cost and price competitiveness and a fairer society. The collective bargaining agenda would include issues such as training, investment, new product development, work restructuring, equal opportunities and health and safety. The purpose of the New Agenda was to make quality of output rather than prices of inputs the centrepiece of talks between trade unions and employers. Pay would be on the bargaining agenda 'but work organisation, training and quality should form the focus' (*ibid*: 8). This approach required unions to press employers for discussions on how management intended to develop the talents of their workforces, the investments they proposed making and how they could encourage employees to ever higher standards of customer service.

The negotiating framework

Though the TUC identified enterprise-level bargaining as the obvious focus for employee relations decision-making, it did not rule out industry and sector bargaining for some matters. Indeed, the TUC emphasised the importance of national framework agreements for establishing minimum rates for jobs or a floor of pay below which no employee may fall, since it believed that decentralised bargaining has not achieved both low inflation and high employment. In its view, a national framework, and bargaining arrangements for minimum standards can help reconcile the need for local flexibility and national standards.

The TUC also supported single-table bargaining, so that the entire job and pay structure could be taken into account in union–employer negotiations. On a wider front, the TUC also believed that there was need for co-ordination at a European level – initially in terms of exchanges of information on 'performance comparisons and agreement on principles' (TUC 1991a: 14). This international role was likely to expand in the future but, in the short term, was to be focused on agreeing bargaining objectives amongst European unions. There was also a case for establishing 'independent comparability arrangements', providing an agreed database for negotiators, especially but not exclusively for public-sector unions.

The 'New Unionism': social partnership and the organising agenda

Prior to the 1997 general election, the TUC (1996a: 1) argued that 'we need a New Unionism so that unions and employers can work together in partnership to make Britain's industries and services more efficient and competitive and to protect people at work.' The New Unionism is rooted in the concept of 'social partnership'. For the TUC, social partnership in the workplace means employers and unions working together to achieve common goals, such as fairness and competitiveness. At national level, this means government discussing issues with employers and unions on an open and fair basis, where it is believed that a common approach can result in benefits to all parties, such as attracting inward investment and promoting training and equal opportunities. The intention is to promote a new approach to employee relations that can deliver secure and worthwhile jobs for trade union members. For the TUC, social partnership in the private sector is based on the assumption that employment security depends on employers operating efficient and effective organisations, providing quality products and services to their customers. In the public sector, the TUC believes that government's agenda for improvement and reform can only be achieved if it engages the skills, talents and enthusiasm of public-sector workers (TUC 1999a).

In 1998, the TUC's Partnership Task Group identified six principles of partnership:

- a shared commitment to the success of the organisation
- a recognition of the legitimate roles of the employer and trade union in the employment relationship
- a commitment by the employer to employment security for all workers and a commitment to engage positively in the process of change
- a focus on the quality of working life, particularly investment in the vocational and non-vocational training of workers
- openness on both sides and willingness by employers to discuss plans and thoughts about the future when they are taking shape
- a shared understanding that the partnership is delivering measurable improvements for all parties – the employer, union and its members.

Subsequently, it was agreed that the Partnership Task Group should consider how information about new partnership arrangements might be collected and disseminated by the TUC to enable unions and employers to learn from best practice. It was also agreed that the Task Group should undertake an analysis of the TUC's training for full-time officials and lay representatives to determine whether these programmes were consistent with the principles of partnership.

The importance of partnership for the TUC is that it has the potential to deliver greater influence over employers' strategic decisions, as well as better jobs for trade unionists. This position is in line with the European Commission's view that maintaining and developing the prosperity of the European economy depends critically on the social partners making progress, at European level, on a shared agenda to develop a partnership for a new organisation of work. According to the Director-General of DG V of the European Commission, partnership is essential for productivity growth in Europe. But this has to be underpinned by minimum standards and willingness by the social partners to promote excellence. In his view, this requires 'a culture of adaptation and anticipation of change', which in turn demands 'trust and co-operation on the basis of informed choices'. For him, structured and dynamic partnership is an essential ingredient of economic success (TUC 1999a: 60).

The TUC's case for partnership is set out in its policy document, *Partners for Progress* (TUC 1999b). The document draws together a statement of the principles of partnership and gives practical examples of how partnerships operate in practice. It notes that successful partnerships require: leadership; understanding of the need to change the culture of employee relations; investment of time and effort in relationship-building; and training and education for participants. The report shows that effective and principled partnership can make a value-adding contribution to enterprises in the following areas:

- change management
- communications
- training and development
- disseminating best practice
- improving personnel performance.

Although the report shows good examples of partnership throughout the private and public sectors, the TUC accepts that only a minority of employers works in partnership with the unions.

The other dimension of the New Unionism is its concern with the organising agenda. This is seen as being the key to union success in rebuilding its organisational basis. Among trade union leaders there is an increasing recognition that successful delivery of services to union members, and improvement in union retention rates, depend upon the creation of a positive organising culture within trade union organisations. The New Unionism project has four principal objectives. These are to:

- promote organising as the top priority of trade unions and build an organising culture
- boost investment of resources – people and cash – into organising and strengthen lay organisation

- help unions strengthen their existing membership bases and break into new jobs and industries and win recognition rights
- sharpen union appeal to 'new' workers to include women, youth, blacks and especially those workers at the roughest end of the labour market.

The overall aim of the New Unionism project, then, is to set the organising agenda alive, against the existing and future industrial and legislative environment confronting trade unions.

It is recognised that one of the key roles in the change process is that of the 'dedicated organiser' and that one of the prime features in need of attention by unions in developing a union 'organising culture' is to recruit union activists. It is also accepted that the union movement has to set its sights on attracting new workers into the unions, as well as moving into new sectors of employment. This means concentrating union efforts on organising typical workers needing a union, signing up those workers who have never been asked to join unions and organising workplaces that have traditionally been difficult to collectivise.

A major TUC initiative in this area is the creation of its 'Organising Academy'. This is modelled on the experiences of the American Federation of Labor-Congress of Industrial Organizations (AFL-CIO) in the United States and the Australian Congress of Trade Unions in Australia. The TUC developed its Organising Academy training programme, with teams of specially selected organisers to spearhead union recruitment campaigns, in order to change the union culture to one of actively recruiting and organising new members. Following the initial activities of the Organising Academy, the TUC's New Unionism Task Group and the Organising Academy Steering Group made a number of proposals regarding the future of union recruitment and the TUC's organising campaign:

- The Organising Academy should be flexible in allowing unions to recruit trainees through their own selection programmes, as well as using the New Unionism selection programme.
- Trainees from sponsoring unions should continue to be jointly sponsored by the TUC and sponsoring unions.
- The recruitment process should move to two intakes per year.
- The Organising Academy should have the remit of including the development of best-practice training for full-time and other union staff.
- Consideration should be given to how the Organising Academy and unions could work more closely, especially in activist training.
- Consideration also needs to be given to increasing the existing salary level of organisers.

For the TUC, then, given the immense labour market, product market, legal and technological changes over the past two decades, strong, reformed trade unions are needed to ensure that the most vulnerable at work benefit from a national minimum wage, through either collective bargaining or a statutory minimum. In this way, minimum standards can be achieved in the labour market. Further, inherent in the social partnership model is the need to minimise industrial disputes and encourage unions and employers to reach employment security agreements together. The TUC concludes (1996a: 22) that by acting in partnership with employers on matters such as jobs, training, investment and minimisation of industrial disputes, unions can ensure that they can help tackle the problems government faces and ensure that 'trade unions can be part of the solution', rather than the problem.

Medium-term principles and priorities

The TUC's and union priority is jobs: good-quality, well-rewarded and secure ones. In the private sector, this implies firms that are prosperous, profitable and competitive. In the public sector, it implies good-quality, secure jobs providing high-quality public services, held in esteem by those using them and wanting to use them. The TUC sets out an agenda for achieving this, underpinned by the belief that the Labour Government's early actions must lay the foundations for economic success and create a greater spirit of national common purpose. It adds that the more trade unions can be seen as part of the solution, the more government and employers will take up their ideas.

In the TUC's view, the economic priority must be to return to full and fair employment, based on:

- active economic policy by government
- active labour market policies regarding training, the long-term unemployed and helping individuals cope with unemployment
- building social partnership between employers and trade unions and delivering investment in people, greater job security and best practice to secure quality products and services
- increased public investment in social housing, urban regeneration and environmental improvement
- providing help for the long-term unemployed and the young
- promoting workplace skills and security.

As sustainable growth continues, the TUC argues, more resources need to be released to support the drive towards full employment, without risking the stability of public finances.

Jobs

Here the TUC is keen to promote the concept of 'best practice' and show how unions and employers can develop the most effective models of work organisation, with the aim of enhancing productivity and competitiveness and protecting individuals. Another area is the organisation of working time and enriching job content to alleviate the problem of monotonous, unchallenging jobs. The TUC would also like to encourage the social partners to explore the scope for 'job security' collective agreements. Another proposal is for public-sector bodies to set best practice in terms of job objectives. Action to which the public sector could contribute includes:

- helping combat sex, race, disability and age discrimination at work
- setting the pace in terms of single-status collective agreements to remove discrimination against the low paid, women and manual workers
- creating employment and training opportunities for young people
- promoting youth training and modern apprenticeships offering high-quality training for young people
- targeting the long-term unemployed.

Investment

To ensure the foundations for steady growth, the TUC believes that economic policy should aim at limiting consumption growth to a slightly lesser rate than growth of gross domestic product (GDP). This is to ensure that resources are available for investment and exports. The priority areas for investment identified by the TUC are: transport; information technology; social housing; and health and education. Whilst acknowledging that government is still a major player in the field, the TUC supports the injection of private finance and development of private/public partnerships, which offer ways of protecting public investment and, at the same time, promote additional investment.

Training and education

The TUC's view is that Britain will only be able to exploit new investment if it becomes a learning society; that is why education has to be a priority of government. The TUC therefore supports lifelong learning and the integration of education and training into a single system. It also argues that employers that involve unions in their training decisions are the most successful in managing change. In this sense, unions can be part of the solution to closing the skills gap experienced by employers.

Quality in the public services

With new approaches to public-sector management being introduced into public organisations (Farnham and Horton 1996, Horton and Farnham 1999, Storey 1992), and increasing emphasis being placed on 'service quality', the TUC (1992) has become increasingly conscious of the need for the unions to address quality as an issue. It distinguishes three approaches to service quality in the public services. These are:

- 'quality management', which requires all members of staff to clarify their products and services so as to identify their customers, and to be given measurable goals to achieve that are monitored on a regular basis (see Chapter 6)
- 'customer care', which clarifies the provider–user relationship by setting out the quality of service to be provided and the rights of redress

- 'quality assurance', which attempts to improve the quality of standards through the application of the British Standards Institution quality assurance standard BS 5750 (now BS EN ISO 9000).

Each of these makes demands upon the unions, in their response to the search for quality in the public services.

Union participation

The unions argue that most quality programmes are management-driven; consequently they are not designed to accommodate union involvement. The TUC has proposed, therefore, that if service quality is to be significantly improved, it requires more direct involvement of employees in decision-making about the way services are provided and managed. According to the TUC, a key challenge for the unions 'is to confront the call for more open communications, devolved self-management and active employee participation'. The unions claim that management sets quality agendas, with the strategy for enhancing employee involvement designed and executed with minimum consultation with staff. Similarly, employee empowerment is often more concerned with the obligations and duties of individual employees rather than with collective rights and representation. 'The main objective is usually to tie the employee's performance more closely to [the] overall goals of the organisation.' What public service unions are arguing are the benefits of a 'partnership approach to improving quality service', especially at workplace level and that the key to responsive and effective public services is a well-trained workforce (TUC 1992: 20–22).

A Quality Work Assured (QWA) Service Mark

Public-service unions want to raise the union profile and articulate more precisely the commitment of staff to quality and to define what improving service quality means from the workers' perspective. They believe that it is important to grasp the language of service quality and stress their commitment to partnership, openness, accessibility, flexibility and choice. But the unions have also wanted to formulate a mechanism for identifying the quality component in service provision in relation to the quality of working conditions and the quality of the workforce. The aims of the TUC's QWA Service Mark were to (1992a: 26):

- increase citizen and customer awareness and evaluation of the conditions and way in which a service is provided
- expose the competence and commitment of the workforce and management
- illustrate best practice in terms of employee participation and involvement
- identify the employer's commitment to training and equal opportunities
- facilitate a close relationship and understanding between staff and service users
- ensure compliance with health and safety and other employment legislation
- increase employee awareness of good management practice

- inform users of an employer's industrial relations record
- help develop quality standards at work
- widen choice and preference
- inform users of staff behaviour and attitudes
- identify labour costs for a public service.

It was hoped, in short, that the QWA Service Mark would provide a benchmark by which quality of public-service inputs and outcomes might be measured, for the benefit of both users and providers of services.

The union response

The key quality objective identified for public-service unions since the 1990s has been to exert a positive influence on the development of public services to the benefit of users and producers. It is suggested that unions must work much closer together and that further consideration needs to be given, in managing quality, to union relations with management and service users. The unions have stressed the importance of education and training programmes to equip staff, and union officials, to deal with demands for high-quality services and ensure that programmes of performance measurement and appraisal are implemented in a fair and systematic way. In campaigning for quality, the unions are arguing that their 'vision' is one of a high-quality workforce producing high-quality services.

Inter-union disputes

In 1988, the TUC amended its rules on inter-union relations and a new code of practice was approved by Congress to mitigate inter-union rivalry, as a result of the recommendations by a Special Review Body appointed after the 1987 Congress.

The amendments to 'Principle 5' provided that no union is to organise where another union has the majority of workers employed and negotiates terms and conditions, unless by arrangement with that union. Where a union has members but not a majority and does not negotiate terms and conditions, another union seeking to organise should consult with the existing union. If there is no agreement, the matter should be referred by either union to the TUC. Where a disputes committee adjudicates, it takes into account:

- the efforts that the union opposing entry of another union is making to retain membership and the degree of organisation over this period
- any existing collective bargaining arrangements
- the efforts that the union seeking entry is making to secure majority membership
- the provisions of the code of practice.

The code of practice is designed to set standards for affiliated unions organising and seeking recognition with an employer on new sites. It requires affiliated unions that are negotiating single-union agreements to give prior notification to the TUC of their intention to do so. The code goes on to say that (TUC 1988: 19):

> Unions must not make any agreements which remove, or are designed to remove, the basic democratic lawful rights of a trade union to take industrial action in advance of the recruitment of members and without consulting them.

Unions are also expected to co-operate with any procedures operated by the TUC and related bodies concerning inward investing authorities. This is to avoid inter-union competition that could damage the attractiveness of the area. When negotiating recognition agreements, which have implications for substantive agreements, affiliated unions are expected to take into account the general level of terms and conditions that are already agreed with the company and to take all possible steps to avoid undermining them.

The relative weakness of this procedure meant that inter-union relations were regularly discussed within the TUC. At the TUC's Annual Congress in 1999, the General Council reported that if there were too many unions operating in one industry in competition with one another, they would end up competing on the basis of price rather than quality. Since the ability of specialist unions to participate in all TUC activities was reduced because of their relative lack of resources, the TUC argued that it could set up umbrella alliances, based on trade groups such as the Federation of Entertainment Unions. The General Secretary of the TUC made it clear to Congress that the TUC would not try to impose mergers on specialist unions. But current structures were often bewildering for young people considering joining a union. It was also clear that the length of time for affiliated unions going through TUC procedures for dispute resolution made the process unsatisfactory. In the General Council's view, discussion was needed on the proposal to establish a network of union officers for handling inter-union issues. It was considered that unions should continue to try to sort out conflicts for themselves and that TUC involvement should be seen as a means of last resort. It was decided therefore that the TUC should come up with proposals, but that this would require a degree of openness amongst affiliated unions (TUC 1999a).

Unions and Europe

British unions, acting primarily through the TUC and the ETUC, recognise that the evolution of the EU poses immense challenges for trade unions and trade unionists. For the unions, the essential challenge of EU policy is to make a reality of Europe's social dimension, so that worker and citizen interests are taken into account within the EU, as well as those of the business community. The TUC is participating with the ETUC in developing economic and social policies aimed at maximising prosperity and economic security for working people in the Union's member states (TUC 1991b; 1996b).

Achievements

Trade unions at both national and European level claim to have achieved a number of their goals on behalf of their members, through European legislation and the courts. These include:

- advances in health and safety legislation and equal treatment between men and women on pay and retirement age
- new rights to maternity leave for women and removal of the upper limit on compensation in sex discrimination cases
- improved rights for part-time workers to claim unfair dismissal and redundancy payments and rights to written particulars
- protection of workers' terms and conditions when businesses change hands
- protection for young workers
- introduction of the Working Time Directive
- introduction of the European Works Council Directive, which, despite the former Conservative Government's opt-out, now covers over 100 UK-based multinational companies and hundreds more based elsewhere in Europe but with subsidiaries in the UK
- introduction of the Posting of Workers Directive, under which pay and working conditions applying in an EU country will be extended to workers from other member states working there under contracts
- introduction of the Parental Leave Directive
- introduction of the Part-Time Workers' Directive and Fixed-Term Contracts Directive
- progress between the social partners relating to part-time, temporary and fixed-term contract workers.

Further, the European Commission has produced measures in which the TUC had worked closely with the European Parliament regarding:

- the right to information and consultation in national undertakings employing more than 50 workers
- the right to continued vocational training
- equal treatment for third-world country workers
- inclusion of a labour clause in public works contracts
- measures to strengthen legal guarantees for trade union freedoms and collective bargaining
- the right to a minimum income
- legislation on poverty, social exclusion and housing
- measures to combat racism and xenophobia.

The TUC's General Council also supports the ETUC's wish to generate more impetus behind the social action issues, especially against employers and governments wanting to block its momentum.

Employment, social and economic policy

The TUC considers that there can be no greater priority than reducing unemployment throughout the EU. In its view, the problems associated with unemployment need to be tackled at the European level. The TUC therefore supported the Swedish Government's proposal that an Employment Chapter be included in the Treaty of Amsterdam 1997. This was subsequently agreed at Amsterdam and employment strategy is now to be co-ordinated amongst member states of the EU. Its provisions are aimed at:

- enabling men and women to attain a secure livelihood through freely chosen productive employment
- preventing long-term unemployment and social exclusion
- ensuring that demand grows at an adequate rate to ensure sustainable growth
- promoting flexibility by providing workers and job-seekers with the skills to adapt to a constantly changing economy.

Other decisions taken at the intergovernmental conference at Amsterdam in 1997 included:

- agreeing a human rights declaration outlawing discrimination on the basis of gender, race, religion, sexual orientation and age
- guaranteeing free movement of persons throughout the EU, except the UK and Ireland, who keep their national border controls
- co-operating over immigration, visas, political asylum, civil and judicial issues and harmonising divorce laws
- agreeing a stability pact regulating participating states' budgetary deficits once a single currency is introduced
- integrating the Social Chapter into the Treaty of Amsterdam, following the UK's signing of it
- co-ordinating common foreign and defence policy through senior civil servants, not politicians
- providing more powers and a simplified co-decision-making role for the European Parliament.

On labour market policy, the TUC strongly supports the rolling review of governments' economic policies beginning at Essen in 1994. This includes:

- complementing the employers' wish to see greater flexibility at work with new protections for workers, especially those working atypically
- making education and training a priority in the workplace
- reorganising and reducing working time to ensure that economic recovery is more employment-intensive
- re-appraising the effectiveness of EU structural funds in terms of employment generation
- focusing employment programmes on those sections of the population where help is particularly needed

- strengthening job placement services to encourage labour market mobility throughout the EU.

Action on unemployment at European level is also focused on the proposal for a Confidence Pact for Employment. This involves discussions between the social partners (ETUC and UNICE), European Commission, member states, European Parliament and Social and Economic Committee. The aim is to create more effective macroeconomic policies, including:

- stimulating public and private investment and using European funds to this end
- using private-sector profits to raise currently low levels of investment in member states
- reducing real interest rates
- establishing wage-bargaining policies seeking a more equitable balance between wages and profits, while recognising the productivity gains being achieved by employees in many sectors of the economy.

The TUC and European unions also want increased provision for education and training for workers and investment in innovation and research.

Economic and monetary union (EMU)

The TUC and ETUC believe that the basic objectives of EMU must be to promote sustainable growth, full employment and stable prices. They want economic policies leading to greater convergence among member states in terms of industrial performance, job creation and living standards. Policy on EMU is illustrated in Exhibit 29.

Exhibit 29 **ETUC policy on EMU**

- to strengthen regional policy in the EU and transfer resources to regions in economic difficulty
- to ensure that the European Central Bank is democratically accountable and that the social partners are regularly consulted through an advisory committee
- to use European institutions to create a European industrial relations area as part of the social dimension
- to make member states not complying with agreed economic and employment objectives lose EU financial assistance

---

Thus the decision of whether or not the UK should take part in EMU is of major importance for the economy, trade unions and trade unionists. It is likely to have a lasting effect on the economy, living standards and the collective bargaining framework. With the continuing globalisation of the economy, and relentless moves towards commercial integration, the unions see the advantages of EMU as including:

- lower-risk premiums on cross-border investment
- comparability of prices within the euro area
- ending uncertainties and the destabilising speculation that is linked to exchange rate variability
- the ability to influence European and global monetary policy
- lower transaction costs on trade and travel.

On the other hand, the potential disadvantages of EMU are:

- ending exchange rate adjustments as a means of adapting to variations in economic performance among countries within the euro area
- reduction in influence over domestic monetary policy
- the costs of changing over to the single currency
- the impact on the UK/US dollar rates, which are relatively more important for the UK than for other EU countries.

In encouraging debate and dialogue in the UK about the EMU issue, the TUC keeps in dialogue with the CBI, Bank of England, consumers and others, in order to work towards a national consensus. The TUC is also seeking real economic convergence in employment, GDP, productivity and competitiveness – as opposed to nominal convergence in budget deficits, public debt and rates of inflation. For these and similar reasons, the General Council of the TUC believes that the balance of advantage is in the UK joining EMU (TUC 1996b).

Institutional reform

Exhibit 30 **Reforms to the Community treaties supported by the ETUC**

- ensuring that social and employment policies are a basic EU activity
- giving ethnic minorities and third-world country nationals equal rights
- defining the undercutting of some terms and conditions of employment as unfair competition
- restricting the exclusion from qualified majority voting to fiscal provisions only
- extending qualified majority voting to:
    - job creation and employment protection
    - employment law
    - working conditions
    - equality of treatment
    - initial and continuing training
    - social security and welfare
    - health and safety at work
    - trade union law and collective bargaining
    - information and consultation of workers
    - working environment
    - the environment
- strengthening regional policy

The ETUC seeks a number of measures to make EU institutions more democratic and accountable. These include:

- creating an enhanced law-making role for the European Parliament
- giving the European Parliament authority to move towards political union, in association with national governments
- giving the European Parliament power to elect the president of the European Commission.

Exhibit 30 illustrates the ETUC's support for reforms to the European treaties.

THE LAW AND TRADE UNION MEMBERSHIP

The law now provides a series of statutory rights for trade union members (see Chapters 3 and 4). The first set of rights, to join and organise trade unions (the right to associate), emerged slowly and took place in two phases. Phase one removed statutory criminal prohibitions, with the state allowing workers and unions to use 'self-help' measures to achieve 'voluntary' employer recognition for collective bargaining purposes. Phase two was the creation of positive legal rights for trade unionists against employers. Workers in Britain now have the right to join an independent trade union and not to be dismissed, or have action short of dismissal taken against them, because of their trade union membership. Such actions by employers are automatically unfair in law and where individuals think these rights have been infringed, they may make a complaint to an employment tribunal.

The law also provides protections for those who do not want to join a trade union or a particular union (the right of dissociation). This makes it automatically unfair for employers to dismiss individuals where they refuse to belong to a union. This is a relatively new right which, apart from the period of the Industrial Relations Act 1971 (IRA 1971), has been built into public policy since the early 1980s (see Chapter 9). The strategy pursued has been to remove the legal props to the closed shop, built into the unfair dismissals legislation under the Trade Union and Labour Relations Act (TULRA) 1974 and 1976, and provide a right for employees not to be union members, even where there is no closed shop arrangement. These rights are also enforceable through employment tribunals (ETs), with the right of appeal to the Employment Appeal Tribunal (EAT). Obviously, strengthening the right not to join a union can be done only at the expense of weakening the right to become a union member and the ways these rights are reconciled vary from country to country (von Prondynski 1987).

The legal relationship of unions to their members

A third and extended group of statutory rights provided to trade union members is to take part in trade union activities and trade union decision-making and to restrain certain trade union actions that are unlawful (intra-union rights). Traditionally, the 'freedom' for members to participate in union activities, and for unions to operate within boundaries of the law, was provided in the union rulebook. These common-law rights still exist and can be enforced in the courts, under the common law, where individuals consider that the rulebook is not being applied by the union or its officials. Further, under the ERA 1999, the Certification Officer (CO) has powers to examine complaints from trade union members of alleged breaches of trade union law or that their union has failed to observe the requirements of the union rulebook, as an alternative to the courts (see Chapter 2). The statutory rights of trade unionists in relation to their unions have been extended in recent years and are summarised below.

Industrial action ballots

Union members have the right to participate in industrial action ballots when a union is contemplating, authorising or endorsing industrial action and it would be lawful for the union to organise such action, if the statutory requirements of the ballot are satisfied. The law also gives union members the right to apply to the courts for an order restraining a union from inducing them to take any kind of industrial action in the absence of a properly conducted ballot. Where appropriate, the courts will make an order requiring the union to take steps to withdraw any authorisation or endorsement of the action, and to leave its members in no doubt that it has been withdrawn. If the court order is not obeyed, anyone who sought the order can return to the court, asking that the union be declared in contempt of court. Unions in contempt of court can be fined, and refusal to pay fines can lead to the sequestration of union assets (Department of Employment 1990; see also Chapters 4 and 10).

Union elections

Union members have the right to elect by secret ballot all members of the principal executive committee of their union at least once every five years. Unions must keep a register of their members' names and addresses and ensure that entries on the register are accurate and reasonably up to date. An independent scrutineer can inspect registers, where this is felt to be appropriate. Someone independent of the process must undertake the distribution, counting and storage of voting papers. All candidates seeking election must be given the opportunity to prepare an election address and have it distributed at no cost to themselves. Elections must be under independent scrutiny, with the scrutineer being responsible for supervising the election and producing a report. If a union fails to comply with these statutory requirements, members can make a complaint to the CO or to the courts, where the CO's procedures are less formal than those of the courts.

Union political funds and political fund review ballots

Members of unions have the right to vote, by secret ballot, if their union intends to set up a political fund – and then in political fund review ballots, at least once every 10 years. If a union with a political fund fails to hold a review ballot after 10 years, its authority to spend money on political objects automatically lapses. The rules for conducting political fund ballots must be approved as rules of the union and be approved by the CO. The CO gives approval only where: every member is entitled to vote; there is a postal ballot; and the ballot is subject to independent scrutiny. Where unions fail to comply with the balloting rules approved by the CO, members may complain to the CO or the courts. Union members also have the right to complain, to the CO or to the courts, if a union unlawfully spends money from its general funds on 'political objects'.

Misuse of union funds

Union members have the right to prevent the unlawful use of their union's funds or property. These include the right to seek a court order against union trustees in order to prevent them applying, or permitting the application of, union funds to any unlawful purpose. They also have the right to inspect their union's accounting records, accompanied by an accountant. Further, there is the right to prevent a union's funds or property being used to indemnify anyone for fines or other penalties imposed on them for any criminal offence or for contempt of court. Unions must also take all reasonable steps to provide their members, within eight weeks of sending the annual return to the CO, with a statement covering: income and expenditure; income represented by membership fees; salary and benefits paid to senior officers and the executive committee; and the report of the auditor(s) on the return.

Union membership registers

Union members have the right to ensure that their union maintains a membership register. Unions must allow any members who have given reasonable notice to check, free of charge, at a reasonable time, whether they are included in the register. They must also supply members with a copy of their register entry on request. Either the CO or the courts deal with any complaints on these matters.

Unjustifiable discipline

Union members have the right not to be disciplined, by being expelled, fined or deprived of membership benefits by their union, where that discipline is unjustifiable. Discipline is unjustifiable in law where the individual's conduct is concerned with any of the reasons illustrated in Exhibit 31.

Individuals who believe that they have been unjustifiably disciplined by their union may make a complaint to an employment tribunal. If, after conciliation with the Advisory, Conciliation and Arbitration Service (ACAS), the tribunal finds that the complaint of unjustifiable discipline is well founded, it makes a declaration to that effect. An application for compensation may also be made to the EAT if the union does not lift the penalty imposed, with the award being 'just and equitable in all the circumstances'.

Exhibit 31 Unjustifiable union discipline

It is unjustifiable for a union to discipline its members where they:

- fail to take part in or support any strike or other industrial action
- show opposition to or lack of support for the above
- fail to break, for any purpose connected with the above, any obligation imposed by a contract of employment
- encourage or assist other individuals honouring their contracts of employment
- assert that the union or its officials has broken, or is proposing to break, any requirement imposed by the union rulebook or the law
- encourage or assist other individuals in making, defending or vindicating such assertions
- fail to agree to or withdraw from an agreement with an employer for the deduction of union dues
- resign from the union, refuse to join another union, belong to another union or propose to do so
- work or propose to work with members of another union or non-union members
- work or propose to work for an employer who employs non-union members or members of another union
- refuse to comply with any penalties imposed by the union following unjustifiable disciplinary action
- propose to do any of the above.

Enforcing union membership rights

The bodies with the responsibility for enforcing the rights of trade members are the courts, the CO and ETs. The role of the CO, for example, is to deal with complaints by union members that trade unions have failed to comply with one or more of the provisions that impose the duty on trade unions to hold secret postal ballots for electing members of their principal executive committees. The CO also deals with complaints that a union has failed to maintain an accurate register of its members. In 1996, for example, a typical year, the CO dealt with only 15 decisions of this sort and there was only one outstanding claim at the end of the year (Certification Office 1997).

The Commissioner for the Rights of Trade Union Members (CRTUM) previously had the duty of providing material assistance to union members who were contemplating taking legal proceedings against their union in any complaint coming within his statutory remit. The CRTUM also had the

Table 14 Applications to the CRTUM for assistance regarding the statutory rights of union members, 1996–97

Statutory right	Number of applications	Outcome
Trustees permitted unlawful application of union property	1	not assisted
Failure to allow access to union's accounting records	3	not assisted
Failure to comply with statutory requirements regarding elections to office	6	not assisted

authority to grant assistance to union members who claimed that their union had breached its rulebook in certain matters. Section 28 of the ERA 1999 abolishes the office of the CRTUM, some of whose functions have been taken over by the CO. Tables 14 and 15 show the relatively light workload of the CRTUM in a typical period, 1996–97. Table 14 analyses the assistance provided by the Commissioner in the first category of applications and shows that the Commissioner received only 10 applications, with assistance being provided in not a single case.

Table 15 shows the number of applications for assistance received by the CRTUM for the period 1996–97, in which union members complained that their union had failed to observe the requirements of their rulebook. Of the 57 applications received, the Commissioner assisted only seven.

Table 15 Applications to the CRTUM for assistance in union rulebook issues, 1996–97

Rulebook issue	Number of applications	Outcome
Trustees permitted unlawful application of union property	1	not assisted
Failure to allow access to union's accounting records	3	not assisted
Failure to comply with statutory requirements regarding elections to office	6	not assisted
Appointment, election of a person or removal of person from union office	7	2 assisted
Disciplinary proceedings by union	7	not assisted
Balloting of members	8	not assisted
Application of union's property/funds	5	2 assisted
Constitution or proceedings of committees/conferences	20	3 assisted

The workload of the Commissioner was therefore not very heavy. Summing up the situation in 1996–97, the Commissioner granted only seven applications out of 74 complaints. Four of these seven cases were resolved successfully, one receiving a favourable court order and the other three being resolved without the need for legal proceedings to be commenced. The three remaining cases were ongoing in the following spring. Thirty applications were found to be outside the scope of the Commissioner and one applicant did not progress his application further. At the end of the year 1996–97, seven applications were under consideration by the Commissioner. The remaining 29 applications, though within the scope of the Commissioner's power to grant assistance, were not assisted (Commissioner for the Rights of Trade Union Members 1997).

VOLUNTARY UNION RECOGNITION

Recognition of trade unions by employers, for the purposes of collective bargaining on terms and conditions of employment, is a critical stage in the development of employee relations within an organisation. The act of recognition demonstrates a decisive level of acceptance by management of the union role in employee relations and represents a fundamental change in the nature of the employment relationship between employers and employees. It shifts from one based on unilateral management prerogatives, individualist employment practices and unitary personnel management principles to one based on joint regulation, collectivism and pluralism in those areas covered by procedural agreements between the employer and the union(s) (see Chapter 3).

Table 16 shows the extent of union recognition in Britain as a proportion of all establishments for 1980, 1984, 1990 and 1998, based on the workplace surveys for these years. From these figures, it is clear that union recognition generally declined in the two decades from 1980 until 2000. Now union recognition is more likely to take place among:

Table 16 Union recognition in Britain, 1980, 1984, 1990 and 1998

Percent of all establishments

	1980	1984	1990	1998
Private manufacturing	65	56	44	30
Private services	41	44	36	22
Public sector	94	99	87	87

Source: Millward *et al* 1992, Cully *et al* 1999

- manual rather than non-manual workers
- private manufacturing rather than private service establishments
- larger establishments rather than smaller ones
- 'old' establishments rather than 'new' ones
- public-sector rather than private-sector establishments.

In 1998, for example, there was a lower incidence of union recognition in almost all types of establishment in the private sector than in 1990. All sizes of workplaces exhibited declining incidence of union recognition in the 1990s, but smaller workplaces had a greater rate of decline than larger ones. Size of enterprise also had a bearing on the declining incidence of union recognition, and between 1984 and 1998, union recognition in workplaces belonging to enterprises of less than 1,000 employees more than halved, from 35 per cent to 15 per cent. 'By comparison, for workplaces belonging to enterprises with 10,000 or more UK employees the incidence of union recognition dropped from 70 per cent to 50 per cent.' WERS 1998 also demonstrated that less than a fifth of private-sector workplaces under 10 years old had recognised trade unions, compared with around two-fifths in the early 1980s. In the researchers' views, 'the lower rate of recognition among these newer workplaces was unquestionably the principal reason for the fall in recognition among the generality of workplaces between 1990 and 1998' (Cully *et al* 1999: 240–41).

In the public sector, in contrast, union recognition was very much the norm in most establishments, remaining at 87 per cent in both 1990 and 1998. It was pay determination by pay review bodies that largely accounted for the small proportion of workplaces in the public sector not recognising trade unions in 1998.

Discussion in this section therefore focuses largely on union recognition in medium to large-scale private-sector establishments, although it also has implications for parts of the public sector. These sectors include hospital trusts, civil service agencies and the educational services where, with the decentralising of management decisions and personnel management responsibilities, some recognition issues could arise between certain employers and trade unions locally.

Multi-union recognition

Multi-union recognition is still the norm in British employee relations, because of the number of trade unions in Britain, trade union structure and the history of the employment relationship. It is these distinctive factors of British employee relations that result in distinctive patterns of employee representation and bargaining structures in establishments where trade unions are recognised. The WERS 1998 concluded, for example, that 'multiple unionism is a feature for a majority of unionised workplaces', with around a quarter of unionised workplaces having four or more unions present. 'Put in the context of all workplaces, about a half have no unions present, a quarter have members from only one union, a tenth have members from two unions, and the remaining fifth have members from more than two unions' (Cully *et al* 1999: 91). In 1998, two principal sets of bargaining patterns existed in multi-union situations. In about a fifth of all unionised workplaces, multi-union recognition involved multiple bargaining units and separate negotiations with each of the unions. In about a quarter of all unionised workplaces, some three-fifths of workplaces recognising two or more unions conducted joint negotiations or 'single-table bargaining' with all of the unions, although single-table bargaining was over three times more likely in the public than in the private sector. Table 17 shows trade union presence in Britain, in 1998, by some of its main characteristics. From Table 17 it is clear that union recognition is predominantly a public-sector phenomenon. Within the private sector, union recognition is closely associated with two factors: workplace size and size of the organisation.

Table 17 Trade union presence in Britain by sector, organisational status and industry, 1998

	No union present	Union present but not recognised	Recognised union
	% of workplaces	*% of workplaces*	*% of workplaces*
All workplaces	47	8	45
Sector			
Private	64	11	25
Public	3	3	95
Organisational status			
Stand-alone workplace	70	11	19
Part of wider organisation	38	7	54
Industry			
Manufacturing	60	10	30
Electricity, gas and water	2	0	98
Construction	55	8	37
Wholesale and retail	70	8	22
Hotels and restaurants	88	5	7
Transport/communications	41	7	52
Financial services	33	1	65
Other business services	74	7	19
Public administration	1	0	99
Education	5	9	86
Health	29	14	57
Other community services	51	8	42

Source: Cully *et al* 1999

Union recognition in Britain is largely a voluntary process and demand for recognition is usually a union-driven process. Recognition claims are made where a union, or a group of unions, with members within an establishment, approaches an employer to negotiate what is called a 'recognition and negotiating procedure' or, more simply, a 'recognition agreement'. In essence, a recognition agreement is one between an employer and the signatory union(s) that provides representational rights for a specified group of employees, through the agency of the union(s), in a defined bargaining unit, on agreed matters. This suggests, in all but a minority of cases, that British employers deal reactively with recognition claims made by trade unions, rather than initiating recognition agreements themselves. The employer then has to decide whether to reject, consider or accept a recognition claim on its merits. This is done on the basis of what management perceives to be in the best interests of the company and its employees. Recognition ranges from full regulation of the employment relationship through rights to collective bargaining, representation rights in the consultative process and representation rights in grievances and disciplinary issues.

In deciding whether to move towards a recognition agreement with the union(s), employers take a number of factors into account. These include: union strength and effectiveness, including their labour market position; employee attitudes and preferences; and employer policies and objectives. The risks of recognition and non-recognition are normally evaluated by management too, including the need to avoid industrial action, inter-union conflict, fragmented bargaining units and the loss of employer initiative in employee relations decision-making (Institute of Personnel Management 1977). Where, on balance, an employer decides to concede a union claim for recognition – and negotiate an agreement – a number of decisions need to be taken between the parties in the interests of stable employee relations.

Determining the bargaining level

A crucial issue to be decided is the level at which collective bargaining is to take place. This is normally at employer level in single-site companies or, in multi-plant companies, at either central or site level. The factors influencing this decision include: what, if any, other bargaining arrangements already exist within the company; what comparative advantage management and unions see in bargaining at a particular level; and size and distribution of the potential bargaining group. Other factors are extent of union membership and potential membership, organisational structure, the company's financial control system and corporate personnel policies (see Chapter 7).

Determining the bargaining unit

Bargaining units are fundamental to collective bargaining and precise definition of a bargaining unit is important for a number of reasons. The bargaining unit:

- establishes rights of collective representation for individual employees in the unit
- defines the area in which procedural and substantive agreements negotiated between the employer and the union(s) apply
- enables employees to know with whom they are grouped for negotiating purposes.

In general, employers want bargaining units appropriate to their organisational structures and employment policies, whilst avoiding workforce fragmentation, and unions want bargaining units based on their recruitment policies and patterns of membership.

A number of factors affect the determination of bargaining units. These are typically grouped into three categories (Commission on Industrial Relations 1974: 22):

(a) Factors relating to the characteristics of the work group
job skills and content; payment systems; other common conditions of employment; the training and experience of employees; qualifications and professionalism; and physical working conditions
(b) Factors introduced by the presence of trade union membership and collective bargaining arrangements
employee preferences of association; general employee wishes towards collective bargaining; the maintenance of existing collective bargaining arrangements which are working well; and membership of unions or staff associations
(c) Factors based on management organisation and areas of decision-making
the presence of procedures unilaterally operated by management; management structure; promotion patterns; geographical location; and recruitment source.

Bargaining units, in short, have to be appropriate to the situation in each case. This includes the circumstances of the workgroups concerned, existing collective bargaining arrangements and the needs of efficient management.

The key issue to be resolved in determining recognition claims is identifying the 'core group' of employees for recognition purposes, with the above factors being taken into account in doing this. The core group of employees is the one with strong common interests, around which a possible bargaining unit can be formed. For bargaining units to be stable and viable in the long term, it is essential that they are based on the common interests of the employees covered by the collective bargaining arrangement. The core group is central in determining bargaining unit issues, since each unit needs to be based on at least one core group with sufficiently strong common interests to support effective collective bargaining procedures.

Four questions have to be addressed when a core group, or groups, is being considered for inclusion in a bargaining unit. These are its potential in terms of:

- organisational coverage

- geographical coverage
- vertical coverage
- horizontal coverage.

The first two questions are commonly linked together, as are the second two. Once a core group is identified it can be extended, by including additional groups of employees within it in one or more of the four directions listed above. In this way, bargaining units can be designated that cover as wide a common interest group as possible. This avoids creating too many small bargaining groups, which can result in fragmented negotiations and treating related groups of employees inconsistently.

Determining union bargaining agents

Employers normally prefer negotiating with a single union, rather than with several. Apart from the special case of 'single-union' recognition, however (see below), the majority of bargaining units contain more than one union within them. Two main factors influence the efficacy of the bargaining agents in union recognition claims: employee support for the unions, and the unions' effectiveness as negotiating bodies. Potential employee support can be assessed in terms of: actual union membership within the proposed unit; the number of employees supporting the union(s) claiming recognition; and the number who would be prepared to join the union(s) if recognition is agreed. Union effectiveness is the ability of the unions to organise members, maintain membership and represent members in dealings with the employer. While some employers deal with staff associations, especially for some groups of non-manual workers, most, with few exceptions, prefer negotiating with bona fide unions. Union effectiveness can be assessed in terms of: financial viability; experienced officials; research and legal expertise; and negotiating record.

Drafting the agreement

The types of clauses contained in a recognition agreement negotiated with trade unions are illustrated in Exhibit 32.

Exhibit 32 **Clauses in recognition agreements**

These include:

- names of the employer and the bargaining agent(s)
- a description of the bargaining unit and any sub-units
- the terms and conditions that are negotiable
- union membership and non-membership
- numbers of, constituencies of and facilities for union representatives
- negotiating procedures and procedures for handling grievances and avoiding disputes
- other provisions
- provisions for varying and terminating the agreement.

Single-union recognition

Single-union recognition is where a company recognises only one union for collective bargaining and related purposes. In traditional collective bargaining arrangements, companies may recognise only one union per bargaining unit, but single-union recognition, in the sense that it is used here, provides for only one union bargaining agent, covering all employees with representational rights in the company. This practice is associated with what are called 'new-style' collective agreements or 'new-style' bargaining (see Chapters 3 and 7), although the newness of such activities is questionable. The rationale of single-union recognition is that employers might wish to avoid fragmentation in the collective bargaining structure and unions wish to secure members and avoid demarcation disputes with other unions. In the WERS 1998, about a quarter of unionised workplaces recognised only one trade union, and single-union deals were twice as likely in the private sector than in the public sector (Cully *et al* 1999).

Management and single-unionism

The major difference between the process of single-union recognition and that of multi-union recognition is that it is management and commercially driven, not union driven, although the unions involved in single-union deals would dispute this. One of the first recorded single-union recognition agreements was between Toshiba Consumer Products (UK) and the EEPTU, at Plymouth in April 1981 (Bassett 1986). This agreement arose out of the closure of Rank Toshiba Ltd in 1980 and was negotiated when the new company was established as a single-site operation that was assembling colour television sets (Rico 1987). Since then, the numbers of such agreements have increased.

It is generally recognised that where management negotiate and consult with trade unions, they often prefer to deal with one union rather than with many. The advantages of this include: having one representational channel for all employees through which all discussions are focused; avoiding inter-union competition and inter-union disputes within the workplace; and simplifying the bargaining structure within which the parties operate. Over and above this, management claims that single-union recognition is beneficial where a company is aiming at teamwork, quality and flexibility amongst its workforce – as in 'high-tech', 'greenfield' site companies. In these circumstances, single-union recognition, with its emphases on harmonised terms and conditions of employment and a committed workforce, is seen as facilitating a common purpose within the company and good working relations between the company and its workers.

On greenfield sites, employer selection of an appropriate union is rooted in the management dictum: 'Talk to every union that could conceivably have an interest in representing your employees and then make a decision as to which union best fits . . . Those not selected will respect that decision' (Wickens 1987: 133). Management's recognition objective is a clear one: to negotiate with one union, on terms, conditions and procedural issues for all workers in the bargaining unit. This necessitates early discussions with the various unions wishing to represent the bargaining group, whether or not they already have members within the bargaining unit, with management emphasising that it alone will take the final decision as to which union will be invited to sign the draft recognition agreement.

That decision takes account of a number of factors. One is the attitudes and experience of the local union officials, who are normally invited to present their union's case for recognition, each arguing why their union is likely to give the 'best deal' to the company – the so-called 'beauty contest'. Even before this, it is customary for the company to investigate the backgrounds and policies of the unions, both locally and nationally, to 'make an assessment of the "comfort" factor which ranks very highly in the decision-making process' (Wickens 1987: 134). These factors are likely to include the national and local politics of each union, the reputations of the local union officers and the employee relations records of the unions. Information for this is gathered from local companies, employers' associations and media sources. In this respect, the experiences of employers with single-union recognition arrangements is particularly useful, as are those of companies that have not gone down this path – and the reasons why.

Another factor to consider is which union is likely to be the most acceptable to the employees within the bargaining group. Some judgement has to be made by the company about the potential willingness of employees to join the selected union. There are a number of indicators here: existing levels of membership; the respective membership bases of the competing unions; how these relate to the bargaining group; and the degree of occupational homogeneity within the bargaining unit. In some cases, the company surveys its employees, using a secret ballot to assess their preferred union and choice of bargaining agent.

Unions and single-unionism

Union attitudes to single-union recognition are ambivalent. In some sectors, single-union recognition has always been the norm: for example, in retailing and in parts of the white-collar civil service. In other cases – union recognition on greenfield sites – it is generally accepted that there are advantages in having the entire workforce in one establishment in a single union in a single bargaining unit. On the other hand, there is hostility among some unions to the practice, incorporated in most single-union, new-style agreements, of including so-called 'no-strike' or 'final offer' arbitration arrangements (Burrows 1986). These, it is claimed, remove the basic democratic rights of trade unions and their members to take legitimate industrial action against employers when they deem this to be necessary, and they should be resisted.

The other concern that unions have with single-union agreements is to do with infringing the recruiting and negotiating freedoms of other unions with membership interests in the bargaining unit. According to the TUC (1988: 9), single-union agreements cause particular differences amongst unions where they:

(a) exclude other unions who may have some membership in the unit covered by the agreement; or exclude unions which previously held recognition or bargaining rights;
(b) exclude other unions who, while having no members in the unit concerned, have recognition agreements in other UK units operated by the same employer;
(c) represent an intrusion by one union into areas considered to be the province of an industrial union(s), or the exclusion by an industrial union of unions representing particular occupations;
(d) are agreed by one union, where another has been previously campaigning for membership perhaps over a long period;
(e) lead unions to compete with each other for employers' approval which encourages dilution of trade union standards and procedures.

Union derecognition

Though it is still a relatively rare employee relations occurrence, union derecognition is nevertheless practised by some employers. It takes place where an employer partially or fully withdraws union negotiating rights from the union(s) in a particular bargaining unit by giving notice of the intention to terminate an existing recognition agreement. Full derecognition is where negotiating rights for a whole bargaining group are withdrawn – as was the case for teachers in 1987, when the Burnham Committee was abolished by the government who first replaced it with an interim pay advisory committee and then with a pay review body (Farnham 1993). In other cases, full derecognition takes place, as among white-collar staff in some insurance companies, where there is lack of support for the union or staff association among the staff concerned. Partial derecognition takes place where the employer unilaterally withdraws the number or coverage of the negotiating groups, and/or union negotiating rights, but at least one recognised union, and one bargaining unit, remains in the establishment or enterprise.

Claydon (1989) presents a more sophisticated analysis of union derecognition. He has analysed derecognition in terms of a matrix and distinguished between breadth and depth of derecognition. Breadth of derecognition can be 'general', 'grade-specific' or 'plant-specific'. There are five types of depth of derecognition:

- 'partial', where the union retains some bargaining rights
- as 'a bargaining agent', where the union retains only rights to consultation and representation
- 'collective', where the union can represent only members in individual grievances
- 'complete'
- 'deunionisation', where union membership is discouraged.

The most common forms of derecognition appear to be collective 'grade-specific' and complete 'grade-specific'.

The reasons given by Claydon for union derecognition by employers included: external pressures; ownership, management and reorganisation;

315

company objectives; and union organisation and industrial relations history – with corporate objectives probably lying at the heart of union derecognition. According to Claydon (*ibid:* 219) it is 'greater pay flexibility, more flexible working practices, and heightened commitment', especially amongst managerial and staff grades, that are the main employer goals associated with union derecognition.

STATUTORY UNION RECOGNITION

Statutory union recognition is where the law provides a legally enforceable union recognition procedure on an employer, where the employer refuses voluntary union recognition and a majority of the workforce wants it. The prototype of statutory union recognition is the USA, where the National Labor Relations Act 1935 – as amended by the Taft-Hartley Act 1947 – provides a series of rights for American workers. These include the rights:

- to join unions and organise for collective bargaining purposes
- to vote whether or not to be represented by a union by means of a secret ballot, enforced by the National Labor Relations Board
- to be protected from 'unfair labor practices', on the part of employers, which might interfere with their rights as workers regarding trade union organisation (Kochan 1980).

This results in more proactive employee relations policies by American employers than in Britain, leading to either union avoidance strategies or pre-emptive union recognition strategies, even though union recognition in the USA is the lowest in OECD countries (Kochan *et al* 1984).

In its election manifesto in 1997, the Labour Party pledged itself to legislate for a statutory procedure for union recognition if it were elected to office (Labour Party 1997). Subsequently, the Labour administration, led by Tony Blair, enacted the Employment Relations Act (ERA) 1999, following considerable debate within Parliament, outside Parliament and forceful lobbying by employer and union interests. The ERA 1999 introduces three new areas of employment law: a new framework of better rights for individual workers, including the important area of 'family-friendly policies'; support for union members by their unions in the workplace; and, most controversially, a new statutory right to union recognition. In general employers were hostile to the statutory union recognition procedure and unions were supportive towards it. For example, Mike Emmott, Policy Advisor on Employee Relations at the then IPD, went on record as saying: 'One thing is clear beyond any doubt: most employers are opposed to the idea of a law on trade union recognition' (1999: 54). The TUC, in contrast, welcomed the publication of the Employment Relations Bill and, while recognising that it fell some way short of what the TUC had hoped for, accepted that the Bill nonetheless offered 'new and very important opportunities for the trade union movement' (TUC 1999a: 19). But there were two aspects of the

ERA 1999 which even the unions viewed as setbacks: the 40 per cent threshold of statutory recognition (see below) and the exclusion of firms with fewer than 21 workers from the statutory recognition provisions.

The first trade union recognition ballot conducted under the provisions of the ERA 1999 was for cabin staff crew at Airtours, the British holiday company, in spring 2000. Although the union involved, the AEEU, claimed to have had a membership of 55 per cent among Airtour's 1,200 cabin crew, it agreed with the company to test staff opinion through a ballot. In the event, in a turnout of 82.4 per cent, 81.9 per cent voted in favour of the union to represent them. This participation rate was over twice as much as the 40 per cent threshold of those voting, as required under the Act (see below), to obtain recognition and, due to an energetic campaign of the union in alliance with the employer, the result was a clear-cut, authoritative one (Taylor 1999). The procedures of statutory union recognition are complex and complicated, but the main provisions of the legislation are outlined and summarised below. For the purposes of the statutory scheme, collective bargaining refers to negotiations relating to pay, hours and holidays, and any other issues agreed by the parties.

A union request to the employer

The union (or unions in a joint application), which must be independent, has to make a written request for union recognition to any employer employing over 21 workers, stating the proposed bargaining unit. The employer has 10 days to respond to the union request. Where the employer responds positively to the request, indicating willingness to negotiate on the issue, 20 days are allowed for talks, although the period may be extended by agreement. If negotiations fail, the union may submit its application to the Central Arbitration Committee (CAC) and ACAS can be invited to assist the negotiations. Where the employer refuses recognition, or fails to respond to the request, the union can then proceed to the CAC and seek its determination of the bargaining unit and whether the union has the support of the majority of workers in that unit.

A union request to the CAC

The CAC will reject an application for statutory union recognition where:

- the union has rejected or failed to respond within 10 days to an employer's proposal to use ACAS to negotiate on the issue
- the CAC is satisfied that another independent union is already recognised for collective bargaining on behalf of any workers in the proposed bargaining unit
- more than one union(s) applying jointly cannot show to the satisfaction of the CAC that they will work together and, where the employer wishes, enter into single-table bargaining arrangements
- there are competing applications prior to a bargaining unit being determined and at least one worker falls within both proposed bargaining units

- a different union attempts to get recognition for a bargaining unit that is substantially the same as the one for which recognition was given within the past three years
- a union that was granted statutory union recognition is derecognised under the derecognition arrangements (see below)
- a union has applied to the CAC for recognition for the same (or substantially the same) bargaining unit within the past three years
- union membership is under 10 per cent of the proposed bargaining unit
- more than one union each has 10 per cent membership in the relevant bargaining units or none of the unions can show that it has 10 per cent membership.

CAC determination of the bargaining unit

Once an application has been accepted by the CAC, it has 20 days to help the parties reach an agreement on the bargaining unit, though it can extend this period. Where there is no agreement, the CAC has 10 working days to determine the bargaining unit. The key issue is that the bargaining unit must be compatible with effective management. Other factors to be taken into account by the CAC, provided they do not conflict with the above requirement, include:

- the views of the employer and union
- existing national and local bargaining arrangements
- the desirability of avoiding fragmented bargaining
- the characteristics of workers falling within the proposed bargaining unit
- the location of the workers.

Once the bargaining unit has been determined by the CAC, and where the unit differs from the originally proposed one, the CAC has to decide whether all the qualifications apply, including the 10 per cent test. If the application is now invalid, the CAC will not proceed with the application.

Demonstration of majority membership

Where the union can demonstrate that a majority of the workers in the bargaining unit are members of the union, the CAC must issue a declaration that the union is recognised for collective bargaining purposes. However, where the following three qualifying conditions are satisfied, the CAC must arrange a ballot to be conducted by an independent person:

- The CAC is satisfied that a ballot should be held in the interests of good industrial relations.
- A significant number of union members inform the CAC that they do not want the union to conduct collective bargaining on their behalf.
- Membership evidence is produced that leads the CAC to conclude that there are doubts whether a significant number of union members want the union to conduct collective bargaining on their behalf.

Ballots on union recognition

Where the union cannot show majority membership, or where the CAC has ordered a ballot for the reasons set out above, the CAC must give notice to the parties that it intends arranging a secret ballot on recognition. If the CAC is notified that the union or union and employer do not want a ballot, it takes no further steps. If it is not so notified, the CAC must arrange the ballot, giving a period of notice of 10 days. An independent qualified person conducts the ballot within 20 working days of that person's appointment, though the CAC can specify a longer period.

The ballot can be a workplace, postal or mixed one. The employer has a duty to co-operate with the CAC in relation to the ballot and to supply the names and home addresses of relevant workers. The employer is also under a duty to allow the union reasonable access to the workers. Where an employer fails to fulfil these duties, the CAC can order the employer to take reasonable steps to remedy that failure. Alternatively, the CAC can issue a declaration without a ballot that the union is recognised for collective bargaining on behalf of the bargaining unit. The costs of the ballot are shared equally between employer and union.

There is a requirement that the union must obtain a 40 per cent 'yes' vote to gain recognition. This means that the union needs not only a majority of those voting in the ballot but also at least 40 per cent of those entitled to vote. Where this happens, the CAC issues a declaration that the union is recognised for the purposes of collective bargaining. Where the union does not get the necessary level of support, the CAC issues a declaration that the union is not recognised.

The procedure agreement

Where union recognition is awarded, it covers pay, hours and holidays and the parties have 30 days to agree a method by which they will conduct collective bargaining, a period that may be extended by agreement. If there is no agreement at the end of this period, either party can apply to the CAC for assistance. A further 20 days is provided for the CAC to try and assist the parties in this purpose. If there is still no agreement, the CAC must specify to the parties the method by which they will conduct collective bargaining. The method specified has the effect of a legally enforceable contract and the CAC may assist where one of the parties fails to carry out the agreed method. Specific performance is the remedy for breach of a legally enforceable contract of this sort, on application to the courts.

The CAC can also impose a procedure agreement where a voluntary agreement is concluded after an application for statutory recognition has been made to the CAC and before any of the above processes have taken place. This provision is intended to deal with situations where an employer concludes a voluntary agreement on recognition as a means of avoiding statutory recognition but then fails to honour the terms of the voluntary agreement. The employer may not terminate a procedure agreement for recognition made under these circumstances for three years. If the parties cannot reach an agreement, the CAC specifies the method to the parties by which they are to conduct collective bargaining. The parties can agree that the specified method will not be legally enforceable. If they do not, specific performance is the legal remedy in case of breach of contract.

Requests for union derecognition

Derecognition may be requested by an employer, a worker or workers. In general, the derecognition procedure applies where the recognition procedure was the result either of an award by the CAC or of a voluntary procedure agreement and the CAC specified the method by which the parties were to conduct collective bargaining, as outlined above. An application for derecognition cannot be made until at least three years after the date of the recognition award or the date of the agreement on recognition.

There is provision for quick derecognition where the number of workers employed by the employer falls below 21. Where this happens, the employer can give notice of this to the union and if the union does not object, derecognition follows within 35 days, as long as the CAC accepts the application.

In cases where the employer wants derecognition and the union was recognised after winning a ballot, the process is as follows:

- the employer must make a written request to the union for derecognition
- the union has 10 days to reply by agreeing to derecognition, indicating a willingness to negotiate about it for up to 20 days, or refusing the request
- where there is a failure to respond within 10 days or a refusal to accept derecognition, the employer can apply to the CAC for a ballot on derecognition
- the CAC will not accept an application if the employer had rejected a union proposal to seek ACAS assistance with negotiations
- the CAC will not accept an application if there has been another application for derecognition from any party in the last three years
- the CAC will not proceed with an application unless it decides that at least 10 per cent of the workers in the bargaining unit favour ending the bargaining arrangements and a majority of the relevant workers favour ending the collective bargaining arrangements.

The CAC must decide whether the employer's application is valid or not. In doing this, it must consider any evidence presented by the union or employer. Where it decides the request is not valid, the application falls. Where it decides that the application is valid, it must give notice to the parties that it intends proceeding with a derecognition ballot.

In cases where a worker or workers in a bargaining unit want derecognition, an application can only be made if no other application for derecognition has been made in the past three years. The CAC must apply the 10 per cent test and the union and employer may submit evidence to the CAC, which must either reject the application or accept it and give the parties notice of a ballot. In this case the CAC must help the parties seek an agreement on the issue.

Ballots on union derecognition

The voting requirements are as follows:

- the ballot is conducted by an independent person, within 20 working days of that person's appointment
- workplace, postal or mixed ballots can be used, with the CAC taking the decision on the same grounds as for recognition ballots
- the employer is under a duty to comply with the organisation of the ballot and allow union access to the workers
- where the CAC is satisfied that the employer has not complied with the above, the derecognition application is cancelled and the union remains recognised
- ballot costs are shared by the employer and union
- where a majority of those voting, and at least 40 per cent of those entitled to vote, support the ending of the bargaining arrangements, the CAC issues a declaration that the union is derecognised.

Workers are protected against detriment or dismissal for campaigning for or against derecognition or recognition or not voting in a ballot. Such dismissals are automatically unfair, with the burden of proof resting on the employer.

ASSIGNMENTS

(a) Read Millward *et al* (1992: 57–77). (i) Identify union membership trends in Britain 1984–90 and (ii) examine the factors explaining these trends. How do these trends relate to your own organisation?
(b) Read Cully *et al* (1999: 84–94). What trends in union membership and trade union recognition do they identify?
(c) Examine the latest Annual Report of the CO and explain the legal rules relating to union mergers and amalgamations. Report and comment on recent amalgamations and mergers in Britain and their implications for employee relations.
(d) From the TUC's last Annual Report, identify three key issues of concern to the TUC during this period and indicate how the TUC is attempting to address these issues.
(e) What are the main features of multi-unionism in Britain identified by the Workplace Employee Relations Survey in 1998 (Cully *et al* 1999: 90–94)? What sort of problems associated with multi-unionism occur in your organisation?
(f) Read the Webbs (1913: Part II, Chapter V). Analyse and comment on the role of 'the standard rate' as a trade union rule. How significant is the concept of the 'standard rate' for trade union negotiators today?

(g) Read the TUC (1999a) and identify and analyse what you think were some of the main issues of concern to Congress during 1998–99.

(h) Read the TUC (1992a: 30–47). What are the employee relations implications of the case studies outlined in the report? Comment on the survey of quality initiatives provided in Chapter 8.

(i) Examine the view put forward by Anderman (1992: 248) that:

> The right to dissociate currently embodied in UK legislation has been introduced in recent years as part of a wider legislative programme designed to promote individualism at the expense of established collective structures...it calls into question the legitimacy of trade unions as collectivities enhancing the freedom of their members as individuals by the use of collective institutions.

(j) An employer is in dispute with the union representing the technical staff who are taking strike action over a pay claim. One of the strike leaders, who has both a full-time and a part-time contract, has been informed by her departmental manager – on the instruction of the chief executive – that he is not to renew her part-time contract. This is due for renewal at the beginning of next month for a further one-year period. What do you do? And why?

(k) Provide some examples of individual conduct that the law would regard as reasons for unjustifiable union discipline, in the case of a lawful trade dispute. What would be some of the employee relations implications of such conduct for (i) management and (ii) the union(s) in such cases?

(l) Read Kochan (1980) and outline the main provisions for union recognition in the USA under the Wagner Act 1935, as amended.

(m) Outline the steps to be taken by the employer in responding to a union recognition claim by factory workers in a non-union company, operating on a single site, with 250 employees in the factory, 150 administrative and supervisory staff and 50 technical staff. The union claims 'over 40 per cent membership' amongst the factory workers, '25 per cent' of administrative and clerical staff and 'substantial support' among technicians.

(n) Read Wickens (1987: 127–61). Examine how the companies discussed in this chapter went about getting single-union agreements and why. What distinguishes the approach to management–union relations outlined in this chapter from (i) non-union companies and (ii) companies with multi-union representation?

(o) Read Burrows (1986: 52–62) and examine and evaluate trade union attitudes to single-union deals.

(p) Read Claydon (1989: 214–22) and examine the reasons why employers use union derecognition strategies.

(q) An employer recognises a single trade union in a negotiating unit comprising its supervisory and shop-floor staff. Management wishes to withdraw recognition arrangements for the supervisors and to put them on personal contracts and performance-related pay. Outline a strategy for how this might be done and examine some of its implications for employee relations in the company.

(r) On what grounds do most employers oppose a statutory right to union recognition?

REFERENCES

ANDERMAN S. (1992) *Labour Law*. London, Butterworth.

BAIN G. (1970) *The Growth of White Collar Unionism*. London, Oxford University Press.

BASSETT P. (1986) *Strike Free: New industrial relations in Britain*. Basingstoke, Macmillan.

BURROWS G. (1986) *No-Strike Agreements and Pendulum Arbitration*. London, Institute of Personnel Management.

CERTIFICATION OFFICE (1992) *Annual Report of the Certification Officer 1991*. London, HMSO.

CERTIFICATION OFFICE (1997) *Annual Report of the Certification Officer 1996*. London, HMSO.

CERTIFICATION OFFICE (1999) *Annual Report of the Certification Officer 1998*. London, HMSO.

CLAYDON T. (1989) 'Union de-recognition in Britain in the 1980s'. *British Journal of Industrial Relations*. 27 (2).

COMMISSION ON INDUSTRIAL RELATIONS (1974) *Trade Union Recognition: CIR Experience*. London, HMSO.

COMMISSIONER FOR THE RIGHTS OF TRADE UNION MEMBERS (1988–97) *Annual Reports*. London, Central Office of Information.

CULLY M., WOODLAND S., O'REILLY A. *and* DIX G. (1999) *Britain at Work*. London, Routledge.

DANIEL W. (1987) *Workplace Industrial Relations and Technical Change*. London, Policy Studies Institute.

DEPARTMENT OF EMPLOYMENT (1990) *Code of Practice on Trade Union Ballots on Industrial Action*. London, Central Office of Information.

EMMOTT M. (1999) 'Collectively cool'. *People Management*. 5 (2), January.

FARNHAM D. (1993) 'Human resources management and employee relations', in D. Farnham and S. Horton (eds), *Managing the New Public Services*, Basingstoke, Macmillan.

FARNHAM D. *and* HORTON S. (1996) *Managing People in the Public Services*. Basingstoke, Macmillan.

FLANDERS A. (1961) 'Trade unions in the sixties', in A. Flanders, *Management and Unions*, London, Faber & Faber.

FLANDERS A. (1968a) 'Collective bargaining: a theoretical analysis', in A. Flanders, *Management and Unions*, London, Faber & Faber.

FLANDERS A. (1968b) 'What are trade unions for?' in A. Flanders, *Management and Unions*, London, Faber & Faber.

GENNARD J. (1990) *The History of the National Graphical Association*. London, Unwin Hyman.

GMB *and* CWU (1991) *A New Agenda: Bargaining for prosperity in the 1990s*. London, GMB/CWU.

HORTON S. and FARNHAM D. (EDS) (1999) *Public Management in Britain.* London, Macmillan.

HYMAN R. (1975) *Industrial Relations.* Basingstoke, Macmillan.

INSTITUTE OF PERSONNEL MANAGEMENT (1977) *Trade Union Recognition.* London, IPM.

JACOBI O., KELLER B. and MUELLER-JENTSCH W. (1998) 'Germany: Facing new challenges', in A. Ferner and R. Hyman (eds), *Changing Industrial Relations in Europe*, Oxford, Blackwell.

KOCHAN T. (1980) *Collective Bargaining and Industrial Relations.* Illinois, Irwin.

KOCHAN T., MCKERSIE R. and CAPELLI P. (1984) 'Strategic choice and industrial relations theory'. *Industrial Relations.* 23 (1).

LABOUR PARTY (1997) *New Labour: Because Britain deserves better.* London, Labour Party.

MILLWARD N. and STEVENS M. (1986) *British Workplace Industrial Relations 1980–1984.* Aldershot, Gower.

MILLWARD N., STEVENS M., SMART D. and HAWES W. (1992) *Workplace Industrial Relations in Transition.* Aldershot, Dartmouth.

RICO L. (1987) 'The new industrial relations: British electricians' new-style agreements'. *Industrial and Labor Relations Review.* 41 (1), October.

STOREY J. (1992) *Developments in the Management of Human Resources.* Oxford, Blackwell.

TAYLOR R. (1999) 'AEEU wins recognition at Airtours'. *Financial Times.* 8 March.

TRADES UNION CONGRESS (1966) *Trade Unionism.* London, TUC.

TRADES UNION CONGRESS (1974) *Trade Union Strategy.* London, TUC.

TRADES UNION CONGRESS (1981–90) *Annual Reports.* London, TUC.

TRADES UNION CONGRESS (1988) *Meeting the Challenge.* London, TUC.

TRADES UNION CONGRESS (1991a) *Collective Bargaining Strategy for the 1990s.* London, TUC.

TRADES UNION CONGRESS (1991b) *Unions and Europe in the 1990s.* London, TUC.

TRADES UNION CONGRESS (1991c) *Annual Report.* London, TUC.

TRADES UNION CONGRESS (1992a) *The Quality Challenge.* London, TUC.

TRADES UNION CONGRESS (1992b) *Quality Work Assured.* London, TUC.

TRADES UNION CONGRESS (1994) *Human Resource Management: A trade union response.* London, TUC.

TRADES UNION CONGRESS (1995) *General Council Report for 1995.* London, TUC.

TRADES UNION CONGRESS (1996a) *Partners in Progress: New steps for the new unionism.* London, TUC.

TRADES UNION CONGRESS (1996b) *The European Union: Trade union goals.* London, TUC.

TRADES UNION CONGRESS (1999a) *General Council Report for 1998.* London, TUC.

TRADES UNION CONGRESS (1999b) *Partners for Progress.* London, TUC.

VON PRONDYNSKI F. (1987) *Freedom of Association and Industrial Relations.* Dublin, Mansell.

WEBB S. *and* WEBB B. (1897) *Industrial Democracy.* London, Longmans Green.

WEBB S. *and* WEBB B. (1913) *Industrial Democracy.* New York, Longmans Green.

WICKENS P. (1987) *The Road to Nissan.* Basingstoke, Macmillan.

9 Public policy and the European social dimension

Public policy is concerned with how the state impacts on employee relations. The state consists of those institutions and offices of state that provide the machinery of government. In the UK, these include:

- the cabinet and government ministers who comprise the executive authority of the state
- Parliament, which is a representative assembly that makes law, raises revenue and is a scrutinising body
- central government departments, governmental agencies, public bodies, public enterprises and the local authorities that administer governmental policies
- the state's agencies of law enforcement and adjudication, such as the courts, tribunals and the police.

In contemporary market economies, like those of western Europe, North America and Australasia, because relations between employers and employees have become part of the public domain, the state is also an employee relations policy-maker. Public policy in this area relates to the ways in which the state seeks to influence the parties, processes and outcomes of employee relations. The state acts in a number of roles, including:

- as an actor in the labour market and in the determination of wages and employment
- as a regulator of industrial conflict
- as an employer
- as a lawmaker and law enforcer.

Another and increasing policy influence on employee relations practices in the UK is the EU. In recent years, the single market programme of the EU has led to the expansion of the 'social dimension' within the EU. This includes employment-related policies and objectives concerned with improved living conditions in general. This commitment to social progress is not new in western European politics. It has been a feature of national and supranational politics in EU member states for many years. Issues such as job security, employee protection, paid leave from work and comprehensive social security schemes have been a much more important feature of western European states than in the USA and Japan.

Another feature of western Europe is the protection given to individual employees' rights to organise and take part in industrial action and the legal regulation of employee relations. In addition, politics in western Europe has had, and retains, a strong corporatist dimension, with the 'social partners' – employers and unions – having a formalised consultative role in national policy-making. According to one student of Europe, 'social policy in the widest sense is very much a hallmark of politics in Western Europe, regardless of country or government. Social policy is indeed a European invention' (Holmstedt 1991: 39). It is the twin issues of state employment policy and the European social dimension that are addressed in this chapter.

EARLY PUBLIC POLICY: *LAISSEZ-FAIRE* AND THE EMERGENCE OF COLLECTIVE *LAISSEZ-FAIRE*

An embryonic modern public policy on employee relations in Britain developed in the early nineteenth century, rooted in the ideas of *laissez-faire*. *Laissez-faire* was based on the assumption that market decisions were preferable to political fiats in determining the allocation, distribution and exchange of economic resources in society. As applied to the free labour market, *laissez-faire* policy meant that market freedoms took precedence over political decisions in determining the procedural arrangements and substantive outcomes of the wage bargaining process. The state's role was a minimalist one of providing a framework of contract law within which the primary parties to the wage–work bargain conducted themselves. Wage-fixing was regarded as a private matter, between the individual 'master' and individual 'servant', in which there was no role for the state or state institutions to intervene.

The state's attitude to trade unions in the early part of the nineteenth century was one of outright hostility and opposition. Unions were seen by both the state authorities and employers as 'criminal conspiracies' and illegitimate combinations acting 'in restraint of trade' (Pelling 1987). Unions, it was argued, distorted the workings of the free labour market and took away the freedoms of the primary parties to negotiate terms and conditions individually, in pursuit of their own advantage and self-interest. Accordingly, both Parliament and the judges declared unions to be criminal combinations. It was only after Parliament relaxed its outright ban on unions in 1824 and after emancipating statutes were enacted – in 1859, 1871 and 1875 – that trade unions were relieved from the worst consequences of criminal liability. The judges then turned to the development of civil liability, which, in turn, was only relieved by the Trade Disputes Act 1906 (see Chapter 4). This gave trade unions blanket immunity from liability in tort, provided immunities to individuals inducing breaches of contracts of employment and legitimised peaceful picketing.

By the early twentieth century, trade unions were well established as collective wage-bargaining agencies, covering a number of well-organised trades and industries (Clegg, Fox and Thompson 1964). But while Parliament had legitimised trade union activities, the state excluded itself from the joint wage-fixing process between autonomous employers and independent unions – just as it had done in the individual wage–work bargain between

327

master and servant and employer and workman. Collective agreements were negotiated voluntarily between the secondary parties to employee relations, they were legally unenforceable and there was no legally binding, national minimum wage. A policy of collective *laissez-faire* and 'voluntarism' – embodied in the concepts of 'free collective bargaining' and the exclusion of the judges and the courts from relations between employers and trade unions – began slowly to replace individual *laissez-faire* as the dominant ideology underpinning British employee relations. It was a 'public' policy that suited government, employers and trade unions alike.

Gradually, however, the policy of collective *laissez-faire* incorporated a series of incremental, interventionist policies by the state. First, the state found that it could not stand aside when standards of cleanliness, overcrowding, ventilation and working conditions in factories and mines, especially those affecting women and children, were unsatisfactory, dangerous to health and safety or offensive to 'public morality'. Accordingly, there was the piecemeal enactment of a series of factory and safety legislation, starting as early as the Factory Act 1833, which aimed to deal with these matters on a trade-by-trade and industry-by-industry basis.

Second, the state also found that it could not stand aside when disruptive industrial conflict appeared to threaten either social stability within the community or the established political order. In 1896, the Conciliation Act was passed. This enabled provision to be made for the registration of boards of conciliation and arbitration and for the Board of Trade to inquire into the causes and circumstances of a trade dispute, or nominate a person to do so, or appoint conciliators or arbitrators to try to resolve it. This was followed by the Industrial Courts Act 1919, which extended the provisions for voluntary arbitration in Britain beyond those embodied in the 1896 Act (Wedderburn and Davies 1969). This effectively provided the legal basis for state intervention in the regulation of industrial conflict until the Advisory, Conciliation and Arbitration Service (ACAS) was created by the Employment Protection Act 1975.

Third, the state also found itself having to intervene to protect the terms and conditions of employment of those in the labour market unable to look after themselves and who were likely to be exploited in the wage-bargaining process by unscrupulous, greedy employers. There was particular concern about the so-called 'sweated trades' at the beginning of the twentieth century. Sweating was associated with home workers who had very low wage rates, excessive hours of work and insanitary working conditions. It was the Trade Boards Acts 1909 and 1918, followed by the Wages Councils Acts after 1945, which sought to remedy these abuses. These Acts set up wage-fixing bodies, comprised of equal numbers of employers and worker representatives with independent members, to establish minimum, legally enforceable, hourly wage rates and other conditions of employment for workers in trades and industries where wages were low and there was no collective bargaining. The intentions were, initially, to protect the low paid and, later on, to encourage the development of collective bargaining in unorganised industries (Bayliss 1959).

THE EMPLOYEE RELATIONS CONSENSUS 1945-79

The inter-war years, from 1919 to 1939, were watersheds in the development of public policy on employee relations. Deep economic recession and high unemployment resulted in hard labour markets (from the sellers' point of view), weakened trade unions and the strengthening of the right to manage in the workplace. However, with the steady growth in the scope and size of the state and of state activity in economic and social affairs in the twentieth century, government could no longer abstain from employee relations decision-making, as it had done for much of the nineteenth century. This was especially the case during World War I, World War II and after 1945. During the two World Wars, for example, the state developed active labour market and wages policies. These were necessary to ensure that labour was allocated and directed to essential industries and occupations, to maximise industrial output and gain the collaboration of the unions and their members in the war effort.

The state built on these policies in the post-war period, after 1945. Besides the policy of being a 'model' and 'good practice' employer (see below) and, after 1965, of developing a statutory floor of employment protection rights (see Chapter 4), Britain's post-war governments up to 1979, excepting the Heath government 1971-74, tried to develop a consensus on employee relations policy. It aimed at being acceptable to employers, trade unions, their members and the wider community alike and comprised three interrelated elements:

- maintaining full employment in the labour market
- searching for an incomes policy
- supporting voluntary collective bargaining.

The attempt to achieve an employee relations consensus incorporated a policy, where trade union power was strong, based on free collective bargaining. This was modified at other times by a policy of bargained corporatism (see Chapter 1), when the state authorities tried to constrain union wage-bargaining power, in conditions of full employment, by making concessions to the unions and their members on social and economic policy and employment law. An attempt was made to move away from a liberal state organised on free market principles to a more corporatist state. Corporatism is where the state authorities try to integrate the interests of capital, labour and government through centralised political institutions so that wage, economic and related policy issues are discussed centrally (Schmitter and Lehmbruch 1979).

Maintaining full employment

Market *laissez-faire* economic policies in the inter-war years resulted in mass unemployment, widespread poverty and social deprivation (Taylor 1965). The popular demand at the end of World War II for 'full employment',

329

which had been an economic reality from 1939 to 1945, was in part a reaction by the British people to the economic and social distress experienced by millions of them a decade earlier.

The rationale for full employment

With the extension of the political franchise and gradual democratising of society during the twentieth century, the democratic imperative began to challenge the market imperative as the motivating influence on state policy in both economic affairs and employee relations. After World War II, the democratic imperative became even more pressing.

One impact of the democratic imperative was from below. It arose from the fact that a generation of workers emerged – from 1945 until the mid-1970s – with the expectation that governments would pursue, amongst other measures, a labour market policy of full employment. The power of the ballot box now meant that the electorate could replace any government failing to deliver the policy objective of full employment and the extension of a comprehensive welfare state. This political fact was not lost on government ministers and public policy-makers in determining their economic, employment and labour market priorities after 1945.

A second impact of the democratic imperative immediately post-1945 was from above. This derived from the demands of some political reformers and social theorists, especially within the Labour Party. They attacked the five pre-war social evils of 'Want, Disease, Ignorance, Squalor and Idleness' and wanted 'full employment in a free society'. They not only accepted the principle but also wished to implement the policy of full employment in practice. Indeed, by the 1950s, full employment had become a bipartisan public policy to which both major political parties, the Conservatives and Labour, were committed. The reasons for this bipartisanship were partly political. The realities of democratic politics meant that unless cabinets and ministers actively pursued full employment as a policy goal, neither they nor the government of which they were members would be re-elected at the next general election.

There were also intellectual reasons for governments supporting the policy of full employment, since the arguments supporting the full employment agenda had been put and won earlier by individuals such as Keynes (1936) and Beveridge (1944). For Beveridge (1944: 15–16) unemployment was an 'evil'. But the greatest evil of all 'is not physical but moral, not the want it may bring but the hatred and fear which it breeds'. In his view, to look to individual employers to maintain aggregate demand and full employment was absurd. They were not within the power of employers to determine. 'They must therefore be undertaken by the State, under the supervision and pressure of democracy, applied through...Parliament.'

By 'full employment' Keynes, Beveridge and their supporters did not mean 'no unemployment at all' but 'unemployment reduced to a minimum and for as short a time as possible'. This required government stimulating aggregate demand in the economy (see Chapter 4) and ensuring that those seeking jobs would be certain that they would be re-employed after only a short period of being out of work. To facilitate the transition between jobs, the unemployed would receive unemployment benefit while looking for new employment, and be provided with state-funded employment services to assist them in doing this. Using combinations of fiscal and incomes policies, successive governments, both Conservative and Labour, fine-tuned the economy for some 30 years – 1945–75. This ensured, certainly until the early 1970s, that unemployment in Britain remained low, at some 2–3 per cent of the working population, or around 300,000 to 500,000 unemployed persons.

The consequences of full employment

The Government's economic policy goal of full employment had three main consequences for employee relations. The first was that with the economy expanding, private-sector employers were often faced with labour shortages, particularly of skilled, trained workers. Employers normally responded to this by bidding up wage rates, or by supplementing the earnings of their workforces locally, in order to compete in local labour markets with other employers. The result was 'wages drift', or a gap between nationally negotiated wage rates and what was actually earned by workers at workplace level. Furthermore, when government dampened down the economy, because of inflationary pressures, employers would hoard labour, rather than lose it to other employers. This was in the expectation that when the economy began to take off again, firms would have the necessary labour resources to enable them to deal with rising demand for their products or services.

The second, related, consequence of 'soft' labour markets (from the sellers' point of view) was the increased wage-bargaining power provided to trade union negotiators. Local labour market shortages also undermined the regulative authority of national, multi-employer collective agreements. This resulted in the spread of plant or workplace bargaining, led from the union side by local, autonomous shop stewards, accountable largely to their members at plant level (see below). They often bargained toughly with local managers and were generally more willing than full-time union officers to threaten and use industrial sanctions in the wage-bargaining process. In consequence, during the 1960s, there was an increase in the number of unconstitutional strikes (in breach of agreed negotiating procedures) and unofficial strikes (not supported by the unions nationally). Governments became increasingly concerned about the economic efficiency and efficacy of British collective bargaining arrangements, processes and outcomes.

A third, knock-on effect of tough wage bargaining in the private sector was that these wage increases provided the benchmarks by which the public-sector unions made their wage claims to the employers. This provided governments with a series of dilemmas. Resisting such wage claims could result in industrial conflict among the state's workforce, damage to the state's reputation as a fair employer or the loss of staff to the private sector. On the other hand, conceding such claims could result in: rises in public spending and therefore in taxation and/or public borrowing; 'wage-price-wage' inflation; and state employers being seen as weak, ineffective parties in the wage-bargaining process, providing a bad model for private-sector employers to follow.

Searching for an incomes policy

The potentially inflationary effects of collective bargaining in conditions of full employment led post-war governments to search for an industrial consensus on the levels of annual wage increases compatible with price stability, economic growth and balance-of-payments equilibrium. The first attempt was that of the Labour Government in 1948, following an economic crisis during summer 1947. It issued a White Paper (Cmd 7321, 1948) arguing for no general increase in money incomes unless justified by labour shortages. The Trades Union Congress (TUC), though initially sceptical, gave the policy its qualified approval, but its annual Congress in 1949 voted for an end to wage restraint and the policy ceased to have effect during 1950. The last attempt at an agreed incomes policy was at the beginning of 1979. The Labour Government and the TUC published a joint statement that, while placing no limits on wage increases, expressed a joint commitment to reduce inflation to the level of Britain's overseas competitors over the following three years. With the return to power in May 1979 of a Conservative government, led by Margaret Thatcher, the policy lapsed.

Between 1950 and 1979 there were over 20 attempts to create a wage-bargaining consensus acceptable to employers and unions (ACAS 1980). Some were unilaterally initiated and imposed by government for given periods, such as between 1966 and 1969 and, under the Counter Inflation Act 1972, between 1972 and 1974. Other attempts, for example in the mid-1960s, sought the voluntary support both of the unions, through the TUC, and of the employers, through the Confederation of British Industry (CBI). Yet others, such as the 'social contracts' between the Labour Government and the TUC between summer 1975 and August 1977, were jointly monitored, government–union attempts at limiting wage increases for limited periods.

The nub of the incomes policy issue was trying to get a central agreement on annual wage increases. This involved developing a wages consensus among government, the unions and the employers by which the economic outcomes of voluntary collective bargaining (increasingly conducted at company and factory levels in the private sector) would be broadly in line with annual increases in national productivity and output.

If neither company wage negotiators nor union negotiators could be persuaded to agree to limit money wage increases in line with rises in real productivity at factory level, this would have a number of effects. First, private-sector employers that conceded such wage rises would have to increase their product prices to remain profitable. This would contribute to wage-price or cost-push inflation. Second, these wage increases, in turn, would provide benchmarks for other wage bargainers to follow in the private sector, especially those operating in the same labour markets. Unless the outcomes of these wage bargains were in line with productivity increases, these too would add to wage-price inflation. Third, the rates of increase in private-sector wages provided reference points for union negotiators in the public sector. Where these increases were conceded without productivity strings being attached, these in turn would fuel wage-cost inflation, creating demands for even higher wage increases by wage bargainers in the next pay round.

In these circumstances, there were few incentives for union wage bargainers to restrain their members' wage claims for any substantial period. If union leaders failed to satisfy their members' wage expectations, their members might take unofficial industrial action anyway. Employers, too, were unlikely to be convinced of the merits of wage restraint by resisting the wage demands of their unionised workforces. They would generally want to avoid expensive and disruptive industrial action and would also be concerned that they might lose some of their labour force if their company's wages were not competitive with those of other employers. And in any case, they were able to pass on rises in wages costs to their customers, in the form of higher product prices, in soft product markets. The only employers likely to resist excessive wage claims were public-sector ones. They needed to set examples to the private sector and keep public spending under control but they employed only a minority of the labour force.

It is clear, in retrospect, that in the period of the employee relations consensus, the one area of public policy where consensus proved to be elusive was in constraining wage bargaining 'in the national interest'. After 1965, the efforts were virtually continuous and a number of approaches were tried. These included voluntary and statutory pay norms (see Chapter 4), but none was successful in restraining wage increases for any length of time. With strong trade unions operating in conditions of full employment, various attempts by governments to adopt a policy of 'bargained corporatism' (see Chapter 1) failed to persuade union leaders, and their members, to accept any variant of public wage policy other than that of 'voluntary collective bargaining'. When national pay guidelines existed, national union leaders lacked the authority and control to get local shop stewards and full-time officers to comply with pay norms, other than in the short term. Unlike the Swedish and German experiences at this time, incomes policies in Britain failed miserably to deliver what was intended.

Supporting voluntary collective bargaining

State support for voluntary collective bargaining, or collective *laissez-faire*, as a process for determining the outcomes of the market relations between employers and employees, can be traced back to the late nineteenth century. Indeed, the final report of the Royal Commission on Labour Laws (1894) had supported the growth of strong, voluntary organisations of employers and employees, industry-level collective bargaining and a role for government in helping to minimise and settle industrial disputes. It was during the period 1945–79 that this policy reached its apotheosis.

Whitleyism

The Whitley Committee (1916–18) reinforced state support for voluntary collective bargaining as a method of conducting employee relations. During World War I there had been a great expansion, reorganisation and flexibility expected in manufacturing industry in response to the demands of the war economy. There had been a significant growth in the numbers and powers of local shop stewards who had challenged the authority of full-time union leaders, had used local bargaining to undermine national wage agreements and had made demands for 'workers' control' of industries and factories.

In the light of these pressures for change, the Committee recommended the establishment of standing joint councils of voluntary employers' associations and union organisations at industry, district and workplace levels. The power to bargain was to be concentrated at national level and it was recommended that the machinery should concern itself with a wide range of issues, including:

- determining wages
- agreeing terms of employment
- promoting efficiency
- encouraging 'joint co-operation' between employers and workers at all levels.

To encourage the development of collective bargaining, the Committee further recommended the setting up of a permanent, voluntary arbitration body and inquiry machinery (Farnham 1978).

In the inter-war years, Whitley councils were established in a number of private and public industries. These included the civil service, electricity, gas, building and printing – largely where collective bargaining had not existed previously (Charles 1973). With the encouragement of the Ministry of Labour and National Service, further joint industrial councils, or similar bodies, were established or re-established in the period immediately following World War II. These included the NHS, local government, railways and water supply industry. Furthermore, with full employment, steady economic growth and rising union membership, the numbers of workers whose terms and conditions of employment were directly determined by collective bargaining increased, mainly through industry-level multi-employer bargaining. By the mid-1960s, the Ministry of Labour (1965) estimated that upwards of 18 million employees, out of a workforce of 24 million, had their terms and conditions of employment determined by voluntary collective bargaining or statutory wage-fixing machinery.

The Donovan Commission

Between 1965 and 1968, the Royal Commission on Trade Unions and Employers' Associations (the Donovan Commission) undertook an examination of British employee relations, at a time when collective bargaining was being conducted in conditions of full employment and strong union bargaining power. Its report epitomised the support that the liberal state wished to give to voluntary collective bargaining. It concluded (Donovan 1968: 50) that:

> Collective bargaining is the best method of conducting industrial relations. There is therefore wide scope in Britain for extending both the subject matter of collective bargaining and the number of workers covered by collective agreements.

Donovan's analysis concentrated on private manufacturing industry. The Commission identified the central defects in British employee relations at that time as the disorder in employer–union relations, pay structures and collective bargaining procedures within factories. This was the result of the conflict between formal industry-wide bargaining at multi-employer level and informal factory bargaining at company or plant level. The formal system purported to settle the terms and conditions of employment of workers. But in practice it was fragmented, competitive wage bargaining within factories between managers and shop stewards, outside the control of employers' associations and national trade unions, which determined actual earnings. This bargaining provided local additions to national wage rates, such as piecework, bonus and overtime payments. In the Commission's view, companies also lacked effective internal procedural arrangements to curtail unofficial and unconstitutional industrial action by their workforces.

The Commission's main recommendations (*ibid*: 262–64) for the reform of collective bargaining were:

- Collective agreements should be developed within factories to regulate actual pay and procedural matters at this level, whilst industry-wide agreements should be limited to those matters that they could effectively regulate.
- At corporate level, boards of directors should develop comprehensive collective bargaining machinery and joint procedures for the settlement of grievances, discipline, redundancy and related issues.
- Companies with over 5,000 employees, including the public sector, should be required to register their procedural agreements with the Department of Employment and Productivity.
- A Commission on Industrial Relations (CIR) should be established that (a) would investigate and report on problems arising out of the registration of procedural agreements, and (b) would consider problems referred to it concerning companies not large enough to be covered by the registration arrangements.

The Royal Commission also argued that new measures were needed to encourage the extension of collective bargaining in Britain, and it recommended that:

- any stipulation in a contract of employment that an employee was not to belong to a trade union should be void in law

335

- the CIR should deal with problems of trade union recognition where employers refused to negotiate with unions
- wages councils legislation should be amended to encourage the development of voluntary collective bargaining machinery
- legislation under which an employer was required to observe relevant terms and conditions for an industry should be amended
- unilateral arbitration should be available on a selective basis, where it could contribute to the growth or maintenance of sound collective bargaining machinery.

Donovan's prescriptions for change epitomised the state's support for the development of voluntary collective bargaining in Britain and for extending its scope. Although voluntary reform proceeded on a piecemeal basis after Donovan, its proposed programme of legislation to promote voluntary collective bargaining was not acted upon immediately. This was because the Labour Government that had established the Commission lost the general election of 1970 and, even before then, it had difficulty getting its post-Donovan White Paper accepted by the TUC and Parliamentary Labour Party (Jenkins 1970). The Heath government that replaced it was committed to major reforms of the law on employee relations. Though the Industrial Relations Act 1971 claimed to promote the principle of collective bargaining freely conducted between workers' organisations and employers, it sought in fact to extend the influence of the law on employer and union behaviour, but markedly failed to do so (Weekes *et al* 1975). Its principles challenged those of the employee relations consensus and, largely as a result of this, the vast majority of employers and unions ignored the Industrial Relations Act 1971. They continued to conduct their employee relationships as they always had done, through voluntary collective bargaining.

The Employment Protection Act 1975

With the Labour Party re-elected to office in 1974, state support for the reform and extension of voluntary collective bargaining continued and, in retrospect, reached its highest point. It was facilitated by the Employment Protection Act (EPA) 1975, the Employment Protection (Consolidation) Act (EPCA) 1978 and related legislation. Part I of the EPA 1975 focused on the machinery for promoting the improvement of employee relations, within which ACAS had a pivotal role, while the EPCA 1978 consolidated the employment protection rights of individual employees, including those of trade unionists. In establishing ACAS, the EPA 1975, section 1(1), stated:

> [ACAS] shall be charged with the general duty of promoting the improvement of industrial relations, and in particular of encouraging the extension of collective bargaining and the development and, where necessary, reform of collective bargaining machinery.

The legislation drafted to do this was aimed at:

- *Encouraging trade union membership and activities.* Employees were given statutory protection from being prevented or deterred by employers from joining or taking part in the activities of an independent union or being compelled to join a non-independent union. Where employers infringed these provisions, employees had the right to go to an industrial tribunal.
- *Providing statutory time off work for those involved in trade union duties.* Officials of independent, recognised trade unions were given the right to time off work with pay for undertaking certain union duties, such as approved training, and time off without pay for certain union activities. Where employers infringed these rights, individuals could make a claim to an industrial tribunal.
- *Facilitating trade union recognition by employers.* Under the section 11 procedure of the EPA 1975 (repealed by the Employment Act 1980), independent trade unions could approach ACAS where an employer refused to recognise them. It was ACAS's duty to examine the issue, consult with the parties, conduct inquiries and report its findings. Where ACAS recommended recognition and an employer refused to comply with it, the Central Arbitration Committee (CAC) could make an award on terms and conditions which became incorporated as implied terms in the contracts of employment of individual workers. This was a form of compulsory arbitration, but there was no direct legal enforcement of union recognition.
- *Obliging employers to consult with and provide information to recognised independent unions.* Recognised independent trade unions were provided with statutory rights to be consulted on proposed collective redundancies and occupational pensions. They were also entitled to be provided with information by employers where it would be in accordance with good practice to disclose or where it would assist in the conduct of collective bargaining. There was, additionally, a statutory duty on employers to consult with recognised independent unions on health and safety matters. These included the appointment of safety representatives, appointment of safety committees and provision of information to safety representatives.
- *Providing legal procedures for extending terms and conditions of employment where unions were not recognised.* Schedule 11 of the EPA 1975 (repealed by the Employment Act 1980) enabled claims to be made to ACAS by independent unions (or employers' associations) that an employer was observing terms and conditions of employment less favourable than the recognised terms and conditions or, where there were no recognised terms and conditions, less favourable than the general level in any trade, industry or district. Failing settlement by ACAS, the CAC, if it found the claim to be well founded, could make an award for the appropriate terms and conditions to be observed as implied terms in the contracts of employment of workers. This too was a form of compulsory arbitration.

PUBLIC POLICY 1979–97: THE CHALLENGE TO COLLECTIVE *LAISSEZ-FAIRE*

Between 1979 and 1997, successive Conservative governments rejected Keynesian economic theory and Beveridge social welfare principles (see Chapter 4). This had considerable implications for public policy on employee relations, which shifted from one focused on voluntary collective bargaining, in conditions of full employment and strong trade unions (with attempts at bargained corporatism through 'social contracts') to a policy of neo-laissez-faire. It was a policy rooted in market liberal economic principles (see below) and weak trade unions (see Chapter 1). The *employee relations consensus* had emphasised:

- state intervention in the labour market
- state support for employee relations collectivism, whilst using the law as a 'prop' to promote collective bargaining
- excluding the courts and the judges from intervening in the internal affairs of trade unions and the regulation of industrial conflict.

Neo-*laissez-faire*, in contrast, emphasised:

- deregulating the labour market
- individualising employee relations, with the legal props to collective bargaining being loosened or removed and legal restrictions on trade unions being enacted
- de-politicising the trade unions.

The policy instruments used included: legislation, economic measures, government example in its own spheres of responsibility, the creation of the Commission for the Rights of Trade Union Members (Farnham 1990), and the appointment of a Commissioner for Protection Against Unlawful Industrial Action.

The theoretical and moral underpinnings of economic, social and employee relations policy after 1979 were rooted in market economics and liberal individualism, or 'market liberalism'. Market economics assumes that supply and demand in the market place, acting through the price mechanism, are preferable to political rationing by politicians in deciding what to produce in an economy, how to produce it and how goods and services are to be distributed among the population. Liberal individualism pinpoints the individual, not interest groups or pressure groups, as the prime decision-making authority, with the freedoms and natural rights of the individual being inalienable and non-negotiable. Free markets lead to economic efficiency and equity, it is argued, and independent, free-thinking individuals in doing what is best for themselves maximise economic welfare generally.

The market economic model makes three assumptions about the relationship of the market to the individual:

- individuals act rationally in pursuing their own self-interest in the market place
- the free play of impersonal, decentralised market forces is the best way of increasing the prosperity and welfare of the individual and of the wider community
- the individual consumer is sovereign in the market place because of freedom of consumer choice and market competition among producers.

For market liberals, because the individual is central to economic decision-making, and because it is assumed that he or she knows what is best for him or herself, the role of government is limited to providing an economic and constitutional framework for individuals to pursue their own self-interest. The state intervenes only to protect the individual's rights to property, liberty and access to free markets. Market liberal – or neo-*laissez-faire* – economic, social and employee relations policy, in short, aims at optimising market efficiency, minimising government intervention in private affairs and protecting individual rights against so-called vested interests.

Deregulating the labour market

There is some debate over whether there is 'a' labour market in Britain or a series of 'segmented' labour markets. Market liberal *macro*economists emphasise the contexts of the general labour market; market liberal *micro*economists try to explain how rational agents in disaggregated labour markets produce different responses to changes in wage levels and unemployment. The macroeconomists focus on how factors independent of the labour market – such as inflation, the exchange rate and mortgage interest tax relief – are likely to influence wages and unemployment; the microeconomists try to evaluate the influence of institutional factors affecting them. To simplify the market liberal analysis, this section focuses on the micro-issues of labour market policy, rather than the macro-issues.

The micro-issues

Labour market deregulation was a central plank of government policy from 1979. Given that labour services are commodities that are bought and sold by 'rational' employers and 'rational' workers in the market place, market liberals argue that levels of wages and employment are determined by the forces of supply and demand in the market. In a free labour market, the quantity of labour supplied equals the quantity demanded at the market wage. Unemployment is symptomatic of labour market rigidity and means that the price of labour is too high, so that wages need to be adjusted downwards if the labour market is to clear. Where there are barriers to a freely operating labour market, it is necessary to deregulate it to make it more competitive. This, it is argued, is in the interests of economic efficiency and individual freedom.

One cause of unemployment and labour market rigidity identified by market liberal economists is institutional. Where, for example, employers have to take account of the costs of compensation for unfair dismissal, they are deterred, it is claimed, from increasing demand for new employees. Extending employment protection rights thus has the overall effect of bringing about a fall in labour demand and an increase in unemployment. Second, fiscal factors, such as changes in taxation and social security, are also claimed to increase unemployment. This is because higher taxes reduce labour supply, whilst higher social security payments result in people being unemployed longer, with more time being spent in job searches.

A third cause of unemployment, in the view of market liberals, is collective action by workers organised into trade unions. Unionised workers are viewed as restricting labour supply and limiting access to jobs for non-union workers who are likely to drive wage rates down. A rise in demand for unionised labour results in higher wages but not in higher employment, because the supply of labour is fixed in the short term. Indeed, market liberals argue that trade unions contribute to higher unemployment because they restrict labour supply, whilst union wage rates do not reflect changes in labour supply or labour demand. More than that, the unionised sector is the benchmark for the whole economy, setting wage norms for other workers to follow. In the non-unionised sector, in contrast, labour supply is seen as being responsive to changes in wage rates. An increase in labour demand there will be reflected in both higher wages and higher levels of employment.

The policy prescriptions

According to market liberals, government can reform and deregulate the labour market by improving the supply side of the market. It can do this in four ways. First, it can reduce the time spent unemployed and in job searches by reducing the rates of social security payments. Second, government can increase labour supply by reducing personal taxation rates. These two measures aim to increase incentives to work, so that more people make themselves available for employment and join the labour market. A third measure is removing wages councils and minimum wages legislation, since these are likely to increase the price of labour to employers thus resulting in a fall in labour demand. The fourth way in which government can act is by reforming trade union immunities. The aim here is to make it more difficult for trade unions to take lawful industrial action without incurring severe financial costs in doing so. Conservative governments during the 1980s and 1990s adopted these measures, to varying degrees, by a series of legislative and economic initiatives.

Individualising employee relations

The necessary conditions for employee relations collectivism are:

- freedom of association for workers to join trade unions
- 'free' trade unions independent of employers and the state
- employer recognition of trade unions
- bargaining in good faith.

Between 1979 and 1997, one plank of public policy aimed at the de-collectivisation of employee relations, with employers being encouraged to use more individualist methods of determining and implementing the wage–work bargain. This policy, stemming from the precepts of market liberalism, took three main forms, with government attempting to:

- weaken union organisation
- strengthen the right to manage
- discourage union militancy.

Weakening union organisation

Although freedom of association and independent trade unions continued to exist in Britain, union organisation was weakened dramatically after 1979 in at least three respects. First, union density, expressed as the percentage of the potential workforce who are union members, fell drastically, especially in the private sector (see Chapter 7). This was largely as a result of structural reorganisation of the economy and high levels of unemployment during the 1980s and 1990s (Daniel and Millward 1983, Millward and Stevens 1986, Millward *et al* 1992, Cully *et al* 1999). Smaller employment units and reduction in size of the manufacturing sector adversely affected union organisation. High unemployment also weakened union bargaining power with employers, making the retention of union members more problematic and recruitment of new members a more difficult task for union organisers (Martin 1992).

Second, as a result of a series of changes in employment law in the 1980s and 1990s, closed-shop agreements, or union membership agreements (UMAs), between employers and trade unions were made unlawful. A UMA is any arrangement by which employees are required to be members of a union as a condition of employment. Pre-entry closed shops are where jobs are restricted to individuals who are already members of the appropriate union, while post-entry closed shops require employees to join a specified union within a set period of starting work. Where individuals claim that their legal right not to belong to a union is infringed, they have a right to make an application to an employment tribunal and seek compensation.

Outlawing the closed shop weakened union organisation. UMAs covered some quarter of the employed workforce in the late 1970s (Dunn and Gennard 1984). Although it is difficult to calculate the extent of the closed shop currently, and despite the continuance of some informal closed shop arrangements, legislation both ended the enforcement of the practice and debilitated union organisation.

Third, other legal measures – originally incorporated in the Employment Act (EA) 1988 and the Trade Union Act (TUA) 1984, now embodied in the Trade Union and Labour Relations (Consolidation) Act (TULRCA) 1992, as amended – provided rights for union members to elect union executive committees and union leaders by postal ballot, at least once every five years. These legislative changes in union election procedures, outlined in a Green Paper in 1983, stemmed from the Government's desire to ensure that

341

trade union members were truly representative of their memberships. Because the unions had not reformed themselves voluntarily, the Government claimed that it 'had reluctantly come to the conclusion that some legislative intervention is necessary' (Department of Employment 1983: 16). Another interpretation of these provisions, however, is that they were seen by government as a further means of weakening collective links among trade unionists, and between union members and the union, thus loosening union cohesion and collective solidarity.

Strengthening the right to manage

The right to manage is that area of corporate decision-making that management considers to be its alone and is not constrained by collective bargaining or the law (see Chapter 3). The boundaries of the right to manage are the interface between unilateral management control and the ability of employees, individually or collectively, to influence or counterbalance those decisions most affecting their working lives. Given government commitment to the enterprise culture and free market economy between 1979 and 1997, one of its policy goals was to strengthen the right to manage. Its rationale was to provide managers, in both the private and public sectors, with more autonomy in organisational decision-making and to restrict union activity and collective action. It was aimed at enabling employers to react more swiftly to changing product markets, obtain greater flexibility from their human resources and have more control over worker productivity. Companies and public-sector organisations, in turn, would then become more efficient, effective and competitive, thus boosting the economy, growth and employment.

The pressure for employers to recognise unions for collective bargaining purposes was considerably weakened after 1979. One of the first measures taken by the Government was to repeal, in the EA 1980, the section 11 procedures embodied in the EPA 1975. This meant that ACAS no longer had a statutory duty to investigate and make recommendations on union recognition. ACAS's only remaining duty was to conciliate on trade union recognition claims, on a voluntary basis. The number of requests for this fell dramatically in the next two decades (ACAS *Annual Reports*).

The powers of wages councils to set wage rates for those aged under 21 and other conditions were abolished by the Wages Act 1986, which limited wages councils to setting minimum adult hourly rates and overtime rates. Subsequently, the Trade Union Reform and Employment Rights Act 1993 abolished the remaining 26 wages councils completely. Fair Wages Resolutions (see below) were rescinded and the comparable terms and conditions procedure – schedule 11 of the EPA 1975 – repealed. Where 10–99 employees were to be made redundant, the minimum period for trade union consultation was reduced. Further, union-only or union recognition clauses in commercial contracts were now to be void in law. It was also unlawful to discriminate against or victimise contractors on these grounds.

All the above public policy changes enabled employers to be more flexible and autonomous in determining the terms, conditions and working arrangements of their employees. The emphasis was on strengthening the right to manage, at the expense of employee and union rights and weakening the legal props to collective bargaining.

Discouraging union militancy

Changes in collective labour law by Conservative governments during the 1980s and 1990s were aimed at reducing union ability to take part in lawful trade disputes (see Chapter 4). Legal immunities, the legal definition of a trade dispute and industrial action ballots are at the root of the issue. Where employees take industrial action, they are normally in breach of their contracts of employment. Under common law, it is unlawful to induce people to break a contract, to interfere with the performance of a contract or to threaten to do so. Without legal immunities, unions and their officers could face legal action for inducing breaches of contract when organising industrial action. Legal immunities provide protections for unions and individuals so that they cannot be sued for damages for inducing breaches of contract when furthering industrial action in certain circumstances (see Chapter 1). The Employment Acts 1980 and 1982, however, withdrew immunities from certain types of industrial action, opening up the possibility of unions and individuals having injunctions issued against them, or being sued, where their actions are unlawful. These legal provisions are now incorporated in the TULRCA 1992.

The law also provides that those organising industrial action are only protected when acting 'in contemplation or furtherance of a trade dispute'. To remain within the law, those calling industrial action must be able to show that there is a dispute and that the action supports it. Lawful disputes are those between workers and their own employers and must be concerned with matters 'wholly or mainly' connected with terms and conditions, negotiating machinery and so on. The following types of disputes are now unlawful:

- inter-union disputes
- 'political' disputes
- disputes relating to matters occurring overseas
- disputes with employers not recognising unions or employing non-union labour
- 'secondary' or 'sympathy' disputes between workers and employers other than their own.

Where unions act unlawfully, they lose their legal immunity (see Chapter 10).

Unions are also required to ballot union members involved in a trade dispute before authorising the action. Under the TUA 1984 (now incorporated in the TULRCA 1992), it became a condition of legal immunity that, before organising industrial action, the union holds a secret ballot in which all those about to take the action are entitled to vote. The action is only lawful where a majority of those voting support it. The EA 1988 went further by providing union members with the right to apply to the courts for an order restraining their union from inducing them to take industrial action without a properly conducted ballot. The Trade Union Reform and Employment Rights Act 1993 requires unions to give seven days' notice to the employer of their intention to hold an industrial action ballot, which must normally be a full postal ballot and be independently scrutinised. Where an unlawful act is authorised by a union official, or by a committee to which such officials report, the union is liable for its members' actions unless it disowns the unlawful act in writing.

The effect of removing legal immunities from certain industrial action is to provide those damaged by the action, such as employers or union members, with the right to take civil proceedings against the union, or in some cases the individual, responsible. The remedies are:

- seeking an injunction to prevent or stop the action
- claiming damages from the union for conducting unlawful action.

Under the TULRCA 1992 and the Trade Union Reform and Employment Rights Act 1993, union members have the statutory right not to be unjustifiably disciplined by their union. They specify the actions that count as discipline and the conduct for which discipline is justifiable. Conduct incurring unjustifiable discipline for union members includes:

- refusing to take part in balloted industrial action
- crossing a picket line
- refusing to pay a levy for supporting a strike or other industrial action
- failing to agree or withdrawing from an agreement with an employer regarding deductions of union dues
- working or proposing to work with members of another union or with non-union members
- working or proposing to work for an employer who employs non-union members or members of another union.

De-politicising trade unions

Union political activity, though difficult to define in practice, has always been a sensitive and ambivalent issue for the Conservative Party to deal with. On the one hand, the Conservatives want the votes of trade union members in local, national and European elections. On the other hand, there are many in the Conservative Party who are distinctly hostile to unions on not only political but also economic grounds. The political objections of many Conservatives to the trade unions are the close political affiliations of some unions to the Labour Party. Trade unions affiliate members to the Labour Party, support Labour Members of Parliament financially and participate in Labour Party decision-making. The economic objections of many Conservatives to the trade unions are that they distort the working of the free labour market, inhibit economic efficiency and weaken management authority in the workplace.

The underlying assumption of Conservative public policy-makers in seeking to de-politicise the trade unions is that the economic and political roles of trade unions can be dissociated. This analysis accepts the unions' economic role as legitimate, up to a point, but asserts that their political role needs to be circumscribed, by law. Market liberals argue that this is necessary, first, on the grounds that it makes politicians democratically accountable to their constituents, not to special interest groups such as trade unions. Second, the unions can concentrate on their more rightful and more legitimate role of protecting their members' employment interests in the labour market. De-politicising the unions could also facilitate an ideological change on the part of the unions and their members, enabling them to identify more closely with the goals of a dynamic free market, operating in a competitive enterprise culture.

Political strikes

The definition of a trade dispute in the TULRCA 1992 now requires trade disputes to 'relate wholly or mainly to' the subjects listed. This raises doubts about the lawfulness of any dispute having political elements. This change in the legal definition of a trade dispute, in seeking to exclude those with a political element, effectively restricts some types of actions aimed at defending or improving terms and conditions of employment. An example is where workers decide to take industrial action in protest at their industry or organisation being privatised.

Political fund review ballots

The TULRCA 1992, as amended, requires unions with 'political objects' and political funds, which are normally used to support the Labour Party and conduct political campaigns, to ballot their members, at least once every 10 years, on whether they wish their union to continue to spend money on political matters. Ballots must be by post and are subject to independent scrutiny. The scrutineer has access to a union's membership register and must inspect the register or a relevant copy where it is felt appropriate to do so. The distribution, counting and storage of voting papers must be undertaken by independent scrutiny. If ballots are not held, the authority to spend money on political objects lapses.

Privatisation

This was a leading policy initiative of the Thatcher and Major administrations. Privatising substantial parts of the public sector, and contracting out certain services in public-sector organisations, has transferred large numbers of workers out of public employment (see below). This means that government is no longer their employer. These businesses cannot therefore call upon government to increase public spending to finance their wage settlements with their employees. They are now required to have regard to market and financial considerations when responding to terms and conditions claims. This takes wage determination in these sectors out of politics, thus in effect de-politicising their wage-bargaining process.

Settling trade disputes

Between 1979 and 1997, successive Conservative governments publicly rejected any role in industrial peacekeeping. Government ministers abstained from directly intervening, by conciliating or mediating, in intractable trade disputes, even in the public sector, no matter how bitter the disputes were. This approach assumed that dispute resolution should be left to the direct employers and trade unions to settle themselves. The outcome could then be determined by powerful employers relying on market forces to generate financially prudent wage settlements and a sense of economic reality amongst the workforce and their union leaders in the wage-bargaining process.

Rejecting corporatism

The Conservative governments' public policy after 1979 resulted in exclusion of the TUC from industrial policy-making. Governments refused to consult directly with the TUC on economic, employment or social policy decisions and they have abandoned top-level meetings with TUC officials. A succession of government Green Papers on trade union law reform, for example, was not used for consultative purposes but as draft legislation, enacted subsequently in virtually the form in which they had been presented. Indeed, the only remaining corporatist body, the National Economic Development Council, was formally wound up in 1991.

THE LABOUR GOVERNMENT'S EMPLOYEE RELATIONS POLICY SINCE 1997

Immediately after being elected to office by a landslide majority in the general election of May 1997, the new Labour Government's employee relations policy remained, to some extent, indeterminate and uncertain. The central issue was to what extent was it likely to be a continuation of existing policy, a return to Labour's traditional policy or a policy in its own right? By late 1999 and early 2000, the direction of its policy was more apparent and some indicators of where the Government was going in terms of employee relations and regulation of the employment relationship were emerging. In essence, its policy direction appeared to be moving away from its former wholehearted commitment to state support for voluntary collective bargaining. It had clearly rejected the bargained corporatist model, which was still alive in Ireland. But it was moving away from the Conservative's anti-union, neo-*laissez-faire* approach, and in its place it seemed to be developing a 'new deal' and modernising approach to employee relations. This emergent policy appears to be based upon a mixture of voluntarism, both individually between employers and employees and collectively between employers and unions, supplemented by increased legal intervention and state and European regulation.

In outline, the Labour Government appears to be shifting to an employee relations policy that appears to be based on five basic pillars. These are: encouraging employment flexibility, protecting minimum employment standards in the workplace, promoting family-friendly policies at work, supporting partnership at work and supporting union recognition, where employers refuse it voluntarily. The main policy instruments being used in furthering its objectives are legal enactment and signing up to the Social Chapter of the EU (see below). The Labour Government's 'new deal' on employee relations, therefore, appears to be incorporating support for a flexible labour market, underpinned by an extended but limited range of legal protections at work, largely for individuals but, to a lesser degree, for trade unions too.

Encouraging employment flexibility

The starting point for Labour's new employment policy (Labour Party 1997a: 150) was that healthy profits are 'an essential motor of a dynamic market economy'. But these depend on 'quality products, innovative entrepreneurs and skilled employees'. Since many fundamentals of the British economy remain weak – such as low pay, low skills and low-quality jobs – there was no future, in Labour's view, in Britain's following this pathway, since she cannot compete with countries paying 'a tenth or a hundredth of British wages' in free market economies. Instead, Britain 'needs to win on higher quality, skill, innovation and reliability'. Labour therefore wants British and inward investors to find the UK an attractive and profitable place in which to do business.

Accordingly, Labour believes in a flexible labour market serving employers and employees alike. But, Labour argues, flexibility is not enough; what is needed is 'flexibility plus'. This includes:

- higher skills and higher standards in our schools and colleges
- policies to ensure economic stability
- partnership with business to raise investment in infrastructure, science and research in order to back small firms
- new leadership from Britain to reform Europe, replacing a policy of drift and disengagement from our largest market
- guaranteeing Britain's membership of the single market – indeed opening up further markets inside and outside the EU – making Britain an attractive place to do business
- minimum standards of fair treatment, including a national minimum wage
- an imaginative welfare-to-work programme to put the long-term unemployed back to work and to cut social security costs.

To sustain economic opportunity and prosperity in a global economy, the Labour Government argues that Britain needs to use the talents of its workforce fully, as evidenced by leading-edge companies that recognise that high performance is directly associated with maximising the potential of every employee. Labour thus believes that 'the way to achieve this is through trust, consultation, teamworking and offering people [at work] real security' and 'a highly educated and skilled workforce able to succeed in the labour market'. Labour further recognises that competitive success is achieved through partnership between employers and employees, not confrontation, with business success depending upon avoiding rigidity in labour market regulation and 'promoting the flexibility we require' (Labour Party 1997b: 1). As a result of this approach:

> There will be no blanket repeal of the main elements of the 1980s' legislation. What there will be is a new deal for people at work, which will avoid rigidity but give people a decent threshold of fair treatment, recognising that social partnership is at the heart of the successful company of the future.

The Labour Government therefore believes that the labour market of the 1990s and 2000s, with its growing emphasis on the importance of flexibility, can bring positive, fresh opportunities for people at work in ways better suited to their own needs. This means, for example, that they can combine atypical work with caring for children or elderly relatives, or they can learn new skills and take on new responsibilities. Labour supports, too, the Social Chapter of the EU and seeks to deploy its influence in Europe to ensure that it develops so as to promote employability and competitiveness, not inflexibility.

Protecting minimum employment standards

Labour also argues (*ibid*: 17) that 'there must be minimum standards for the individual at work, including a minimum wage, within a flexible labour market.' With weakened trade unions, a changing labour market and a shift to service-sector employment, the Labour Government believes that the most effective way in which minimum standards of employment practice can be enforced is through the law. It is therefore developing a balance in employment law where rights and duties go together. To this end, the Labour Government wants the key elements of the trade union legislation of the 1980s to remain on statute, covering ballots, picketing and industrial action. But it believes that people should be free to join or not to join a union and every person at work should be entitled to basic minimum standards of fairness, properly enforced, based largely on the notion of individual rights (Labour Party 1997b).

A national minimum wage

Labour believes that there should be a statutory wage level beneath which pay should not fall. Most other OECD countries have a wages floor, including the United States, Japan and France, but apart from agriculture Britain has had none since abolition of the last wages councils in 1993. Labour argues that the minimum wage should not be decided by a rigid formula but according to the economic circumstances of the time, with the advice of an independent Low Pay Commission, chaired by Professor George Bain, including representatives of employers, small businesses and employees. Labour believes that a statutory minimum wage will remove the worst excesses of low pay, particularly benefiting women, while cutting some of the benefits budget by which taxpayers subsidise companies paying very low wages. In the event, the Low Pay Commission decided on setting a minimum hourly rate of £3.60 for workers over 21 years of age through the National Minimum Wage Act 1998, which was raised to £3.70 per hour in 2000.

Those opposed to a statutory minimum wage argued that it would result in job losses, raise employment costs and therefore result in price rises, and have a knock-on impact on pay differentials. Those favouring the introduction of a statutory minimum wage, on the other hand, argued that Britain has among the fewest basic legal standards to protect the working conditions of employees. Labour's objective is to establish a framework of minimum standards in the labour market and at the workplace that seeks to support flexibility as well as providing protection against unfair treatment. The minimum wage issue fits this agenda and forms a central plank in Labour's attempts to set basic standards at work, 'which should be regarded as part of fundamental citizenship' and 'as natural as the rule of law' (*ibid:* 3)

Research by the TUC (1995) into the arguments for introducing a statutory minimum wage in Britain demonstrates that:

- women are twice as likely to be low paid as men
- more than half of those paid less than £2.50 an hour are part-time workers
- 85 per cent of those on less than £2.50 an hour work in the private sector
- income inequality has increased dramatically in the past 25 years
- basic hourly rates have fallen in all industries previously covered by wages councils
- the cost of means-tested benefits for people in work is estimated to be £2.4 billion per year
- more than a third of those who would benefit from a national minimum of £3.00 an hour live in the poorest 10 per cent of households.

Further, although the case for a minimum wage has been dominated by economic arguments, for and against it, there is also a moral case for raising minimum pay levels.

Health and safety

Labour is committed to continue working with employers and employees so as to promote best practice in health and safety throughout industry and the service sector. It intends working with employers' and employees' organisations to improve occupational health, reduce absenteeism and ensure that independent advice and support is available to those wishing to improve the situation in their workplaces. Labour also believes that health and safety protection at work is an area where partnership between employers and employees has been successful in setting minimum standards. In its view, the social partnership approach to health and safety can be extended with positive benefits for companies, employees and everyone concerned. There is an overwhelming economic case for high standards of occupational health care, with 31 million working days lost through work-related illness, 23 million of them because of industrial injury.

The Social Chapter

The Social Chapter, or Social Policy Agreement, was a protocol to the Treaty on the European Union 1993, which set out the broad objectives on improving the working and living conditions of workers in member states of the EU but excluded the UK. The Social Chapter was originally incorporated in the Treaty of Rome 1957 and Single European Act 1987. The Labour Government signed into the new Social Chapter as part of the package of measures that were incorporated into the Treaty of Amsterdam 1997. A number of directives are being introduced. One gives workers in multinational companies the right to be informed of corporate changes through European works councils (EWCs). A second is the parental leave ruling, which member states had to enforce by June 1998. This gives both parents the right to a minimum of three months unpaid leave but is not to be confused with maternity leave. Other measures are in the pipeline. The Labour Government says that future proposals for legislation under the Social Chapter will be measured against their impact on competitiveness.

Age discrimination

Labour also believes that all people at work should be treated fairly, building on existing entitlements. It sees the case for employing a balanced workforce, including older and younger workers, as an overwhelming one. This mixes skills and experience and brings a wealth of accumulated talent to employers, enabling older employees to assist in the development of younger staff. Labour has backed off legislating against age discrimination, however, and issued a 'code of practice' on age discrimination in employment. The purpose of the *Code of Practice on Age Diversity in Employment* (1999) is to encourage employers to stop using age as a criterion in personnel policies. It identifies six stages in the employment process in which good practice is required to create an age-diverse workforce and reduce age discrimination: recruitment, selection, promotion, training and development, redundancy, and retirement. But to what extent the code is likely to end age discrimination in the workplace is yet to be determined.

Promoting family-friendly policies at work

The Employment Relations Act (ERA) 1999 introduced new legal provisions for promoting family-friendly policies in the workplace, by creating statutory rights to leave for family and domestic reasons. These provisions include improvements to maternity leave, rights for parents of young children and a right to time off work for employees to look after dependants. On maternity leave the Act provides for three periods of leave:

- ordinary maternity leave for 18 weeks for all women workers, during which the contract of employment continues; on returning to work, female employees have the right to return to the same job that they had before their leave of absence
- at least two weeks' compulsory maternity leave, around the time of the birth, to satisfy health and safety requirements
- additional maternity leave for women with one year's service by the eleventh week before the expected week of childbirth, allowing 29 additional weeks after the 18 weeks ordinary maternity leave.

The procedure for giving notice of the beginning and end of maternity leave has also been simplified.

Following the EU directive on parental leave, parents have a statutory right to a minimum period of 13 weeks' leave to care for a child, with a maximum age of five. During the period of parental leave, the employment contract continues. The intention is that employees should not lose seniority or pension rights and they have protections in the cases of redundancy and dismissal. Parental leave schemes are intended to be self-regulating in individual workplaces and employers are not required to keep records of them. Collective agreements or workforce agreements can provide rights that are better than those laid down by law. Where such agreed schemes are written into contracts of employment, they are legally enforceable.

Schedule 4 of the ERA 1999 sets out the right to 'time off for dependants', giving employees the right to take reasonable time off to deal with situations where:

- a dependant falls ill, gives birth or is injured or assaulted
- arrangements have to be made to care for a dependant who is ill or injured
- care arrangements have broken down
- there is a problem at school.

The definition of a dependant includes spouses, children, parents or someone living in the same household who is not an employee, tenant or lodger and 'anyone' who reasonably relies on the employee. These legal rights are enforceable in employment tribunals.

Supporting partnership at work

The Labour Government's enthusiasm for partnership at work focuses on two key areas: partnership between employers and employees, and partnership between employers and unions. As its 1997 manifesto put it (Labour Party 1997a: 17):

The best companies recognise their employees as partners in the enterprise. Employees whose conditions are good are more committed to their companies and are more productive. Many unions and employers are embracing partnership in place of conflict.

The main implications of adopting this approach to the employment relationship are, first, that the Labour Government is keen to encourage a variety of forms of partnership and enterprise by spreading ownership and encouraging more employees to become owners through employee share-ownership plans and co-operatives. Second, it is assumed that by promoting more conflict-free employer–union relations, the need for damaging and costly strikes and other forms of industrial action can be avoided. Section 30 of the ERA 1999 allows government to spend money, directly or through other organisations, to encourage employers and employees to work in partnership together.

Supporting union recognition

Incorporated within its 'partnership at work' perspective is Labour's commitment to supporting the right of unionised workers to have their union recognised by non-union employers who refuse recognition. Up to 85 of Britain's top 100 companies negotiate pay and conditions with unions, but the proportion of workplaces where unions are recognised has fallen from around two-thirds in 1979 to under 40 per cent in the mid-1990s. Among the best-known firms in the UK refusing union recognition are Marks & Spencer, IBM, McDonalds, Honda, United Utilities and the Body Shop. Labour's proposal, that 'the union should be recognised' where 'a majority of the relevant workforce vote in a ballot for the union to represent them' (Labour Party 1997a: 17), has now been enacted in the ERA 1999. This, it believes, will promote stable and orderly employee relations, and where an employer refuses to grant recognition, an independent union can invoke a legal procedure that can ultimately lead to statutory union recognition (see Chapter 7).

A 'third way' in employee relations policy?

The final question needing to be addressed in this section is the extent to which the Labour Government's employee relations settlement outlined above is a 'third way' in employee relations policy, which is analogous to 'New' Labour's political settlement post-1997. The latter, it is claimed, transcends both social democracy and neo-liberalism and is a 'third way' alternative to state socialism, supported by 'old' Labour, and the free market supported by the New Right in the 1980s and 1990s (Giddens 1998). Advocates of the 'third way' in employee relations thesis argue that Labour's support of the national minimum wage, its policy of enhancing job protection rights, its creation of statutory union recognition procedures and its signing up to the Social Chapter do not add up to enthusiastic acceptance of neo-liberalism. Rather, they argue, these measures demonstrate Labour's concerns with enhancing social partnership at work, extending social justice in the workplace and aligning itself with a more western European model of employee relations, without damaging employer interests in terms of labour efficiency, flexibility and individualised employment practices. Arguing along these lines, Taylor (1998) has concluded that the election of the Blair Labour Government in 1997 was likely, in retrospect, to be seen as a turning point in the history of British employee relations.

Undy (1999: 333) has taken a more sceptical view of New Labour's employee relations settlement and has rejected the third way thesis on two grounds. First, he argues that New Labour's wider interests and the decline of trade union power mean that employee relations are no longer viewed as posing a major problem for government or employers. They do not, therefore, warrant the effort of a considered and consistent approach, as suggested by third-way thinking. Second, in his view, New Labour's employee relations settlement is primarily a product of a decision-making process involving 'Old' and 'New' Labour. 'Indeed, it may be taken as a *final* settlement because it is the last act of Old Labour' (my italics). On this basis, the third-way influence is reflected in the decision 'to retain much of Mrs Thatcher's anti-union legislation, dilute the pre-election commitment to union recognition and reject the EU's proposed national-level works councils'. On this basis, Undy concludes, New Labour's third way in employee relations policy 'may be much closer to neo-liberalism than the substance of the legislation would suggest'.

THE STATE AS AN EMPLOYER

As the role of the British state expanded during the twentieth century, so the number of people employed by the state and its public agencies also increased, until the early 1980s. An outline summary of the structure of state employment by major sectors, for selected years since 1961, is provided in Table 18. From this, it can be seen that state employment rose steadily until 1981, when it reached over 7 million employees. By 1998, however, employment in the public sector had fallen to its lowest level in the post-war period: just over 5 million. Between 1961 and 1998, employment in public corporations (excluding NHS trusts) had fallen by 1.78 million. In central government, employment had fallen to under 1 million by 1998, compared with 2.4 million in 1981, the civil service having only just over half a million staff in 1998 ('other' central government) and the armed services just over 200,000, compared with 878,000 and 334,000 in 1981 respectively. Another significant change was the proportion of NHS staff working in NHS trusts in 1998. This represented an increase of over 800 per cent between 1991 and 1998, now that NHS trust staff are no longer classified as central government employees but as employees of public corporations. The numbers employed in local authorities, in contrast, were relatively more stable between 1981 and 1998, although there was a redistribution of staff within this sector, with the numbers employed in construction falling dramatically, those in education and social services falling slowly and those in the police rising steadily.

Table 18 Numbers employed in the UK public sector: by headcount 1961, 1971, 1981, 1991 and 1998

(000s)

	1961	1971	1981	1991	1998
Public corporations	2200	2009	1867	723	1539
NHS trusts	..	..	..	124	1122
Other	2200	2009	1867	599	417
Central government	1790	1966	2419	2178	885
HM forces	474	368	334	297	210
NHS	575	785	1207	1098	77
Other	741	813	878	783	598
Local government	1869	2652	2899	2947	2578
Education	785	1297	1454	1416	1204
Social services	170	276	350	414	395
Police	108	152	186	202	207
Construction	103	124	143	106	59
Other	703	803	766	809	713
Total public sector	5859	6627	7185	5848	5002

Source: McGregor 1999

The state as a model good-practice employer

One of the traditional roles of the state in employee relations, from the late nineteenth century until the late 1970s, was to be a 'model', 'good-practice' employer. Although the concepts overlap, they may be distinguished analytically. As a 'model' employer, the state adopted what were deemed to be progressive employment practices, such as encouraging union membership and recognising trade unions, in order to enhance 'best practice' in the public sector and to act as an example for the private sector to follow. As a 'good-practice' employer, in contrast, the state adopted certain of the employment practices of the best private-sector companies, such as wages comparability, so as to be able to recruit, retain, reward and motivate the sort of staff it needed in the public sector. As a 'model' employer, the state played a 'lead' role in employee relations, whilst as a 'good-practice' employer, the state had a 'following' role (Farnham and Horton 1993, 1996).

The model employer concept of the public sector can be traced back some 100 years. In 1893, for example, the House of Commons passed a resolution stating that 'no person in Her Majesty's Naval Establishments should be engaged at wages insufficient for proper maintenance.' It added that 'the conditions of labour as regards hours, wages, insurance against accidents, provisions for old age, sickness, etc., should be such as to afford an example to private employers throughout the country' (White 1933:

156). Examples of model employment practices adopted by public-sector employers – certainly after 1945 and, in some cases, earlier – include:

- job security
- jointly agreed employee relations procedures with the public-sector unions for handling grievances, discipline, dismissal and redeployment
- equal opportunities policies and equal pay
- occupational pensions
- training and career development opportunities
- the recruitment of disadvantaged workers.

To varying degrees, these model practices applied across the public sector. When compared with private employers, the public sector demonstrated a rich pattern of relatively homogeneous, consistent and standardised employment practices, aimed partly at influencing 'bad' practices in the private sector (Beaumont 1981).

A prime example of a model employment practice was in relation to 'fair wages' principles, linked with union membership. The Fair Wages Resolutions of the House of Commons (1891 and 1946, but rescinded in 1983) obliged private firms contracting to the public sector to pay 'fair wages' to their employees and recognise their rights to be union members. The principle underlying these resolutions was that it was the government's duty to use its bargaining position with private contractors to ensure that they observed at least minimum standards of fairness in the terms and conditions of employment provided to their employees. The outcome of collective bargaining was acknowledged to be the relevant standard of fairness to be met by the contractors' terms and conditions of employment (Beaumont 1992). These arrangements, it was believed, would eliminate unfair wage-cutting by government contractors and influence the development and growth of union organisation and collective bargaining in these parts of the private sector.

One facet of being a good-practice public employer meant providing terms and conditions of employment comparable with those provided by the best private employers. As the Priestley Commission wrote regarding Civil Service pay (Priestley 1955: para. 172):

> We consider that the Civil Service should be a good employer in the sense that while it should not be among those who offer the highest rates of remuneration, it should be among those who pay somewhat above the average...the Civil Service rate should not be lower than the median but not above the upper quartile.

This principle of 'pay comparability' was incorporated in guidelines provided to the Civil Service Pay Research Unit, formed as a result of the Priestley Commission. It was a principle legitimised more generally in the public sector in the late 1970s by the Standing Commission on Pay Comparability (SCPC). Although abolished in 1981, the SCPC – set up by the Prime Minister, James Callaghan, in March 1979 – had a distinctive role in public-sector employee relations. Its remit was to examine the pay and conditions of employment of groups of public-sector workers referred to it by the government, with the agreement of the employers and unions concerned, and to report on these. In each case, the SCPC had to make recommendations 'on the possibility of establishing acceptable bases of comparison with terms and conditions for other comparable workers and of maintaining appropriate internal relativities' (Standing Commission on Pay Comparability 1981: iii).

The related roles of the model and good-practice employer in the public sector were not always compatible. One example was public-sector employers acting as leaders of wage restraint in their own sector during periods of incomes policy, but at other times acting as followers of private-sector wage levels in order to recruit and retain staff. However, providing a lead in some employment practices and in others following the best private employers were crucial elements in the employment policy of the state to its employees up to 1979.

The reasons for state employers' adopting these policies were partly practical and partly ethical. First, they had the relative freedom to develop innovative employment policies and practices because they were unconstrained by the short-term pressures of profit-making and financial stewardship acting on private employers. Second, such practices were seen as contributing to public sector efficiency by attracting the right staff, minimising industrial conflict and retaining a well-qualified workforce. Third, government considered that public employers had a social duty to provide examples of model and good employment practices that might be copied by less progressive employers in the private sector.

Converging with the private sector?

Since 1979, public-sector employment policies and practices have shifted as a result of government initiatives, although the changes must not be exaggerated. Put briefly, rather than public-sector employment practices being used by state employers to influence the private sector, a number of private-sector employment practices – such as performance-related pay, personal contracts, the removal of wage-bargaining procedures and compulsory competitive tendering – have been introduced into the public sector. There is thus increasing convergence between the public and private sectors, but with the public sector following the lead of some leading private employers, rather than vice versa. These changes in employee relations policies and practices in public-sector organisations are complementary to the changes in macro public policy – based on neo-laissez-faire principles – since 1979.

Compared with the private sector, the specialist personnel management function came into the public sector relatively late. It was not until the 1970s, partly as a result of local employee relations problems, that the establishment function, certainly in the civil service, NHS and local government, began to be superseded by specialist personnel managers. Although part of the management structure, personnel managers saw themselves as mediating between employers and employees, and seeking to accommodate both management needs for efficiency and fairness and employee needs for fairness and job satisfaction. Since the 1980s and during the 1990s and the early twenty-first century, this traditional personnel management role, in turn, has been challenged by an increasing emphasis on styles of management and employee relations more associated with those of the private sector – namely high employee commitment strategies and human resources management (HRM).

There is a lively academic debate about the differences between personnel management and HRM (Guest 1987, Storey 1989, Beardwell and Holden 1998). However, it is generally recognised that HRM differs from traditional personnel management in a number of ways:

- HRM focuses on employees as resources that, like other resources, need to be used efficiently.
- Employees are viewed as a key resource, with employers actively pursuing employee commitment to corporate goals and values. Only through a systematic set of policies on recruitment, rewards for performance, staff appraisal, training and development, and effective communication, it is argued, can commitment and excellence be achieved.
- HRM assumes that personnel management is the responsibility of all line managers rather than of personnel specialists.
- There is a preference for management communication with employees individually, rather than relying on collective forms of information exchange through trade unions.
- HRM assumes a unitary model of employee relations, in contrast with the pluralist model underpinning traditional personnel management.

A central focus of HRM, compared with traditional personnel management, is improving employee performance. This necessitates selecting the 'right' people to do the job, rewarding them accordingly, appraising their performance and training and developing them to do their existing and future jobs better and more efficiently. As in the private sector, public-sector employers are responding to these issues in a number of ways (Farnham and Horton 1993, 1996, Horton and Farnham 1999).

Recruitment and selection

In parts of the public sector, responsibility for recruitment is being decentralised to agency and workplace level, innovations are reducing the time taken to recruit new staff and better selection techniques are being introduced to assess staff on their competencies and how these relate to job requirements. 'Headhunters' and assessment centres are also being used and greater use is being made of psychometric testing, bio-data sifting and wider sources of potential recruitment, such as ethnic minorities. The latter is being achieved by opening up competition to top posts, recruiting from the private sector and using short-term contracts. Another recruitment and employment strategy borrowed from the private sector is that of implementing more flexible working arrangements (Management and Personnel Office 1987). These challenge the public-sector model of lifetime employment, enabling public employers to reduce costs, improve productivity and compete with the private sector for some staff.

Rewarding performance

One of the most significant HRM innovations in the public sector since the mid-1980s has been the introduction of performance-related pay (PRP). PRP is an individualised form of payment providing for periodic rises in pay reflecting assessments of individual performance and personal value to the organisation. Such increases may determine the rate of progression through pay scales or be increments added to existing pay scales or lump sums. Copied from the private sector, PRP is predicated on the belief that rewarding 'high performers' by paying them more helps to focus attention on achieving corporate objectives, improves performance and encourages 'a more decisive, competitive and entrepreneurial spirit' (Murlis 1987: 27). PRP was first introduced into the Civil Service in 1985 and has been extended radically since then. In the NHS, the recommendations of the Griffiths Report (Department of Health and Social Security 1983) resulted in the introduction of PRP for general managers and, in the 1990s, PRP was extended to other professional groups. In 2000, it was planned to introduce performance pay for teachers in England and Wales, despite objections to the principle of it by most of the teaching unions.

Staff appraisal

With increased emphasis on improved performance in the public sector, staff appraisal systems are becoming widespread for many groups of staff. Based on private-sector practice, staff appraisal was triggered in the NHS by the Griffiths Report and led to the introduction of an 'individual performance review' for some senior staff. The emphasis was on sharply defined individual responsibilities for achieving objectives, combined with the need to develop a stock of potential general managers from within the service. As in other parts of the public sector, staff appraisal is seen as playing a key role in redefining roles, generating clarity of purpose and building commitment to a new sense of corporate identity. Performance appraisal, together with staff development (see below), has been used by both Conservative and Labour governments as an instrument for inducing cultural change, measuring performance and introducing flexible reward systems in the public sector, based on private-sector experience (Farnham and Horton 1993, Horton and Farnham 1999).

Staff development

Part of the drive to enlarge the training function in the public sector since the 1980s has derived from the need to provide staff with the skills and competences necessary for operating the new management systems being introduced. In the civil service, NHS and local government, many of these new systems are computer-based, and staff therefore need appropriate training.

New management development programmes have been introduced in the civil service, some offered jointly with private-sector organisations. In the NHS, the National Health Service Training Agency was established in 1985 to provide health authorities with leadership and support 'as they develop, implement and manage education and training programmes to help achieve the goal of cost-effective high-quality health services' (Annandale 1986). In local government, a key role has been taken on by the Local Government Management Board, which resulted from a merger between the Local Government Training Board and Local Authorities Conditions of Service Advisory Board. (It became the Employers' Organisation for Local Government in 1999.) To raise the quality of public service provision, public organisations are also using another 'big idea' borrowed from the private sector – 'total quality management' – and training their staff to implement it (see Chapter 9).

Relations with employees

The new employee relations in the public sector since 1979 have manifested themselves in a number of ways. Wage-negotiating machinery was removed from nurses and the NHS professions allied to medicine in 1983, and from teachers in 1987. As a result, about half the staff in the NHS have their pay determined by pay review bodies, and about 400,000 teachers in England and Wales now have no national wage-bargaining arrangements. The principle of comparability of public-sector pay with that of the private sector, as embodied in the Priestley Commission (1955), was effectively destroyed by the abolition of the Civil Service Pay Research Unit in 1981. Since then, the ability of the employer to pay, value for money and market forces have become the dominant criteria for determining collective pay increases in all parts of the public sector. National collective bargaining came under further attack in 1990 when the Government signalled its intention to encourage decentralised wage bargaining in the public sector, modelled on private-sector practice, even if in reality it did not effectively take root. Structural changes in the civil service, NHS and education provide the opportunity for changing bargaining structures (see Chapter 8) and changes have taken place in local government with the establishment of a single bargaining unit for administrative, professional and technical staff and manual workers in the mid-1990s. NHS trusts may set their own terms and conditions for staff, while 'Next Steps' agencies in the civil service are breaking down Whitleyism.

Competitive tendering and best value

Compulsory competitive tendering (CCT) and 'contracting out' are not new to the public sector. But earlier, under the Fair Wages Resolutions

(FWRs), any private employer subcontracting to the public authorities had to ensure that its terms and conditions of employment were not less favourable than those existing in the public sector, or those which were the norm in the industry through collective bargaining. With the rescinding of the FWRs in the 1980s, there was a general deterioration of the terms and conditions for those workers covered by CCT arrangements.

Until the Trade Union Reform and Employment Rights Act 1993, there appeared to be no legal protection for such workers. The Government claimed that the European Community's Acquired Rights Directive, implemented in Britain through the Transfer of Undertakings Regulations 1981, applied only to commercial undertakings. In the European Court of Justice in 1992, however, the Redmond case confirmed that the Directive applied to employees in both the private and public sectors. This decision was incorporated in the 1993 Act. This means, in any transfer of undertakings, that: contracts of employment are transferred to the new employer, together with existing terms and conditions; collective agreements, where they exist, are transferred; union recognition is transferred; and dismissals that result from such transfers are automatically unfair.

The 'New' Labour Government has replaced the requirement for CCT in local authority services with 'best value' (BV). This requires providers of public services, whether internal or external providers, to do so in the most effective ways, balancing quality and cost, so as to meet the objectives of their clients and customers. Councils have greater discretion in choosing delivery mechanisms, but BV applies to a wider range of services than did CCT. According to Rouse (1999: 90), there is no presumption that private or public provision is superior and encouragement is given to developing multi-agency partnerships and collaborative networks. 'It is also rooted in the principle of democratic renewal, with councils deciding on their priorities and standards of service in consultation with their communities and other partners.' Fundamental performance reviews of all local authority services are required over a five-year period, with BV being seen as a culture change aimed at achieving commitment to continuous improvement in service standards and efficiency. The Audit Commission and Best Value Inspectorate are charged with establishing that BV has been achieved. Authorities achieving excellence will be awarded 'beacon' status.

THE SOCIAL DIMENSION OF THE SINGLE EUROPEAN MARKET

EU policies on employment and social issues do not form a coherent or comprehensive programme but a patchwork of different policy areas. They include legislation, action programmes and funding, and cover such diverse subjects as employment protection, health and safety, equal opportunities and training. The rationale for EU legislation in the field of employment and social issues is threefold. The first reason is to try and harmonise provisions in member states to produce a 'level playing field' for enterprise across member states within the EU in order to prevent 'social dumping'. This is a situation where companies operating in different countries could attempt to reduce their employment and social costs, by investing their businesses in those countries where employment and social costs were lowest and most attractive to the business community. This would be detrimental to the interests of other countries and their workers, who could lose their employment opportunities. The second reason is to facilitate freedom of movement of people within the EU and this requires some regulation and protection of workers' rights. A third reason is the need to create a community relevant to the people of Europe, as well as to its entrepreneurs and business sector.

In the area of health and safety, for example, which is already covered by extensive legislation, the European Commission is proposing a continuing list of future legislation. In other areas, in contrast, such as trade union rights and collective agreements, recommendations rather than legislation are proposed and the European Commission is taking no co-ordinated action but intends leaving matters to governments, without seeking to enforce minimum safeguards.

This lack of cohesion in EU policies on employment and social policy is a consequence of the EU political institutions not being the machinery of an integrated nation state, nor even of a federal one, but having circumscribed political powers. EU institutions are limited to framework legislation and pilot projects, without powers of command that national, regional or local administrations have. Political power is still largely the prerogative of national governments. Despite the political difficulties attached to harmonising provisions in the area of labour law and employee relations, the European Commission has been active in developing legislation in this field for many years.

The roots of the social dimension of the EU run deep. The Treaty of Rome 1957 stated a commitment to common action on economic and social progress, as did the European Coal and Steel Community 1951, which had extensive powers to fund and promote improvements in the working and living conditions of coal and steel workers. Various European treaties contained a number of articles authorising Community institutions to take action in different areas of social policy, while the European Social Fund provides funding for retraining or settlement allowances for workers threatened by loss of employment. Successive Social Action Programmes have laid the foundation for action in the social sphere for over two decades.

The single market programme, operationalised through the Single European Act 1987, brought a new momentum to the development of EU social policy. The roots of social policy lie in the belief that achieving support for a single market from both sides of industry, and all major political parties, requires parallel efforts in the social field. The single market programme has included measures to extend the traditional aims of Euro-legislation, such as full freedom of movement for people. It has also committed member states to encourage improvements in social policy. There has been a general commitment to strengthen EU economic and social cohesion, especially by reducing disparities between various regions and the backwardness of the

Exhibit 33 **Major developments in European integration since 1951**

Treaty of Paris 1951
- created the European Coal and Steel Community
- promoted living and working conditions of coal and steel workers

Treaty of Rome 1957
- created the European Economic Community (EEC) by removing barriers to the free movement of labour, capital, goods and services (the 'Common Market')
- created the European Atomic Energy Community
- included the Free Movement of Workers Chapter enshrining the right of citizens of member states to live and work where they wished
- included the Social Chapter promoting improved working conditions and better standards of living for workers and the right to equal pay for equal work between men and women

Single European Act 1987
- set a deadline for establishing the single European market
- replaced unanimity in the voting procedures of members states by qualified majority voting (QMV), through allocating votes according to the populations of member states, thus removing the power of veto by single member states
- formalised the European Community's commitment to involving the 'social partners' in European decision-making procedures
- enabled health and safety provisions to be harmonised by QMV

Treaty on the European Union 1993
- created the European Union (EU)
- provided for the creation of a common currency, starting in January 1999
- restated the principle of 'subsidiarity', giving competency to the EU when common objectives could be better achieved by harmonised action rather than by member states acting alone
- formalised the EU's commitment to involving the 'social partners' in EU decision-making machinery
- amended the Social Chapter, so that through the Social Policy Agreement member states (except the UK) could extend the employment and social issues to be harmonised by QMV

Treaty of Amsterdam 1997
- empowered the Council of Ministers to combat discrimination on the grounds of sex, ethnic origin, religion or belief, age and sexual orientation
- pledged to remove remaining restrictions on the free movement of labour
- introduced an Employment Chapter making the achievement of high and sustainable employment opportunities in the EU a strategic goal
- required EU institutions to encourage 'social dialogue' on employment, working conditions, the right to work, training and social security
- incorporated the Social Policy Agreement into the Treaty as the Social Chapter, making it applicable to all member states of the EU (including the UK)

least favoured ones. Freedom of movement, health and safety, and reform of the structural funds were included in the Single European Act 1987, as were various programmes for combating unemployment and emphasising the need for social progress towards a 'people's Europe'.

The UK joined the European Economic Community in 1973, and since then there have been a number of treaties by which member states have agreed to extend the scope of EU law, including those covering employment and social issues. The major developments in European integration since 1951 are summarised in Exhibit 33.

EU law includes regulations and directives. Regulations tend to be broad in nature and are directly applicable to all member states. Most EU legislation takes the form of directives, however, which are the normal way in which employment law is introduced into member states. In this sense, directives are legislative instruments requiring member states to transpose their contents into national law, with member states normally being given two years to do this. European legislation is a complex process, but is basically determined in the following ways, depending upon the issues concerned (Farnham 1999):

- unanimous vote of the Council of Ministers
- qualified majority voting (QMV) in the Council of Ministers
- a co-decision procedure involving the Council of the EU and European Parliament
- a 'framework agreement' involving the 'social partners', who can *either* suggest that the European Commission draft a directive for approval by the Council of Ministers (by unanimous decision *or* QMV) or jointly negotiate an EU-level framework agreement.

Under the framework agreement procedure of the Social Chapter (see below), the social partners can negotiate an EU 'framework agreement' over a nine-month period, which can be extended by agreement between them and the European Commission. Where agreement is reached, it can be implemented in member states by a national collective agreement. Alternatively, it can be the basis of a proposal by the European Commission for adoption as a legally binding instrument by the Council of Ministers, either by unanimous vote or QMV – depending on the subject – for transposing into national law. The framework agreement procedures were used in enacting the Parental Leave Directive 1996, Part-Time Workers Directive 1997 and Fixed-Term Contracts Directive 1999.

The Social Chapter

The founder members of the EEC (later the EU) never saw their 'European project' solely in terms of a free market for goods, services, labour and capital. They also saw it as establishing a stable economic and political community in which a 'social dimension', involving social regulation and protection of its free trade area, was an important, parallel development. In the light of costly European wars in the twentieth century, in terms of numbers of people killed and economic devastation, the European project was seen as a means of promoting prosperity, preserving peace and investing in the future. Economic opportunities for business and social protection for its people were the twin pillars of the 'new' Europe. Market competition would take place, but within the framework of a level playing field of minimum social conditions, to protect against social dumping. The Treaty of Rome 1957 therefore incorporated a 'Social Chapter', later amended by the Single European Act 1987 and Treaty on the European Union 1993, which set out clear commitments to harmonising social conditions among member states. In outline, the objectives of the Social Chapter are to:

- promote employment
- improve living and working conditions
- encourage dialogue between management and labour
- develop human resources
- combat social exclusion.

Member states are also required to maintain the principle that men and women have equal pay for equal work.

The Social Chapter became operational in the UK on 1 May 1999, but it is not a set of detailed regulations. It merely allows member states to make legislation at EU level on a range of social issues by a variety of institutional means, which member states have to implement. Exhibit 34 shows the coverage of the Social Chapter, although the issues of pay, right of association, right to strike and right to lock out are formally excluded from it.

Exhibit 34 Coverage of the Social Chapter

Unanimous vote in Council of Ministers

- social security and protection of workers
- protection of workers where employment contracts are terminated
- representation and collective defence of interests of workers and employers, including co-determination
- conditions of employment for third-world country nationals legally resident in the EU
- financial contributions for promoting employment

Qualified majority voting in Council of Ministers

- health and safety
- working conditions
- information and consultation of workers
- equal opportunities for men and women
- integration of persons excluded from the labour market

The main areas where EU law impinges on British employee relations practice are equality, employment protection, health and safety, and consultation and information. The origins, timing and implementation of the main pieces of this legislation in these areas are summarised and outlined in Table 19.

Table 19 Main EU legislation since 1975

Area	EU Directive	Implemented in UK
Equality		
	Equal Pay 1975	Equal Pay (Amendment) Regulations 1983
	Parental Leave 1996	Employment Relations Act 1999
	Sex Discrimination 1997	(to be implemented)
	Part-Time Workers 1997	(to be implemented)
	Fixed-Term Contracts 1999	(to be implemented)
Employment protection		
	Collective Redundancies 1975	Employment Protection Act 1975
	Collective Redundancies 1992	Collective Redundancies and Transfer of Undertakings (Protection of Employment) (Amendment) Regulations 1999
	Transfer of Undertakings 1977	Transfer of Undertakings (Protection of Employment) Regulations 1981
	Transfer of Undertakings 1998	Collective Redundancies and Transfer of Undertakings (Protection of Employment) (Amendment) Regulations 1999
	Insolvency 1980	Employment Protection Act 1975
	Proof of an Employment Contract 1992	Trade Union Reform and Employment Rights Act 1993
Health and safety		
	Working Time 1993	Working Time Regulations 1998
Consultation and information		
	European Works Council 1994	(implemented after 15 December 1999)

The Working Time Directive 1993, for example, came into force in the UK on 1 October 1998 through the Working Time Regulations 1998. Their main provisions are:

- working hours are limited to a maximum of 48 per week during a 17-week reference period
- rules cover night work, rest periods and annual leave
- individuals can agree to opt out of the 48-hours-per-week rule
- rules governing the 48-hour week can be determined by collective agreements and workforce agreements (see Chapter 7)
- employers must allow lay officials of independent recognised trade unions to take reasonable time off, with pay, to undertake their union duties
- members of independent recognised trade unions are entitled to reasonable time off during working hours for trade union activities
- young employees not in full-time education are entitled to time off to study for certain qualifications
- individuals who have been continuously employed for two or more years,

and are under notice of dismissal on the grounds of redundancy, are entitled to time off work during working hours to look for new work.

It may be concluded that the extent and coverage of EU legislation are wide-ranging, comprehensive and growing in importance. Areas covered by EU legislation include collective redundancies, transfer of undertakings, health and safety, European works councils, maternity and paternity leave, and working time. Clearly, European-driven employment rules are having an increasing impact on employee relations at company and workplace levels. Draft Euro-legislation is always in the pipeline. This necessitates continual vigilance by personnel specialists to keep ahead of such changes in the law insofar as they impact on their organisations and personnel policies.

The European Community Charter of Fundamental Social Rights of Workers

Discussion about the social dimension of the single European market has led to the adoption of the European Community Charter of Fundamental Rights of Workers by member states of the EU except the UK (see Chapter 3). This 'Social Charter' is not to be confused with the Social Chapter and simply proposes a floor of rights for workers to be implemented by member states. It has no legal force and was intended only as a bill of rights for European citizens in the social sphere, although it is no more than a series of recommendations on minimum standards. What it provides, in effect, is a collection of targets for European action and minimum standards for member states to achieve. The Charter also underpins the importance that the majority of member states attach to the social dimension of the EU.

The Social Charter proclaims the major principles underlying the following declared rights of individuals in the EU. In outline, these rights can be summarised as follows (Commission of the European Communities 1990):

- *Freedom of movement.* Every worker shall have the right to freedom of movement throughout the EU and to engage in any occupation or profession in accordance with the principles of equal treatment and access.
- *Employment and remuneration.* Every worker shall be free to choose their occupation and all employment shall be fairly remunerated, with workers having a wage sufficient to enable them and their families to have a decent standard of living.
- *Improvement of living and working conditions.* This principle states that completion of the internal market must lead to an improvement in the living and working conditions of workers in the EU. Workers shall have the right to a weekly rest period and paid annual leave. The conditions of employment of every worker shall be stipulated in laws, a collective agreement or a contract of employment, according to the arrangements applying in each country.
- *Social protection.* Every worker shall have a right to adequate social protection and shall enjoy an adequate level of social security benefits. Persons

unable to enter the labour market must be able to receive sufficient resources in keeping with their circumstances.

- *Freedom of association and collective bargaining.* Employers and workers shall have the right to associate and their organisations shall have the right to negotiate and conclude collective agreements together. Dialogue between the two sides at European level must be developed. There shall be a right to strike and utilisation of conciliation, mediation and arbitration machinery should be encouraged.
- *Vocational training.* All workers must be able to have access to vocational training and benefit from it throughout their working lives. There should be leave for training purposes to improve skills or to acquire new skills.
- *Equal treatment for women and men.* Equal treatment must be assured and equal treatment for women and men must be developed. Equality of access should be provided to employment, remuneration, working conditions, social protection, education, vocational training and career development.
- *Information, consultation and participation of workers.* These principles must be developed along appropriate lines and shall apply especially in companies operating in two or more member states. These processes should be implemented particularly during technological change, corporate restructuring, collective redundancies and when transfrontier workers are affected.
- *Health protection and safety at the workplace.* Every worker must enjoy satisfactory health and safety conditions in the working environment. The need for training, information, consultation and the participation of workers in this area is stressed.
- *Protection of children and adolescents.* The minimum age of employment must be no lower than the minimum school-leaving age. The duration of work must be limited, night work must be prohibited and initial vocational training must be an entitlement.
- *Elderly persons.* All retired workers must be able to enjoy resources affording them a decent standard of living. They must also be entitled to sufficient medical and social assistance.
- *Disabled persons.* The disabled must be entitled to additional concrete measures aimed at improving their social and professional integration.

ASSIGNMENTS

(a) Why did 'free collective bargaining', or collective *laissez-faire*, have such an appeal to employers, the unions and the state? Does it still do so?

(b) Read Wedderburn (1986: 21–5) and examine why legal immunities, rather than positive legal rights, became incorporated in the English legal system affecting employee relations.

(c) Critically examine the Donovan Commission's presumption (1968: 54) that: 'Properly conducted, collective bargaining is the most effective means of giving workers the right to representation in decisions affecting their working lives, a right which is or should be the prerogative of every worker in a democratic society.' What are some of the implications of this statement for managing employee relations?

(d) Read Farnham (1978) and analyse the main characteristics of Whitleyism as a model of employee relations practice.

(e) What were the goals of neo-laissez-faire public policy on employee relations between 1979 and 1997? Evaluate the effectiveness of this policy and examine some of its implications for the management of employee relations.

(f) Interview a number of public-sector employees and find out why they joined public-sector organisations. Ask them what they understand by the terms 'model' employment practices and 'good' employment practices, giving examples of each. Ask them what they regard as the main differences between public-sector employment practices and those of the private sector.

(g) What features of state policy on employee relations, in the 1980s and the 1990s, influenced the emergence of 'human resource management' practices among some British employers? How have these HRM practices manifested themselves?

(h) How is the Labour Government's employee relations policy similar to and different from (i) the 'employee relations consensus' and (ii) the Conservatives' neo-*laissez-faire* approach?

(i) Describe and analyse the introduction of best value in a local authority known to you.

(j) What are the cases for and against UK employers supporting the social dimension of the EU?

(k) Identify two current EU directives and discuss their impact on British employee relations policy and practice.

REFERENCES

ADVISORY, CONCILIATION AND ARBITRATION SERVICE (1980) *Industrial Relations Handbook*. London, HMSO.

ADVISORY, CONCILIATION AND ARBITRATION SERVICE (1981–92) *Annual Reports*. London, ACAS.

ANNANDALE S. (1986) 'The four faces of management development'. *Personnel Management*. July.

BAYLISS F. (1959) *British Wages Councils*. Oxford, Blackwell.

BEARDWELL I. *and* HOLDEN L. (1998) *Human Resource Management: A contemporary perspective*. London, Pitman.

BEAUMONT P. (1981) *Government as Employer – Setting an example?* London, Royal Institute of Public Administration.

BEAUMONT P. (1992) *Public Sector Industrial Relations*. London, Routledge.

BEVERIDGE W. (1944) *Full Employment in a Free Society*. London, Allen & Unwin.

CHARLES R. (1973) *The Development of Industrial Relations in Britain 1911–1945*. London, Hutchinson.

CLEGG H., FOX A. *and* THOMPSON A. (1964) *A History of British Trade Unions since 1889. Volume 1 1889–1910*. Oxford, Clarendon.

CMD 7321 (1948) *Personal Incomes, Costs and Prices*. London, HMSO.

COMMISSION OF THE EUROPEAN COMMUNITIES (1990) *The Community Charter of Fundamental Social Rights for Workers*. Brussels, European Commission.

CULLY M., WOODLAND S., O'REILLY A. *and* DIX G (1999) *Britain at Work*. London, Routledge.

DANIEL W. *and* MILLWARD N. (1983) *Workplace Industrial Relations in Britain*. London, Heinemann.

DEPARTMENT OF EMPLOYMENT (1983) *Democracy in Trade Unions*. London, HMSO.

DEPARTMENT OF HEALTH AND SOCIAL SECURITY (1983) *NHS Management Inquiry* (the Griffiths Report). London, HMSO.

DONOVAN, Lord (1968) *Royal Commission on Trade Unions and Employers' Associations: Report*. London, HMSO.

DUNN S. *and* GENNARD J. (1984) *The Closed Shop in British Industry*. London, Macmillan.

EMPLOYMENT PROTECTION ACT 1975.

FARNHAM D. (1978) 'Sixty years of Whitleyism'. *Personnel Management*. July.

FARNHAM D. (1990) 'Trade union policy 1979–89: restriction or reform?' in S. Savage and L. Robins (eds), *Public Policy under Thatcher*, Basingstoke, Macmillan.

FARNHAM D. (1999) *Managing in a Business Context*. London, Institute of Personnel and Development.

FARNHAM D. and HORTON S. (1993) 'Human resources management in the public sector: leading or following the private sector?' *Public Policy and Administration*. Special edition, Spring.

FARNHAM D. and HORTON S. (1996) *Managing People in the Public Services*. London, Macmillan.

GIDDENS A. (1998) *The Third Way*. Cambridge, Polity Press.

GUEST D. (1987) 'Human resource management and industrial relations'. *Journal of Management Studies*. 24 (5).

HOLMSTEDT M. (1991) *Employment Policy*. London, Routledge in association with the University of Bradford.

HORTON S. *and* FARNHAM D. (EDS) (1999) *Public Management in Britain*. London, Macmillan.

JENKINS P. (1970) *The Battle of Downing Street*. London, Knight.

KEYNES J. M. (1936) *The General Theory of Employment, Interest and Money*. London, Macmillan.

LABOUR PARTY (1997a) *New Labour: Because Britain deserves better*. London, Labour Party.

LABOUR PARTY (1997b) *Building Prosperity: Flexibility, efficiency and fairness at work*. London, Labour Party.

MCGREGOR D. (1999) 'Employment in the public and private sectors'. *Economic Trends*. No. 547, June.

MANAGEMENT AND PERSONNEL OFFICE (1987) *Working Patterns*. London, MPO.

MARTIN R. (1992) *Bargaining Power*. Oxford, Clarendon.

MILLWARD N. and STEVENS M. (1986) *British Workplace Industrial Relations 1980–1984*. Aldershot, Gower.

MILLWARD N., STEVENS M., SMART D. and HAWES W. (1992) *Workplace Industrial Relations in Transition*. Aldershot, Dartmouth.

MINISTRY OF LABOUR (1965) *Written Evidence of the Ministry of Labour to the Royal Commission on Trade Unions and Employers' Associations*. London, HMSO.

MURLIS H. (1987) 'Performance-related pay in the public sector'. *Public Money*. March.

PELLING H. (1987) *A History of British Trade Unionism*. Harmondsworth, Penguin.

PRIESTLEY REPORT (1955) *Royal Commission on the Civil Service*. London, HMSO.

ROUSE J. (1999) 'Performance management, quality management and contracts', in S. Horton and D. Farnham (eds), *Public Management in Britain*, London, Routledge.

ROYAL COMMISSION ON LABOUR LAWS (1894) *Final Report of the Commission 1991–94*. (Chairman: Duke of Devonshire). London, HMSO.

SCHMITTER P. and LEHMBRUCH G. (1979) *Trends Towards Corporatist Intermediation*. London, Sage.

STANDING COMMISSION ON PAY COMPARABILITY (1981) *Final Report*. London, HMSO.

STOREY J. (1989) *New Perspectives on Human Resource Management*. London, Routledge.

TAYLOR A. J. P. (1965) *English History 1914–45*. Oxford, Clarendon.

TAYLOR R. (1998) Annual review article. *British Journal of Industrial Relations*. 36 (2).

TRADE UNION AND LABOUR RELATIONS (CONSOLIDATION) ACT 1992.

TRADE UNION REFORM AND EMPLOYMENT RIGHTS ACT 1993.

TRADES UNION CONGRESS (1995) *Arguments for a National Minimum Wage*. London, TUC.

UNDY R. (1999) Annual review article. *British Journal of Industrial Relations*. 37 (2).

WEDDERBURN, Lord (1986) *The Worker and the Law*. Harmondsworth, Penguin.

WEDDERBURN, Lord and DAVIES P. (1969) *Employment Grievances and Disputes Procedures in Britain*. Berkeley, University of California Press.

WEEKES B., MELLISH M., DICKENS L. and LLOYD J. (1975) *Industrial Relations and the Limits of the Law*. Oxford, Blackwell.

WHITE L. (1933) *Whitley Councils in the British Civil Service*. Chicago, Chicago University Press.

WHITLEY COMMITTEE (1917–18) *Reports*. London, HMSO.

10 Collective industrial action

Collective industrial action or a 'trade dispute' takes place whenever an employer and/or the trade union organisations with which it deals are unable to resolve their differences peacefully and constitutionally in determining, regulating or terminating the wage–work bargain. In law, a trade dispute means any dispute between 'employers and workers, or between workers and workers, which is connected with one or more of the following matters' (Trade Union and Labour Relations (Consolidation) Act (TULRCA) 1992, section 218):

(a) terms and conditions of employment, or the physical conditions in which any workers are required to work;
(b) engagement or non-engagement, or termination or suspension of employment or the duties of employment, of one or more workers;
(c) allocation of work or the duties of employment between workers or groups of workers;
(d) matters of discipline;
(e) the membership or non-membership of a trade union on the part of a worker;
(f) facilities for officials of trade unions; and
(g) machinery for negotiation or consultation, and other procedures, relating to any of the foregoing matters, including the recognition by employers or employers' associations of the right of a trade union to represent workers in any such negotiation or consultation or in the carrying out of such procedures.

Where a trade dispute takes place, this results in a temporary breakdown of the employment relationship between employer and employee, the imposition of industrial sanctions by the employer and/or the union against the other party and the manifestation of overt industrial conflict between them.

Kornhauser and his colleagues summarise the nature of industrial conflict neatly and succinctly (1954: 13) when they describe it as: 'the total range of behavior and attitudes that express opposition and divergent orientations between individual owners and managers on the one hand and working people and their organisations on the other hand'. In taking industrial action against one another, the secondary parties to employee relations (employers and unions) are using the economic and social power that they have to coerce the other side to take a decision against their will. They use this power to try and force the other party into conceding an employment decision – whether over wages, conditions, job security or working arrangements – which cannot be resolved by negotiation, compromise or third-party intervention. Collective industrial action and use of industrial sanctions, therefore, involves the application of naked force by one or both of the secondary parties to employee relations – employers and unions – against the other. This undermines good working relations between them, imposes financial costs on both sides, and might even threaten the social order, if matters get out of control.

Because of this, the state takes an active role in regulating industrial conflict. If the state cannot achieve industrial peace by persuasion, argument or third-party intervention, it provides certain legal backstops to contain and constrain what it defines to be legitimate industrial action. These are aimed at protecting those damaged by industrial action, keeping sanctions within acceptable constitutional bounds and discouraging what the state defines as politically destabilising employee relations conflict (see Chapters 3, 4, 8 and 9).

FUNCTIONS AND FORMS OF INDUSTRIAL ACTION

The taking of industrial sanctions by either employers or unions represents the breakdown of trust, co-operation and goodwill between them. Industrial sanctions, therefore, tend to be the means of last resort used by the parties in attempting to resolve their differences arising from conflict over the wage–work bargain. When employers or unions take collective industrial sanctions against one another, it is because they believe that it is only by imposing their unilateral power on the other side that they can achieve their employee relations objectives.

The aim of industrial sanctions is to weaken the other side's resolve in opposing what is on offer at the bargaining table. If employees are not unionised, then the employer's ability to impose its unilateral decisions on them is less likely to be resisted, because they have no countervailing collective power against management. If employees are unionised, however, the employer is obliged to take account of the employees' collective power and its potential impact on the outcome of the conflict, in taking its decision. It also has to listen to what is being proposed by the union leaders on behalf of their members.

Similarly, in deciding whether to take industrial sanctions against their employer, employees and their union leaders have to take account of the likely outcome in terms of the potential costs to them. They particularly have to decide whether a successful outcome to the action is possible and the consequences of the action for employee relations in the future. In all trade disputes, the potential for coercive power between employer and unions is a crucial determinant of the propensity to apply industrial sanctions, the form that the sanctions take and the likely outcomes of the conflict between the parties.

Theories of industrial conflict

There are three main, competing sets of theories seeking to explain the nature of industrial conflict between employers and employees and between management and unions (Farnham and Pimlott 1995). These are:

- structural or Marxist theory
- unitary or 'human relations' theory
- functionalist theory.

In outline, Marxist theorists see industrial conflict between employers, representing the interest of 'capital', and unions, representing the interests of 'labour', as inevitable and deep-rooted, since it emerges out of the class and power relations within capitalist, market economies. Human relations theorists see industrial conflict as anti-social, dysfunctional and disruptive of enterprise harmony and effectiveness. Functionalist theorists see industrial conflict as having positive benefits for the parties to employee relations, as long as it is channelled into appropriate institutional mechanisms and resolved accordingly.

Marxist theory

Marxist theory views industrial conflict as rooted in the economic structures of capitalist societies. It is a theory of social change, and although there are a number of schools of Marxian scholarship, Marxism is essentially a method of analysing power relationships in society. It assumes that:

- the capitalist mode of production is but one stage in the development of human society
- class conflict is the catalytic source of change within capitalism
- out of the dialectical conflict between the social classes, with opposed economic interests, social change takes place, leading eventually to the socialist state.

As Allen (1976: 21) has written:

> When reality is viewed dialectically it is seen as a process involving interdependent parts which interact on each other. When reality is also viewed materialistically it is seen as phenomena predominantly influenced by economic factors. The dialectical relationship between economic factors, therefore, provides the prime motivation for change. This briefly is what Marxism in the first instance is about.

In the bourgeois capitalist state, the competing class interests are those of profit-seeking capitalists and the wage-earning proletariat. The struggle for economic hegemony between them is deemed to be inevitable, irrevocable and irreconcilable. Industrial conflict between employer and employee, and between management and union, is merely a reflection of the dominant class interests within capitalism and is synonymous with class conflict. As such, employee relations conflict, between those buying labour in the market place and those selling it, is seen as a permanent feature of capitalism (Hyman 1975). Industrial conflict, in its various forms, in short, arises out of economic contradictions within the capitalist mode of production and is a means for advancing and fighting the class struggle and class war. The

373

protagonists are those owning and representing private capital and those supplying their skills for wages in the labour market. In an economic system driven by market forces, private ownership of the means of production and profit-seeking, mutual accommodation between capital and labour is impossible and continuous class conflict between them is inevitable. In Marxist analysis, it is the trade union function to uphold and protect the class interests of working people, through direct and indirect action, and union militancy, against the owners of industrial capital, including the bourgeois state.

Human relations theory

The unitary or human relations theory of industrial conflict is at the opposite end of the theoretical spectrum. This set of theories holds, in essence, that conflict at work between employer and employee is dysfunctional, that trade unions cause industrial conflict and that industrial conflict in any form is a corroding and disruptive social influence in the workplace and the wider society. The ideas and concepts associated with what is sometimes misleadingly called the 'Human Relations School' were first gestated and publicised by American industrial sociologists, such as Mayo (1946), Roethlisberger (1946) and Warner and Low (1947). Their ideas were further refined and developed by more sophisticated 'neo-human relations' theorists, such as McGregor (1960) and Argyris (1964). The main implications of their analyses are that conflict at work is unnatural, subversive and destabilising and, as it cannot be suppressed, that enlightened management policies and participative styles of management should eradicate it.

All of Mayo's research was carried out with the permission and collaboration of management. For Mayo, management embodies the central purposes of society and, with this initial orientation, he never considered the possibility that organisations might contain conflicting interest groups, such as management, workers and unions, as distinct from different attitudes or 'logics'. For him, industrial conflict was a social disease, while the promotion of organisational equilibrium, or a state of 'social health', should be management's prime aim and objective. The issue that Roethlisberger sought to address was (1946: 112): 'how can a comfortable working equilibrium be maintained between the various groups in an industrial enterprise such that no group . . . will separate itself out in opposition to the remainder?' Warner and Low (1947) had similarly overwhelmingly negative connotations of industrial conflict. The subjective bias in their writing towards stability, harmony and social integration within organisations meant that they saw conflict exclusively as a dissociative and disintegrative phenomenon, although they conceded that 'frictional' conflicts could arise from personality differences, poor management and bad communications. Industrial conflict, by this view, is a pathological social condition, upsetting the 'normal' state of organisational equilibrium, and must be avoided at all costs by enlightened management policies and 'good' management practices.

Functionalist theory

The functionalist theory of industrial conflict, in contrast, sees conflict as inevitable in any human situation. Individuals group together in society for associative purposes – such as in politics and employee relations – and inter-group conflicts arise that, if resolved, result in new behavioural norms, thus eliminating the sources of dissatisfaction among the groups involved. Moreover, as Coser (1956: 31) wrote: 'Far from being necessarily dysfunc-tional, a certain degree of conflict is an essential element in group formation and the persistence of group life.' In employee relations, this means that conflict creates links between employers, management and unions. It mod-ifies the norms for readjusting these relationships, leads each party to match the other's structures and organisation, and makes possible a reassessment of their relative power in achieving consensus or agreement among them-selves. In this way, industrial conflict serves as a social balancing mechanism maintaining and consolidating the instrumental relationships that exist amongst employers, employees and unions.

For functionalists, therefore, it is the divergent interests of the parties in the employment relationship that generate industrial conflict. With indus-trial enterprises being the dominant institutions of modern society, 'where few command and many obey', Dahrendorf (1959: 250–53) has taken issue with the scientific management and human relations views that the 'true interests' of management and workers are identical. He has asserted that:

> Taylor's exclusive emphasis on the community of interests among all partici-pants of the enterprise is plainly insufficient for the explanation of certain phe-nomena, such as strikes, and that it is therefore necessary to assume a conflict of latent interests in the enterprise emerging from the differential distribution of authority.

The significance of the functionalist theory of industrial conflict for em-ployee relations is the need for the parties to the wage–work bargain to accept the inevitability of any potential conflict between them, institution-alise it and resolve it through appropriate constitutional mechanisms. Under these conditions, it is only likely that either or both parties will resort to uni-lateral force, and use of industrial sanctions, to achieve their employee rela-tions goals where institutionalised relations between them have broken down. And then, only after the institutional arrangements between them have been exhausted. It is then the state's role to attempt to mediate between the parties and get them to resolve their differences constitutionally and peacefully. Furthermore, the application of industrial sanctions by any of the parties to employee relations is possible only within the limits of the law.

Manifestations of industrial conflict

In practice, industrial conflict takes a variety of forms. Writers such as Kornhauser and his colleagues (1954) and Hyman (1989) distinguish between industrial conflict that is individual and unorganised and that which is collective and organised. Individual and unorganised conflict, for example, takes place at the personal and interpersonal levels and involves certain types of worker behaviour and managerial behaviours which manifest themselves in a variety of ways, as outlined in Figure 15. The essence of unorganised industrial conflict is that it is unpredictable, is not directed into conflict-resolving channels and is difficult to manage.

Examples of how collective and organised industrial conflict manifest themselves (the central theme of this chapter) are provided in Figure 16. These relate to management–union conflict and are formalised types of industrial conflict. Although strikes are often considered to be the main manifestation of organised conflict, it is clear from Figure 16 that collective industrial conflict is not limited to strike activity alone. Nor does collective conflict manifest itself only in the workplace. It also takes place in the socio-political spheres through elections, lobbying, public relations activities and educational propaganda by both employers and unions.

PATTERNS OF STRIKE ACTIVITY IN THE UK

Strike activity is not an easy term to define and the official statistics of the United Kingdom (UK), collected by the Department for Education and Employment (DfEE) (formerly the Employment Department, Department of Employment and earlier still the Ministry of Labour) cover only what are described as 'stoppages of work'. Technically, a stoppage of work is any trade dispute between employers and workers, or workers and workers, that is connected with terms and conditions of employment. The official statistics exclude disputes not resulting in stoppages of work, such as working to rule or going slow, and stoppages involving fewer than 10 workers or those lasting one day or less, except where the total number of working days lost is greater than 100. The statistics also include lockouts by employers and unlawful strikes. But they do not distinguish between strikes and lockouts, 'lawful' and 'unlawful' stoppages and, since 1981, 'official' and 'unofficial' disputes.

Figure 15 **Manifestations of individual and unorganised industrial conflict**

Worker behaviour	Management behaviour
absenteeism	autocratic supervision
withholding effort	tight discipline
time-wasting	harassment of workers
industrial sabotage	discrimination at work
labour turnover	demoting individuals
complaints	one-sided propaganda
rule-breaking	speeding up work
low morale	anti-union propaganda
'griping' against management	'slagging off' the workforce

Figure 16 Manifestations of collective and organised industrial conflict

In the workplace	In society
restrictions of output	political lobbying
going slow	union political affiliations
working to contract	corporate political donations
removal of overtime	political demonstrations
strikes and lockouts	using the media
closing down plants	educational propaganda

In practice, a strike is any stoppage of work, or withdrawal of labour, initiated by workers, while lockouts are stoppages of work initiated by employers who prevent employees working by refusing them entry to the workplace. A lawful strike is one undertaken in accordance with the legal requirements of the TULRCA 1992, as amended. To be lawful, strikes must be between workers and their direct employer, must relate to matters covered in section 218 of the Act and can take place only after a properly conducted strike ballot has been held, thus providing legal immunities to the strike leaders and the union(s) involved. Unlawful strikes are not protected by legal immunities and can result in injunctions and fines being awarded against the unions. An official dispute, or more properly a 'constitutional' one, is where strike action occurs that is in accordance with agreed negotiating procedures between the employer and the union(s). Unofficial or 'unconstitutional' disputes, in contrast, are in breach of agreed procedures for avoiding disputes.

Another meaning sometimes given to an 'official' dispute is one that is supported by the union(s) and is in accordance with union rules. 'Official' disputes of this sort normally involve the payment of strike benefits to the workers taking industrial action. Similarly, the term 'unofficial' disputes can also refer to industrial action not normally in accordance with union rules where the unions pay no benefits to striking workers.

Strike statistics

In analysing stoppages of work annually, the DfEE uses three measures of strike activity. These are: number of working days lost, number of workers involved in stoppages of work and number of stoppages.

Working days lost

The number of working days lost is the total time in the basic working week lost as a result of trade disputes over a given period, usually a year. Overtime and weekend working are excluded, with allowances being made for public and known annual holidays and for absences from work due to sickness and unauthorised leave. Where strikes last less than the basic working day, hours lost are converted to full-day equivalents. Similarly, days lost by part-time workers are also converted to full-day equivalents. The number of working days lost in a stoppage reflects the actual number of workers involved at each point in the stoppage. This is generally less than the total derived by multiplying the duration of the stoppage by the total numbers of workers involved at any time, because some workers would not have been involved throughout the dispute. In disputes where employers dismiss their employees and subsequently reinstate them, the total working days lost figure includes the days lost by the workers during the period of dismissal. Where employers dismiss their workers and replace them with another workforce, the statistics cannot assume that the working days lost by the dismissed workers continue indefinitely. In such cases, the statistics measure the number of days lost in terms of the replacement workforce during the period of the stoppage.

Workers involved

The number of workers involved in stoppages of work covers those individuals directly and indirectly involved at the establishment where the dispute occurs. Workers indirectly involved are those who are not themselves party to the dispute but are laid off because of it. Workers at other sites who are indirectly affected are not counted, because of the difficulty of deciding the extent to which a particular employer's reduction in output or services is due to the effects of a strike elsewhere or to some other cause. Workers involved in more than one stoppage during the year are counted for each stoppage in which they take part. Part-time workers are counted as whole units.

Number of stoppages

This records the total number of stoppages lasting more than one day, over the year. Because of recording difficulties, the number of working days lost per year is normally regarded as a better indicator of the impact of trade disputes than the number of recorded stoppages.

Stoppages of work

A time series of stoppages of work in the UK for the period 1971–98 is shown in Table 20 (Davis 1999a). A number of conclusions may be inferred from it. First, the number of working days lost per year varied widely over this 28-year period, with relatively high figures for some years – such as 1972, 1979 and 1984. There were also some low ones, especially since 1985, followed by a dramatic fall in working days lost between 1991 and 1998, apart from 1996. The unusually high number of working days lost in certain years was due, in the main, to large individual stoppages. In 1972, for example, a miners' strike over a national wage increase accounted for 10.7 million (45 per cent) of the 23.9 million working days lost for that year. Similarly, in 1979, a strike by engineering workers accounted for 16 million (54 per cent) of the 29.5 million working days lost in that year. And in 1984, the days lost in the miners' strike, in protest against pit closures, accounted for 22.4 million (83 per cent) of the 27.1 million working days lost during that year (Bird 1992). It is important to consider, therefore, the size of the major stoppages in each period when making comparisons between individual years.

Second, the annual average number of working days lost per 1,000 employees declined substantially during the 1980s compared with the 1970s. For the 10 years 1971–80, the annual average was 572 working days lost per 1,000 employees; for the 10 years 1981–90, it was 288 working days; and for the eight years 1991–98, it was remarkably lower, at 25 working days. If the miners' dispute is discounted in 1984, then the annual average for the period 1981–90 falls to only 160 lost working days per 1,000 employees. The 1980s, and especially the 1990s, were clearly times of relatively low levels of industrial conflict in the UK compared with the 1960s and 1970s (Smith *et al* 1978).

Third, the average number of workers involved annually in stoppages of work for the five years 1971–75 was 1,375,000. This rose to 1,765,000 workers per year, on average, for the five years 1976–80, falling to 1,289,000 workers per year for the five years 1981–85. For the five years 1986–90, the annual average fell even more dramatically to 684,000 workers, while for the eight years 1991–98, the annual average fell even further to 197,000 workers per year.

Fourth, the number of recorded stoppages during the 1970s averaged around 2,300 per year. During the 1980s, they fell to a little over 1,000 stoppages per year on average and, for the five years 1986–90, to an average of about 840 stoppages per year. For the years 1991–98, the average fell substantially to 237 stoppages per year.

Causes of industrial action

Ever since the nineteenth century, government has recorded information on the principal causes of industrial stoppages in the UK. Government officials review the available information from employers, conciliation officers and newspaper reports and then identify what the parties identify as the main reason for each strike. Table 21 shows that the dominant issue in the strikes occurring in the UK during the period 1925–98 was pay. Over this 73-year period, pay was cited as the main reason for over three-quarters (76.5 per cent) of working days lost. Although the relative importance of pay issues declined progressively up until the immediate post-war period (1945–54), it subsequently recovered in the 20 years after 1955. During the 1980s, pay once again declined in relative importance but still remained the most important single cause of working days lost annually, at around 58 per cent of the total, and in the 1990s at around 53 per cent.

The pay issues causing disputes between employers, employees and unions are wide-ranging, including union demands for:

- increases in wage rates or bonuses
- restoration of pay differentials
- special rates for particular jobs or for the conditions in which the work is performed
- guaranteed earnings.

Table 20 **Stoppages of work in progress: the UK, 1971–98**

Year	Working days lost (000s)	Working days lost per 1,000 employees	Workers involved (000s)	Stoppages
1971	13,551	612	1,178	2,263
1972	23,909	1,080	1,734	2,530
1973	7,197	317	1,528	2,902
1974	14,750	647	1,626	2,946
1975	6,012	265	809	2,332
1976	3,284	146	668	2,034
1977	10,142	448	1,666	2,737
1978	9,405	413	1,041	2,498
1979	29,474	1,272	4,608	2,125
1980	11,964	520	843	1,348
1981	4,266	195	1,513	1,344
1982	5,313	248	2,103	1,538
1983	3,754	178	574	1,364
1984	27,135	1,278	1,464	1,221
1985	6,402	229	791	903
1986	1,920	90	720	1,074
1987	3,546	164	887	1,016
1988	3,702	166	790	781
1989	4,128	182	727	701
1990	1,903	83	298	630
1991	761	34	176	369
1992	528	24	148	253
1993	649	30	385	211
1994	278	13	107	205
1995	415	19	174	235
1996	1,303	57	364	244
1997	235	10	130	216
1998	282	12	93	166

Source: Office for National Statistics

Pay disputes also commonly occur over reductions in earnings, changes in payment systems and job grading or regrading. Other pay issues that have been identified as likely to cause disputes between management and workers include conflicts over cash allowances, holiday pay and fringe benefits.

Table 22 provides a detailed analysis of the percentage of working days lost by principal cause of dispute, for all industries in the UK, for the years 1981–98. Again, stoppages over pay accounted for most of the working days

Table 21 Number and percentage of working days lost over pay: the UK, 1925–98

Period	Number (000s)	Over pay (000s)	Over pay per cent
1925–34	200,935	175,751	87.5
1935–44	18,956	11,405	60.2
1945–54	20,694	10,293	49.7
1955–64	38,910	27,586	70.9
1965–74	90,164	74,217	82.3
1980–90	78,118	45,309	58.0
1991–98	4,451	2,374	53.3

Source: Department of Employment, Employment Department and National Office for Statistics

Table 22 Working days lost in the UK by cause of dispute, 1981–98

Year	Pay	Hours	Redun- dancy	Trade union matters	Conditions of work	Staffing	Dismissal/ discipline
1981	62	5	15	7	1	4	6
1982	66	5	16	2	1	6	3
1983	58	3	17	2	4	8	8
1984	8	0	87	1	0	2	1
1985	25	3	67	1	1	2	2
1986	59	3	15	3	3	13	4
1987	82	2	5	1	2	5	4
1988	51	0	7	4	1	33	3
1989	80	8	4	2	1	4	1
1990	58	25	2	2	3	8	3
1991	41	2	33	1	9	8	7
1992	37	0	37	2	9	10	5
1993	23	5	60	1	0	10	1
1994	58	3	5	0	0	30	4
1995	49	7	17	1	1	21	4
1996	82	4	3	0	7	3	1
1997	55	3	29	0	3	8	2
1998	59	1	19	1	5	6	10

Cause – percentage of total

Source: Employment Department and Office for National Statistics

lost in every year, except for 1984, 1985 and 1993, when redundancy issues predominated, whilst in 1992 pay and redundancy issues were in joint first place. In 1991, pay was the major issue causing disputes (41 per cent of the total) and redundancy was a close second (33 per cent). It is also noticeable that in 1988 and 1994 about a third of all working days lost were caused by issues relating to staffing and the allocation of work.

Industrial action over time

Table 23 shows strike rates over time for the mining, energy and water supply industries, manufacturing and service sectors. Between 1982 and 1993, the mining, energy and water supply industries had the highest rate in each year, except in 1989, when there was a large strike in public administration. Up until the late 1980s, the strike rate for manufacturing industries had been significantly higher than that for the service sector. During the 1990s, however, strike rates were relatively low and fairly similar, with

Table 23 Working days lost per 1,000 employees in the UK, 1978–98

Year	Mining, energy and water	Manufacturing	Services	All industries and services
1978	372	1,135	77	413
1979	232	3,347	422	1,272
1980	259	1,691	42	520
1981	374	396	117	195
1982	649	352	211	248
1983	2,212	345	39	178
1984	38,425	529	114	1,278
1985	7,518	183	86	299
1986	293	220	46	90
1987	482	124	181	164
1988	536	339	116	166
1989	165	156	199	182
1990	245	228	44	83
1991	87	52	30	34
1992	97	23	24	24
1993	91	28	31	30
1994	2	15	13	13
1995	6	17	20	19
1996	8	24	70	57
1997	9	21	7	10
1998	1	8	13	12

Source: Office for National Statistics

the exception of 1996, when the service sector rate was almost three times that for manufacturing. The low rates make it difficult to work out any particular pattern between the two sectors, and in 1998, manufacturing had the lowest strike rate on record.

International comparisons

From the analysis provided so far, it is clear that number of working days lost, number of workers involved and number of recorded stoppages in the UK vary annually and over time, due to a variety of complex economic and related factors. It is also apparent that the principal causes of trade disputes in the UK vary over time too. To obtain a balanced overview of the UK's strike rate, or its numbers of working days lost per 1,000 employees, comparisons can be made with the strike rates in the EU's 15 member states and nine other member states of the Organisation for Economic Co-operation and Development (OECD). This is done for all industries and services in Table 24 for the period 1988–97, although some care must be exercised in interpreting the data, due to differences in the methods used for selecting and compiling data on industrial disputes in the countries represented. Also, since there are considerable variations between years in the incidence of working days lost, international comparisons based on the average for a number of years in strike-prone industries are more useful than annual comparisons alone, as shown in Table 25. This is because some years are heavily influenced by a small number of very large stoppages in particular industries.

First, it can be seen from Table 24 that there are wide differences in strike rates amongst each of these countries within given periods and in different periods of time. For the whole period 1988–92, for example, 11 countries – Finland, Greece, Ireland, Italy, Spain, Sweden, Iceland, Turkey, Australia, Canada and New Zealand – consistently had higher strike rates than the UK. Similarly, in the period 1988–97, the UK ranked twelfth out of the 24 countries, whilst in the period 1993–97, it ranked only sixteenth (Davis 1999b).

Second, some countries have consistently high strike rates and others relatively low ones. Iceland, Spain, Greece and Canada are in the former category. Switzerland, Austria and Japan – with less than five lost days per 1,000 employees – and the Netherlands, with an average of 12 lost days per 1,000 employees, are in the latter category for the period 1988–97. Countries like the UK, the USA and Portugal lie in the middle range of strike activity over this period.

Third, there was a general downward trend in the incidence of working days lost per 1,000 employees in EU and OECD countries for the period 1993–97, compared with the earlier period 1988–92, with strike rates being generally higher for the period 1982–86 than for the years 1987–95. Iceland was an exceptional case, where working days lost per 1,000 employees doubled between the periods 1988–92 and 1993–97. The period 1993–97, therefore, appeared to be less strike prone than the earlier period 1988–92.

Table 24 Average numbers of working days lost per 1,000 employees in all industries and services in EU and OECD countries, 1988–97

	1988–92	1993–97	1988–97
UK	98	26	62
Austria	7	2	4
Belgium	46	n/a	n/a
Denmark	33	48	40
Finland	184	175	180
France	85	n/a	n/a
Germany	16	n/a	n/a
Greece	627	47	327
Ireland	165	82	120
Italy	248	151	201
Luxembourg	0	n/a	n/a
Netherlands	15	27	21
Portugal	66	23	44
Spain	644	295	469
Sweden	102	54	80
EU average	138	n/a	n/a
Iceland	341	609	479
Norway	68	77	73
Switzerland	0	1	1
Turkey	366	147	249
Australia	211	92	150
Canada	313	194	253
Japan	4	2	3
New Zealand	189	33	108
United States	66	42	54
OECD average	103	n/a	n/a

Source: International Labour Organisation, OECD and Office for National Statistics

One feature of trade disputes is the variation in strike activity among different industrial sectors. Some industries are particularly strike prone, such as mining and quarrying, manufacturing, construction, and transport and communication (see below). This variation and the contrasting industrial structures of different countries in part explain why some countries have relatively high or low rates of strike activity compared with others. To help reduce this effect, Table 25 compares the working days lost per 1,000 employees in these four strike-prone sectors in 20 of the OECD's 24 member states, for the period 1982–91. Overall, for the period 1982–91, the incidence of working days lost per 1,000 employees in these strike-prone

Table 25 Industrial disputes in OECD countries: working days lost per 1,000 employees in strike-prone industries, 1982–91

Country	Averages		
	1982–86	1987–91	1982–91
UK	980	240	610
Denmark	560	90	330
France	150	80	120
Germany	100	10	50
Greece	920	5,360	4,470
Ireland	510	350	430
Italy	280	440	360
Netherlands	40	40	40
Portugal	270	110	200
Spain	520	770	650
Japan	20	10	10
United States	310	210	260
Canada	940	760	850
Austria	–	–	–
Finland	760	180	470
Norway	300	30	170
Sweden	10	170	90
Switzerland	–	–	–
Australia	610	530	570
New Zealand	2,740	520	890

Note: averages for Greece, Italy, Portugal and Japan are based on incomplete data
Source: Employment Department

industries was between one-and-a-half times to twice as high as for all industries and services, although it was three times as high in the United States. Nevertheless, like all industries and services, these strike-prone ones also experienced a general decrease in strike rates over this period.

INFLUENCES ON INDUSTRIAL ACTION

Employee relations are not conducted in a vacuum (see Chapters 1, 4 and 5) since they take place in specific economic, institutional and political contexts. It is these broad categories of factors that have been identified by scholars as the main ones influencing industrial action, patterns of strike activity and the outcomes of industrial conflict between employers and unions. There is, however, no general theory of strikes or industrial action.

As Jackson (1987: 149) has concluded: 'Strikes are enormously complex and are themselves a classification of a variety of different kinds of activity under one head.' Each strike is undertaken 'for different reasons at different times and has a different meaning for different participants'. Because strikes are the most obvious form and most quantified type of industrial action, this section, like the previous one, focuses selectively on the main factors influencing strike activity rather than other manifestations of industrial conflict.

Economic factors

A number of studies use economic variables to explain strikes or stoppages of work, including inter-industry comparisons, unemployment and the business cycle.

Inter-industry comparisons

Kerr and Siegel (1954) undertook an early comparative study of the major variations in strike incidence among different industries in 11 countries. Their focus was on why industrial conflict was prevalent in some industries and absent in others. Previous studies had concentrated on labour market and product market factors, management and union policies, procedures for adjusting disputes and the influence of dominant personalities on industrial conflict. Kerr and Siegel showed that these factors did not explain why some industries are strike prone in many parts of the world and others are not. Their central explanation of strike propensities (see Figure 17) was in the location of workers in society, with the nature of their jobs acting as a secondary influence. Isolated masses of workers, insulated from society at large, were identified as being most likely to take strike action, frequently and bitterly, especially when employed on unpleasant tasks. Individuals and groups who are integrated into the general community, on the other hand, through a multiplicity of associations, were identified to be least likely to strike.

The Department of Employment undertook another more detailed study of variations of inter-industry strike activity in the UK for the period from the mid-1960s to the mid-1970s (Smith *et al* 1978). It had six main conclusions:

- There were very considerable differences between industries in terms of their propensity to strike, with five industries – coal mining, docks, car assembly, shipbuilding, and iron and steel – accounting for at least a quarter of stoppages and a third of the days lost.
- Stoppages were overwhelmingly a manual worker phenomenon, although stoppages among non-manual workers were increasing at that time.
- On average, over the period 1966–73, almost three-quarters of stoppages, accounting for over half of the working days lost, involved members of only one union. Furthermore, six unions, accounting for about half of total union membership, were involved in about 80 per cent of stoppages.
- Strike activity was concentrated in a very small number of plants, with the incidence of strikes rising strongly with plant size.

Figure 17 General pattern of strike propensities

Propensity to strike	Industry
high	mining seafaring and docks
medium high	lumber textiles
medium	chemicals printing leather manufacturing construction food
medium low	clothing gas, water and electricity services
low	railways agriculture trade

Source: Kerr and Siegel (1954)

- There were regional differences in strike proneness, over a considerable period of time.
- High average earnings, high labour intensity and large average establishment size were associated with relatively high strike frequency, and high strike incidence, whilst a high proportion of female employees was associated with low strike proneness.

Unemployment

Another key economic variable claimed to be linked with patterns of industrial action has been unemployment. Hibbs (1976), for example, looked at data for 10 countries between 1950 and 1969 and found that there was a negative relationship between unemployment and strike activity (ie as unemployment fell, strike activity rose). He concluded that the inverse relationship between industrial conflict and unemployment demonstrated considerable sophistication by workers and unions in their use of the strike weapon, since they sought to capitalise on the strategic advantages provided to them by tight labour markets. Furthermore, strikes were responses by workers to movements in real wages, rather than money wages. When unemployment was low, workers had the opportunity to seek alternative jobs that might offer higher rates of pay. But as the cost of labour mobility was high, they would first try to increase their wages in their present jobs, by striking if necessary. He also argued that both unions and their members were more able to withstand stoppages of work during periods of prosperity, since their financial resources were relatively buoyant then and the costs incurred in striking tended to be lower than in periods of recession.

Creigh and Makeham (1982), in contrast, suggested a positive relationship between unemployment and strike activity (ie as unemployment rises, strike activity rises). Their study examined data relating to 15 countries between 1975 and 1979 and focused on the role of employers in trade disputes. They argued that during periods of high unemployment employers may be less willing to resist industrial action or take countervailing steps to avoid disruption caused by strikes. Consequently, where strikes occurred during periods of high unemployment, strikes were likely to last longer. However, with unemployment inversely related to levels of economic activity, an employer's strike costs in terms of lost production were likely to increase as unemployment fell. So employers tended to avoid strike action in these conditions. Indeed, during periods of prosperity, employers were able to pass on increased costs to their customers. Low unemployment might increase worker demands for high pay rises but it also induced employers to raise their pay offers to them.

A third set of writers claimed that there was no correlation, either negative or positive, between unemployment and strike activity (Knight 1972, Shorey 1976, Smith et al 1978). Clearly, the relationship between the two is complex. But to date, a definitive general relationship between unemployment rates and measures of strike activity, either at industry level or nationally, does not appear to have been demonstrated.

The business cycle

It has long been recognised that there are cycles of strikes and that they are possibly related to the business cycle. Rees (1952) identified a pronounced positive correlation between them, with strikes increasing in frequency during periods of prosperity and diminishing in frequency during recessions. The timing of the relationship appeared to be such that strikes typically turned down before business activity reached a peak and turned up some time after recovery had begun. Rees's explanation was based on the assumption that the strike weapon had become the strategic tool of well-organised 'business unions', rather than the spontaneous protest of aggrieved workers, and that union strategy was the driving force in the situation.

According to Rees, the strike peak represented a maximum divergence of expectations between unions and employers. As the business cycle rose, unions were influenced by the wage increases of other unions, increases in the cost of living and a buoyant labour market. Employers, in contrast, sought higher sales, higher profits and new markets. They were, therefore, likely to resist wage demands for which the unions were prepared to fight and this could result in union strike action. Issues of special interest to employers, normally preceding the peak of the business cycle, were rises in the number of business failures, falls in investment and declines in orders.

The matter of special concern to the unions was future employment prospects. As the business cycle peaked, some union leaders had more pessimistic expectations of the economy and strikes fell off. The lag in strikes at the troughs of business cycles represented a 'wait and see' policy by union leaders, who wanted to be sure that the revival was genuine before risking their members' jobs.

Institutional factors

These are another set of factors that are claimed to influence industrial action. Those supporting the institutional approach have explained particular aspects and patterns of industrial conflict by reference to the institutions of conflict resolution, especially that of collective bargaining. The Donovan Commission (1968), for example, sought to explain the number of unofficial strikes in Britain in the 1960s in terms of the inadequacies of multi-employer collective bargaining machinery (see Chapter 9). The Commission identified the growing gap between industry-wide pay rates and actual earnings at the workplace and argued that existing procedural agreements were failing to cope adequately with the resolution of disputes between management and workgroups within workplaces. The Commission went on to recommend the reform of company and factory-level collective bargaining machinery. This was to be based on comprehensive company-wide agreements aimed at regulating pay, grievances, discipline and redundancy, and providing facilities for shop stewards within the firm.

The idea that collective bargaining helps to identify, regularise and institutionalise industrial conflict is based on a number of assumptions:

- It is argued that collective bargaining regulated conflict between employers and employees by keeping it within acceptable bounds, providing a forum for resolving it and legitimising the joint decisions made between the representatives of the two sides.
- When there is a dispute, collective bargaining enables management and unions to pause, think and reflect upon the consequences of their actions before taking industrial sanctions against each other.
- Collective bargaining absorbs energies that might otherwise be directed into more destructive channels of industrial or social conflict.
- Collective bargaining, in providing a forum for communication between management and unions, facilitates not only improved working relations between them but also peaceful change in society generally.

Collective bargaining is predicated, however, on the premises that employers recognise and accept the nature of industrial conflict, that they agree to institutionalise it and that there are appropriate agents of worker representation.

A seminal study was that of Ross and Hartman (1960), who examined patterns of industrial conflict in 15 countries between 1900 and 1956. Although their methodology and their findings have been challenged subsequently (Eldridge 1968, Ingham 1974, Edwards 1981), Ross and Hartman's analysis was important for two main reasons. First, their research provided a useful framework for analysing industrial conflict. Second, they were instrumental in influencing further studies on the institutionalisation of industrial conflict and its implications for the parties to employee relations (Kassolow 1969, Clegg 1976).

Ross and Hartman's central thesis was the 'withering away of the strike'. They argued that there was a general reduction in strike activity over the period they studied. The reasons given for this were: employers had developed more sophisticated policies for dealing with employees; the labour movement was forsaking strike action in favour of political action; and the state had become more prominent as an employer. In fact, strike activity did not wither away but started to grow in the 1960s and 1970s, although, as indicated above, it diminished again in the 1980s. It has been difficult to identify consistent trends across different countries since they wrote, but their thesis was persuasive for the period they reviewed.

It is important to recognise the differing contexts of employee relations during the 1960s, 1970s, 1980s, 1990s and 2000s. In Britain at least, the 20 years after the publication of Ross and Hartman's work were characterised by full employment, Keynesianism and a large public sector. The years since the late 1970s, in contrast, have featured deregulated labour markets, supply-side economic policies, a smaller public sector and far greater legal regulation of industrial action (see Chapters 4, 8 and 9). These factors affected the institutions of employee relations and the willingness of the parties to become involved in industrial action. It is not surprising, in the circumstances, that industrial action was particularly centred on the public sector during the 1980s, as it was subjected to compulsory competitive tendering, privatisation and new styles of personnel management (Farnham 1993). Since then, however, the incidence of industrial conflict has fallen in both the public and private sectors in Britain.

The second main theme of Ross and Hartman's study was the identification of distinctive patterns of industrial conflict and the linking of them to different employee relations systems. They identified five categories of employee relations, each with its own forms of strike activity. These were: two northern European patterns; a Mediterranean-Asian pattern; a North American pattern; and three special cases – Australia, Finland and South Africa. The first northern European pattern incorporated Denmark, the Netherlands, Germany and the UK. These were characterised by a nominal propensity to strike, with strikes of low or moderate duration. The second northern European grouping of Norway and Sweden featured infrequent but long strikes. The Mediterranean-Asian pattern, comprising France, Italy, Japan and India, had high participation in strikes, but these were of short duration. Finally, the North American pattern of the USA and Canada had a moderately high propensity to strike and disputes were of relatively long duration.

In comparing different employee relations systems, Ross and Hartman identified five key features that, at their time of writing, were claimed to be associated with distinctive patterns of strikes, which are summarised in Figure 18. Denmark, the Netherlands, Germany and the UK were characterised by mature trade unions, stable union memberships and subdued union leadership conflicts. There was a wide acceptance of trade unions by employers and centralised collective bargaining. These countries had important Labour parties and while governments rarely intervened to regulate terms and conditions of employment, they did intervene in the resolution of industrial disputes. Norway and Sweden shared many of the above characteristics but had less active government intervention in management–union relations.

The Mediterranean-Asian countries, in contrast, had relatively young trade union movements, low union membership and continual union leadership conflicts. Collective bargaining was weak, left-wing parties were divided and there was considerable government intervention in industry. In North America, there was an old trade union movement, with a stable membership and little factionalism. Unions were increasingly accepted by employers, collective bargaining was decentralised, terms and conditions were largely determined privately and there was no Labour party in North America.

Figure 18 Principal features of comparative employee relations systems

---

1 Organisational stability of the labour movement

   1.1   age of labour movement
   1.2   stability of membership

2 Leadership conflicts in the labour movement

   2.1   factionalism and rivalry
   2.2   strength of communism in the unions

3 State of management–union relations

   3.1   degree of union acceptance by employers
   3.2   consolidation of bargaining structure

4 Labour political activity

   4.1   a Labour party as a leading political party
   4.2   Labour governments

5 Role of the state

   5.1   extent of government activity in defining terms of employment
   5.2   dispute settlement procedures

Source: Ross (1959)

Political factors

Some scholars have seen political power as a major variable determining long-term patterns of strikes and industrial action. Korpi and Shalev (1979:

181) have argued, for example, that where labour movements have been organised effectively and co-ordinated politically, they have tried to achieve their goals not only through collective bargaining but also through political rather than strike action. On the other hand, where labour movements have been fragmented, have been politically weak and have had little or no political influence, strikes have been likely to remain high. Thus in Scandinavian countries and Austria, which have had well-organised union movements and where democratic socialist political parties have been in power for many years, strikes have been rarely used to pursue union goals and objectives. In countries like the United States, Canada and Ireland, on the other hand, where labour movements have been less well organised and socialist parties were weak or non-existent, strikes were more common.

> In these instances, conflicts between buyers and sellers of labour power continue to be manifested primarily within the employment contract, something which is no longer the case elsewhere. The long duration of strikes in these countries has contributed to give them very high relative volumes of strikes (man-days idle) in the postwar period.

In countries like Britain, Belgium and Denmark, the relationship between the political activities of their labour movements and strike activity was claimed to be more complex. Up until the late 1970s in Britain, for example, though the Labour Party gained periods of political power, its control of and its long-term impact on the political system were relatively insecure. Labour governments were therefore unable to manage class conflict through 'political exchange' for any long period of time. Consequently, Britain's post-war strike record was similar to that of the pre-war period and the strike weapon, as a union tactic, failed to wither away. In post-war Belgium, despite labour's involvement in government, strike mobilisation was as high as it had been in the pre-war period. In Denmark, although organised labour had periodic influence in Danish governments in the years up until the late 1970s, its power was less stable than in the rest of Scandinavia. According to Korpi and Shalev (1979: 182): 'This instability may well have contributed to the continuing wave-like incidence of industrial conflict in post-war Denmark, at what is nevertheless a relatively low level by international standards.'

Another political analysis of strike activity has been provided by Shorter and Tilley (1974). They argued, first, that trade unions have had a crucial role in channelling worker dissatisfaction into strike action, and second, that strikes have had political aims that did not simply express economic interests. Where trade unions have not had political power through representation in the political system, strikes have been used to put direct pressure on governments to change their existing policies or to initiate new ones. In this sense, strikes were an expression of class conflict between workers and their organisations and the political authorities, with 'strike waves' often coinciding with periodic political crises as they have done in France and Italy.

In Shorter and Tilley's analysis, strike activity prior to World War II was of a similar intensity throughout western Europe. After the war, however, patterns differed. In countries such as those in Scandinavia, where labour gained political power, strike activity declined. Where labour failed to gain political power, such as in France and Italy, strikes continued at relatively high levels and expressed the political aspirations and expectations of the working class. The United States, in contrast, was seen as a special case, because strike activity did not wither away as it had done in northern Europe. This was explained in terms of the failure of successive Federal governments to substantially protect workers' interests through interventionist political reforms. As a result, North American 'labor unions' drew a sharp dividing line between free collective bargaining, used to protect their members' job interests, including the use of strike action if necessary, and ad hoc 'interest-coalition' politics used to advance union political action.

MANAGING COLLECTIVE INDUSTRIAL ACTION

Nowadays collective industrial action in Britain is normally initiated by trade unions. Industrial action initiated by employers, such as lockouts, is very rare, although to what extent plant closures, transfers of businesses and large-scale redundancies are regarded by trade unions and their members as covert forms of 'industrial action' by management is a matter of debate. This section therefore concentrates on the main issues to be considered by employers when they face organised industrial action from trade unions. These involve both legal and non-legal issues, although the suitability of any management response depends on the nature of the dispute, estimated costs of pursuing any particular course of action and the balance of bargaining power between the two sides (Martin 1992).

Preparing for industrial action

Every trade dispute is unique. The type of action threatened by the trade unions, the extent and scope of the expected action and the nature of the issue in dispute, all affect the ways in which management is likely to respond and plan its own counteractions to the situation. Once it seems likely that unions and their members are planning collective industrial action, management has to prepare and consider its possible responses. There are four key points:

- *Assess the scale of the problem.* Management needs to identify the scope of the dispute, estimate its possible support amongst the workforce and assess the potential difficulties and costs of resolving it. This includes considering the likelihood of a settlement in the short term.
- *Make contingency plans.* The decisions that management has to take include: how any work is to be covered during the dispute; how adequate health and safety standards are to be maintained; and how any relevant property of the employer, such as keys, vehicles or other equipment, is to

be returned to management before industrial action takes place.

- *Extend the communication systems*. Over and above existing communication channels, new communication systems may be necessary while the dispute is in progress. This is to ensure: effective management co-ordination of the dispute; publicity to employees and the press; and open channels of communication with the unions and their members.
- *Plan actions in response*. This should include considering what sort of warnings are to be given to employees, unions and customers about the legal and non-legal implications of the dispute.

Some of the key points to be considered by management prior to industrial action being taken are summarised in Exhibit 35.

Exhibit 35 **Key points for management in preparing for industrial action**

These include:

- making plans before industrial action takes place
- assessing the effects the action will have
- remembering that industrial action is normally in breach of the contract of employment
- ensuring that strikers do not get paid during the dispute
- bearing in mind that picketing must be peaceful and at the employees' place of work
- not using the disciplinary procedure in response to industrial action
- remembering that the law on industrial action is normally invoked by the employer
- laying off employees without pay is only lawful where there is a term in the contract that allows it
- keeping in touch with those co-ordinating management action and seeking advice where necessary
- remembering that management and employees have to work together after the dispute is settled.

The legal issues

The main legal issues arising from industrial action that employers have to consider are: legal immunities, balloting, and picketing.

Legal immunities

Where employees take industrial action, they are normally in breach of their contracts of employment. Also, when trade unions, their officials or others organise industrial action, they are calling for breaches of, or interferences with, the performance of employment contracts. They may also be interfering with the ability of employers to fulfil commercial contracts. It is unlawful, under the common law, to induce individuals to break or interfere with a contract, so the legal device of statutory immunities enables unions and individuals organising industrial action to do so without being sued in the courts (see Chapters 4, 8 and 9). These are sometimes referred to as 'trade union' or 'legal immunities'. Legal immunities do not, however, protect individual strikers, or those taking action short of a strike, from being dismissed, or from having legal proceedings taken against them by their employer, because they have broken their employment contracts.

For unions and strike leaders to be protected by legal immunities, the following conditions are necessary. First, there must be a trade dispute and a properly conducted industrial action ballot. Second, the action must not: be secondary action, which does not involve the primary or direct employer; promote a closed shop; or support employees dismissed while taking unofficial industrial action. Further, the action must not involve unlawful picketing.

Legal immunities only apply where a union or its officials are acting 'in contemplation or furtherance of a trade dispute' (the 'golden formula'). In law, a trade dispute must be: (i) between workers and their own employer; and (ii) wholly or mainly about employment-related matters. This legal definition does not cover actions:

- between groups of workers or inter-union disputes
- between workers and employers other than their own
- between a union and an employer where none of its workforce is in dispute with it
- not 'wholly or mainly' relating to employment-related matters
- relating to matters taking place overseas.

Where legal immunities do not apply, employers (and customers and suppliers) damaged by the industrial action may take civil proceedings in the courts against the union or the individuals concerned. They have to show that:

- an unlawful act has been done or is threatened
- a contract to which they are a party has been or will be broken or interfered with
- they are likely to suffer loss because of it.

Unless legal immunities apply, a union is held responsible for any acts that are done, authorised or endorsed by its principal executive committee, general secretary, president or any other committee of the union. To avoid legal liability, a union or its agents must repudiate the act as soon as is reasonably practicable after it has come to their notice. They must give written notice of the repudiation to the committee or individuals concerned. And they must do their best to give written notice of the fact and date of the repudiation to every member involved in the action and to the employer.

Where legal immunities do not apply, those damaged may seek an injunction from the courts. This may be issued on an interim basis, pending a full hearing of the case. The courts also have the authority to require any union found in breach of the law to take such steps to ensure that:

- there is no further inducement to take or continue the action
- no further action is taken after the injunction is granted.

If an injunction is not obeyed, the employer may return to court and ask that those concerned be declared in contempt of court. Any party found in contempt may be fined or have other penalties issued against it. Unions may be deprived of their assets, through the sequestration of their funds. This means that union funds are placed under the control of a person, appointed by the court, who may pay any fines or legal costs incurred as a result of the court's proceedings. It is also possible for employers (and others) to claim damages for any losses resulting from the unprotected industrial action. There are, however, upper limits on these damages in any proceedings and these are according to the size of union membership.

Balloting

Where a union calls on its members to take part in or to continue industrial action, it must hold a properly conducted secret ballot to maintain its legal immunity. Unless all the relevant statutory requirements are satisfied, the ballot does not preserve this immunity. The ballot must always be held before a union calls for or otherwise organises industrial action. Those entitled to vote are all the union members who the union reasonably believes are, at the time of the ballot, to be called upon to take industrial action. There must normally be a postal ballot. The ballot paper must contain a question requiring the voters to indicate if they are prepared to take part in the action. The law requires that the following statement should appear on every voting paper: 'If you take part in a strike or other industrial action, you may be in breach of your contract of employment' (Employment Department 1990: 11). Following the enactment of the Employment Relations Act 1999, however, schedule 3 adds to this a sentence describing the new protection given to workers against unfair dismissal during the first eight weeks of lawful industrial action. Dismissals during this period are automatically unfair.

Unions are required to give the employer seven days' notice of the intention to hold a ballot, the date of the ballot and a description of the employees voting. Not later than three days before the ballot paper is sent to any union member, the employer must be provided with a sample of the voting paper or, where there is more than one, of each voting paper. Majority support must be obtained in response to the question(s) asked. Votes must be accurately and fairly recorded and an independent scrutineer must be appointed. As soon as is reasonably practicable after the ballot, the employer must be informed of the result and the scrutineer must make a report. Written notice must be given to the employer before the action commences. Where a union is calling out members in different places of work, unions may aggregate votes where:

- at least one member affected by the dispute works in each workplace to be balloted
- the union has a reasonable belief that the members have the same occupation and are employed by the employer with whom the union is in dispute
- the ballot is restricted to those employed by the employer with whom the union is in dispute.

Picketing

To be protected legally, pickets must comply with the basic rules embodied in the law. This is to ensure that picketing is organised lawfully and in accordance with good practice. According to the Employment Department (1992: 5), the law requires that picketing may only:

(i) be undertaken in contemplation or furtherance of a trade dispute;
(ii) be carried out by a person attending at or near his own place of work; a trade union official, in addition to attending at or near his own place of work, may also attend at or near the place of work of a member of his trade union whom he is accompanying on the picket line and whom he represents.

Furthermore, the only purpose involved must be peacefully to obtain or communicate information or peacefully to persuade individuals to work or not to work. Picketing that is not peaceful and leads to violence, intimidation, obstruction or molestation is likely to involve offences under the criminal law.

Responding to employees

An employer's response to industrial action is normally aimed at preventing the action or, if this fails, achieving a return to work on acceptable terms as early as possible, whilst at the same time avoiding an escalation of the dispute. For these purposes, employers need to develop action plans that are coherent, flexible and effective. Considered responses need to be given to employees individually and to their unions.

Responses to individual employees are normally preceded by a written warning to them, by either a personal letter or a general circular, with some means by which they can acknowledge its receipt. Ideally, this communication should make clear the nature of the employer's response to the proposed action and should provide sufficient time for the employees to change their minds. Since employees refusing to take industrial action cannot be 'unjustifiably disciplined' by their unions, employers sometimes include information to this effect in the warning letters sent to individuals before and during industrial action.

When deciding how to respond to industrial action, employers need to answer two key questions (Local Authorities Conditions Advisory Board 1991: 13):

- Has the action led to a breach of the terms of the individual's contract?
- How important is any breach that may have occurred?

Where a strike is involved, this is a fundamental breach of the employment contract, since the employees are refusing to do the work required of them, even though work is available. Action short of a strike is not so straightforward. It depends on the form of action and its effects. With go-slows, work-to-rules or bans on voluntary overtime, there appear to be no breaches of contractual terms. Where overtime is customary, however, and the ban is severely disruptive to the employer, it may be possible to argue that this has breached an implied term of the employment contract.

The nature and extent of the breach of contract, therefore, are major factors in determining an employer's responses to industrial action by some or all of its workforce. A summary of the possible responses available to employers faced by industrial action is provided in Exhibit 36. In adopting any of these actions, employers have to bear in mind the legal implications of what they are doing and any likely reactions by employees to the employer's initiatives. When employees are taking strike action, for example, there is no legal obligation on the employer to pay them, since they are not ready and willing to work under the terms of their contracts. In other cases, such as when employers propose taking disciplinary action against employees for breach of contract, the situation is less clear-cut, and indeed there are disadvantages to doing this. For example, the stage at which disciplinary action is invoked depends on the relevant procedure. Furthermore, the individual employee may not take any notice of formal warnings and then the employer may be forced to take further disciplinary action without really wanting to.

Exhibit 36 **Possible responses by employers to industrial action**

These include:

- deducting pay for strike action
- deducting pay for action short of a strike
- refusing partial performance of the contract
- sending employees home
- suspending with pay
- suspending without pay
- using the disciplinary procedure
- locking-out
- summary dismissal
- taking civil action against individual employees.

There are important statutory provisions regarding dismissal for industrial action. These provide that employees dismissed whilst taking part in industrial action will not be able to make a complaint to an industrial tribunal unless:

- at the date of the dismissal one or more of the employees also taking industrial action was not dismissed
- one or more of the other employees dismissed for taking part in the action was subsequently offered re-engagement within three months of their date of dismissal, and these employees were employed at the same establishment as the employee claiming dismissal.

Where, however, the call to take industrial action has been repudiated by the trade union, no union member who is sacked while continuing to take action is able to claim unfair dismissal, even if there has been selective dismissal or re-engagement.

Dismissals of workers for taking strike action are automatically unfair during the first eight weeks of a dispute. Where a union repudiates industrial action during the course of a dispute, making the industrial action illegal, if employees continue to take action then they lose their right to bring a claim of unfair dismissal to an employment tribunal. But even where a union has not repudiated the action and an employer dismisses selectively from among those taking part in the dispute, it has to be shown that it was reasonable to do so in the circumstances. Similarly, where an employer re-engages selectively, the dismissal of other employees may not necessarily be declared unfair. The question is whether it was reasonable to re-engage some but not others. In practice, however, employers normally re-engage all sacked strikers once a dispute is settled, provided that their jobs remain after the dispute has ended.

The general effect of industrial action on conditions of employment is clear-cut as far as strike action is concerned. Employees unavailable for work cannot expect to receive any employment benefits. For example, the employer is under no legal obligation to provide occupational sick pay should an employee fall sick during the strike action. However, if an employee has taken annual leave and strike action starts during this period, then in the absence of evidence to the contrary, that individual should be deemed to be on leave, not on strike. Similarly, employees who are on sick leave before industrial action starts should be assumed to be on sick leave, provided that the necessary certification is produced. Also, the operation of the Health and Safety at Work Act 1974 is not suspended during a period of industrial action and employers continue to owe a duty to any employees remaining at work and to others. The employer may need to come to an arrangement with employee representatives ensuring that essential safety measures are carried out before the strike action takes effect.

Responding to trade unions

An employer's responses to the trade unions, when a trade dispute is either threatened or takes place, tends to centre on the issue of whether or not to take legal action against the union(s) involved. What the employer does is as much a matter of management judgement as of legal technicalities. The central issues are:

- What will be the likely long-term effects on relations between the employer and the union(s) if the employer initiates legal action?
- What will be the likely outcome on the dispute of legal intervention by the courts?

The key legal issue is that successful legal action by an employer against trade unions in the courts depends on a union losing its legal immunities when it and its members take part in what is deemed to be 'unlawful' or 'unprotected' industrial action (see Chapter 4). Legally, employers need to determine in the first instance whether (Employment Department 1992):

- a trade dispute is taking place
- the 'golden formula' applies (ie that the action is 'in contemplation or furtherance of a trade dispute')
- a proper industrial action ballot has been conducted
- the action is authorised by the relevant trade union(s)
- the action is primary, not secondary
- picketing is peaceful and in accordance with the Employment Department's code of practice.

The normal civil law remedies are available to employers when unlawful industrial action takes place or is threatened. Proceedings against individual employees are rare but liability for civil claims extends beyond those taking part in industrial action. Those organising the action may also be liable, including the union officials and the union, except where they are protected by legal immunities. But legal immunities only have the effect of protecting employees as union members, not as individual employees who have no immunity for the act of breaking their individual contracts of employment.

The immediate civil remedy is an injunction. This is a court order seeking to stop the industrial action and is normally granted only if the court decides that such action is unlikely to be shown to have immunity on the full hearing of the case. An injunction is a holding measure, until a full trial decides the matter properly. An injunction is usually sought as a way of immediately preventing the action from taking place, since a full trial is only possible some time after the intended action has been carried out. The courts are generally ready to grant injunctions to employers, provided that the proposed action might not have immunity. They do this by taking account of the 'balance of convenience' between the parties. This means that judges tend to favour the party that is likely to suffer the most if the injunction is not granted. Normally, this is deemed to be the employer. However, the courts also consider the likelihood of the union establishing at full trial that legal immunity does apply and they give the union the opportunity to put its side of the case, before granting an injunction.

Many employers, in practice, are very reluctant to use the law to resolve industrial disputes because of the detrimental long-term effects it can have on employee relations. Much depends on the damage being done by industrial action. Moreover, the union or individuals concerned may disregard an injunction and then the employer has to consider whether to institute contempt of court proceedings against the union. These may lead to fines, damages or other penalties against the union. Employers, therefore, need to give very careful consideration to the consequences of invoking the law in an industrial dispute before making a definitive decision to proceed with it.

The return to work

Once a settlement has been reached between management and unions, a full return to normal working as soon as possible is essential. Where action has been short of a strike, there is no great difficulty. With strikes, a phased return may have to be arranged. The formal terms of the return may have to be negotiated at the time of settlement and employers should try to seek reciprocal arrangements with trade unions on the terms of the return to work. But written agreements do not always reflect all aspects of the employment relationship. For example, as far as possible, employers should ensure that there is no victimisation of union members who did not take part in the industrial action. This might mean advising employees of their rights of appeal under trade union rules and the law, such as the right not to have 'unjustifiable discipline' taken against them.

It is normally important to restore the pre-existing employee relations climate, so that the return to work can take place without any recriminations on either side. On the employer's side, this means the job or career structures of employees should not be prejudiced by the fact that they took industrial action. The employer has to decide whether disciplinary warnings arising from misconduct during the industrial action should be kept on record or deleted. It also needs to decide what effect any break in continuous service is to have on employee benefits and conditions of employment. Employees who have been dismissed and subsequently re-engaged are normally reappointed on the same terms and conditions, provided their posts still exist. Overall, then, employers and management have a prime role in ensuring that the return to work proceeds smoothly, fairly and in accordance with what has been formally agreed with the trade unions.

ASSIGNMENTS

(a) Read Dahrendorf (1959: 241–79). What is his theory of industrial conflict and what are its implications for the managing of employee relations? Also read Jackson (1987: 155–84) and compare his explanations of industrial conflict with Dahrendorf's analysis.

(b) Report and comment on any forms of individual and unorganised conflict in your organisation.

(c) Describe and analyse a strike with which you are familiar. Get your material either from a situation that you have directly experienced yourself or from the literature of employee relations, newspaper reports, television documentaries or individuals who have actually been involved in a dispute.

(d) Read the latest annual report on industrial stoppages in *Labour Market Trends*. What were the trends for the past year? What were the principal causes? And what were the duration and size of stoppages?
(e) Read Smith *et al* (1978: 84–90). What are their main conclusions about the nature of strike activity in Britain for the period of review (1966–75)? To what extent do you think that their analysis is still relevant today?
(f) Read Clegg (1976). What is his explanation of strike proneness?
(g) What guidance does the Employment Department's (1992) code of practice on picketing provide relating to numbers of pickets on picket lines and the organisation of picketing? What is the legal status of the code?
(i) Your organisation has been informed by the unions of their intention to take strike action as a result of a properly conducted industrial action ballot. Consider the responses you will advise the employer to take in the circumstances and draft a letter to the employees concerned warning them, individually, of the employer's intended responses.
(j) An organisation has informed the unions of its intentions of closing its manufacturing plant, and of instituting compulsory redundancies if they do not accept lay-offs and a reduction in the terms of the present lay-off agreement. The unions are now in dispute with the company, having taken a properly conducted industrial action ballot. The company has proposed rotating lay-offs for its staff for six months, with access to independent arbitration, a 10 per cent cut in employee benefits and a profit-sharing scheme. The unions have rejected this and the 400 staff have been dismissed by the management and replaced by a new workforce. (i) What is the legal position? (ii) What advice would you give to senior management at this stage of the dispute?

REFERENCES

ALLEN V. (1976) 'Marxism and the personnel manager'. *Personnel Management*. December.
ARGYRIS C. (1964) *Integrating the Individual and the Organisation*. Chichester, Wiley.
BIRD D. (1992) 'Industrial Stoppages in 1991'. *Employment Gazette*. May.
CLEGG H. (1976) *Trade Unionism under Collective Bargaining*. Oxford, Blackwell.
COSER L. (1956) *The Functions of Social Conflict*. London, Routledge & Kegan Paul.
CREIGH S. *and* MAKEHAM D. (1982) 'Strike incidence in industrial countries: an analysis'. *Australian Bulletin of Labour*. 8 (3).
DAHRENDORF R. (1959) *Class and Class Conflict in Industrial Society*. London, Routledge & Kegan Paul.
DAVIS J. (1999a) 'Labour disputes in 1998'. *Labour Market Trends*. 107 (6), June.
DAVIS J. (1999b) 'International comparisons of labour disputes in 1997'. *Labour Market Trends*. 107 (4), April.

DONOVAN, Lord (1968) *Royal Commission on Trade Unions and Employers' Associations*. London, HMSO.

EDWARDS P. (1981) *Strikes in the USA, 1871–1974*. Oxford, Blackwell.

ELDRIDGE J. (1968) *Industrial Disputes*. London, Routledge & Kegan Paul.

EMPLOYMENT DEPARTMENT (1990) *Trade Union Ballots on Industrial Action*. London, COI.

EMPLOYMENT DEPARTMENT (1992) *Code of Practice on Picketing*. London, COI.

FARNHAM D. (1993) 'Human resources management and employee relations', in D. Farnham and S. Horton (eds), *Managing the New Public Services*, Basingstoke, Macmillan.

FARNHAM D. *and* PIMLOTT J. (1995) *Understanding Industrial Relations*. London, Cassell.

HIBBS D. (1976) 'Industrial conflict in advanced industrial countries'. *Political Science Review*. 70 (4).

HYMAN R. (1975) *Industrial Relations*. London, Macmillan.

HYMAN R. (1989) *Strikes*. Basingstoke, Macmillan.

INGHAM G. (1974) *Strikes and Industrial Conflict*. London, Macmillan.

JACKSON M. (1987) *Strikes*. Brighton, Wheatsheaf.

KASSOLOW E. (1969) *Trade Unions and Industrial Relations*. New York, Random House.

KERR C. *and* SIEGEL A. (1954) 'The interindustry propensity to strike – an international comparison', in A. Kornhauser, R. Dubin and A. Ross (eds), *Industrial Conflict*, New York, McGraw-Hill.

KNIGHT K. (1972) 'Strikes and wage inflation in British manufacturing industry 1950–1968'. *Bulletin of the Oxford Institute of Economics and Statistics*. 34 (3).

KORNHAUSER A., DUBIN R. *and* ROSS A. (EDS) (1954) *Industrial Conflict*. New York, McGraw-Hill.

KORPI W. *and* SHALEV M. (1979) 'Strikes, industrial relations and class conflicts in capitalist societies'. *British Journal of Sociology*. 30 (2).

LOCAL AUTHORITIES CONDITIONS OF SERVICE ADVISORY BOARD (1991) *Employers' Responses to Industrial Action*. London, LACSAB.

MCGREGOR D. (1960) *The Human Side of Enterprise*. New York, McGraw-Hill.

MARTIN R. (1992) *Bargaining Power*. Oxford, Clarendon.

MAYO E. (1946) *The Social Problems of an Industrial Civilization*. London, Routledge.

REES A. (1952) 'Industrial conflict and business fluctuations'. *Journal of Political Economy*. 60 (5).

ROETHLISBERGER F. (1946) *Management and Morale*. Cambridge, Mass., Harvard University Press.

ROSS A. (1959) 'Changing patterns of industrial conflict', in G. Somers (ed.), *Proceedings of the 12th Annual Meeting of the Industrial Relations Research Association*.

ROSS A. *and* HARTMAN P. (1960) *Changing Patterns of Industrial Conflict*. New York, Wiley.

SHOREY J. (1976) 'An interindustry analysis of strike frequency'. *Economica*. 43, No. 172.

SHORTER E. *and* TILLEY C. (1974) *Strikes in France 1830–1968*. Cambridge, Cambridge University Press.

SMITH C., CLIFTON R., MAKEHAM P., CREIGH S. *and* BURN R. (1978) *Strikes in Britain*. London, Department of Employment.

WARNER W. *and* LOW J. (1947) *The Social System of the Modern Factory*. New Haven, Yale University Press.

11 The skills of employee relations

Stephen Pilbeam and Marjorie Corbridge

The management of people, and in particular the resolution of conflict that arises in the workplace, requires not only knowledge of the law, organisational policies and procedures, but also acquisition of appropriate skills to enable the conflict to be resolved to the satisfaction of all. Employee relations skills, in common with other managerial skills, must be identified, learned and practised by managers if managers are to be effective. Negotiation is a core employee relations skill and is a process whereby individual or collective differences between the parties are reconciled. This occurs through a process of persuasion, with the aim of reaching agreement. Employees also raise formal grievances with managers. These grievances may arise from their jobs, the application of policies and procedures or from their terms and conditions of employment. This potential for conflict needs to be resolved, which requires managers using relevant procedures, interview skills and judgement to ensure that issues are dealt with fairly and effectively. Harassment is a potentially difficult situation that can arise in the workplace, which requires specific policies and managerial skills in order to deal effectively with the issues arising from it. Similarly, managers who are concerned about the conduct or job performance of their employees may need to take corrective or disciplinary action against them. This action could ultimately result in the termination of their employment contracts. Where organisations are being restructured or skill mixes changed, or where demand for a product or service falls, job losses can occur and a redundancy programme may need to be implemented and managed. It is this range of employee relations activities that is addressed in the present chapter, with a particular focus on the skills required to deal with these activities effectively.

THE BASICS OF NEGOTIATING

Negotiation is a process whereby two or more interested groups seek to reconcile their differences through attempts to persuade the other group to move from their initial position, with the overall aim of reaching an agreement. Implicit in this process is an intention and willingness to compromise in pursuit of an agreement which, although it may be less than ideal, is acceptable to the groups involved. The precise definition of acceptability is subject to many influences and the contingencies of the negotiating situation, not least of which is the balance of bargaining power between the negotiating groups. It could be argued that the relative power between the negotiating groups influences the outcome of the process to a much larger

405

extent than the skills and abilities of the negotiators. Negotiation is therefore a conflict-resolving activity and involves concessions and compromise, but can incorporate collaboration, confrontation, accommodation and avoidance. Chapter 7 explored some of the main theories associated with negotiation; this section concentrates on the basic skills involved in the negotiation process.

Negotiations pervade organisational life and essential negotiating skills developed within an employee relations framework are transferable to many other areas of management. More flexible organisational structures, with reduced emphasis on hierarchical relationships, necessitate effective intra-organisational negotiation between teams, groups and individuals. Managers in the private sector may be involved in negotiating contracts or in negotiating for resources. In the public sector the development of purchaser and provider relationships, coupled with the pursuit of 'best value', heightens demand for effective negotiation skills. In short, managers need to be able to negotiate effectively with other managers, with workers, with customers and with suppliers. The aim of any negotiating process, therefore, whether formal or informal, is to reconcile conflicting viewpoints through concessions, compromise and exchanges between the parties involved. To analyse the negotiation process three distinctive and sequential elements can be identified: preparation, negotiation and implementation. Negotiation also incorporates certain skills, such as tactical adjustment, listening skills and professional competencies. Much of what follows is focused on team negotiations in an employee relations context, although, as indicated above, the skills of negotiation can be deployed in many other contexts (Gennard and Judge 1999).

Preparing for management negotiation with a trade union

Preparation includes:

- defining negotiation objectives, the development of group cohesiveness, information-gathering and the allocation of roles
- achieving intra-group consensus
- considering the abilities and skills of the other negotiating team
- determining the relative power balance, tactics and strategy
- defining negotiating parameters in terms of optimum and minimum outcomes
- predicting the expectations, arguments, counter-arguments and strategies of the other side.

Thorough and careful preparation is a key element in successful and effective negotiation. The definition of clear negotiation objectives is essential because it enables negotiators to distinguish between the important and the less significant issues they wish to address and it serves to clarify and synchronise individual expectations. A by-product of good planning can be the development of effective working relationships and cohesiveness within the negotiation team.

A starting point in negotiation is the identification, clarification and consideration of the specific issues involved. Until a common understanding is achieved, it is inappropriate to make any strategic or tactical decisions. This exploration of the issues needs to be accompanied by information-gathering activity. This activity is largely self-explanatory but involves accessing appropriate information sources, including any facts surrounding the issue, employer information relevant to the negotiation, statistical material, and organisation rules and agreements. It also includes external information, for example market rates in the case of pay negotiations and any relevant legislation. There needs to be an assessment of who should be involved in the negotiations and consideration given to the size of the negotiating team. The larger the team, the greater the resources and expertise available, but there is also a consequent increase in complexity because more people are involved. The need for particular skills, knowledge and expertise in relation to the particular negotiation influences the composition of the negotiating team.

Allocation of roles within the negotiating team is of critical importance and can be addressed by answering the following questions: Who will take a lead role? Where will the locus of decision-making lie? What control mechanisms are necessary to ensure a co-ordinated approach? Should a lead negotiator, observer and note-takers be allocated in advance? Who will have the authority to call adjournments? In essence, the decisions revolve around creating a cohesive team with members who are able to present a united front, or at least avoid overt disagreement, in dealing with the other side. The negotiation process starts in the preparation stage because it enables intra-group negotiation to take place prior to actual negotiations with the other interest group or party. The achievement of intra-group consensus, through agreement on key issues, objectives and tactics, gives confidence to the negotiating team. It also reduces the possibility of exposing weaknesses, or any apparent dissonance within the team, which might have a negative impact on the negotiating position, during the negotiations.

In assessing the strength of the other side, negotiators need to take account of the skills, experience and expertise of the other team. In parallel with this, an important judgement to make is the level of commitment to the issue likely to be exhibited by the other side and its significance for them. The validity and logic of their arguments needs to be predicted and assessed and the power balance, as defined by the ability to impose unilateral action or take sanctions against the other side, is a crucial factor. Identifying the comparative strengths of negotiating positions is a prerequisite to the determination of strategy and tactics. The negotiating team also needs to focus upon the outcomes it seeks in relation to its predetermined objectives. Identifying the team's optimum and minimum acceptable outcomes facilitates this process. These polar points can be refined by considering what the team would like to achieve, what it intends to achieve, and what it must achieve – 'likes', 'intends', 'musts' or 'LIMs' (Kennedy et al 1984).

Some writers describe these as the ideal solution, realistic settlement point and fall-back position (Adam-Smith 1998). Adam-Smith suggests that the settlement point can be found in an area where the negotiating objectives of the two sides overlap and this is illustrated in Figure 19. Clearly where there is no overlap, there is much less scope for a negotiated outcome which is acceptable to both parties. For example, if the management pay offer ranges from 1 per cent to 3 per cent, and the trade union objective ranges from 3.5 per cent to 5 per cent, lack of overlap will prevent an agreement being reached. Alternatively, it will result in expectations being revised or provoke an attempt to exploit a power advantage. These ideas about bargaining range can also be applied to qualitative issues such as the negotiation of policies and procedures, in which case the 'likes', 'intends' and 'musts' apply to words rather than numbers. Salamon (1998) agrees that the negotiator, as well as gathering and analysing quantitative and qualitative data, must also determine the bargaining limits on the issues to be negotiated. Whatever analytical tool is used, the principle remains the same: defining the negotiating parameters is a focal point for the negotiating team. These parameters allow some flexibility, provide a framework for negotiating and give direction to the negotiation activity. Such decisions, or more accurately expectations, are not, of course, disclosed to the other side. But they are subject to probing and speculation by the other party during the negotiation process.

Figure 19 **Negotiating objectives and parameters**

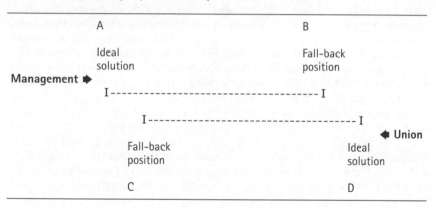

It is useful to try to perceive and evaluate your own expectations from the standpoint of the other side. Thus an associated aspect of preparation is predicting the parameters and expectations of the other group and the responses and arguments likely to occur, in order to plan appropriate counter-responses and counter-arguments. This predictive process can include an assessment of the potential strategies available to the other side.

Decisions have to be made about the nature of the negotiations. Some are problem-centred or integrative. Others are competitive or distributive. Which predominates is determined largely by the negotiation issue. Integrative negotiation exists where the parties believe that co-operation and a problem-solving approach will produce a mutually acceptable outcome. The negotiations are more likely to be characterised by openness and a degree of trust between the parties. It is potentially a 'win–win' situation. In contrast, distributive negotiation is more likely to be perceived as a 'win–lose' situation because of the incompatibility of negotiation objectives between the parties and the behaviour within the negotiations is likely to be influenced by this conflict perspective. There are rarely pure forms of either integrative or distributive negotiations. A more realistic strategy is to attempt to define the likely mix and develop an awareness of oscillation and fluctuation during the negotiation process. Within these limits, there is advantage in appreciating that the purpose of negotiating is the pursuit of mutual benefit rather than just the scoring of points by one side at the expense of the other. Also, within the preparation it is useful to consider the implications of a failure to agree within the negotiation process and what action may become necessary if this happens.

While detailed preparation is vital, this should not predispose the negotiating team to developing a rigid position. Flexibility and the ability to manoeuvre within the negotiating process are essential and desirable characteristics. A further caveat is that the attitudes, personalities and relationships of the negotiators are likely to influence the negotiations independently of the strength of argument, because negotiations are a psychological encounter. Additionally, within each negotiating team the power, influence and accountability of the participants in relation to each other create an internal dynamic that should not be discounted. These factors suggest that the negotiation process and the negotiation cycle should be viewed through an interactive and behavioural, rather than a purely mechanical, frame of reference.

Negotiation phases

An awareness of the negotiating cycle offers valuable insights to the manager. This cycle involves a number of phases that, although initially sequential, often oscillate in order to reflect the ebb and flow of the negotiations, which are also likely to be punctuated by adjournments and side meetings. The three phases can be described as arguing, proposing, and exchanging and agreeing.

Arguing

This formative phase begins with the opening statements and supporting arguments from the negotiating parties. The party presenting first has considerable influence in setting the tone of the negotiations. Initial negotiating positions are established by the rejection of demands and demonstrations of inflexibility. This phase can be highly ritualistic and challenging, but affords an opportunity to test commitment, identify tactics and assess strengths. The arguing phase reasserts itself throughout the negotiations. It is manifest each time one side seeks to convince or persuade the other side of its strength of argument. Arguing is an inevitable precursor to compromise and agreement.

Proposing

Having established their relative positions, the negotiators enter an exploratory phase in which each side seeks to discover some potential for flexibility and movement away from initial statements of position. This incorporates tentative offers and concessions of a highly conditional nature. The proposing stage is characterised by probing and encouraging the other side to reveal their real expectations, whilst to some extent concealing your own. Positions are summarised and attempts are made to move forward by finding common ground. It is a delicate phase with progress often dependent upon allowing the other side to concede certain points without necessarily losing face. Concession may be implicit and disguised by the appearance of not having given way and this should be respected. Triumphalism is to be avoided as it may set back the negotiations to the arguing phase. A patronising approach is also likely to have negative consequences.

Emotional language can undo a fragile, emerging or embryonic agreement. As well as avoiding emotionally charged words, personal attacks and put-downs, negotiators need to focus upon the positive and constructive rather than the negative and destructive, in terms of language and approach. It is also important during this phase to listen actively, observe behaviour and make appropriate judgements to enable progression to the next phase of the negotiations.

Exchanging and agreeing

This phase, which typically consumes the most time, is about exchanging concessions, giving and receiving, and consequently it moves negotiations towards agreement. It is dependent on an overlap in the predetermined expectations of the parties involved. Clearly, if there is too wide a gap between negotiating positions, exchange is unlikely to occur. However, if concessions are made, a degree of convergence characterises the negotiations as the parties seek areas of agreement through trading their concessions to gain something in return. The exchange process can generate a momentum of its own. The optimism and relief of concluding negotiations can result in concessions that may have been unthinkable earlier in the negotiations. Experienced negotiators may bide their time and seek to exploit this situation, although they may pay a price for this if any exploitation becomes apparent to the other side.

As it becomes evident that compromise is possible, negotiations can move quickly to the agreement phase. The exchange process is checked, precise statements are made and potential misunderstandings are addressed. A written record serves the purpose of promoting common understanding of the outcomes to the parties – an agreement is not an agreement until it is agreed in writing.

Implementation

Ultimately negotiation has little benefit or value to those involved unless the negotiated outcomes are converted to action. This action has two aspects.

The first is the effective communication with and dissemination of information to those affected by the agreement. The second is the devising of a programme of implementation that includes allocating responsibility, determining resources required and setting timescales. Part of the implementation strategy is to evaluate the outcomes of the negotiations in relation to the agreed objectives and to make an assessment of negotiating performance. This reflective evaluation may include learning points for future negotiations.

Sometimes there is a failure to agree in negotiations, which largely unsatisfactory outcome prompts a reassessment of the options available and an evaluation of whether or not agreement remains a viable proposition. If agreement appears unlikely, an examination of the alternatives becomes necessary. These may include an imposition of terms by one party, should it have the unilateral power to do so – although there are clearly implications for the relationship between the parties if this course of action is pursued. Alternatively, the parties can consider the value and practicability of third-party intervention, either internal or external to the organisation, in order to conciliate, mediate or arbitrate according to the situation (see Chapter 3).

Tactics and skills

As a general principle, making concessions in negotiation without gaining something in return is to be avoided – if negotiation is about giving and receiving, why give away something for nothing? Where a concession is unavoidable some conditions for acceptance can be attached. These conditions should be injected into the negotiations prior to indicating a willingness to concede, because they are then likely to stand more chance of being accepted. Once given, concessions cannot be withdrawn without inflicting some damage on the negotiation process and losing good faith. On the same basis, final offers must be final offers or credibility is affected.

Whilst it is potentially attractive to separate out the negotiating items within a set of negotiations and deal with each in turn, this imposes a constraint on exchanges and concessions. A holistic approach incorporating all the negotiating items, whilst not necessarily as easy to manage as a segmented approach, is ultimately likely to be more balanced and fruitful. Threats and posturing are not illegitimate tactics within the ritualism of negotiation. 'Trickery', however, may be destructive and can affect not only the immediate negotiations but also future negotiations by eroding mutual trust and confidence.

Adjournments are a valuable tactic for negotiators, but their value and scope goes beyond the tactical level. The skilled use of adjournments can have a significant impact upon the progress of the negotiations. Some potential uses of adjournment are shown in Exhibit 37.

Exhibit 37 Uses of adjournments during negotiations

These include:

- to consult privately when it is apparent that there is divergence or disagreement within the negotiating team
- to discuss privately when a new argument becomes evident
- to evaluate progress or lack of it
- to allow an opportunity to consult with others not directly involved
- to consider whether or not to reject an offer
- to take a break in order to regroup or relieve fatigue
- to allow a cooling-off period if breakdown appears to be a probability
- to consider the breaking-off of negotiations, or unilaterally withdrawing, when negotiations have turned sour
- to afford an opportunity for off-the-record communication between negotiation teams.

Frequent adjournments can be disruptive and may suggest a weakness of argument or lack of cohesion or co-ordination on the part of the side asking for them. It can also give the impression that the negotiators are not empowered to make decisions. Adjournments can also be an undesirable irritant to the other party if they are too frequently used, unless of course the aim is to cause irritation. It is advisable to set a time limit for reconvening the negotiations in order to focus effort and ensure that the negotiations are not protracted unnecessarily. This timescale must be realistic, as failure to adhere to an agreed resumption time can be a source of considerable antagonism, with negative implications for the tenor of the negotiations when resumed. This latter point is more likely to apply in the case of adjournments during negotiations in process. It is less likely where a formal adjournment until another day is agreed.

The importance of listening skills in negotiation warrants special attention. It is self-evident, although not always appreciated, that most information can be gathered and obtained through listening actively. There is a good argument for allocating some team members to exclusively listening roles or even allocating observers to listen to specific members of the other side. Examples of active listening skills are indicated in Exhibit 38.

Exhibit 38 Active listening skills

These include:

- concentrating on what is being said
- observing and interpreting associated body language
- encouraging speakers through appropriate verbal and non-verbal responses
- seeking clarification of your understanding
- using pauses and silences through conscious attempts to avoid jumping in
- using appropriate questioning techniques and valuing the importance of open questions
- drawing appropriate and accurate inferences from what may be coded language.

Clearly, natural ability features as a variable in determining negotiation competence. However, there are elements of competence that can be developed through exposure to negotiations, training and experience. Some of the necessary interpersonal and analytical skills are indicated in Exhibit 39. A skill that is a prerequisite for effective negotiation is that of multi-sensory perception – ability to listen, observe, assimilate, reflect, respond, predict and control behaviour simultaneously.

Exhibit 39 Interpersonal and analytical skills in negotiation

---

These include:

- effective oral communication skills
- interpreting non-verbal cues
- awareness and control of body language
- active listening
- sensitivity to people and situations
- ability to think on one's feet (or seat) and articulate appropriately
- creative thinking and problem-solving
- persuasiveness and personal authority
- awareness of power relationships
- judgement
- assertiveness
- quality of presentation
- information processing and evaluation
- teamwork and group dynamics
- recognition of the ritualistic nature of the negotiation encounter.

Effectiveness as a negotiator is founded on these competencies, which include not only practised skills but also a firm knowledge base.

Stress in negotiation

Linked with the idea of negotiating competencies is the concept of 'negotiation stress'. The degree of stress is likely to influence the degree of competence exhibited in negotiations. Pressure, or stress, is a natural facet of negotiation but it is useful to identify the potential sources of stress. First, there is the pressure associated with the need and desire to achieve the predetermined negotiation objectives in the face of opposition. Additionally, in the case of team negotiations, there is the desire to be seen to be making an effective contribution to the team effort. Second, personal credibility is at risk in negotiation. Personal performance may enhance or diminish this and has implications not only for the next negotiation but also for the negotiator's general organisational reputation. The stress derives from wanting to preserve individual credibility and reputation. Third, the negotiating process itself is fertile ground for stress. This may be produced by the environment, disparity in objectives, the emotional context, general fatigue or being the object of personal inference or attack. The skill for the negotiator

413

is to recognise these possibilities and to adopt appropriate compensating and personal adaptation strategies. To the list of general competencies can be added the ability to manage stress.

HANDLING GRIEVANCES

It is important that managers recognise, acknowledge and resolve issues when employees feel dissatisfied and unfairly treated. A failure to do this may result in employees taking action themselves, which can range from poor attendance and poor work performance to leaving the organisation. Action like this is costly and can still leave matters unresolved. Good communication may encourage the informal raising and resolution of concerns and this will reduce the number of formal concerns that are raised with management. However, a small number of formal grievances do not mean that there are no problems; it may be an indication that employees feel that these will not be taken seriously or that they fear repercussions.

The culture of the organisation affects the way in which grievances are received and handled. In a unitary or neo-unitary organisation where there is an assumption of common values and shared objectives, the 'right to manage' is accepted. In this organisational type, conflict can be seen as dysfunctional and employees may feel inhibited about raising formal grievances for fear of being labelled as 'difficult' or 'deviant' and the effect that this labelling may have on their career or work prospects. In a pluralist organisation, where conflict is seen as inevitable and part of everyday working life, it is more likely to be accepted that employees have a right to question managerial decisions. In this case the grievance procedure is more likely to be used as a legitimate mechanism for the resolution of conflict.

A grievance is a formal expression of a perceived dissatisfaction that an employee feels towards an employer. It is based on a procedural right of individuals at work to express their concerns about any aspect of their work situation with their employer. Employers are not required by law to have a grievance procedure. But they are required to provide, within the terms and conditions of employment, the name or job title of a person to whom the employee can apply when seeking redress of any grievance relating to his or her employment (Employment Rights Act 1996). There is no legal requirement for a staged procedure or for the grievance to be resolved to the employee's satisfaction.

In addition, the Employment Relations Act 1999 (ERA 1999) gives an employee the right to be accompanied at a grievance where 'a grievance hearing is related to the performance of a duty by an employer in relation to a worker' (ERA 1999: section 13.5). This means, in practice, that the employer has to look carefully at the detail of the grievance to ensure that this requirement is met and the employee is not denied the legal right of accompaniment. Alternatively, the organisation may decide to give employees the right of accompaniment, or even representation, at all grievance hearings. In addition, under the Employment Rights Act 1996, as amended by the Public Interest Disclosure Act 1998, employers should provide within their grievance procedures the opportunity for workers to raise concerns about workplace malpractice, suspicions of criminal acts, miscarriages of justice and dangers to health and safety. Workers who 'honestly and reasonably' raise these issues have some protection against suffering a detriment.

Grievance procedures

Grievance procedures should be set down in writing, preferably in the employee handbook, and provide an accessible, easily understood framework for the resolution of workplace dissatisfaction. All employees should be made aware of the procedures and how they operate. This is best done at the induction of new employees into the workplace. Exhibit 40 indicates the basic elements that should be incorporated within grievance procedures.

Exhibit 40 **Basic elements of a grievance procedure**

These include:

- there should be a formal procedure
- the procedure should be in writing
- the procedure for raising grievances and for settling them promptly and effectively should be agreed with employee or union representatives
- if there is a separate disputes procedure then the two procedures should be linked
- an individual grievance should be settled as close to the point of origin and within as short a timescale as possible
- the right of accompaniment should be addressed
- confidentiality should be assured.

Grievance procedures should set out the stages through which a grievance is heard and this will normally reflect the organisational hierarchy. The number of stages in the procedure will depend on the size of the organisation and the structure of its management. This provides a structured approach to resolving difficulties and recognises the authority and responsibilities of the parties to the grievance. A staged approach should provide a defined timescale for the resolution of the problem and a review at each stage. There are normally three levels in a staged procedure. The first is at departmental level, where the written formal grievance is presented to and heard by the departmental manager. The line manager should ask the employee to attend the formal meeting, with the right of accompaniment, and to present his or her grievance. This hearing should be held and a response given by the manager within five working days. If the matter is unresolved, the procedure moves on to the second stage – the functional manager stage – when the grievance is raised with a more senior or functional manager. This manager should make arrangements to hear the grievance, giving the right of accompaniment, and respond to the grievance within a further five working days. A failure to resolve the grievance at the second stage will result in a movement on to the third stage, which allows the employee to raise the grievance with the chief executive or a director. At this stage, the employee is again allowed to present the problem, accompanied in line with the procedure, and this hearing should be held and the response should normally be given within 10 working days. Exhibit 41 provides an example of a grievance procedure.

Exhibit 41 **Example of a grievance procedure**

If you feel dissatisfied with any aspect of the application of policies and procedures or with terms and conditions of your employment and how it applies to you, you have the right to raise this issue formally through the grievance procedure. It is expected that you would raise these issues informally with your line manager in the first instance. If any situation is not dealt with to your satisfaction informally, you should take it up formally using the grievance procedure. You have the right under section 10 of the Employment Relations Act 1999 to be accompanied by a recognised trade union official or by an employee of your choice. Your companion has the right to address the hearing and to confer with you during the hearing but is not permitted to answer questions on your behalf.

Stage 1: You should inform your manager, in writing, of the issue that you wish to raise through the formal grievance procedure. Your manager will arrange to meet with you to hear your grievance within five working days.

Stage 2: If the issue remains unresolved following the meeting with your manager, you may progress the matter to your functional manager or your manager's manager. A further meeting will be held within a further five days.

Stage 3: If the issue remains unresolved, the matter may be progressed to the Chief Executive or member of the senior management team as appropriate. This meeting will take place within 10 working days.

Any issue of a sensitive nature that directly involves your line manager may be raised in the first instance with the human resources manager.

If at any time it is not possible to adhere to the timescale agreed in the procedure, agreement should be sought between the two parties for a mutually acceptable date for the hearing and the response. Full records of all stages of grievance procedures should be kept, in line with the Data Protection Act 1998. Written records should also be copied to the employee.

The grievance interview

Any dissatisfaction raised formally through the grievance procedure needs to be taken seriously. If employees feel sufficiently strongly about an issue to use formal processes, this is an indicator of the seriousness of the situation from the employee's perspective and they have the right to a fair and respectful hearing. Issues raised informally should also be taken seriously to reduce the use of formal processes. The grievance interview requires the manager holding the hearing to use a range of skills. The skills required to conduct an effective grievance interview are common to other types of interview. Interviewers should undertake to:

- *Prepare.* A grievance is initiated by the employee and, apart from carefully reading the formal grievance and gathering relevant facts, there may be little that the manager can do to prepare for the first interview. However, the manager should be mindful of setting precedents regarding the decision and therefore it is important that any manager is fully familiar with all relevant policies, procedures and practices associated with the issue under discussion.
- *Provide an appropriate physical environment.* The grievance interview should be held in private; therefore, a room where the hearing can be held without interruption should be made available. This indicates that the grievance is being taken seriously. The employee should be notified of the date, time and place and informed of his or her right under the ERA 1999 to be accompanied.
- *Listen to, and hear, what is being said by the aggrieved individual.* The grievance interview, in common with all interviews, requires good active listening skills to be displayed. This includes appropriate body language and good eye contact to be maintained if the employee is to be reassured that the issue is being listened to and heard fairly.
- *Ask appropriate questions in the appropriate way.* Empathetic questioning is essential so that the manager can understand the nature of the grievance and how the aggrieved feels about it. The nature of the complaint must be fully explored and this will need careful probing so that all the facts are identified and clarified. Questions should be asked in a calm and non-threatening way to encourage the employee to speak openly without feeling that it will disadvantage the case. It is valuable to identify the outcome that the aggrieved person is seeking because it is not uncommon for the situation to require a negotiated settlement; compromise may be the only way forward.
- *Analyse the facts and take a decision.* Having listened to and heard all of the facts of the case, consulted the appropriate policies and procedures and looked for similar cases that may have set precedents, the manager has to take a decision. It may be necessary to take advice or seek clarification from a personnel specialist or another line manager. But care must be taken not to jeopardise the fairness of treatment of the employee by discussing the case with a manager who may be called upon to hear a later stage of the grievance. A manager works within a framework of organisational policies and procedures and any decision taken may set precedents and in effect contribute to organisational 'case law'. Therefore any management interpretation must be one with which the employer can live. If further time is needed for full investigation, employee agreement should be sought for extending the timescale to avoid further complaints of not adhering to the agreed procedure.

Communicating and monitoring decisions

The individual grievance ends with an outcome that is accepted by the individual or the procedure is exhausted, but the situation does not end there. It is important that the decision is communicated clearly to the employee, within the procedural timescale, and that both parties fully understand what exactly has been agreed. The decision should be communicated to the employee in a face-to-face situation and followed up in writing. It is important that the organisation monitors grievances, as they provide useful information for more effective management of people. For example, complaints about a particular policy may be an indicator that it needs to be rewritten so that it is clearer to employees. All managerial decisions taken as a result of formal grievances should be analysed to assess their impact on the organisation and the establishment of precedents. This requires a formal system of monitoring that requires all decisions to be notified to a central point so that they can be aggregated, evaluated and communicated anonymously to all managers. Grievance incidents can provide positive opportunities for formal management development programmes.

HARASSMENT AND BULLYING AT WORK

Harassment at work can have serious implications for the well-being of individual employees and for the organisation in which they work. Individuals may suffer stress, and the resultant ill health, increased rates of absence and reduced productivity could lead to the loss of good employees. The culture of the organisation may become damaged by ignored allegations of harassment and bullying with a potential decline in public image. Dealing with allegations of harassment or bullying requires separate procedures from grievance procedures. They also need particular managerial skills. The EU Code of Practice and the Commission for Racial Equality (CRE) defines harassment as 'unwanted conduct of a sexual (racial) nature, or other conduct based on sex (race), affecting the dignity of men and women at work'. Harassment can occur on other factors, such as religion, sexual orientation or age. Ishmael and Alemoru (1999) define bullying as 'persistent, offensive, intimidating, malicious or insulting behaviour, which amounts to an abuse of power and makes the recipient feel upset, threatened, humiliated or vulnerable'. Although there are notable differences between harassment and bullying, they are both demonstrations of unacceptable behaviour affecting the dignity of men and women at work and need to be dealt with accordingly. A policy needs to clearly define what constitutes harassment and the definition identifies the issue of unwelcome conduct as a deciding criterion. A recent Employment Appeal Tribunal (EAT) gave the following guidance: 'The essential characteristic of sexual harassment is that it is words or conduct which are unwelcome to the recipient and it is for the recipient to decide for themselves what is acceptable to them and what they regard as offensive.' In other words, it is a subjective test rather than an objective test.

The recipient therefore needs to make it clear that the behaviour is unacceptable and, provided any reasonable person would understand the conduct to be rejected, that 'continuation of the conduct would, generally, be regarded as harassment'.

The development of a policy on Dignity at Work based on the EU Recommendation and Code of Practice on the Dignity of Men and Women at Work provides a framework for the management of these issues in the workplace. The recommendation proposes policies and procedures, preferably agreed with employees, that outlaw harassment and bullying, set out managerial duties to implement the policy, require all employees to comply and give employees the right to complain. Managers need to be responsive to complaints and allegations, maintain confidentiality and put a stop to victimisation following any complaint. A procedure for the resolution of complaints of harassment and bullying needs to be agreed and in place to enable allegations to be handled fairly, confidentially and in a timely way. The grievance procedure may be an inadequate way to handle these issues, as the alleged perpetrator may be in direct line of management with the recipient. The procedure should provide practical guidance on what to do, provide the opportunity for informal resolution, offer advice through counselling services and link with disciplinary procedures.

The process of handling allegations about harassment and bullying should cover the following issues:

- The formal or informal report should be handled sensitively and the recipient encouraged to explore the options for action. The options range from doing nothing to formally reporting the incident through the appropriate complaints procedure.
- The alleged harrasser should be seen and told of the alleged behaviour causing distress, that it is considered harassment and that it must stop. Natural justice principles demand that the harasser should know of the allegation, be given the opportunity to respond or to change the behaviour. However, it is worth reflecting that there is some behaviour that is so serious that it contravenes criminal law, in which case the harasser should be informed that it is to be reported to the police.
- The employee suffering harassment or bullying should be advised to keep a diary or other record of incidents. The precise details from diary notes with specific dates, times, places and descriptions of events increases the credibility of the allegation and may increase the confidence of the recipient to proceed to the formal procedure.
- If the harassment stops, the recipient may decide to take no further action and this decision should normally be respected. If the employer has evidence that this is not an isolated incident, a discussion with the employee may bring about a change in behaviour.
- If the harassment does not stop, the employee being harassed may choose to proceed to the formal policy. This will require a full investigation, interviewing witnesses and taking of full statements. Confidentiality is vitally important at this stage of the investigation

- Proven cases of harassment or bullying can lead to advice but no punitive action, a disciplinary penalty, action short of dismissal or dismissal. It may be appropriate to redeploy either the harasser or the recipient, but whichever course of action is taken, the recipient of the harassment should not be disadvantaged or this may constitute discrimination.

The grievance procedure should make reference to the Dignity at Work Policy and in particular draw attention to the existence of a different reporting procedure. Disciplinary procedures should also include reference to harassment and bullying and their relationship to these procedures.

DISCIPLINE AT WORK

Discipline at work incorporates concepts of self-discipline, peer discipline and managerial discipline. Managerial discipline is the focus of this section, as a disciplinary procedure emphasises managerial values and standards. Discipline can be defined as constructive action instigated by management against an employee who fails to meet reasonable and legitimate expectations in terms of performance, conduct or adherence to rules (Corbridge and Pilbeam 1998). Ethics, professionalism and effective managerial practice argue for an emphasis on problem-solving, prevention and constructive approaches to discipline issues, as these are more likely to encourage a positive response from the employee. It also maximises the opportunity for acceptance of the problem, correction of the behaviour or performance, and reconciliation of the parties, thereby protecting the organisation's investment in its human capital. A disciplinary process can therefore be viewed as an individual conflict-resolving mechanism within the employment relationship, with an emphasis on improvement and remedy rather than on punitive measures. Where encouragement, guidance, support or training do not result in employee improvement to an acceptable managerial standard, punishment may, however, be necessary. Sanctions against the employee can act as a deterrent to the individual behaviour or conduct and, by example, for the workforce as a whole. Fairness, equity and consistency in the management approach to discipline will minimise disagreements and benefit employee relations within the organisation. The Advisory, Conciliation and Arbitration Service Code of Practice (ACAS 2000a: 6) states: 'Disciplinary procedures should not be viewed primarily as a means of imposing sanctions. Rather they should be seen as a way of helping and encouraging improvement amongst employees whose conduct or standard of work is unsatisfactory.'

Disciplinary rules and procedures

Disciplinary rules are necessary for promoting order and avoiding ambiguity and inconsistency in employee relations. By setting standards, rules determine acceptable and unacceptable employee behaviour and importantly let employees know where they stand. Because managers are primarily responsible for the maintenance of discipline at work, disciplinary rules are normally initiated and formulated by management, although they may be subject to consultation, negotiation or co-determination. If rules are to be effective, they need to be perceived as reasonable by employees and employee representatives, and accepted as workable by line managers who have to enforce them. Rules reflect legitimate managerial authority, based on the common-law duty of employees to obey reasonable and legitimate instructions given by the employer, and enable managers to obtain compliance to instructions in the pursuit of organisational effectiveness. While management principally determines disciplinary rules, they encompass obligations incurred under statute law, for example in relation to health and safety and non-discrimination on the grounds of sex, race or disability. They also reflect 'acceptable behaviour' within a wider societal sense, for example, values associated with honesty, propriety and non-violence.

Disciplinary rules are also influenced by the development of custom and practice, and so it is evident that rather than being characterised as stable rules, they are subject to continuous change. These forces for change in terms of organisation rules have implications for the ongoing process of managerial communication of the rules. Managers therefore face the challenge of ensuring that disciplinary rules are clear, accessible and understood. Managers must also communicate clearly the consequences of breaking the rules, particularly where the breaking of a rule may threaten continued employment. The communication issues are, first, appropriate use of language and, second, the effective means of communication. The communication process encompasses prominent display, word of mouth, team briefings and incorporation of rules into an employee handbook or other documents. While managers cannot specify a rule for every occasion, the aim should be to specify clearly and precisely those rules necessary for the efficient and safe performance of work and for the maintenance of satisfactory relations within the workforce and between employees and management. Also, rules should not be so general as to be meaningless (ACAS 2000a). The design of effective rules is more likely to be based on the principle of voluntary compliance, rather than on the imposition of sanctions for breaking the rules.

Rules set standards and a disciplinary procedure provides a means of ensuring that these standards are met and a method for dealing with a failure to meet them. The Employment Rights Act 1996 (ERA 1996) creates an employer obligation to ensure that the principal statement of employment conditions makes reference to rules, disciplinary procedures and appeals procedures. A disciplinary procedure should include a general statement regarding the employer's attitude towards discipline. This should indicate that a precursor to formal disciplinary action will be counselling or informal managerial intervention, with the aim of resolving disciplinary problems at the lowest possible level as a normal part of effective day-to-day management. Only when this informal approach fails will it be necessary to escalate the matter and enter a formal disciplinary procedure.

Disciplinary procedures should conform to the 'principles of natural justice'. These principles have emerged from ideas of equity, due process and model legal practice and are therefore associated with citizen consent to the rule of law within civilised societies. In the employee relations context, the advantage is in the employee, as corporate citizen, consenting to abide by managerial rules because justice will be dispensed fairly. An illustration of these principles in an employment context is provided in Exhibit 42. Incorporation of these principles into disciplinary procedures is therefore likely to enhance the perceived equity of the procedures and foster voluntary compliance with the rules. Any perceived unfairness may create resentment and militate against compliance or correction. The principles of natural justice are also important in enabling an employer to demonstrate 'reasonableness in the circumstances' in relation to employee dismissal. In order to command respect and support, and to operate effectively, disciplinary procedures must also be accepted as fair and equitable by line managers and facilitate consistent managerial action.

Exhibit 42 Principles of natural justice in employment

These incorporate:

- knowledge of the standards or behaviour expected
- knowledge of the alleged failure and the nature of the allegation
- an investigation to establish a prima facie case should normally precede any allegation
- an opportunity to offer an explanation and for this explanation to be heard and considered fairly
- an opportunity to be accompanied or represented
- any penalty should be appropriate to the offence and take account of any mitigating factors
- an opportunity and support to improve behaviour, except when misconduct goes to the root of the contract, should normally be provided
- a right of appeal to a higher authority.

According to the ACAS code of practice on disciplinary and grievance procedures, disciplinary procedures should:

- be in writing
- specify to whom they apply
- be non-discriminatory
- provide for matters to be dealt with quickly and within specified time limits
- address the issue of confidentiality
- indicate the disciplinary actions that may be taken
- specify the levels of management that have the authority to take the various forms of disciplinary action (ensuring that immediate superiors do not normally have the power to dismiss without reference to senior management)
- provide for employees to be informed of the complaints against them and

any relevant evidence before any hearing, and to be given an opportunity to state their case before decisions are reached

- inform workers of their statutory, and any other, right to be accompanied
- ensure that, except for gross misconduct, no employees are dismissed for a first breach of discipline
- ensure that disciplinary action is not taken until the case has been fully investigated
- ensure that the individuals are given an explanation for any penalty imposed
- provide a right of appeal – normally to a higher level of management – and specify the procedure to be followed.

The ACAS code of practice on disciplinary practice and procedures is not legally binding upon employers. But it is admissible in evidence and any provision of the code which appears to an employment tribunal to be relevant to any question arising in the proceedings is required to be taken into account (ACAS 2000a). The word 'required' signifies that great store should be placed on the code by employers. Even if disciplinary rules are instigated and primarily formulated by managers, there is a case for disciplinary procedures being agreed through consultation or negotiation with employees or their representatives in order to enhance moral authority, to command respect and to work effectively.

A disciplinary procedure should normally be incremental and should provide for a range of progressive actions against employees, with a view to correcting the problem. If a disciplinary issue is not resolved at an informal level, it may be necessary to enter the formal disciplinary procedure. The first stage of the formal procedure may be a recorded oral warning. Warnings should always make clear the consequences of a failure to improve or a repetition of the offence. The next stage of the procedure should be a written warning that, depending upon the severity of the case, may or may not be a final written warning. The final stage may be either 'ASOD' (action short of dismissal, including disciplinary transfer, or reduction in status and responsibility) or termination of employment. An indicative outline of the stages in a disciplinary procedure is provided in Figure 20, but the stages should not be viewed as a strict sequence, for managerial flexibility to enter at an appropriate stage, depending on the seriousness of the allegation, is both legitimate and necessary. The importance of having and following a proper procedure was highlighted by *Polkey* v. *A E Dayton Services* (1987 IRLR 503), where a dismissal was found to be unfair because of a procedural failure. Failure to follow a fair and reasonable procedure is, therefore, not only ineffective managerial practice but may also affect the legitimacy of the disciplinary action itself.

Disciplinary hearings

The importance of thorough investigation in disciplinary matters cannot be overemphasised. Before disciplinary action is initiated, there needs to be a

Figure 20 **Principal stages of a disciplinary procedure**

Disciplinary matter and the procedural stage	Management response	Management level, with advice from personnel
1 Misconduct that is not serious	Oral warning	Team leader or supervisor
2 More serious misconduct or repeated misconduct	Written warning	Supervisor or line manager
3 Serious misconduct or repeated misconduct	Final written warning and/or action short of dismissal	Line manager and/or senior manager
4 Gross misconduct or further misconduct	Dismissal or action short of dismissal	Senior manager

prima facie case of misconduct, breach of rules or unacceptable standards of work. It may be appropriate to suspend the employee during the investigation, particularly in cases of apparent gross misconduct. However, unwarranted suspension will be to the detriment of the problem-solving approach and to perceptions of equity. The investigation should include the objective collection of both oral and written evidence. Checking the employee's record is also essential and may contribute to the decision of whether or not to proceed. If the evidence suggests that an allegation is justified, the employee should be informed and a suitable time and place arranged for the hearing. The right to be accompanied or to be represented should be pointed out to the employee and any relevant evidence should be given to the employee before the hearing. As well as the right to a companion at a grievance hearing, section 10 of the ERA 1999 gives workers (not just employees) the right to make a reasonable request to be accompanied at a formal disciplinary hearing. The worker chooses the companion, who can be a fellow worker or a certified trade union official (or certified workplace representative). The role is one of companion rather than representative. The companion can confer with the worker during the hearing and is permitted to address the hearing but has no legal right to answer questions on behalf of the worker. The worker may propose an alternative date for the hearing if the chosen companion is not available on the date proposed for the hearing. In this case the employer is required to postpone the hearing to the date proposed by the worker, provided that the alternative date is reasonable, has regard for the availability of the manager and falls before the end of five working days of the date proposed by the employer. The companion is entitled to reasonable time off during working hours in order to fulfil his or her responsibilities (Temperton 2000, Lewis and Sargeant 2000).

The disciplinary hearing is potentially an emotional encounter and requires sensitive handling. Professionalism and good interpersonal skills are crucial. An introduction of those present and reasons for attendance should precede the hearing. The employer should explain the purpose of the hearing and where it fits into the formal disciplinary procedure. The allegation should be clearly stated, going through the evidence and concentrating on the facts. The employee should be given the opportunity to respond to the allegation and explain any actions. The employer must listen to and consider the employee's response to the allegation. If it is apparent that there is no case to answer, the hearing should be terminated and no further action taken against the employee. If the employee does not offer an acceptable explanation or justification, a discussion should follow during which the problem is clarified and an acceptance of employee responsibility for resolving or improving the situation is encouraged.

If disciplinary action seems necessary, due consideration of all the circumstances is normally achieved by adjourning the hearing. During the adjournment, proper weight should be given to the employee's explanation and also to any special factors that have emerged or are known. Employers are able to act upon the establishment of a reasonable belief based on the information available at the time. There is no obligation to prove an allegation beyond 'reasonable doubt'. The decision or outcome of the disciplinary hearing should be clearly and unambiguously communicated to the employee, as should the right to appeal against the decision if there is dissatisfaction with the outcome.

This simple description of the hearing process belies the managerial skills required. The potential for conflict between employer and employee perspectives militates against a smooth process, despite the emphasis on thorough preparation and professionalism. The interviewing manager can be confronted with a range of responses from aggression or distress, on the one hand, to passiveness and disinterest on the other. The employee may reject the allegation outright or engage in self-denial behaviour. It is important in these circumstances to be able to remain calm and rational and demonstrate a professional, sensitive and objective approach. The information-gathering nature of the hearing requires good questioning skills and active listening. The ability to weigh the balance of probabilities, make an objective judgement and decide on appropriate action are skills that will determine the success or otherwise of the disciplinary process. Managers need to recognise and accept the responsibility associated with being 'prosecutor, judge and jury'. The process should not be treated merely as a means for confirming managerial concerns but as an opportunity for resolving conflict in the employment relationship through corrective action.

The result of the hearing needs to be formally communicated to the employee, with copies to the employee's representative, if appropriate. Clearly this requires effective writing skills, not only because of the need to have an accurate record for the employee's file and to demonstrate procedural fairness, but also to ensure that the employee understands the decision. Any communication should be constructed in language and style that the employee understands. Performance or conduct should be monitored and reviewed and the employee either told of a satisfactory outcome or, failing this, the next stage of the procedure may need to be invoked. Warnings, except in extreme cases, should expire and be 'spent' after a predetermined period. This is in the interests of natural justice so that the employee, having made a mistake and paid the appropriate penalty, has the opportunity to 'wipe the slate clean' in due course. In relation to substandard performance, as opposed to misconduct, some organisations have separate capability procedures. There are, for example, restoring-efficiency procedures in the civil service, in order to communicate a more positive, problem-solving and partnership approach to managing the return to effective performance, although ultimately the disciplinary procedure may need to be invoked. A positive approach coupled with fairness and consistency in individual matters of discipline are likely to contribute to good employment relations and perhaps a corrective action procedure is a more appropriate name for a disciplinary procedure.

THE LAW AND DISMISSAL

The right of an employee not to be unfairly dismissed originated in the Industrial Relations Act 1971. It was consolidated most recently in the ERA 1996, sections 94–134 in Part X. The law provides an employee with a limited job property right and affords some protection against unreasonable behaviour by the employer ending in loss of employment. The employer is in no way denied the freedom to dismiss individuals; in fact, legislation ensures that employers can legitimately dismiss employees for 'fair' reasons in 'reasonable circumstances' by providing, in effect, a set of rules for the employer to follow. Thus the law actually legitimises dismissal by defining it as fair and reasonable in certain circumstances, through providing a set of rules and guidelines allowing employers to dismiss employees without fear of adverse consequences. And, in this way, the right of managers to dismiss is made legitimate (Corbridge and Pilbeam 1998).

However, employment protection legislation serves to encourage effective employment practice and is, in reality, aimed at persuading employers to act reasonably and fairly in the circumstances. The legislation enhances the role of ACAS as a conciliator and ACAS has a statutory obligation to intervene at the request of either party or on its own initiative when a claim of unfair dismissal is lodged. This has a significant impact upon the number of cases that are settled or withdrawn before reaching an employment tribunal, with only 30 per cent of claims actually being heard (ACAS *Annual Reports*). The legal remedies for employees are best viewed as a backstop.

Employees are now protected against unfair dismissal after one year's continuous service, unless they have reached state retirement age or normal retirement age for the organisation, although this age discrimination is the subject of legal challenge. This one-year qualification may be subject to further reduction, either through precedent created by particular cases, through interpretation of European Union Directives, or another change in government policy. Since the ERA 1999, employees with fixed-term contracts can no longer waive their right to protection against unfair dismissal in the case of non-renewal of the contract. This makes fixed-term contracts a less flexible employment arrangement for employers. The Fixed-Term Contracts Directive, which seeks to ensure parity of treatment for those employed on fixed-term contracts, while good for workers, is likely to further erode employer flexibilities. There is normally no service requirement in cases of inadmissible reasons for dismissal. Indicative examples of potentially inadmissible reasons include dismissal on the grounds of:

- pregnancy, maternity, sex, race or disability
- spent convictions
- refusal to work on a Sunday in the case of protected workers
- asserting a statutory employment right
- trade union membership, activity or non-membership
- the relevant transfer of an undertaking
- health and safety activities or action
- no reason being given.

Dismissal takes place when either the employer terminates the contract, with or without notice, or when the employee resigns by reason of the employer's behaviour and the employee considers the employer to have repudiated the contract by its actions or behaviour. Constructive dismissal, as this second case is known, may consist of a serious single act that is deemed to have destroyed the contract or alternatively it may constitute a series of smaller incidents that cumulatively add up to repudiation of the contract. Indicative examples of constructive dismissal include:

- issuing unjustified warnings or undermining authority or expressing unwarranted suspicions
- using provocative or defamatory language or engaging in physical or psychological abuse
- preventing access to pay increases, promotion or development opportunities
- making unreasonable and substantial changes to job duties or terms and conditions
- failing to respond effectively to genuine grievances or failing to provide effective support to victims of harassment, bullying or unfair discrimination
- insisting on unsafe working practices
- insisting on excessive workloads.

427

For a dismissal to be fair it has to exhibit the twin characteristics of being for a fair reason and being reasonable in the circumstances. The five potentially fair reasons for dismissal are related to:

- conduct of the employee
- the employee's capability or qualification
- redundancy
- a statutory duty that will be contravened, by the employee or the employer, if employment continues
- some other substantial reason of a kind justifying dismissal.

Although these reasons provide convenient categories, it is the substantial merits of each incident or case that determine whether or not the dismissal is for a fair reason. The reasonableness of each decision relates to whether the dismissal is based upon sufficient factual evidence, whether the correct procedures have been followed, whether dismissal as a penalty is justified, and importantly whether dismissal fell within the range of responses of a reasonable employer. There is some legal debate about whether employment tribunals (ETs) should continue to use the 'band of reasonable responses' test or whether a strict interpretation of the law requires ETs to substitute their own judgements of the merits of the case (see *Hadden* v. *Van den Bergh Foods Ltd* 1999 IRLR 672). This would tend to favour employees more than employers. Reasonableness is not an objective standard and takes account also of the employer's size and resources.

An employer does not have to prove employee fault beyond reasonable doubt. The burden of proof is one of establishing a genuine and reasonable belief based on information available at the time, following proper investigation; it is a 'balance of probabilities' test as opposed to proving allegations 'beyond reasonable doubt'. As part of any investigation, the employer is expected to talk to the employee, listen and consider any explanations. This makes it essential that dismissals are well documented. Fair reasons for dismissal require that a distinction is drawn between general misconduct, which is dealt with within the incremental framework of a disciplinary procedure, and gross misconduct, which may justify summary dismissal for one occurrence. Gross misconduct may include acts of drunkenness, theft, violence, breach of confidence, serious and wilful refusal to conform to legitimate managerial instructions or serious misconduct outside the workplace. Alleged or suspected gross misconduct does not obviate the need for thorough investigation or the opportunity for employees to offer an explanation for their behaviour, but the serious nature of these offences can go to the root of the contract and effectively destroy it. There is a duty on the part of the employer to ensure that what may constitute gross misconduct, and its potential consequences, are clearly and unequivocally communicated to all employees.

Capability of the employee may be in question if there is a failure to achieve a satisfactory standard of work or of job performance. If this is a failure to exercise competence, this may constitute misconduct. However, if the issue is one of incompetence or relative incompetence, the employer needs to point out the performance shortfall, specify the standard expected, indicate the consequences of a failure to meet the standard and give the employee reasonable time to improve. Within this process, there is an implicit obligation for the employer to provide reasonable and necessary support, training and guidance to the employee.

Incapability through ill health requires particularly sensitive handling and a distinction needs to be drawn between frequent short-term absences and long-term ill health. The issue is ultimately whether the employee is able to give continuous and effective service and each situation requires consultation with the employee and a prognosis in relation to the job before deciding upon a course of action. Availability of alternative work needs to be considered, although there is no obligation upon the employer to create an alternative job. Age of the employee, length of service, likelihood of a return to health and the impact of the absence upon the organisation are all factors to be taken into account. When the employer has exhausted alternatives and can no longer be reasonably expected to accommodate health limitations or hold a job open, then the 'enough is enough' point is reached and dismissal may be fair and reasonable. Reasonable adjustments may need to be made for disabled employees (Disability Discrimination Act 1995).

Redundancy occurs when the requirements for a particular type of work cease or diminish. Selection for redundancy requires employers to act reasonably and from genuine motives. There is a legal requirement to consult employees and their representatives (see below).

Dismissal for the reason that a statutory duty prevents employment continuing relates to a situation where it would be unlawful for an employee to continue working in the position for which he or she was contractually employed. Although this appears straightforward, the experience is that dismissal on these grounds is rarely justified. Indicative examples include loss of a driving licence in certain circumstances or loss of a licence to practice in certain professions or a failure to renew a work permit.

Some other substantial reason (SOSR) is included as a fair reason for dismissal to give employers scope to dismiss an employee for a reason not conveniently falling into one of the other four categories discussed above. The reason for dismissal must be substantial, and not trivial, and it must justify dismissal. Described by some as an 'employer's charter', it has been used for dismissals relating to third-party pressure to dismiss, personality conflicts, relationships between employees and business reorganisation requiring variation to contractual terms. In the latter category, decisions by ETs are generally supportive of the needs of the business, thus overriding the interests of the individual employee where this is justified on commercial or efficiency grounds. This entails an assessment of the balance of advantage to the employer, through reorganisation, against disadvantage to the employee. There remains a requirement for employers to achieve change through consultation, persuasion and agreement. Effectively, SOSR provides a broad category in respect of the managerial prerogative of parting company with unacceptable employees.

Remedies for unfair dismissal

It is important for managers to be aware of the remedies for unfair dismissal and also to be able to prepare effectively for an ET case. Dealing with remedies first, where an ET finds that there has been no unfair dismissal, the matter ends, subject to any appeal by the applicant on a point of law. In cases where a tribunal is satisfied that dismissal is unfair, it has powers to order reinstatement or re-engagement of the employee. Reinstatement involves a return to the employee's previous job and acting as if dismissal had not taken place. Re-engagement involves a return to a comparable or otherwise suitable position. In considering the alternatives of reinstatement and re-engagement, ETs will consider the applicant's wishes and any representation made by the employer relating to practicability. An employer cannot be compelled to take back an employee, but refusal to do so may result in an award of additional compensation to the employee. In reality, fewer than 1 per cent of successful unfair dismissal claims result in re-engagement or reinstatement, principally because the adversarial nature of the legal process, and the time taken to reach a decision, condemn the employment relationship to irretrievable breakdown.

An alternative to reinstatement or re-engagement, and the most commonly exercised remedy, is the award of compensation to the unfairly dismissed employee. This consists of a basic award based upon length of service and calculated on the same basis as redundancy payments. The tribunal may also make a compensatory award to take account of the employee's current and future financial losses arising from the dismissal, although the employee has an obligation to mitigate this loss by actively seeking other work. The compensation awarded takes account of the contribution by the employee to the dismissal and the award may be reduced in proportion to that contribution. An additional award may be made where an employer rejects an order to reinstatement or re-engagement and a special award is available in dismissal that relates to health and safety or trade union matters. Awards are capped at a maximum of £50,000, except in dismissals relating to unlawful sex, race or disability discrimination. However, the median award is only of the order of £3,000 (ACAS *Annual Reports*).

Preparing for employment tribunals

An employee – who is the applicant – with a complaint normally completes form ET1, identifying the employer, indicating the grounds for the claim and the remedy being sought. The application must normally be made within three months of the effective date of dismissal. After an assessment of jurisdiction (the entitlement to claim) by the Central Office of Employment Tribunals, it is sent to the employer (the respondent) and to ACAS, via the regional office. The employer is obliged to respond on form ET3, normally within 14 days. Clearly the response by the employer has to be preceded by several considerations and points of decision, the first of which is to decide whether to concede or to contest the claim. This decision should take account of:

- an appreciation of the legislation that may be relevant to the case
- the skills required to defend the case and whether legal representation is necessary
- a judgement on how well the case has been handled within the organisation in relation to documentation and the conduct of those involved
- the likely consequences and cost of the decision to proceed; importantly, what is the applicant likely to achieve if successful, and would it be better to seek an out-of-court settlement?

If it is decided to contest the claim, it is necessary for the employer to gather the relevant documentation for consideration and also identify and consult the relevant witnesses and parties to the dismissal. This leads to a review of the situation, with consideration being given to the role of an ACAS conciliation officer, who may contact the applicant or the applicant's representative. This is done with a view to reducing the differences between the employer and employee and seeking to identify areas of consensus as a way of progressing towards an acceptable resolution. A pre-hearing assessment may be appropriate as a means of testing commitment and providing guidance on the merits of the case of both parties (Employment Department 1999).

If, despite these efforts, the case goes to a tribunal, the preparation required relates to proper and accurate presentation of the evidence. In addition, a co-ordinated and cohesive approach by those involved is essential, together with determination of a strategy appropriate to the case. The principles relating to negotiation preparation and negotiation activity (see above) are transferable to defending unfair dismissal claims. Tribunal chairs are not generally sympathetic to surprises or court room antics and these should be avoided.

Exhibit 43 Principles of binding arbitration in individual employment disputes

---

- unfair dismissal claims only and where there are no jurisdictional issues
- arbitration as a binding alternative where both parties agree, with no right of appeal, except arbitrator misconduct
- arbitrator to follow the ACAS Code and Advisory Booklet on Discipline at Work
- arbitrator to fix the procedure and rules of evidence with the format being investigative rather than adversarial
- representatives permitted, but not necessarily to be lawyers, and proceedings to be free from legal argument and case law
- arbitrator could make the same awards as an ET
- proceedings are in private and decision is not to be published

---

Ultimately, employers have no grounds for concern if they have acted reasonably, have followed the principles of natural justice, have ensured that disciplinary action is taken according to agreed procedure by skilled interviewers, have documented the case appropriately and have prepared thoroughly for the tribunal. However, this reassurance does not prevent defending a claim from being time-consuming and costly or from generating managerial anxiety. A number of factors are resulting in the development of proposals for a binding arbitration alternative, as shown in Exhibit 43. This is because of the tribunal burden on employers, a return to the principle of a quick, speedy and informal response to claims for employees and concern about the escalating number of tribunal claims. These have increased from 80,000 in 1994 to 120,000 in 1999, with approximately 35 per cent of these relating to unfair dismissal (ACAS *Annual Reports*).

MANAGING REDUNDANCY

Redundancy is one of the potentially fair reasons for dismissal referred to above. Section 139 (1) of the ERA 1996 states that redundancy occurs when the reason for dismissal is wholly or mainly attributable to the employer having ceased or intending 'to cease to carry on the business for the purposes for which the employee was employed'. Alternatively, 'the employer has ceased or intends to cease to carry on that business in the place where the employee was so employed'. Redundancy also occurs where 'the requirements of that business for employees to carry out work of a particular kind, or for employees to carry out work of a particular kind in the place where the employee was employed by the employer, have ceased or diminished or are expected to cease or diminish'. The legal framework for redundancy consists of four elements:

- payment of compensation for job loss
- the requirement for consultation with employees for both collective redundancy and individual redundancy
- protection against unfair selection for redundancy
- other statutory rights.

Redundancy payments

Legislation provides for compensation payments for loss of employment due to redundancy, subject to age, length of service and statutory maximum weekly wage, as shown in Table 26. Entitlement is calculated on completed years of employment subject to a maximum of 20 years' service and subject to a maximum weekly 'pay' of £240. From the age of 64, entitlement calculated on the 41–63 formula is reduced by 1/12 for each month of service beyond 64. The maximum statutory redundancy payment is therefore only just over £7,000. The employee has a right to a written statement of how the redundancy payment is calculated and any dispute over payment can be taken to an ET. Employees need two years' service to qualify for statutory redundancy payments

Requirement for consultation

There is a requirement for consultation between employers and employees in a redundancy situation, regardless of the number of employees to be

432

Table 26 **Statutory minimum redundancy payments**

Age	Number of weeks' pay
18–21	$1/2$ week's pay for every completed year
22–40	1 week's pay for every completed year
41–63	$1^1/2$ weeks' pay for every completed year
over 64	overall redundancy entitlement reduced by $1/12$ for every month worked in the final year of work

made redundant. The Collective Redundancy and Transfer of Undertakings (Protection of Employment) Regulations 1995 require the employer to consult with 'appropriate representatives' when 20 or more staff are to be made redundant. Even when there is only one individual employee being made redundant, there is a statutory obligation to follow a reasonable procedure, including meaningful consultation with that individual. Failure to consult may result in the reasonableness of the dismissal being challenged.

The employer must inform the Department of Trade and Industry of the number of workers to be made redundant. The minimum statutory periods for consultation are as follows:

- where 20–99 employees are to be made redundant within a 30-day period, the consultation must take place at least 30 days before the first redundancy takes place
- where more than 100 employees are to be made redundant within a 90-day period, the consultation must take place at least 90 days before the first redundancy takes place
- where there are fewer than 20 employees or the redundancy is spread over a longer period of time, management is still required to consult.

Specific information must be provided by management to the representatives prior to the consultation. This includes:

- the reason for the proposed redundancy
- the number and types of employees to be made redundant
- the total number of employees of this type employed
- the proposed selection criteria
- arrangements for redundancy payments
- the proposed implementation and the timing.

Although consultation, with a view to reaching agreement, is compulsory, there is no requirement for agreement to be reached with the employee representatives.

Selection for redundancy

The selection criteria to be used by an employer in a redundancy situation are not defined in law. However, the employer should consult on appropriate selection criteria and employees must know the basis of selection. Selection should be based on objective criteria and be reasonable in the circumstances. Care must be taken in determining selection criteria that unlawful discrimination does not take place. Redundancy can be non-compulsory or compulsory. Non-compulsory redundancy requires that employees in effect choose to accept redundancy rather than be forced out of employment. They may, however, need attractive financial incentives to go. This may increase the financial costs for the employer, but this may be offset by a less adversarial approach to redundancy. Difficulties may still arise if there are too few or too many volunteers and the employer may still have to make selection decisions.

Last-in first-out (LIFO) is a method that is transparent, easy to apply and easy for the workforce to understand. Selection based on length of service has a 'felt-fair' appeal but it can lead to skill mix problems and care must be taken to ensure that unlawful discrimination does not occur and that a proportion of the workforce does not suffer a detriment due to taking career breaks.

Employee efficiency and work performance criteria may be used for redundancy selection. These may include attendance and timekeeping, as well as performance appraisal evaluation. Again, care is needed to ensure that up-to-date and accurate data are used for this approach, as it may be argued that the real reason for dismissal is not redundancy but conduct or capability. A matrix of multiple criteria may be used that includes performance and attendance data alongside skills, qualifications and experience. The factors are decided upon, weighted and scored objectively, so that staff can see their position relative to others and hence the criteria are transparent. ETs often favour this 'measured factor' approach. Care is needed with any criteria that includes attendance to ensure that the employer stays within the requirements of the Disability Discrimination Act 1995.

Other statutory rights

Any employee who qualifies for statutory redundancy payment is entitled to 'reasonable' time off with pay to seek future work. The law does not define 'reasonable', but any employer refusing time off to an employee under redundancy notice may be required to demonstrate to an ET that the decision was reasonable. The ERA 1996 allows an employee who is under notice of redundancy to have a trial period of up to four weeks in a job that may be seen as 'reasonable alternative employment' without forfeiting the right to redundancy if the job proves to be unsuitable.

Redundancy policies

In order to plan for redundancy situations, which may occur in any organisation, management should develop a redundancy policy, which will provide a framework for action if and when the occasion arises. If an agreed policy is in place, then employer and employees are not dealing with the details for action whilst under the stress of the situation. The agreed policy should be supplemented by a procedure which in effect provides a plan of action for the implementation. The redundancy policy should form part of the package of employment policies that any 'model' employer has at its disposal. The policy should include:

- an opening statement about management attitude to employment levels, together with recognition that the requirements for labour are not static and that change over time is inevitable
- individual and collective consultation arrangements
- steps to be taken to reduce the likelihood of redundancy
- selection criteria
- details of redundancy payment arrangements
- details of redeployment procedures
- a statement on the appeals procedure
- provision of support systems, such as outplacement, counselling and training.

Handling redundancy

Announcement of redundancy in any organisation gives rise to feelings of anxiety and insecurity in the workforce. Often first indications of organisational difficulties result in the informal communications system coming into operation, with rumour and misinformation exaggerating the situation and increasing anxieties. For this reason organisations may try to conceal the redundancy situation. The timing of an announcement is important and needs careful handling, and if managers get it wrong, it can lead to loss of trust and confidence in managers with consequential problems in the longer term. When the announcement is made, any individuals 'at risk' from redundancy should be seen by their manager. Managers will need the skills and confidence to handle what might be an emotional and difficult situation. They must be prepared for a variety of responses to the situation and feel equipped to handle the range of reactions with which they may be faced. There are various options open to managers for the handling of the redundancy situation following the announcement:

- it can be handled within current management resources
- it can be handled by freeing up permanent managers and bringing in temporary staff
- it can be handled by providing outplacement services.

The choice will depend on the size of the organisation, the extent of the redundancies and the skills and abilities of the managers. The managerial skills required will include: interviewing and listening skills, communication skills and problem-solving skills. Interviewing skills have been covered elsewhere in this chapter, but in redundancy interviews additional skills may be required to enable the manager to recognise and handle individual responses, which may include anger, disbelief, denial, fear and anxiety. The manager will need to know when to speak and when to remain silent and listen. The redundancy interview should not be hurried but should allow time for the employees to express their feelings and be heard. Important information should be provided, in writing, for the employees to take away, as, in times of stress, they may not remember important details of timing and payments. Line managers themselves may be anxious as they too may be under stress about potentially losing their jobs. Communication skills are important in facilitating exchange of information between employee and employer. Managers should have the opportunity to practice both written and oral communication skills in role-play of difficult situations. This could occur as part of general management development. Counselling and support for redundant employees is a key component in the handling of redundancy. Counselling is a specific skill that managers may not possess, in which case either qualified counsellors or outplacement providers may be the best option. Managers should be discouraged from taking on a task that they are not qualified to undertake. Other support that may be provided inside or outside the organisation includes: financial planning, if appropriate, career counselling, skills assessment and job-search skills. Outplacement may provide the redundant worker with the opportunity to work through the range of emotions being experienced from shock and disbelief to hope and success in finding new employment.

Survivor syndrome and rebalancing the organisation

One aspect of redundancy that has had less attention in the past is the issue of rebalancing and reshaping the organisation following a redundancy situation. Those remaining in the organisation also suffer anxiety and stress. There is the relief that 'it is not me – this time', coupled with fear that this may be the start of 'downsizing'. Redundancy happens for many reasons, but one reason for shedding labour is to build an organisation that is in a better position to survive in a changing world. Those employees who remain need to know that a rebalancing plan has been developed and is being communicated in a positive manner, that jobs have been redesigned and work restructured to enable plans to be achieved. They need to know that there is a human resources strategy and plan that reflects the new business and that the organisation either has the skills it needs for the future or that there is a training plan in place to achieve this. A positive managerial response to a post-redundancy experience sends the message that a planned and considered approach is being taken and will contribute to the confidence of the remaining staff, thus reducing the effects of 'survivor syndrome'. This may help to build commitment, renew the psychological contract and ultimately help the organisation to succeed.

ASSIGNMENTS

(a) Address the following 10 questions on negotiation. If possible, undertake this assignment before and after a negotiation activity in order to be able to reflect on your learning points: (i) How would you define negotiation? (ii) In what situations do you have to negotiate and what tactics and skills do you personally deploy? (iii) What is required in preparation for team negotiation? (iv) What is meant by 'like to achieve', 'intend to achieve" and 'must achieve' in relation to negotiation? (v) What are the phases of the negotiation cycle, what happens at each phase, and why might it be useful for negotiators to have an awareness of the phases? (vi) Give examples of negotiation tactics. In what circumstances should they be deployed? (vii) What are the potential purposes of adjournments in team negotiation? (viii) What skills are required for effective negotiation and how can they be developed? (ix) Which factors contribute to the stress of negotiation? (x) Which factors affect the approach and tenor of the negotiations?

(b) Observe or participate in a negotiation in your organisation. Then (i) Analyse the negotiation process in terms of the skills required. To what extent were these skills evident and how effectively were they utilised? (ii) Did adequate planning take place? (iii) Was it possible to detect movement through and oscillation within the phases of the negotiation cycle?

(c) Identify a situation where you have been required to negotiate on a one-to-one basis. (i) Describe the situation. (ii) Was there a successful outcome? (iii) What contributed to the success or otherwise of the outcome?

(d) Identify a situation at work where you will have to negotiate on a particular issue. (i) Decide upon your ideal solution, realistic settlement and fall-back position (or your LIMs). (ii) After the negotiation, review the outcome in relation to your expectations.

(e) Body language or non-verbal cues make a vital contribution to the communication process. Keep a confidential log of body language that you observe in your organisation. (i) How does body language manifest itself? (ii) What do you interpret from the signs? (iii) How does it help or hinder the communication process?

(f) Attend an employment tribunal and observe an unfair dismissal case. (i) Write a brief report on the proceedings and the outcome. (ii) Was a proper procedure followed by the employer? (iii) Comment upon whether the employer acted 'reasonably in the circumstances'. (iv) Discuss whether and to what extent the employee contributed to the dismissal. (v) Using the principles of natural justice outlined in this chapter, examine each one in relation to the case and comment upon whether they have been adhered to.

(g) Obtain a copy of disciplinary procedures from two or more organisations. (i) Discuss to what extent they include the features recommended by the ACAS Code of Practice. (ii) Compare and contrast the disciplinary procedures, identifying strengths and weaknesses.

(h) What advice would you give to a newly appointed line manager who has been presented with a formal written grievance? What support would you give to this manager through the preparation for and the conduct of the grievance interview?

(i) Interview a manager who is experienced in disciplinary interviews or hearings. (i) Using open questions, identify the skills required for effective disciplinary interviews or hearings. (ii) Write a brief report on your findings.

(j) Interview a number of managers in your organisation who have potential for involvement in grievance matters. (i) Question them about their understanding of the grievance procedure. (ii) Comment upon whether any training is warranted.

(k) Investigate the number of grievances you have had in your organisation over a specific period. (i) Analyse the subjects of the grievances and the outcomes of the hearings. (ii) Write a brief report on your findings, paying particular attention to any organisational implications.

(l) Design a training programme to prepare newly appointed line managers to recognise and handle conflict in the workplace.

(m) Review a 'dignity at work', harassment or bullying policy. What are the distinguishing features of each of these policies, and can all concerns be addressed with one policy document? Identify and discuss the issues that are important in successfully implementing any of these policies.

(n) Critically evaluate your organisation's redundancy policy. Comment on the effectiveness of the selection criteria identified in the policy.

(o) Identify and discuss the selection criteria that may be used in a matrix model of multiple criteria (the measured factor approach). How might these criteria be weighted to reflect their contribution? What data may be required to measure these criteria, and what difficulties might be encountered in collecting and using this data?

(p) Analyse the skills and competencies that managers require in order to manage the individual redundancy interview effectively. How might these skills be acquired in such a sensitive employment area?

(q) What support does your organisation offer to employees who are being made redundant? Evaluate the effectiveness of this and make recommendations for the support of the staff who 'survive'.

REFERENCES AND FURTHER READING

ADAM-SMITH D. (1998) 'Employment relations processes', in M. Corbridge and S. Pilbeam, *Employment Resourcing*, London, Pitman.

ADVISORY, CONCILIATION AND ARBITRATION SERVICE (2000a) *Code of Practice on Disciplinary and Grievance Procedures*. London, ACAS (periodically revised).

ADVISORY, CONCILIATION AND ARBITRATION SERVICE (2000b) *Discipline at Work – advisory handbook*. London, ACAS (periodically revised).

ADVISORY, CONCILIATION AND ARBITRATION SERVICE (2000c) *Redundancy Handling – advisory handbook*. London, ACAS (periodically revised).

CORBRIDGE M. and PILBEAM S. (1998) *Employment Resourcing*. London, Pitman.

DEPARTMENT OF EMPLOYMENT (1987) *Redundancy Consultation and Notification*. London, ACAS.

DEPARTMENT FOR EDUCATION AND EMPLOYMENT (1999) *Employment Tribunals Procedures – England and Wales*. London, DfEE.

DOHERTY N. (1995) 'Helping survivors to stay on board'. *People Management*. January.

EGGERT M. (1991) *Outplacement*. London, Institute of Personnel Management.

EMPLOYMENT DEPARTMENT (1999) *Individual Rights of Employees: A guide for employers*. London, ED.

EMPLOYMENT DEPARTMENT. *Fair and Unfair Dismissal: A guide for employers*. London, ED. (periodically revised).

EMPLOYMENT DIGEST 270 (1989) 'Preparing for a disciplinary interview'. June.

EMPLOYMENT RELATIONS ACT 1999.

EMPLOYMENT RIGHTS ACT 1996.

FARNHAM D. *and* PIMLOTT J. (1995) *Understanding Industrial Relations*. London, Cassell.

FOWLER A. (1990) *Negotiation Skills and Strategies*. London, Institute of Personnel and Development.

FOWLER A. (1996) 'How to conduct a disciplinary interview'. *People Management*. November.

GENNARD J. *and* JUDGE G. (1999) *Employee Relations*. London, Institute of Personnel and Development.

INDUSTRIAL RELATIONS REVIEW AND REPORT 555 (1994) 'Guidance on Identifying Reasons for Dismissal'. March.

INDUSTRIAL RELATIONS REVIEW AND REPORT 556 (1994) 'EC Equality Law Secures Rights for Part-timers'. March.

INDUSTRIAL RELATIONS REVIEW AND REPORT 566 (1994) 'Sunday Trading Act 1994: Employment protection rights'. August.

INDUSTRIAL RELATIONS REVIEW AND REPORT 570 (1994) 'Inconsistent Treatment Not Decisive in Itself'. October.

INSTITUTE OF PERSONNEL AND DEVELOPMENT (1999) *Harassment at Work – Key Facts*. London, IPD.

INDUSTRIAL RELATIONS REVIEW AND REPORT MANAGEMENT (1993) 'TURERA 1993 – Personnel Practitioners' Checklist'. July.

IRS EMPLOYMENT REVIEW 575 (1995) 'EAT Addresses Limits of 'Polkey' reductions'. January.

ISHMAEL A. *and* ALEMORU B. (1999) *Harassment, Bullying and Violence at Work*. London, Industrial Society.

KENNEDY G., BENSON J. *and* McMILLAN J. (1984) *Managing Negotiations*. London, Business Books.

LEWIS D. *and* SARGEANT M. (2000) *Essentials of Employment Law*. London, Institute of Personnel and Development.

SALAMON M. (1998) *Industrial Relations: Theory and practice*. London, Prentice Hall.

STEPHENS T. (1999) *Bullying and Sexual Harassment*. London, Institute of Personnel and Development.

SUMMERFIELD J. (1996) 'Lean firms cannot afford to be mean'. *People Management*. January.

TEMPERTON E. (2000) 'The right to moral support'. *People Management*. March.

TRADE UNION REFORM AND EMPLOYMENT RIGHTS ACT (TURERA) 1993.

WALTON R. E. *and* McKERSIE R. (1965) *A Behavioral Theory of Labor Negotiations*. New York, McGraw-Hill.

Author index

Subject index